HANNIBAL'S DYNASTY

HANNIBAL'S DYNASTY

Power and politics in the western
Mediterranean, 247–183 BC

Dexter Hoyos

Routledge
Taylor & Francis Group

LONDON AND NEW YORK

First published 2003
by Routledge
11 New Fetter Lane, London EC4P 4EE

Simultaneously published in the USA and Canada
29 West 35th Street, New York, NY 10001

Routledge is an imprint of the Taylor & Francis Group

Typeset in Garamond by The Running Head Limited, Cambridge
Printed and bound in Great Britain by TJ International Ltd, Padstow, Cornwall

British Library Cataloguing in Publication Data
A catalogue record for this book is available from the British Library

Library of Congress Cataloging in Publication Data
A catalog record for this book has been requested

ISBN 0–415–29911–X

CONTENTS

ACKNOWLEDGEMENTS

It is a pleasant task to acknowledge the people and institutions who have helped to make this work possible. My earliest debt is to Richard Stoneman, who expressed interest in the theme of Hannibal's dynasty even before I began writing; and his support since the book was completed has been just as valued. The rest of his team at Routledge, and Frances Brown and Carole Drummond at The Running Head Ltd, have been consistently helpful and informative on every aspect of publication.

I should like to express my appreciation to the scholars, publishers and archivists who made available several of the illustrations for this book. In alphabetical order they are Archivi Alinari and Archivio Brogi of Florence, Italy; CNRS Editions, Paris, and Prof. M. H. Fantar; and Dr Matthias Steinart of the Archäologisches Institut at the University of Freiburg, Germany.

I am grateful too to Sydney University for its continuing commitment to Greek and Roman studies, a rather endangered species in Australia, and its aids to research through grants of study leave and travel funds. Invaluable again have been the interest, courtesy and expertise of the University Library staff at every level, for without these my research task would have been hard indeed.

As always, it has been my wife Jann and our daughter Camilla who made it both possible and worthwhile. Hamilcar, Hasdrubal, and Hannibal and his brothers have not been the centre of their attention, but if Barcid family life was at all similar they were fortunate men.

Dexter Hoyos

1 Hannibal—bust found at Naples in 1667: identification not certain (reproduction courtesy of Archivi Alinari, Firenze)

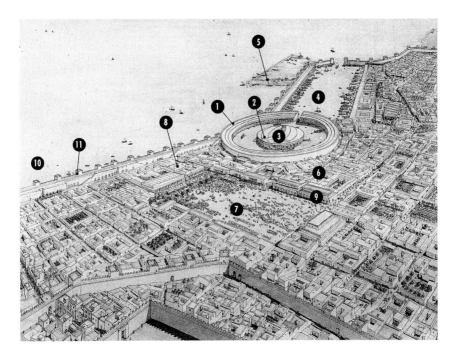

2 Carthage in Hannibal's time: the ports region (reconstruction)

1 Naval port
2 The admiralty island
3 The admiralty pavilion
4 Merchant port
5 The 'Fabre quadrilateral' (ancient quay)
6 Lower city: artisans' and commercial district
7 Agora (central square)
8 Senate house
9 Public buildings
10 Coastline
11 City wall

From M. H. Fantar, *Carthage: La cité punique* (courtesy of CNRS Editions, Paris)

3 Carthage (*ca.* 1890)—View from Byrsa hill towards the lagoons (the ancient
   artificial ports); on the horizon, the Cape Bon peninsula

4 Carthage (*ca.* 1990)—aerial view from the south: in the middle distance, Byrsa hill (Colline de St-Louis) from M. H. Fantar, *Carthage: La cité punique* (courtesy of CNRS Editions, Paris)

5 Antiochus III (l.) and Masinissa(?) (r.)—portraits (presumed) in the Louvre and Capitoline Museums respectively

6 Gallic warrior (third century BC)—detail of the famous statuary-group of a Gallic warrior slaying his wife and himself to avoid capture: from the Altar of Attalus I of Pergamum

7 Marcellus—Hannibal's vigorous opponent, killed in ambush in 208 BC: a late
Republican or early Imperial statue

8 Scipio—presumed portrait, in bronze (reproduced courtesy of Archivio
Brogi/Archivi Alinari, Firenze)

9 Philip V of Macedon—
two coin-portraits of the
king in his prime

10 Polybius—commemorative stele from
Kato Klitoria, in the Peloponnese, set up
by a first-century AD descendant
(reproduced courtesy of Dr Matthias
Steinhart, Archäologisches Institut, the
University of Freiburg)

INTRODUCTION

Hannibal is the only Carthaginian who is still a household name. As leader of the Carthaginians and their empire in the Second Punic War from 218 to 201 BC, he made it touch and go whether they or the Romans would come to dominate the Mediterranean west, and after that, more or less inevitably, the east. He belonged to a remarkable family. Had the Carthaginians won the war and changed the course of ancient history, the victory would have been due in great part to Hannibal and his kinsmen, who had rebuilt Carthaginian power after its catastrophic defeat in 241 at Roman hands.

In taking his city to its most extensive and eventful level of power Hannibal was the third, the greatest and the last of a republican ruling dynasty. His father Hamilcar, nicknamed Barca (hence the convenient family sobriquet Barcid) came to prominence in 247, the year Hannibal his eldest son was born. Hamilcar and his son-in-law Hasdrubal preceded Hannibal between 237 and 221 as effective rulers of Carthage and creators of a land empire that replaced—and outdid—the city's lost island possessions. Hannibal built on their base.

How the Barcids' dominance was founded and how maintained, what each leader in turn aimed to achieve with it, what they actually accomplished, and how and why Barcid supremacy in the end collapsed—and then staged a brief revival—are the themes of this study. The theme involves politics, international relations, strategy and geography, for the Barcid generals were not only Carthage's *de facto* leaders of government but her official commanders-in-chief, and the two rôles were bound closely together.

The Carthaginian state had enjoyed success before, but never on the Barcid scale or with the potential to change all of ancient history. This achievement was the more remarkable as Hamilcar and his successors, uniquely in Punic history, exercised decades of dominance not from their home city but from hundreds of miles away, first in Spain and then in Italy. Hamilcar's adroit handling of the war against rebel mercenaries and subject Libyans in North Africa, from 241 to 237, made him supreme in Punic affairs, and his successes in Spain followed by Hasdrubal's consolidation cemented the Barcid supremacy. Yet they and then Hannibal were not military dictators: all three

1

were elected to their commands by the citizens of Carthage as well as by their armies, and all relied on a supporting network of kinsmen, friends and supporters to sustain their political dominance at Carthage.

Barcid expansionism interestingly involved a measure—or at least a show—of co-operation with their non-Punic subjects and dependants too. Hasdrubal not only struck treaties and practised conciliation, but also arranged to be chosen supreme leader by the peoples of Punic Spain—a symbolic act, but one obviously judged worthwhile for building Spanish loyalty. Marriage-alliances contributed too, in both Africa and Spain: Hamilcar married daughters to Numidian princes, while both Hasdrubal and Hannibal took wives from lordly families in Spain. Alexander the Great and his successor-kings had acted similarly in the east. The Romans by contrast, when their turn at world empire came, took much longer to make use of such methods.

The generals' long-lasting control of home affairs depended on continuing success abroad, which in turn required resources from Africa—officers, soldiers and war-elephants, colonists for new cities in Spain, and funds too at times. The drive to continental empire moreover aimed at benefiting the Carthaginian state, not solely the dominant family and their friends (otherwise the generals could have set up a breakaway state in Spain, and the Carthaginians at home could have ignored Hannibal's later collision with the Romans). The new cities, capped by Hasdrubal's New Carthage, opened handsome opportunities to Punic settlers. Wealth, as Hamilcar's later Roman biographer Nepos noted, flowed in turn from the new conquests to Africa. Carthage's famous enclosed harbours, naval and commercial, which the historian Appian described and archaeologists have excavated, are very likely the most enduring monuments to those Barcid-garnered riches.

The new imperial expansion kept Carthage as a great power on a par with the others around the Mediterranean—most crucially of all with the Romans, who not only had driven the Carthaginians from Sicily in the first war but afterwards took advantage of their weakness to extract Sardinia too. Barcid military activities interacted closely with Punic foreign relations. Both Hamilcar and then Hasdrubal extended Punic control in Spain through treaties and alliances as well as campaigns (though the conventional picture makes Hamilcar do the fighting and Hasdrubal the negotiating). The Romans' sporadic attention to them was always expressed in strategic and territorial terms: the seizure of Sardinia in 237, the Ebro accord 12 years later and, in Hannibal's time, the episode of Saguntum. Each Roman intervention confirmed Barcid political dominance, even at the price finally of a new war with the old enemy.

In its turn, Hannibal's grand design of 218 required not only military victory but ensuing diplomatic successes, and had an equally blended goal: an Italian, or at any rate southern Italian, alliance system backed by Punic arms, to keep the Romans in permanent check and guarantee hegemony over the western Mediterranean to the Carthaginians. In both war and alliance building he was impressively and yet incompletely successful. At the height of their success, between 216 and 209, the Carthaginians held sway over North Africa, the rich southern half of Spain and most of the south of Italy, while continental north Italy and much of Sicily were in revolt against the Romans. Thanks to the Barcids' qualities as generals, paradoxically Carthage the quondam sea-power came close to overthrowing the Roman republic—long dominant in land warfare—through war on land. As a result Roman victory in the second war, even more than in the first, was not preordained or predictable. Many observers reckoned on a Punic triumph. Two Greek states, Macedon and Syracuse, thought it profitable to ally with the prospective victors and share the coming spoils.

That the momentum of victory slowed and then reversed was due as much to Barcid miscalculation—and overconfidence—as to the enemy's dogged perseverance. Another Barcid paradox was their lack of experience as admirals: and as a result the Romans, comparatively new to naval warfare, outclassed the veteran mistress of the seas on the water from start to finish, with the innovative naval port at Carthage no help even if it was a Barcid (or Barcid-approved) creation. Hannibal in his later years was to show a touch of skill and resourcefulness as a naval commodore, but his lack of anything like it during his own war contributed to his and his city's failure in their greatest enterprise.

Stalemate in Italy and a seesawing military situation in Spain, along with inability to master the seas, forced Barcid kinsmen and supporters at home to share supremacy (so it seems) for the first time with another political group, centred on the non-Barcid general Hasdrubal son of Gisco. After Hannibal's return and final defeat, even shared pre-eminence was gone—though not to the son of Gisco's benefit. Still, enough glamour, wealth and nostalgia survived to bring Hannibal back to the helm in 196, and it took yet another hamfisted Roman intervention to dislodge him for good. Even then the Barcids left a legacy: no bloodshed or revolution, and a state and society prosperous and stable enough to endure—at any rate until the Romans chose to act one more time.

The Barcid style in government, exploiting the lustre of successful war and conquest to focus authority on one vivid figure, well fitted the third century— the zenith of the Hellenistic era in the eastern Mediterranean, where great (and not so great) states likewise acknowledged long-term leaders with similar claims to glory. Military command, rather than naval, typified them and equally their Punic counterparts: as just noted, Hamilcar, Hasdrubal and Hannibal, and Hannibal's brothers too—all leaders or deputy leaders of the Mediterranean's oldest sea-power—were devoted land generals. All the same, unlike the major eastern powers which were monarchies with Greek or Hellenized élites, Carthage remained a republic and, while influenced by Hellenistic culture, kept a civilization and leaders that were distinctively home-grown.

Set up through military success, exploiting the charisma of victory and conquest and the profits deriving from these, and relying at home on support from citizens as a whole as well as allied or opportunistic fellow-aristocrats, Barcid dominance of the Punic world in some ways prefigured the supremacy established two centuries later by Julius Caesar and Augustus over Rome—a historical irony, since it was by defeating Barcid Carthage that the Romans began to build their own continental empire which, in time, was to set in train the transformation of Roman republic into Caesarian monarchy. It was appropriate, in a way, that Rome and the Roman world should later come under the rule of Caesars from North Africa and that the first of that dynasty, Septimius Severus, should commemorate the last of the Barcids with a splendid monument on the spot where Hannibal died.

Once they had driven their old enemy to suicide in 183, the Romans chose to remember him with tempered but genuine admiration, a compliment they extended to his family. Hannibal's war was enshrined in memory as the testing-time of the Roman people and their victory as the warrant for world mastery. The Barcids aroused admiration too among Greeks, whose many and fractious states, in losing their own wars against the Romans, cost these nothing like the effort they had needed against Barcid Carthage. The second-century Greek historian Polybius judged Hamilcar the outstanding general of the first war, and plainly reckoned Hannibal inferior to none in the second except Scipio Africanus who finally defeated him (and whose family later befriended the historian).

This impact on Greeks and Romans was much to the Barcids' posthumous benefit. Almost nothing survives of Carthaginian records—a few quotations, paraphrases and references in later authors—and little of contemporary Roman or Greek ones either. But all were used, in varying degrees of detail and prejudice, by later authors whose accounts do remain. These record much about Hannibal, a good deal about his father Hamilcar, and rather less on the other notable Barcids. At the same time they can be problematic.

Some do not survive in full: for instance Polybius', Diodorus', Livy's and Dio's histories of the period. Others are short, like Nepos' biographies of Hamilcar and Hannibal, Plutarch's of Fabius Cunctator and Marcellus, the treatments by Appian of Roman wars in North Africa, Spain, Sicily and against Hannibal, later epitomes of past history like those by Eutropius, Justin and Orosius, and those—late Roman and Byzantine respectively—of Livy and Dio. The farther away from the period, the more necessarily reliant these authors were on previous sources, while their own knowledge of the details of politics, society and warfare (even on the Roman side) varied from extensive to imaginative. Most applied a pro-Roman tint to their narratives because the bulk of their sources had it, or because they accepted a teleology of Roman triumph and Carthaginian defeat. More crucially still, nearly all were writing to illuminate not Punic history but Roman. Features of Punic government, society and economy could be ignored except when some detail was needed to clarify a situation; and then the detail—even if taken from an early and informed source—might not be too accurately relayed.

To interpret the Barcids, and even to reconstruct what they did and how it was done, calls then for careful detective work. Hamilcar's first decade in military affairs (for instance) is known in some detail, but less clearly his political and social connexions. Then for his and Hasdrubal's empire-building in Spain we have to rely on an array—a small one at that—of disconnected notices in Polybius, Diodorus and others. And while the military history of Hannibal's war on the Romans is a well-recorded saga, its technical details (especially in his famous early victories) tend to attract more interest and analysis than the next decade and a half, the years first of Carthage's maximum extent of power and the Barcids' own zenith, and then of decline in both. Hannibal's own deserved reputation as military leader, which loses nothing in Polybius' and Livy's telling, can prompt over-easy generalizations—dogged Romans and unsupportive home authorities—about why he and his city finally failed. In all these areas, and others, established dogmas and issues still under debate both need a fresh look.

As usual in such analyses, much depends on what the ultimate sources were or may have been for the accounts that survive. Yet identifying them solves only part of each problem, for like the survivors even the earliest accounts were partisan to one degree or other. The limited evidence for much of Hamilcar's and most of his successor Hasdrubal's doings compounds the difficulty. The activities of Hannibal and his brothers, while more fully reported, largely come filtered through Roman historical tradition rather than direct from Barcid informants, with much resulting distortion suspected by moderns—and sometimes proved. Even Polybius, our earliest surviving source and a writer not only conscious that objectivity was difficult but still keen to achieve it, needs to be assessed with care. Admiring both the Romans and the Barcids does not guarantee invariable impartiality, clear exposition or persuasive analysis, and one or other of these qualities goes missing rather often in his narrative.

The issues that arise over the Barcids and Barcid-era Carthage are therefore important and taxing. Judgements have to be made according to the quantity of evidence, the coherence of one source compared to another's where different sources make differing claims, how well the various solutions to a problem fit in with factors otherwise known, and occasionally even on how a textual passage is to be read. Much of the time an author has to settle for probable answers rather than certainties, and inevitably they will be subjective to an extent, however great his effort, Polybius-like, for objectivity. For the reasons mentioned earlier, the effort is still worth making.

Citations and references

Hannibal, his family and Carthage interest not only specialists in ancient history but, rightly, a broader range of readers too. In the main text therefore sources are quoted in translation, with the Greek and Latin originals given in the notes when it seems useful. The notes supply detailed references to ancient sources and important modern discussions, with the latter cited by author's name and date of publication (or a few by initials like *CAH²*). Technical points too complex to fit comfortably in the text are likewise discussed in the notes, apart from some that need detailed treatment—these have been reserved to the Appendix. Full details of the abbreviations used in the notes, and all the ancient sources, are included in the Bibliography. All dates, unless accompanied by 'AD', are BC.

I

THE HEIGHTS OF HEIRCTE
AND ERYX

I

The safest time to sail along an enemy coast is at night, so that was probably when the Carthaginian ships entered the little Sicilian bay between its two steep and massive headlands. They anchored close to shore and Hamilcar the general gave the order for his troops to disembark.

The Carthaginians knew this area well. Not far to the south-east on its coastal plain, the city of Panormus had once been the jewel of Punic Sicily but for seven years now had lain in the Romans' hands, along with most of the old Punic province. In the pass leading down to the little bay between the two mountain headlands stood the fort of Heircte, still held for Carthage. The Romans had once tried to capture Heircte and failed. After that they ignored it—something they would now rue.

Probably as dawn broke the troops climbed the tracks up the steep-sided mountain that loomed above Heircte and the bay on the western side, to gain the summit. This was a broad, undulating plateau with a rim measuring 100 stadia—more than 11 miles, or 18 kilometres. The heights had broad meadows, no dangerous creatures, healthy winds from the sea and access to plentiful water. There were only two paths up on the land side and one from the shore; much of the summit was edged by cliffs, the rest easily fortifiable.

A hillock on the plateau gave the occupiers a panorama of north-western Sicily and the Mediterranean beyond: to the east Panormus and its fertile plain bounded by uplands; over to the west a deeply indented coast backed by serried hills; on the south yet more heights, plateaux and valleys dotted with small villages and scattered stone-walled towns. The heights offered a bastion in the heart of Roman-held Sicily, yet one that was virtually impregnable.

The year was 247, the eighteenth of the longest war in Carthaginian history. The war was at a stalemate. Hamilcar, recently appointed to command in Sicily, was trying something new.[1]

II

The Carthaginians had not wanted to fight the Romans in 264. Nor had a Punic war been on the Romans' minds. For two and a half centuries the two states had had trade and treaty relations, and they had recently renewed these. In 264 the Romans meant to intervene in Sicily against the reviving might of Syracuse and in search of easy plunder in the island's east.

But when they made allies of Syracuse's enemies and the Carthaginians' own protégés the Mamertines of Messana, the Carthaginians abruptly turned against both. They allied with the king of Syracuse to keep the Roman legions out of Sicily. But the legions did cross and King Hiero soon came to terms with them. From mid-263 the Carthaginians were faced with Roman dominance over eastern Sicily and no certainty about their ultimate aims.

The Roman republic had come a long way from the medium-sized central Italian state which had made those earlier treaties. By 264 Roman territory covered a third of peninsular Italy, and the republic dominated the rest. Etruscans, Samnites, the Greek colonies of the south and all the other once-independent peoples of the peninsula were its obedient allies. Most of this expansion had taken place in the last forty years and it was barely complete when the Mamertines' troubles with Syracuse gave the Romans an opening into Sicily. The prospect alarmed the Carthaginians; they had not wanted war with the Romans, but did not want them in the island either. By mid-263, with Hiero out of it, the war was purely Carthage versus Rome.[2]

The Romans in turn, to judge from their actions, had had no wish to make war on the premier sea-power of the western Mediterranean. But just as the Carthaginians would not stand for Roman influence in eastern Sicily, so too the Romans would not accept a Punic threat to their alliance with Messana and taming of Hiero. Neither side made a peace move. Instead the war broadened.

Over the years it cost both sides heavily. Sicilian towns and cities were sacked, like historic and splendid Agrigentum (Greek Acragas) which suffered first at Roman hands and later at the Carthaginians'. Each raided the other's coasts in Italy and Punic Africa. Overall the war went badly for the Carthaginians. An unpleasant surprise befell them four years into the war: not only were their enemies militarily superior on land but now they created a major war-fleet for the first time in history, and between 260 and 255 inflicted one naval defeat after another on the one-time masters of the western seas. In Sicily the Carthaginians lost strongpoint after strongpoint, despite some intermittent successes. After 252 they held on to only the heavily fortified west-coast ports of Drepana and Lilybaeum.

The Romans, in spite of their territorial successes, suffered repeated blows too, especially from 255. An invasion of North Africa in 256–255 ended in catastrophic defeat. Two powerful fleets then foundered in storms off North Africa, with huge loss of sailors' and soldiers' lives. In 249 came their worst and the Carthaginians' finest hour. A fleet under one consul was defeated just off Drepana, and soon afterwards the other consul's fleet was manoeuvred by a second Punic commander into a shattering gale off Cape Pachynus south of Syracuse. The losses, both in men and ships, were catastrophic again. All told, the figures reported for losses at sea between 255 and 249 were 550 ships and more than 200,000 men, numbers gigantic in any age—and almost ruinous when the total population of the Italian peninsula hardly exceeded 3 million. Small wonder that the Roman census of 247 recorded a drop in registered male citizens of 50,000 compared to the last prewar census.[3]

Even so the Romans refused to abandon their sieges of Drepana and Lilybaeum, begun not long before. They had taken the decision long before, after capturing Agrigentum in 261, to drive the Carthaginians out of Sicily and they held to it. This was not so much because they wanted to exploit the island for themselves: during the war the Sicilian communities, even apart from Hiero's niche realm of Syracuse, enjoyed a good deal of autonomy, and afterwards the Romans would pay them only limited attention for nearly 15 years. But from the Roman viewpoint even a loose hegemony in Sicily could not coexist with a continuing Carthaginian presence—not even if this stayed in the western region of the island where it was three centuries old. How many times, after all, had the Carthaginians sallied forth from there to make war on Sicily's Greeks and come near to making satellites of them all?

The Carthaginians were no more inclined to compromise. By contrast with the island's Greeks, Sicels and Elymians—their sparring partners or intermittent allies over those centuries—the Romans were uncomfortable neighbours, as the other communities of Italy had found. Entrenched Roman influence in even a corner of the island (the Mamertines had become members of the republic's network of alliances) would be a permanent threat. As early as 263, cities in the Punic-dominated west had made overtures to the newcomers: Segesta for instance, which claimed a shared Trojan ancestry, and Halicyae its neighbour. The Carthaginians could expect some of these ties to have been strengthened in the decade and a half since. Besides, the Romans held a notorious interest in war-booty—it had been one of the enticements proffered by those urging a Sicilian intervention in 264—and this alone would make any neighbour of theirs nervous. If the Carthaginians wished to stay in Sicily, they had to ensure that the Romans left.

Their resolve on this did not waver, it seems, even when the position was most desperate. When the consul Regulus' invasion army was carrying all before it outside their walls, they sought his terms but then rejected them as too harsh. Regulus demanded (according to our limited evidence) an indemnity and Punic withdrawal from Sardinia and Sicily. An indemnity could be haggled over, and Sardinia with its Punic territory in the fertile south was a secondary though valuable possession; if any demand really was too harsh for the Carthaginians, it must have been the one for Sicily. Close to ruin though they were, they went on fighting. They soon turned the tables on Regulus too.[4]

It is a surprise, then, that they did so little to follow up the smashing successes of 249. Good commanders were on hand—Adherbal and Carthalo, the victors at Drepana and Cape Pachynus, and the soon-to-be-appointed

Hamilcar. The enemy was disheartened and short of money. Yet it proved impossible to break the sieges of Drepana and Lilybaeum or Roman mastery of the countryside; and the only other Punic move was a raid on the Italian coast—perhaps near Rome—that fizzled when Roman defenders approached.

The probable reason for this anticlimax was lack of funds. A few known items point to this. Around 250 (according to a late source, Appian) the Carthaginians had sought a loan of 2,000 talents, equivalent to 12 million Greek drachmas or 120 million *asses* in third-century Roman money, from Ptolemy king of Egypt. He politely rebuffed them. In 248, following Carthalo's abortive expedition to Italy, his troops mutinied for lack of pay. He took drastic measures, such as marooning some of them on deserted islands and sending others (ringleaders probably) to Carthage under arrest, but the rest were still rebellious when his successor Hamilcar arrived. Not paying your soldiers, when they constituted more or less your entire overseas army—and numbered little more than 20,000—was an unwise policy: the Carthaginians had to have good reason for it.

Another pointer to money woes is the decrease in the number of Punic ships on active service. The powerful fleet of 170 quinqueremes was moth-balled, apart from the force used for raiding the Italian coasts and keeping Lilybaeum and Drepana supplied. Nor was the docked fleet maintained in fighting trim at Carthage: when relaunched many years later for fresh fighting, it was undermanned and such sailors and marines as it had were newly levied and poorly trained. Plainly not much money had been spent on it. This economy was safe enough at first: Roman losses had been so heavy in 249—by one calculation, they were left with a mere 20 quinqueremes in service—and Roman resources so depleted that the Carthaginians had little naval opposition to face. The best the Romans could do in these years was to lend individual ships to citizens to launch privateering raids on North Africa's coast.[5]

There is other evidence too for financial straits at Carthage. In or not long after 247 another general, Hanno, captured the wealthy inland town of 'Hecatompylus', a Greek name for Theveste, today's Tebessa 160 miles (260 kilometres) south-west of Carthage, with frankly imperialist aims according to the historian Diodorus. Why a war in Africa when the one for Sicily was still unfinished? Strategic and political reasons may have contributed—Regulus' invasion had encouraged Carthage's Numidian neighbours to attack Punic lands—but Diodorus implies the importance of booty and extra revenues in the Carthaginians' thinking around 247. In these same years their own native Libyan subjects were charged taxes so oppressive that in the end they were ready to revolt. The Carthaginians, 'thinking that they had rational grounds, governed the Libyans very harshly', comments the historian Polybius drily. Hanno again was a noted practitioner of such revenue-raising.[6]

Much if not most of Carthage's wealth and revenues flowed from trade—or had flowed before the war. Some of it was exotic: men told stories of barter with tribes on the West African coast, journeys to the Tin Isles north of Spain, far-western sea routes jealously guarded and intruding ships sunk. But the bulk of Punic commerce was with other Mediterranean lands, west and east, and it is very likely that this suffered from the interminable war.

The occasional Roman fleet raiding on the coast would have had only passing effects on trade, but privateers could pose a bigger deterrent if they plundered widely and repeatedly. The biggest blow, though, would have been the closure of Sicily and Italy to Carthaginian merchants. Not only were these lands commercially important themselves, but ancient merchant-ships also needed to put in to land regularly on long trips, for fresh stores or to avoid rough weather. Now no Punic merchant could safely use landing-places under Roman control. Trade especially with the eastern Mediterranean and beyond must have suffered, though it was still possible to get to and from such places by sailing eastward along the Libyan and Egyptian coasts—a longer route. When the Romans finally built a new fleet in 242, the Carthaginians seem to have learned this not from merchants or intermediaries but on its arrival outside Drepana. All this would damage revenues, credit and war-making; and nothing suggests that doubling the Libyans' taxes and annexing new territory made up for all the damage.

Hamilcar, taking over from Carthalo in Sicily, thus had an unenviable mission. He had limited money, limited forces and only two surviving strongpoints. The enemy controlled the rest of the island and every year still sent two consular armies there, some 40,000 Roman and allied Italian troops. Realistically then his task was not so much to win the war as to avoid losing it.

Big battles and large-scale campaigns were out of the question. At best he might wear the Romans down to a point where they were finally willing to make peace. At the least, he must keep the fight going one way or other until the Carthaginians had the means for a major new effort, or till something else turned up: for instance problems for Rome from some other quarter—restiveness among the hard-pressed Italian allies, or moves by their old foes the Gauls in Italy north of the peninsula.

To old, experienced Carthaginian generals this may have looked like a poisoned cup. Hamilcar was young and confident, and had his own ideas of how to carry out his mission.

First he quelled the still-restive soldiers, with methods much harsher than Carthalo's. He 'cut down many of them one night and had many others thrown into the sea', writes Zonaras in his résumé of the historian Cassius Dio. But Hamilcar then, according to Zonaras, failed to recapture one of the islets just outside the harbour of Drepana after the besieging consul seized it. When he tried to retake it, the Romans drew him off by launching an assault on the town. The story looks a little suspicious: Zonaras claims that capturing the islet helped the Romans' siege-efforts against the town, but in fact Drepana remained firmly in Punic hands for years to come. If the islet was lost, the blow was not so damaging after all. Still the episode, if true, illustrates

Hamilcar's problems with manpower and could help explain his coming change in strategy.

Now he led a new naval raid on Italy, moving along the toe of the peninsula through the lands of Locri and the Bruttians, meeting it seems little resistance. There was no Roman navy to worry about and Hiero of Syracuse—despite becoming a permanent friend, *amicus*, of the Romans the year before—no doubt thought it rash to challenge Hamilcar's warships with any of his own. It was on the return trip to Sicily that the new general pounced on the heights of Heircte.[7]

III

Just where Hamilcar's mountain stronghold was is still debated. Not, as originally thought, Monte Pellegrino, the mountain on the shore just north of Panormus: it is too small for Polybius' specification of a 100 stadia rim, not to mention too close to the city, too sheer nearly everywhere, and without access to a proper haven.

More recent candidates lie some 12 miles (16 kilometres) across the mountains to Panormus' west, overlooking the gulf of Castellammare—steep and narrow Monte Pecoraro rising to nearly 1,000 metres above Terrasini or lower Monte Palmita to its south. But again, both are too small, Pecoraro too steep. Since Hamilcar could not have stationed all his army on the heights themselves as Polybius states, some (or most) of it must have camped on the coastal lowlands beside them, and the 100 stadia would then have to include these. Polybius' emphasis on the nearness of Panormus becomes incomprehensible.

The heights of Heircte were most probably the broad and lofty mountain mass bounding the plain of Panormus 5 miles (8 kilometres) west of the city, its highest point being the 809-metre Monte Castellaccio. Much of it is steep-sided but paths, one of them starting from the shore below, lead up to the undulating plateau on the crest. To the south lie even higher mountains. Below its eastern flank a pass separates it from the smaller but even steeper cape of Monte Gallo. The pass may be where the fort of Heircte stood; the small bay and sheltering island at the foot of the two headlands will have been where Hamilcar's fleet moored. Water is available at the harbour, as Polybius states. The heights are about 100 stadia in circumference, with pastures and with a suitable lookout on Monte Castellaccio.[8]

Hamilcar's move was unexpected and debatable. Polybius stresses his isolation from Lilybaeum and Drepana. He could not defend them from assault where he now was; pressure on the enemy could only be indirect. But with the forces available, that was going to be true wherever he was. Carthage's Sicilian field army, which in battle outside Panormus only three years before had numbered about 30,000, now probably amounted to some 10,000 infantry, mostly professional mercenaries from all over the western Mediterranean (including at least 3,000 Gauls, we learn later), and a few hundred cavalry. For at war's end 20,000 mercenaries left Sicily for North Africa and these included the unbeaten garrisons of Lilybaeum and Drepana, who must have numbered 10,000 or more. Losses over the years must be allowed for, but given this total Hamilcar's force too cannot have been substantially bigger. Besides, if it had been, he would have enjoyed much greater flexibility. He could have pounced on Panormus or tried more aggressively to raise the siege of Drepana.

The Romans reacted by camping a force close to his, it seems on a lower hill to the south. Only 5 stadia, or about a kilometre, separated the camps, but not much aggressive Roman élan was shown. Assaulting the Punic eyrie was clearly an option with little appeal even when Hamilcar was away on one of his raids. The Roman force was about the same size as the Punic and served chiefly to protect Panormus, although constant skirmishing occurred. After all, the bulk of the two consular armies sent yearly to Sicily, four legions plus Italian allied contingents, was tied down outside Drepana (where the Romans were also occupying the nearby heights of Eryx) and Lilybaeum. Hamilcar felt secure enough to sail out, no doubt with only part of his force, on a new sweep of the Italian coast, this time as far north as Cumae on the bay of Naples. The resulting booty and prisoners it seems cheered his mercenaries substantially: we hear of no more grumbles.[9]

Further Italian raids may have been made over the next three years, though we are not told of any. The Romans founded new defensive centres on their coasts in these years: citizen colonies, Alsium and Fregenae, on the Etruscan coast near the Tiber in 247 and 245 or 244, and a colony of Latin status at Brundisium on the Adriatic in 244. The first was probably a response to Carthalo's raid, but Fregenae even nearer to the Tiber suggests that still more security was found necessary for the coast close to Rome. Does the colony at Brundisium imply that Hamilcar had made descents in that area in 246–245? Quite possibly: after his visitations to the Tyrrhenian side of Italy it might have been a good idea to try a coast where he was less expected.

At Heircte itself Hamilcar handily held off the enemy troops over the way. Polybius limits himself to generalizing about the two sides' ambushes, stratagems, sorties and counterattacks. The Carthaginians may have operated more widely too. Diodorus, in another opaque and short excerpt, reports 'Barca' attacking 'Italium, a fort of Catana's near Longon' (the outcome is not known). Catana lay on the other side of Sicily, a long way from Heircte though not impossible for a general accustomed to hitting at Italy. But no Longon is known in that area, whereas a town Longane existed by a similarly named river close to Mylae and Messana—the historic river where Hiero of Syracuse had once shattered the Mamertines of Messana in battle and led them to call in the Romans. Diodorus' later copyist may have mistakenly replaced Messana with Catana. Likely enough the Mamertines held the area for their Roman allies to guard the coast-route to the west. The fort's name would fit Mamertine occupiers, as they originally hailed from Italy.[10]

From time to time he may also have sailed over to the besieged towns on the coast to keep up the defence; and occasionally too to Carthage itself. His eldest son had been born in 247 but another arrived during the 240s (both were to be with him on campaign in Spain in late 229 or early 228), and it is not at all plausible that his wife was with him in his mountain camps. The children—there were daughters as well—may have found him something of a stranger, if an affectionate one, but their father must have welcomed the brief respites from warfare, especially the piecemeal kind of warfare he was waging.

Hamilcar may have aimed to obstruct Roman forces and supplies moving to the sieges at Drepana and Lilybaeum, a reasonable strategy as we have seen, given the resources he had. Already his presence near Panormus made the coast road beyond there impossible for the enemy. Inland, the roads zigzagged around one mountain ridge after another (and maybe with Punic attackers lurking round the other side) or else a time-consuming detour was required via Agrigentum and the south coast (the Romans had built a road linking Panormus and Agrigentum some years earlier for other purposes). The sea was a much easier way of travel and transport, but Hamilcar could hit at ships too. Besides, ships had to put in regularly to land, and the sea itself was perilous between autumn and spring of every year. Hamilcar's guerrilla methods thus had promise.

These methods probably earned him his famous nickname. A Carthaginian had only one proper name but nicknames were often used—partly to sort out different bearers of the few names common among leading men. Hamilcar went down in history as 'Barcas' to the Greeks and 'Barca' in Latin. This reflected most likely the Punic word for lightning, like the Semitic *brq* (with vowels added, *baraq*). Hamilcar's swift and scorching sorties by sea and land would fit it well. He had less scope for these, as we shall see, from Eryx later, and so his countrymen probably attached it to him during his Heircte years. Scintillating stories of his exploits circulated at Carthage. Beyond the city too, for a few years later a Numidian prince was keen to ally himself—at some risk—with a leader who had so roused his admiration.[11]

Yet all he achieved was a stalemate. The Romans could not take Drepana and Lilybaeum, but neither could he force them to lift the sieges. Coastal defences in Italy, as mentioned, were being improved. His forces were thinning through military action and because, with funds short and pay already falling into arrears, few recruits came his way. The besieged strongholds on the west coast may have been in worsening straits too. One spring or summer morning in 244 the Roman troops opposite his position awoke to find it empty and no Punic ships in the bay. A fast rider would be sent off at once to inform the consuls besieging Drepana and Lilybaeum, but they knew already: the lightning had struck near Drepana.

IV

Mount Eryx or Monte San Giuliano rises isolated to over 2,000 feet (750 metres), just inland from Drepana: a broad ridge with a vast view over both coastal plain and sea—which may explain Polybius' notion that it was the second highest mountain in Sicily. On its crest stood a renowned temple of the goddess known to Phoenicians as Astarte, Greeks as Aphrodite and Romans as Venus, whose servitors included priestess-prostitutes. On a shoulder below stood a little town also named Eryx, while a low spur jutting in Drepana's direction was called Aegithallus. The Romans had captured the position in 249, their only success amid the disasters of that year (what their view of the priestesses was we do not know).

Hamilcar sailed in at night to another small bay north of the mountain, took his men up the zigzag road to the town and slaughtered the garrison. Captured townsfolk were marched down to the ships and taken over to Drepana—for some of them a second forced removal, as another Hamilcar had shifted the entire citizenry of Eryx to the port 16 years earlier. If he had planned on retaking the summit as well, he failed; Roman troops still held it, and Aegithallus too. But the town of Eryx now became Hamilcar's stronghold.

This was a far more ticklish, and puzzling, position than the heights above Heircte. He was wedged halfway up a mountain, between two tenacious enemy garrisons, with one twisting path down to his anchorage. On the plain below him a Roman consular army was encamped, though facing it were his forces in Drepana. Even if he had captured the summit as well, it would not have added greatly to his flexibility of manoeuvre. Yet Hamilcar both chose this position as his new base and maintained it for more than two years.

The change suggests that Heircte had become too remote and Drepana, at least, too heavily pressed. If his losses were not being replaced then the range and impact of his actions would be narrowing. The alternatives were unappealing: either shut his field forces up in one of the two ports with the garrison there or move around the open country harassing the besiegers and their lines of supply. With his current strength the second option would court disaster: even if the enemy detached only part of their armies against him, one pitched battle could mean the end of his army. The other option would concede all initiative to the Romans and leave the besieged ports with even gloomier prospects.

But the problem at Eryx, which Hamilcar never really solved, was how to use the position to make a real impact. He was supplied by sea, like the besieged ports, but nothing more is heard of naval raids and by mid-242 there were no Punic ships at all in Sicilian waters. On land his numbers and site hardly allowed him to range too far from the area.

At best he eased the plight of the besieged by giving the besiegers plenty of trouble. Polybius again merely supplies unhelpful generalizations about both sides experiencing 'every kind of privation', 'every means of attack and every variety of action'. But an excerpt of Diodorus tells how a Punic officer named 'Vodostor'—probably a version of the Carthaginian name Bostar—after a victory suffered heavy losses by letting his men plunder against Hamilcar's orders; the total loss of his infantry was prevented only by the discipline of his 200 horse. Plunder after victory and cavalry rescuing infantry point to an action on the plain, most likely an attack on the Roman siege-camp.

Hamilcar then sought a truce from the consul in command, C. Fundanius, to bury his dead, thus conceding defeat. Fundanius brusquely refused, only to be forced to make the same request when he in turn suffered heavy losses. He must have tried to follow up his success against Bostar by launching an attack of his own, either on Hamilcar's position or on Drepana, without success. Hamilcar set him an example of civility by granting his request, 'stating that he was at war with the living, but had come to terms with the dead'. This will have been in 243 or early 242, for Fundanius presumably took up office around 1 May 243, the normal period in this era, and left it 12 months later.

Polybius does tell a story, in another place, of the 3,000 Gallic mercenaries in Hamilcar's army. Some at least were notching up 20 years in Punic service, and a thousand or so of them found their situation on the mountainside irksome: no plunder worth mentioning and probably no pay either. They plotted to betray Eryx town, and their comrades, to the enemy. Had they succeeded, Hamilcar Barca would have been led in a consul's triumphal procession through Rome and then put to death. The history of Carthage, Rome and the Mediterranean would have been tantalisingly different.

Instead, but not too surprisingly, the scheme foundered and the malcontent thousand merely deserted to the Romans. These could think of nothing better to do with them than station them on the summit of the mountain in place of its Roman garrison. Embarrassment ensued when the irreverent Celts looted the sacred and wealthy temple. Still, there they had to be left while the war lasted (at its end the Romans hastily sent them packing)—giving, we may surmise, little trouble to their former commander.[12]

The other 2,000 Gauls under their chieftain Autaritus remained loyal. All the same, Hamilcar's force was further reduced. In practical terms he was having no effect on the war. In fact the entire Carthaginian war-effort in Sicily kept going only thanks to Roman forbearance in not building a fleet to cut supply-links from North Africa. This forbearance ended in 242.

V

A patriotic loan enabled the Romans to build a brand-new fleet of 200 ships to an excellent design (ironically, that of a famous Carthaginian blockade-running quinquereme captured back in 249), and in mid-242 the consul C. Lutatius Catulus arrived with it on the western coast of Sicily. This seemingly was the first the Carthaginians knew of the new fleet, a striking sign of the shutdown of their normal overseas contacts.

Their reaction was oddly lethargic. For years the bulk of their war-fleet had been moored in the well-protected harbour of Carthage; yet the sailing season closed in October without it setting sail. When it did sail, as early in the new year as was safe, it was undermanned and its crews untrained. In other words, even after eight or nine more months these had only just been gathered, nor can all that many of the seamen have been veterans of 249. On top of this, the warships were overloaded with supplies for Sicily even though it seems they were accompanied by transports with other supplies. This can only be a sign that the situation in the besieged ports—and maybe at Eryx too—was now truly desperate.

Everything had been left to the last minute. This sorry response to a development that for years had been liable to happen suggests a bemusing level of complacency—if not fecklessness—in the governing élite at Carthage. If this was due to financial reasons it ranks as one of the most disastrous economies in history. Common sense should at least have dictated keeping the fleet in enough trim to be launched as soon as possible once the Romans reappeared on the sea, and in as battle-worthy a condition as possible. Instead Lutatius could blockade both the harbour at Drepana, probably by seizing the islands at its mouth, and the roadstead at Lilybaeum, and press the siege of Drepana even more closely. Too closely for his own health, for he suffered a severe wound in an assault. If this involved Hamilcar, it was the general's last coup—and an unprofitable one again, for Lutatius' deputy, the praetor P. Valerius Falto, was just as energetic.

Hamilcar could not of course have foreseen when the enemy would launch a new naval effort (though this would not deter enemies from blaming him for not foreseeing it). But it would be interesting to know whether he had condoned or criticized the laying-up of the fleet. There must, of course, still have been a few warships in commission down to 242 to maintain a trickle of supplies from and contacts with Carthage, even if raids on Italy had stopped. Perhaps he and like-minded Carthaginians had reckoned that if the main fleet did put to sea it would achieve little while costing much, since the war was now confined to western Sicily and there were no resources to widen it effectively. On the other hand his own experience and good sense would have made him wary of lowering the fleet's combat-readiness to the level it had now reached. If he did criticize, his criticism was discounted.

The Punic fleet in its less than satisfactory condition sailed for Sicily at the very start of the sailing season in 241, under the command of one of Carthage's many Hannos. Despite the Romans' naval presence there must have been intermittent contact with Hamilcar in the previous months, for a plan had been arranged: Hanno would race to Hamilcar's bay, unload the supplies, take aboard the veterans of Eryx as marines and then turn to fight Lutatius' fleet. This called for both luck and enemy incompetence. Instead the consul and praetor intercepted him near the Aegates islands just off Drepana on the blustery morning of 10 March 241. Hamilcar could watch it all from his stronghold.

Lutatius and Valerius had used the months of Punic unresponsiveness to train and exercise their fleet and crews to an unusual height of skill. The Carthaginians fought strenuously but succumbed after a long day. Hanno got away to Carthage with some 50 ships—to meet the usual fate of a beaten commander, crucifixion, which can hardly have surprised him. The Romans sank or captured 120 other quinqueremes and took 10,000 prisoners. As the sun went down behind the Aegates islands, Hamilcar must have recognized that the war was lost.

Later writers fancied not. They supposed that he wanted to carry on, believed victory could yet be won, and was let down by the spineless authorities at home. This is part of the hostile and romantic notion that no sooner was the first war with Rome over than Hamilcar Barca began plotting the second. In reality, not only could hungry Drepana and Lilybaeum (not to mention Eryx) now be starved out before the Carthaginians could hope to build a new navy and find crews for it, but the Romans were in a position to repeat Regulus' invasion of North Africa. Hamilcar could see that as well as or better than anyone over at Carthage. Even if he beat off a new Roman attack on his stronghold, as a late writer implies, it made no difference on the larger scale.

The Carthaginians decided to seek peace terms. Whether they were able to consult Hamilcar is not known, but it was Hamilcar they appointed to negotiate with full powers. His feelings may well have been mixed. He had commanded longer than any previous general in Sicily, knew the enemy well and had earned their respect; nor was he someone easily browbeaten. At the same time he had commanded on a shoestring, his veterans had again not been paid for years, and his political standing at home (as we shall see) had fallen away badly. He would be an easy target if the terms were harsh. But to refuse would mean handing over the decisions on Punic Sicily, his men and himself to some other negotiator, very possibly a political enemy. Hamilcar accepted his appointment.

He sent Gisco, the commandant of Lilybaeum, to ask the consul's terms. Lutatius put various predictable demands: Punic withdrawal from Sicily, the return of all Roman prisoners without ransom (the Carthaginians being of course expected to pay ransom for theirs in the usual way), a guarantee not to make war on the Romans' ally Hiero of Syracuse and an indemnity of 2,200 Euboic talents—13,200,000 drachmas or 132 million *asses*—payable over 20 years. These terms may well have been more restrained than Hamilcar had expected. Sardinia was not demanded too and nothing was said about the Punic fleet or home territory. One other demand he did reject: the handover of all his troops' weapons and all deserters. He was making peace, the Carthaginian stated, not surrendering. It was probably now too that he reconciled his unbeaten but restive men—on the mountain, at Drepana and at Lilybaeum—to defeat by promising them fair treatment once they returned to North Africa.

Lutatius did not press the point. His year of office would expire soon, an agreement still had to be sent to Rome to be ratified, and he could not be sure how far the Carthaginians could be pushed without reviving their will to fight. Regulus had pushed too far and paid for it, and Polybius insists that even now the Carthaginians were ready to fight on but had simply run out of resources. The draft peace terms, minus the offending demand, were sent to Rome.

There they met opposition. The sovereign People thought them too easy on the Carthaginians, refused ratification and sent a commission of ten (no doubt senators) 'to examine the situation', as Polybius puts it. For a while the issue of peace or continuing war hung in the balance. But in the end the commission only heightened the money terms and made a couple of other changes.

One even benefited the Carthaginians: not Hiero alone but all the allies of either signatory should be safe from attack by the other, and neither side should involve itself in the other's territories, recruit troops there or form alliances with the other's allies. This was the only concessive crumb Hamilcar could win for his city. A new clause added the islands 'between Italy and Sicily', in other words the Aegates and Lipara groups, to the Punic withdrawal from Sicily. But the revised indemnity clause made the most difference.

The 2,200 talents must be paid in ten yearly instalments, plus 1,000 (60 million *asses*) payable immediately. This heavy lump sum both made it easier to reimburse the Roman citizens whose loans had created Lutatius' victorious fleet, and at the same time made it harder or impossible for the Carthaginians to renew warfare. Nothing suggests that they would have, but the commissioners could not read minds. They were, after all, letting Hamilcar's veterans go and there was plenty of wood in North Africa for building new fleets. As it turned out, the payment also made it hard or impossible to pay the Punic mercenary forces their long-overdue arrears, with consequences that would be calamitous not only for Carthage but, in the long run, even for Rome.[13]

The People's assembly at Rome ratified the satisfactorily revised treaty. For the first time since 264, the one-time Mediterranean friends were at peace. Hamilcar led his men down from the mountain, and no doubt those from Drepana, over to Lilybaeum. He put the Lilybaeum commandant Gisco in charge of evacuating all 20,000 troops to Africa, and sailed for Carthage ahead of them.

This prompt self-removal from the scene did not impress the veterans and looks unimpressive even now. Hamilcar might argue that, with the war and the negotiations both complete, his generalship had terminated, but no such automatic cut-off of command is known in the Carthaginian republic. True, he now had to undergo an official scrutiny at home on his conduct of affairs;

every general must. But he could have stayed on in Sicily for a time to see what he could do for the men, whose needs and grievances he knew better than most. The pull of homesickness may have been too strong; an even stronger pull, perhaps, the danger developing against him politically and personally as the general who had failed to win the war. At all events he chose to suit himself rather than others.[14]

Polybius judges Hamilcar's performance in the war very highly. 'He put to the test all chances of victory in warfare, if ever a leader did', and was 'the general to be ranked as the best, both in genius and in daring'. These accolades seem excessive. Hamilcar's most notable distinction was that in six years he had never been defeated, either at sea or on land. Yet except for the first couple of years at Heircte, his command had been strategically defensive. He had run essentially a holding operation; but instead of winning time for Carthage's resources to improve or the Romans' resolution to wane, had seen his own strength and opportunities thin out to little more than nuisance value. If the Romans had decided on a new fleet sooner, his command might not even have lasted the six years it did. When it ended he left behind discontented and disaffected troops. Polybius' verdict reflects, partly at least, admiration for Hamilcar based on his later exploits.

The war-effort had been pared down too far. Hanno, the successful general in North Africa, may share the blame, since he seems to have been the dominant political force at Carthage in those years. It is not certain, though, that he was a political rival of Hamilcar's already (as often surmised): we shall see that there is rather more reason to think the opposite. But at all events the home authorities had not been strongly disposed to add to Hamilcar's dwindling strength. His own lack of major successes no doubt had had something to do with this unenthusiasm. Whatever his own political influence at the start of his command, it was much impaired by 241. There were lessons in all this—about politics, leadership and resources—useful to an ex-general in his prime.[15]

II

CARTHAGE

I

Hamilcar Barca belonged more or less certainly to Carthage's ruling élite. His family's social distinction is suggested for instance by the Roman poet Silius' claim that they were descended from a brother of Dido, the exiled princess of Tyre who in legend had founded the city around the year 814. The claim probably dates from Hamilcar's or his sons' time: Belus, Dido's father, has the name not only of the chief Phoenician god Ba'al but also of a known (though later) king Ba'lu of Tyre, while her brother in the tale is named Barca, which was merely Hamilcar's nickname. All the same, his appointment to a major military command while still fairly young suggests, though it does not prove, that his family was already an established one.

Whether he and his father Hannibal were kin to any of the numerous other Hamilcars and Hannibals of Punic history, including several active in the first war against Rome, cannot be known. Those names and a few others—Adherbal, Bostar, Bomilcar, Carthalo, Gisco, Hasdrubal, Himilco, Mago and commonest of all Hanno—were almost the only ones used by the Carthaginian ruling élite. Telling them apart is often a problem. Thus Hamilcar Barca himself: he can hardly be the same Hamilcar as an able general active in earlier years of the war with Rome, but a few writers ancient and modern think he was.[1]

Hamilcar was 'fairly young' when appointed to Sicily, according to Cornelius Nepos' biographical sketch. Nepos probably exaggerates for effect. True, Hamilcar's eldest son later did become general-in-chief in his mid-twenties, but that was to be after more than a decade and a half of his family's dominance in Carthage's affairs. If the later historian Appian can be believed, Hannibal already in 218 had a nephew, Hanno son of Bomilcar, old enough to command a cavalry corps: in other words a sister's son (Hannibal had no brother named Bomilcar) who should by then have been at least twenty years old. This would mean that by 238 Hamilcar had a daughter already married and a mother.

This chimes with other facts. Around 240 he did offer a daughter in marriage to a Numidian prince, and a few years later married another to his close political ally Hasdrubal. In other words by the later 250s he had already become a father. He must have been born by 275, or rather earlier. A man of thirty could still—for literary effect—be called 'quite young'.

When Hamilcar left for Sicily, his wife was expecting another child. Probably late in 247 the birth took place. Hamilcar must have been particularly satisfied: this was a boy, his first son. He named him after his own father, as was customary. But he seldom saw the little Hannibal for years to come. He was at war abroad and it is very unlikely that the boy and his mother went with him—especially as another baby, Hasdrubal, followed around 244. This supports the possibility noted earlier of occasional visits home. A third brother, Mago, was born probably around 241 or 240, as he too held an important command in his brother's army by 218. So as the 230s opened, Hamilcar was the father of three growing sons and perhaps as many daughters, an unusually sizeable brood in ancient times.[2]

The family was not just socially prominent but rich too. Early in the next century, after 40-odd years when most of its male members had been at war away from home, Hannibal owned estates in the fertile territory of Emporia, the later Byzacium by the gulf of Hammamet, 120 or so miles (200 kilometres) south of Carthage. The spoils of war quite likely contributed to such holdings, but from the start it was virtually essential for Hamilcar to be rich if he meant to take part in public life. A century before, Aristotle had reported that Punic officials, especially the highest ones, were chosen on the basis of birth and wealth together—partly because bribery was taken for granted, as it still was in Hamilcar's and his sons' day. At the same time, degrees of wealth no doubt existed, and before he died Hamilcar was to become much richer.[3]

To be appointed general in Sicily against the Romans and hold command for six years implies strong political connexions, especially if the appointee was still relatively young. A well-connected marriage may have helped, though nothing is known of Hamilcar's wife. His father Hannibal too may well have been or still was a man of consequence at Carthage, but it is typical of our limited knowledge of affairs there that all this is guesswork.

As we saw, Hamilcar's appointment coincided with a distinct running-down of his country's effort in the Roman war in favour, it seems, of expansionist campaigning in the Carthaginian hinterland. As we saw too, the leading figure in this expansion was Hanno, mysteriously dubbed 'the Great' by some ancient writers, who is widely suspected of instigating the rundown of the war-effort in Sicily during the 240s. Did Hamilcar, then, already belong to a faction or clique politically at odds with Hanno's, and was he given the Sicilian command as a poison cup to oblivion?

This is possible, but not probable. The slackening of effort there had begun before he arrived, for the victories of 249 were not followed up effectively. It is just as likely, or even likelier, that Hamilcar was appointed because he convinced the Punic senate that he could make a difference with the limited resources available, while expansionism and exploitation at home would build up the resources for a bigger effort to come. Given Hanno's current eminence in the state, it might surprise that he did not block the appointment—if Hamilcar was already his enemy. That the appointment went through and was continued for six years suggests the two were not the foes then that they later became. Hanno's view of the situation very likely chimed with Hamilcar's in those years.

Hanno's was the successful war. He operated close to home and won glamour, plaudits and extra revenues; when the mercenaries rebelled later on he was the obvious choice to command the Carthaginians against them. All points to his being the senior political figure of the day. To gain the command in Sicily, Hamilcar would need his support. Nothing suggests that they were hereditary enemies—certainly no ancient writer does. In 247 Hamilcar may even have been a vigorous new member of Hanno's own political circle. By contrast Adherbal and Carthalo, his predecessors in Sicily who disappear from record after 249–248, may have belonged to a different circle which could not stand up to Hanno's revitalized group.

The young general was able and ambitious, and Punic politics were no more governed by party-affiliations or a permanent pecking-order than Roman or Athenian. He would naturally hope to win a greater level of eminence and influence as time went by. But the war in Sicily brought less and less prospect of these. As suggested earlier, Hamilcar's political standing went down rather than up as the years dragged on. If Hanno failed to support him strongly, that should hardly surprise; Hamilcar was going nowhere. What should be noted is that even so the Carthaginians never moved to appoint a new general, and still judged him highly enough to make him their plenipotentiary in the peace talks during 241.[4]

But the ending of the war and the crisis that it brought on completed Hamilcar's eclipse. He could argue that he had given up nothing that his countrymen had not already lost, that Sardinia and the western seas were untouched, an indemnity was normal, and it was the home government that had failed to pay his troops for so long. His critics, by contrast, could retort that he had made no impact on the enemy's war-effort for years; then had neither bargained the Romans down in the peace talks nor even prevented them from worsening the indemnity; had made promises to the veteran mercenaries in the name of Carthage that Carthage could not possibly honour—and had now given up his post and left the task of coping with the restive men to others.

But these were not indictable failings, and Hamilcar had enemies who wanted to be rid of him. Actual criminal charges were prepared against him for stealing public funds during the war. As he walked the streets of his city in the first weeks of peace, looking for support, Hamilcar must have wondered whether he faced the same fate as so many of his military predecessors—crucifixion for failure.

II

Hamilcar's Carthage stood on the southern side of an arrow-shaped penin-sula beside the gulf of Tunis. On its north side it was bounded by a large bay (now a silted-up swamp); on the south by the gulf and the lake behind this. A broad flat isthmus between these waters joined the arrowhead to the main-land, and a range of low hills edged its coast. At the southern end of the range, on Byrsa hill, stood the temple of one of the Carthaginians' chief gods, Eshmoun. Northwards along the hilltops lay the city's ancient burial-grounds, while on the watery plain between Byrsa and the lake of Tunis was the sacred sacrificial ground, the *tophet*.

The city spread down in narrow, often steep, but straight streets from the hills to the sea, and over the hills westward to the isthmus. The ground between Byrsa and the shore, the Old City, was of course the most closely settled. Temples, public buildings, workshops, houses and high apartment-blocks lined the streets. Over the hills lay the suburb of Megara, a broad domain of villas, gardens and orchards intersected by canals. The massive fortifications ringing the whole city measured more than 18 miles (30 kilo-metres) around.

The best-known feature of Carthage was the pair of landlocked artificial ports in its south-east corner, existing today as a couple of shallow lagoons. Appian vividly describes them as they were in the mid-second century: first a rectangular merchant-haven reached from the sea by a channel 70 feet (22 metres) wide, then, via a further channel from the merchant-harbour, the cir-cular war-haven with the fleet commander's island at its centre (the island too survives). Both the ports and the island were lined with boat-houses framed by columns. The circular port's capacity, according to Appian, was 220 ships.

Archaeology confirms his essential accuracy, though the war-haven's claimed capacity looks exaggerated. At some date the Carthaginians decided that their existing coastal installations were not enough, developed though these were. They then transformed a narrow silted-up channel, which had once extended northwards for about 400 yards (365 metres) from the city's southern shore past the *tophet*, into this elaborate installation. But they did so at a fairly late date: possibly only a few years or decades before the Third Punic War or, more likely on historical grounds, during the Second Punic War. In 241 the project was probably no more than an idea in some enthusiast's head, at best.[5]

The peninsula had been a strong and safe site for Phoenician traders and settlers in early times. Qart-hadasht, 'New City' in Phoenician, was suppos-edly founded earlier than Rome or any western Greek settlement, in 814 or 813 according to the early third-century historian from Sicily, Timaeus. The Greeks and Romans of later ages, probably elaborating a Carthaginian tradi-tion, told the story of Elissa or Dido who established the new city on the site of Byrsa. Archaeological finds do show a city existing by the earlier half of the eighth century, which brings us quite near to Timaeus' date. But Carthage was almost the youngest of the Phoenician settlements in the western Mediterranean; younger for instance than Gades, beside the Atlantic in southern Spain, and Utica a few miles up the coast from Carthage.

Other important Phoenician foundations were Hippou Acra west of Utica, Lepcis on the Greater Syrtes gulf, the gulf of Sirte to the south, Panormus in Sicily and Malaca in Spain. Like Carthage they were created to trade and many did so very successfully. But Carthage prospered more than any of them, thanks to her central Mediterranean position and the Carthaginians' talents in seafaring, commerce and (increasingly) agriculture. The city spread northwards beyond the hill-cemeteries. In the sixth and fifth centuries a Punic empire, too, began to grow.

By the start of the fifth century this embraced the far west of Sicily with its old Phoenician settlements and natural wealth, Sardinia's southern coastal lowlands, and Carthage's own hinterland with its people the Libyans. The Libyans paid taxes and Libyan conscripts were an important component of Punic armies. On the plateaux and in the mountains beyond, the Numidian peoples under their various kings varied between friends and vassals of the Punic republic, depending on distance and Punic assertiveness. The other Phoenician colonies, including the Spanish ones, became allies or friends with degrees of dependency that no doubt lessened with distance. Along the Algerian and Moroccan coasts of Africa a chain of small trading stations— for instance Rusicade, Tipasa, Iol and Lixus—extended Punic trade and influence to the straits of Gibraltar and beyond.

Punic traders ranged more widely still, from working the Atlantic coasts of Africa and Spain to gathering products of Egypt, Phoenicia and Asia Minor. They dealt with the Etruscans of Italy, as inscriptions illustrate from Pyrgi, port of Caere, engraved on sheets of gold in Etruscan and Punic around the year 500: these record Thefarie Velianas, lord of Caere, consecrating a shrine to the goddess Astarte. Near that date too the Carthaginians struck a treaty with the Romans, quoted by Polybius in Greek translation along with its successor of 348. These treaties restricted where and how Romans might trade or get supplies in Punic-dominated territories, and Carthaginians in Roman, while recognizing the Romans' control in their hinterland Latium. As well as showing that trade between the two states went back centuries, they illustrate how Hamilcar's and his fellow-citizens' ancestors dealt with other Mediterranean states less powerful at sea but important enough to deserve respect.[6]

Carthaginians were no more ethnically or racially exclusive than Romans or Greeks. They often found wives or husbands from Numidian peoples and Greek cities, for instance. A King Hamilcar who wrought fire and slaughter in Sicily in 480 had a Syracusan mother. During the war with the mercenaries soon after 241, Hamilcar Barca offered one of his daughters in marriage to his admirer the Numidian prince Naravas, and in a later decade a granddaughter was married to a Numidian king. The famous Sophoniba, daughter of another general during the Second Punic War, was the wife of two other Numidian kings in succession, the second time tragically. Two of Hannibal's agents in Sicily in the same war were born at Carthage, had a Punic mother but a Syracusan exile grandfather, bore Greek names and were at home in both cities. Hannibal himself, and before him his brother-in-law Hasdrubal, married Spanish wives. No Carthaginian, though, is recorded as married to a Roman.[7]

The Carthaginians' relations with their neighbours were not always this pacific. Every so often there were clashes with the Numidians: who for instance took the opportunity of Regulus' invasion in 256 to revolt against Punic domination and afterwards were harshly repressed. On the western seas, the Carthaginians left a reputation to later ages of jealously guarding their supposed monopoly of trade, stories much exaggerated all the same. In Sicily from 480 on, wars were repeatedly waged with the island's Greek states, notably Syracuse and Agrigentum. The Carthaginians won varied and sometimes impressive successes, but were never able to extend lasting control beyond the western quarter of the island.

On the other hand they fought Greeks only in Sicily, where Punic and Greek territorial borders and opportunities met. Cyrene, wealthy but over 1,000 coastal miles (1,600 kilometres) away towards Egypt, and Neapolis, Tarentum and other notable Greek cities of Italy aroused no hostilities. And though in the sixth century the Carthaginians had joined forces with the Etruscans to thwart Greek settlement in Sardinia, only a single clash is heard of with Massilia, the Greek colony in southern Gaul—and that not for certain. Most of the time Punic dealings with the Greek lands were mercantile. In return for products from Punic North Africa—purple dyes and fancy cloths were noteworthy, and pomegranates which the Romans called 'Punic apples'—and goods from other lands merchandised by Carthaginian dealers, the Greeks supplied wine, oil and ceramics to North Africa.

These items were not all they supplied. Greek culture had many attractions to offer even to an independently vigorous community and, from the fourth century on, the Carthaginians showed themselves receptive. In 396 they ceremoniously adopted the cult of Demeter and Core, goddesses of grain. Greek artworks and artistically decorated utensils were among their imports. Greek art motifs were imitated, for instance on Punic glass vessels, ritual razors, grave stelae and sarcophagi, as Egyptian forms already were. Punic houses borrowed Greek features: the peristyles, the pavement mosaic (but in a plainer local style of pottery and limestone fragments embedded in the floor-surface), even bathrooms with bathtub and washbasin. Hamilcar engaged a Greek tutor for his heir and cannot have been the only Carthaginian to do so. Again, from early in the fourth century the Carthaginian state began to issue coins: only in Sicily at first, to pay the mercenary troops, then later in North Africa as well. From the start they were based on Greek models and well produced.[8]

All this did not turn the Carthaginians into a Hellenized community. They had other sources of inspiration, Egypt for instance, and they kept close links with their mother-city Tyre. Above all, language and religion, both descended from Phoenicia, sustained cultural independence. Supreme among Punic deities were Ba'al Hammon the god and his consort Tanit, whom the Carthaginians often entitled *pene Ba'al*, 'Face of Ba'al'. Other divinities included Ba'al Shamim, Melqart whose name means 'lord of the city', Eshmoun with his temple on Byrsa hill, Reshep, and others unsatisfyingly shadowy.

The Carthaginians were strongly religious, not always along lines that appeal to moderns. Notoriously they sacrificed small children to the gods to avert catastrophes: not children of slaves, Libyans or foreigners, but their own. Plentiful archaeological evidence from the *tophet* suggests that the rite, called *molk*, increased over the centuries and that rich Carthaginians were specially assiduous. It may be that only stillborn babies, or those who died very young, were offered, but no ancient writer suggests it. The most striking *molk* on record took place in 310 when the city was menaced by Agathocles' expedition from Sicily—reportedly 500 victims all told, and all from aristocratic families. Melqart must have been appeased: Agathocles' expedition went down to disaster.

Carthage was under threat again half a century later, from the invading proconsul Regulus, but no mass *molk* is reported. Individual child-offerings were certainly made down to Hannibal's own lifetime (so the finds show). Maybe the community had outgrown the need for mass immolations, or was embarrassed by them under the eyes of the Hellenistic world.[9]

III

Carthage was now one of the greatest cities of the Mediterranean. Her state revenues at the outbreak of the war with Rome may be estimated at some 2,000 talents a year—12 million Greek drachmas—sparse though the evidence is. According to the historian Livy, by 193 the wealthy and tributary city of Lepcis was paying one talent a day in tax: our one explicit revenue-figure. Lepcis, later Lepcis Magna famous for its Roman remains, stands east of Tripoli on the Greater Syrtes shore, today's gulf of Sirte: but as Livy sites it by the Lesser Syrtes, today's gulf of Gabès, in the fertile Emporia region, he may have confused it with Leptis Minor, between Hadrumetum and Thapsus, and at any rate not too far north of the gulf of Gabès. Whether Lepcis or Leptis, the tribute may in fact represent what the whole region paid, with one of those cities as the collection-centre (the Emporia coast did stretch as far as Lepcis Magna). At a guess, all the rest of Punic North Africa—Carthage's own customs and harbour-dues, the tribute paid by the Libyans, any dues or levies extracted from allies like Utica and Hippou Acra, and whatever taxes were exacted from Carthaginians themselves—should have added up to maybe three times as much again.[10]

This rough-and-ready calculation gives Hannibal's city an annual revenue of 1,400–1,500 talents in 193: between 8,400,000 and 9 million Greek drachmas or recently established Roman *denarii*. Uncertain though it is, this estimate is plausible. In the early decades of the same century, the Roman republic's income, including indemnities and war-booty, has been reckoned as averaging 13–14 million *denarii* a year, in other words well over 2,000 talents. To Rhodes, a rich trading-city but hardly comparable even with second-century Carthage in size or possessions, her mainland territories in Asia Minor were paying 120 talents a year in the same period and her own customs-duties bringing in a million drachmas or about 167 talents—thus a total of just under 300 till Roman ill-will after the Third Macedonian War took away the former and slashed the latter.

In 264 Carthage's empire had included western Sicily and southern Sardinia, and her trade and agriculture were flourishing, so revenue of well over 2,000 talents in that era seems a reasonable though speculative estimate. This was a sizeable income, larger than the 1,000 talents estimated for Athens at the peak of her power and empire around 431. It would have fallen after 241, but in the 230s and 220s the new Punic empire in Spain as well as the annexations in Numidia must have added sizeably to revenues again, conceivably raising them over 3,000.

The indemnities that the Carthaginians later had to shoulder are compatible with this. After 241—or more probably 237—they had to pay the Romans 220 talents a year for ten years, after an opening payment of 1,000 and with a further 1,200 to be squeezed from them in 237. The indemnity after Hannibal's war, 200 a year, was equivalent to 12 million Roman *asses* or 1,200,000 *denarii*—less than after 241, but the Carthaginians had now lost Spain. By contrast Syracuse in Sicily was required to pay only 100 talents over 15 years when it made peace with the Romans in 263.[11]

In 241 there were probably close to 200,000 Carthaginian male citizens. There are no contemporary statistics but the geographer Strabo reports that at the start of the Third Punic War, a century later, the city was home to 700,000 people. Probably he means free persons, since ancient population statistics (and ancient guesses) rarely include slaves, but whether non-Carthaginian residents are also counted in we cannot say. Strabo must have got his figure from a writer on that war: it could have been Polybius, who was at Carthage in 146 as it died.

The total is impossible for the city alone, whose built-up area was too small on any calculation. Nor can the people living in the spread-out garden suburb of Megara have been very numerous. Modern estimates for the city itself vary widely, from as few as 125,000 residents to more than double that. But if Strabo's statistic means residents and their families living both in Carthage and in its own surrounding territory—distinct from the territories of sister cities like Utica and of the subject Libyans—it may be accepted as a round figure.

As Carthage was formidably prosperous in the last half-century of its existence, between 10 and 20 per cent of residents would be non-citizens (assuming that Strabo includes them, knowingly or not). On a conservative estimate, citizens and their families in Carthage and its surrounding territory would then total around 575,000 in 149, with adult males numbering between 160,000 and 175,000. Ninety-two years earlier, when they were a great power but at the end of a harrowing war with the Romans, the total would hardly be lower. Also to be reckoned in would be a number of citizens living elsewhere—traders, farmers, administrators—in North Africa, Sardinia and Spain, even if Sicily was now closed off. Aristotle in fact twice stresses the Punic state's habit of relieving social strains at home by sending out ordinary citizens to neighbouring towns to 'make them prosperous'. At a very conservative guess, the Carthaginian citizens living elsewhere might total 10,000 to 15,000, plus their families.

Punic human resources naturally included the other peoples under Punic control: the allied Phoenician cities and, above all, the subject Libyans. The wealth of the state also allowed it to hire mercenary troops (something never done by the Romans). Slaves were a further human resource. Little enough is known about them, but at least tens of thousands existed in Punic lands, and probably hundreds of thousands. The Punic state and its empire must have included some millions of people in 241, even after the loss of western Sicily. For comparison, 241,700 Roman citizens—adult males again—were registered in the census of 247, growing to 273,000 twenty-two years later. Polybius perhaps exaggeratedly reckons the Italian allies of military age in 225 at another half-million. In numbers at least, though not in militarized or geographic cohesion, the Carthaginians were still a match for the Romans.[12]

IV

To the contemporary Greek world the Carthaginians were barbarians just like the Romans. Neither people spoke Greek (a fatal flaw) and, even by the mid-third century, neither had anything that could be called a literature. None the less Greeks put the Carthaginians in a special category long before they did the same for the Romans. In the late fourth century Aristotle, analysing and classifying states' constitutions, included the political system of Carthage for discussion—the only non-Greek state to qualify. It had stable institutions with many Greek-like features: elected magistrates, a council or senate, a citizen assembly—all these could be found at Rome too, though Aristotle was uninterested—and even a few social features reminiscent of one Greek city or another. Men's meals in communal clubs recalled those at Sparta, for example. To Aristotle the Carthaginians' political system, in spite of its partiality to money, was 'aristocratic', meaning government by the best men: it had 'a threefold aim, wealth, virtue and the good of the people'. He approves of it.

Details, of course, and emphases differed. Originally the city had had kings like its mother Tyre, but monarchy had eventually given place to aristocratic rule. In Hamilcar's time the republic was presided over by two annually elected *sptm* or *shouphetim*, 'sufetes' in the Latin form (a kin-word to Hebrew *shophet*, judge). Whether these had replaced the king, or whether a nominal king still existed, is one of the many Punic unknowns. Greek and Roman writers often use the term 'king' without making clear whether they mean it literally or as a misnomer for sufete. (A complication is added by various lesser officials also, it seems, called sufetes.) Military commands were entrusted to generals elected by the citizens for particular theatres of campaigning, as Hamilcar was for Sicily. It looks unlikely that someone could be both sufete and general at the same time—no one is known who did—but Aristotle does emphasize that a Carthaginian could hold more than one office at the same time.

The precise powers and range of Punic executive offices, military and civil, are obscure too. Punic generals, according to Greek observers, had 'kingly'— no doubt meaning absolute—authority on campaign. The record shows that they could make pacts with foreign states, though these may then have had to be ratified at Carthage. Their power was matched by the risk they ran if they failed. Unusually in a republic, a defeated general was liable to be recalled and put to death: the fate of Hanno who lost the battle of the Aegates in 241.[13]

The collective political wisdom of the Carthaginians reposed in a council or senate of several hundred, many of them no doubt former sufetes and generals. The senate's formal collective name was 'The Mighty Ones' (*h'drm* or *hadirim*)—a noteworthy forerunner of *de Hoogmogendheden*, 'the High Mightinesses', the formal epithet of the Dutch States-General three centuries ago. How were senators recruited? We are not told. Tenure of one of the various official posts, for instance as a *rab* (a title much attested on Punic inscriptions though its functions are not clear), public scribe, or market inspector, or membership of what Aristotle calls the 'pentarchies', administrative Boards of Five, may have been the regular way in.

The senate, the Mighty Ones, dealt with questions of peace and war, and the overall direction of policy. Apparently it could interest itself in any aspect of internal affairs—once even forbidding citizens to learn Greek (a Roman writer claims), a ban not likely to have lasted long. The senate had an inner 'sacred council' by the third century, apparently 30 strong, whose authority Livy stresses. Just what it did is unknown: it may have organized the agenda of the Mighty Ones, and acted too as an executive committee.[14]

This inner council was an institution peculiar to the Carthaginians. So were some others, above all the tribunal of One Hundred, or One Hundred and Four. This was set up 150 years (or more) before Hamilcar's time to supervise and where necessary to discipline generals. According to Aristotle, members were chosen not by the senate, but by the Boards of Five from among the senators, and purely on merit (process unknown, as usual). He calls the Hundred and Four 'the highest authority' at Carthage—arguably an overstatement since he applies the same term to the chief magistrates. Perhaps by his day the tribunal had extended its jurisdiction, though we can only surmise in what directions: for instance scrutinizing the work of civil magistrates, sufetes included.

Though not mentioned in events of the century and a quarter after Aristotle, it was probably enough the same tribunal which convicted the hapless generals put to death at various times for failure, and likely enough it was the one whose judgement Hamilcar risked facing in 241. Livy's 'order of judges' appointed for life, reportedly the most powerful institution in the state soon after the Second Punic War, was very likely though not definitely the same body. Its powers may have fluctuated over that length of time too, as we shall see.[15]

The ordinary Carthaginian male citizen had a voice in government too. The citizen body was fairly limited: women had no vote, nor of course did slaves. Perhaps too Punic men of low economic status, like poor artisans, were excluded, but the evidence is too indirect to be reliable. Citizens themselves no doubt had to reach legal manhood, whatever age that was, before they qualified as voters. The men of Phoenician towns like Utica and Hippou Acra—not to mention the millions of subject Libyans—were not Carthaginians, though each may have had suffrage in his own community. But nobody expected that even the existing 180,000 Punic citizens would or could all take part in voting, any more than all citizens could at Rome. The central square below the Byrsa hill, however big, would not have held more than a fraction of them. Plainly only limited numbers took part.

The citizen assembly, meeting in the square, elected sufetes and generals, and passed laws. What procedures were followed and what determined a candidate's eligibility for office are predictably unknown, but the lavish spending which our informants insist was taken for granted meant that only rich men could compete. This in turn is a clue, both to sharply marked patron–client relationships between the powerful few in public life and many if not most ordinary voters, and at the same time to constantly fluctuating political cliques and followings—the great men manoeuvring for allies and against opponents; friendships, enmities (and clientships) very changeable; and voters on the lookout for the biggest or most ingratiating offers.

The assembly's powers were oddly qualified. If the sufetes—Aristotle calls them the 'kings'—and the senate agreed on referring a matter to the people, this was done. Likewise if sufetes and senate disagreed over referral; and (presumably) so again if one sufete and the bulk of the senate were at odds with the other sufete. When consulted, the citizens had more freedom to discuss and decide than for instance Romans did in their assemblies. But Aristotle equally implies that sufetes and senate, if they saw eye to eye, could take decisions without consulting the citizens at all. How often this happened we do not know, but happen it did: memorably in 218 when the Romans' declaration of war was vociferously and fatally accepted in the senate.[16]

V

This fairly tidy, and to Greek theorists impressive, political setup must not obscure one important reality. For much of their known history, the Carthaginians had in practice been governed by dominant individuals and their close kin.

Whether or not it was a monarchy in its beginnings, virtually on its first appearance in the historical record the Punic state is reported as falling under the control of a rebellious general, Malchus—a name that seems a Latin version of Phoenician *milk*, 'king.' In rather more detail the same source, Justin, then tells of the rule of Malchus' successor Mago, another general, and Mago's descendants after him. One of his sons was the half-Syracusan Hamilcar of 480, whom Herodotus terms 'king', so these rulers belong to the sixth century and after. They were seen by at least some foreigners as royal: Diodorus describes two of the dynasty as kings 'according to the laws'. Just what this title really meant is not clear, but its implication is plainly that the Magonids dominated the affairs of city and empire. It may be that by now the kingship had become elective, though held for life and remaining in the hands of one family.

The Magonids' known activities were military, and it was military defeat abroad that finally broke the dynasty's dominance at home some time in the early fourth century. For the same reason the tribunal of the Hundred and Four was created, to control future over-mighty generals. Yet not every ambitious Carthaginian was deterred from hopes of Magonid-style domination. Later in the century the most eminent citizen was one Hanno—styled the Great like his namesake a century later—who, after holding high military command in Sicily, was accused of plotting to make himself master of the state and was put to death with many of his kinsmen and supporters. His family remained powerful even so, providing other notable generals (none of them very successful) against the Greeks until Agathocles' time. But in 308, just after Agathocles' invasion failed, one of them conspired to make himself master of the city by a military coup. In an episode vividly recorded by Diodorus, Bomilcar's attempt was thwarted and he was executed on the cross. This was the end of the Hannonid ascendancy.[17]

These later efforts at dominating the state may have been partly encouraged by the examples of successful autocracy that Punic aristocrats could see across the water, not just in Greece (like Jason of Pherae in the 370s and of course the Macedonian kings) but equally in Sicily—above all the triumphant four-decade rule of Dionysius the Elder at Syracuse, later too that of Agathocles. Autocrats and kings were now in the ascendant in much of the Greek world. Their glamour and power might well incite men of wealth, status and following at Carthage, who in any case had the recent memory of Magonid dominance as a spur. But such moves failed against resistance from the bulk of the city élite. These had earlier grown strong enough to limit and then discard entrenched Magonid supremacy. They had refined the complex republican institutions that reinforced oligarchic control and attracted Aristotle's approval. They now showed they could cope effectively with the ambitions of even so eminent a figure as the conspirator Hanno and so unscrupulous a general as Bomilcar. We can infer that whatever these men's resources in funds and followers, they did not outweigh those of the other grandees united against them.

In the more than sixty years since Bomilcar's failure the oligarchic republic suffered no more pressure from over-mighty citizens, or at any rate none is reported. Leading men and lesser ones no doubt competed or co-operated to win office and influence at different levels. Each would have his group of friends and followers, possibly also more formally recognized clients or social dependants. To judge by the past cases of Magonids and Hannonids, and the coming one of Hamilcar and his family, such allegiances were very often hereditary—though it would be rash to suppose that they bound everyone, grandees and ordinary voters alike, in unloosable fetters or for unchanging generations. But how competition and co-operation worked, how changeable or stable the political groupings were, how much based on family allegiances and how much on policy issues—not to mention what family groups existed, where each came from and what it took for a family to rise into, or fall from, prominence—all these issues remain, once again, largely unknown.

It seems likely that the war with the Romans brought about a fair degree of solidarity in the ruling élite. Some defeated generals might be crucified, but even in the darkest days of Regulus' invasion no bickerings among Punic leaders are heard of, and no hints of treachery or unrest. Competition for office, all the same, surely continued; and, after a decade and a half of fighting, views on how to wage the war could well start to diverge. The rundown of effort after the victories of 249, accompanied by the removal of both the victorious commanders in favour of Hamilcar Barca, may signal a change in political fortunes for rival groups: Hanno and his allies—Hamilcar conceivably among them—now winning pre-eminence over whoever had enjoyed it earlier. We have already seen that Hanno's group apparently then kept its pre-eminence until the war ended.

But this was not to last much longer. The loss of the war in Sicily more than counterbalanced the gains in Africa, and brought on a crisis that permanently shifted the structure of Punic politics.

III

THE REVOLT OF AFRICA

I

Not only had the Carthaginians lost the war and their possessions in Sicily; they soon found themselves in danger of losing everything at home too. The 20,000 soldiers evacuated from Sicily—mercenaries from all round the western Mediterranean and conscripts from among the subject Libyans of Punic North Africa itself—had plenty of grievances, especially over their unpaid arrears (the size of which lost nothing in the telling). They were suspicious, unruly and armed.

They found a republic both too impoverished to pay them and too maladroit to fob them off successfully with promises or part-payments. Gisco's careful efforts to prevent them from uniting into one body were discontinued. The men were vexed by being sent inland to the distant city of Sicca and soon marched back to Tunes near Carthage. Then insistent official haggling over the payments combined with agitation among the men to cause an explosion, and their resort to arms gave a signal to the oppressed Libyans. All at once, the lands around Carthage and her fellow-Phoenician cities Utica and Hippou Acra erupted in revolt.

Utica and Hippou Acra, on the coast to Carthage's north, were laid under siege. A rebel corps blockaded Carthage from Tunes a few miles away, cutting access to the city at the western end of the isthmus. Coins and Polybius' account show that the rebels obtained good sources of funds and presented themselves to some extent as a conscious political force—'the Libyans', and perhaps also 'the army'—opposing their oppressors.

The haggler for the Carthaginians had been Hanno, still the general in charge of Libya. He was now given command against the rebels. It is reasonable to infer that the muddle and (in the soldiers' eyes) the bad faith of the Carthaginians' dealings with the returned veterans was his and his faction's doing. That there may have been sound financial reasons for haggling is not much of a defence.[1]

Another mistake, or so the troops saw it, was not to make Hamilcar and Gisco the negotiators from the start. Gisco had finally been sent to them and almost succeeded in reaching an agreement, but feelings ran so high by then—especially among the Libyan troops—that talks broke down. Hamilcar did not put in an appearance at all, partly no doubt because he knew of the troops' irritation with him. Gisco, who had repeated his chief's promises when evacuating them, they arrested when the talks broke down—and he later suffered a hideous fate at their hands. Had Hamilcar been with him, Punic and not only Punic history would have progressed very differently.

But Barca probably had a further reason for not involving himself in the talks. His enemies (it seems) launched a prosecution against him, alleging misconduct during his Sicilian command.

This is an inference from Appian, the only writer to mention a prosecution. He has it happen after the war in Africa ended, thus during 237; but chronology is very much against so late a date. Besides, by then Hamilcar was the saviour of his country. Lodging charges in 237 based on Sicilian events of the 240s would have been a fairly predictable waste of effort. Hamilcar's rather inglorious return in 241 and immediate disappearance from the public scene offer a more convincing context. Appian often gets details in this era confused (for instance, the terms of the original and the revised peace-terms of 241, and the course of postwar relations between Carthage and Rome), so a mistake in chronology may well be another.[2]

Prosecution for wartime misconduct or theft of public funds (Appian has both, in different works) suggests a case before the tribunal of One Hundred and Four. Notoriously a guilty verdict could mean crucifixion or else a flight into exile. But Hamilcar won the support of 'the leading men', writes Appian—or his term may even mean 'the men in power'—and the case failed. Who the enemies were is not stated, and of Hamilcar's rescuers the only one named is Hasdrubal, who then or later became his son-in-law. Appian adds that this young man was 'the most popular' of the ex-general's supporters. Enemies then or later claimed a homosexual relationship originally existed between the two men, but there is no evidence in support.

Hasdrubal is usually thought to have allied himself with Hamilcar only after the war with the mercenaries and Libyans. But this depends on combining Appian's date for the prosecution with Diodorus' report (which clearly comes from a better-informed, or at least better-organized, source) that, after the war, Hamilcar founded a villainously democratic party and thus gained wealth and power. Yet not only is Appian's dating probably wrong but Diodorus does not mention Hasdrubal amid these later events at all. Hamilcar by 237 was popular on his own account. If he needed a popular ally or allies, it would have been in the postwar months of 241.

Another such ally may be suggested: Hanno the Great, the commanding political and (at home) military figure of the day. Although his poor negotiating skills helped to provoke the mercenaries into rebellion, his repute was still high—for he was promptly given the command against the rebels. Had Hanno been one, presumably a leading one, of the enemies behind the prosecution, Appian's phrase for Hamilcar's rescuers is harder to account for and so is Hamilcar's escape from danger. What then about Hasdrubal's superior popularity, if that is what Appian implies? It could be a touch of exaggeration, allowing the author to introduce the future second leader of the Barcid dynasty at a dramatic point.[3]

If not an ally of Hamilcar's over the trial, Hanno probably stayed neutral at least. Whether he owed a favour to the ex-general, or simply thought the attack on him mischievous, or felt that now was not the time to destroy a talented commander whom the state might soon need (the great rebellion was surely looming or had already broken out), we do not know. But it would be a mistake to assume that the two were already divided by bitter rivalry.

II

Hanno had done very well fighting Numidians and taxing the Libyans, but he was a good deal less successful against the veterans. His level of incompetence is no doubt overstressed in Polybius' account, which draws on a strongly pro-Hamilcar tradition. Even so things soon reached a point, probably early in 240, where Hanno's efforts had been stymied and he may even have been cut off from Carthage, on the far side of Utica and, if so, dangerously positioned between the rebels besieging that town and those beleaguering Hippou Acra to the north. The Carthaginians decided to appoint a second general as well. Hamilcar Barca was the choice.

Hamilcar was not given Hanno's army but commanded a second one, which the Carthaginians had been gathering (like Hanno's) from mercenaries, rebel deserters and citizens. He himself may well have been responsible for putting it together. The alternative—Hamilcar, though out of judicial danger, staying in retirement while some other person recruited and trained the force, then stepping forward to take command—seems less likely. As the other top general of Carthage he was the obvious man for the task of raising and then leading a second army. Its original aim may have been to confront the rebels at Tunes who had cut Carthage off from the rest of the country (though not from access by sea) but, if so, Hanno's predicament changed this: Hamilcar broke out towards Utica.

Two generals in the field together for a major campaign was not a novelty. Even three had operated jointly on occasion. At times too, one general seems to have held the superior authority: in 250 and 249 Adherbal apparently had overall authority while others, including Carthalo, were his deputies. This seems not to have happened now. At first Hanno operated on his own and Hamilcar does not seem to have had the power to give him orders. When the rebels murdered Gisco and his fellow-prisoners, the authorities at Carthage urged each general to take action; they did not urge one to do so and leave it to him to direct the other. Hamilcar did then 'call Hanno to him' so as to unite the two armies, but this was probably a request or suggestion. For when the two did join forces only to quarrel bitterly, the only solution that the authorities in Carthage could devise was to let their two armies decide who should stay in command and who should retire.

Later on, with Hanno holding a command once again, it took a delegation of senators to persuade the two to bury their antagonism in the national interest. It looks, then, as though the two men were originally equals in command. This, plus the fact that their quarrel seemingly took the Carthaginians by surprise—hence the desperate and unprecedented solution of letting the troops decide—also adds some support to the view that the two men, up to then, had been political allies or at least had co-operated politically.[4]

III

Once appointed general, Hamilcar won some quick successes. He raised the siege of Utica—and probably gave back to Hanno his strategic freedom of movement—by a victory on the bank of the river Bagradas nearby, then reconquered parts of the Libyan hinterland. This endangered rebel supplies and reinforcements, so forces from Tunes set out after him, led by two of the original ringleaders of the revolt, Spendius the Campanian and Autaritus the Gaul. This reaction may have been one of Hamilcar's hopes in marching inland: as well as recovering subject territory and harassing supply-routes to the enemy, he was dividing rebel forces, which could make them easier to destroy. If Polybius is correct that 70,000 Libyan recruits had joined the 20,000 veterans—or even if he exaggerates—thinning such forces offered the Carthaginians the only hope of conquering them.[5]

Very luckily for the Carthaginians, they had the Romans on their side. They nearly did not. When the revolt broke out, the Carthaginians still had enough naval strength to begin intercepting traders from Italy (probably from other lands too) who supplied goods to the rebels, and the haul of Italians and Romans had reached more than 500 when a stiff protest arrived from Rome probably in spring or early summer 240. Hanno, Hamilcar and the other Carthaginian leaders recognized that to antagonize their ex-enemies would be the last word in folly. The offenders were set free, no doubt with apologies as fulsome as could be penned.

The soundness of this response was soon proved. The Romans in turn released 2,700 remaining Punic prisoners of war ransom-free (the Carthaginians had not the money to ransom them), banned Italians from doing business with the rebels, and complied with other requests—for instance, so Appian and Zonaras report, waiving the clause in Lutatius' treaty forbidding one state from hiring mercenaries in the lands of the other. The freed veterans look like Carthaginian citizens, who would be a welcome addition to the city's hard-pressed military resources.

Roman goodwill turned out to be one of the decisive factors in a struggle that grew more and more bitter. It also encouraged Hiero of Syracuse to

continue his own helpful efforts, which were equally vital. His motive, prag-
matically set forth by Polybius, was to make sure that Carthage remained in
existence as some sort of balance to the might of Rome. The Romans too
were hardly motivated by simple generosity: they took an austere view of
rebellion by subjects and allies (they had had to crush one themselves just
after Lutatius' peace) and probably worried too about a dangerous power-
vacuum in North Africa if the Carthaginians were overthrown. Not to
mention that they would not be paid their yearly war-indemnity, though they
may have waived its payment during the revolt.

Hamilcar's operations were not risk-free. Spendius shadowed him but kept
to higher ground, avoiding pitched battles and harassing the Punic army on
its march—tactics much like those later followed by Fabius Cunctator against
Hamilcar's son. When Libyan and Numidian reinforcements joined him he
was even able to entrap Hamilcar's army, and with superior numbers.[6]

Hamilcar may well have expected destruction, but his carelessness or error
was counterbalanced by his good fortune. One of the Numidian leaders, the
young prince Naravas, brought his 2,000 horsemen over in eagerness for the
general's friendship. Hamilcar's anxiety about the situation he had got into is
suggested by his enthusiastic reaction—he promised not only to make Naravas his partner in action but also to give him a daughter in marriage. The two
of them then smashed the rebels and their remaining Numidian allies in a
spectacular victory. Having pulverized this enemy army Hamilcar began a
much-publicized policy of freeing prisoners unharmed and even accepting
them into his own forces if they wished.[7]

What Hanno was doing meanwhile we are not told. Polybius is our only
source and his strongly pro-Hamilcar account has little time for other generals or operations. The other rebel leader, Mathos, had taken charge of the
forces blockading Hippou Acra while a third rebel force remained at Tunes.
Most likely then Hanno made himself useful by offering threats to both sets
of rebels—possibly using Utica, halfway between them, as his base—to prevent them from pressing their own efforts or sending reinforcements to
Spendius. They certainly made no progress against Hippou or Carthage.[8]

IV

But at this point, probably around the end of 240, the struggle took on an
even uglier colour. To counter Hamilcar's successes, and stimulated by the
mercenaries in Sardinia who had seized that island for themselves, the rebel
leaders tortured to death their long-held Punic prisoners (including their old
and respected commandant from Lilybaeum, Gisco) and began to treat other
Punic captives in the same way. Hamilcar, still operating away from Carthage,
abandoned his mercy policy for one of no quarter to prisoners—which
meant putting some to the sword and throwing others under the feet of war-
elephants, following a precedent from Alexander the Great's time.

Polybius sees this change as not just understandable but necessary, but it may well have been counterproductive. Rebels now had to choose between being slaughtered and fighting on. Some rebel areas that had previously yielded may have taken up arms again: for much of Libya and 'most of its cities' were still in revolt well over a year later.[9]

Hamilcar plainly found himself under some pressure again, for he now thought it desirable for Hanno to join forces with him. This may also have been how he interpreted a new message from the authorities at Carthage, urging both generals to avenge Gisco and his companions, and in any case he would be forming plans for the new campaigning season of 239. Just what move he had in mind for the joint army we are not told—it would still have been fairly small, probably not much over 20,000 men—but at a guess he aimed to pounce on the different rebel camps in turn before they could try any union of forces in turn. Instead and ironically, the union of the two Punic armies led to disunion between the two generals.

It may have been due to an entirely personal matter. But, rather likelier, they may have disagreed on strategy and methods. Hanno, for instance, may not have liked his colleague's unalloyed frightfulness: whatever his talents for squeezing taxes out of subjects, in his capture of Theveste he had shown a preference for leavening severity with moderation. Or—even though he had agreed to join Barca—he may have felt they ran a serious risk in taking the bulk of Carthage's field forces well away from the city and the coast, while Tunes remained a rebel centre and Hippou under siege.

On both of these counts Hanno would have had good grounds for criticism. He may well have been unhappy too about his colleague's strategy for the coming campaign. At all events he refused to co-operate with Hamilcar, and without Hanno Hamilcar thought it too risky to act. The paralysis was broken only when 'the Carthaginians'—we may infer the senate seconded by the people's assembly—ordered the troops to determine which of the two should stay in command and which step down.

Just who did the choosing we are not told. Maybe the entire army, Carthaginians, mercenaries, allies and any Libyan levies: after all who their leader was would have a direct bearing on whether they all won or lost. Yet legally the position was a Carthaginian office, and normally the citizen body of Carthage chose the holder. Mercenaries were hired professionals; allied and Libyan troops served because they had to. Most likely then it was the citizen soldiers and officers who decided between Hanno or Hamilcar—though their choice was probably encouraged by the other troops too.

The men kept Hamilcar. This was testimony, from the judges best qualified, to the quality of his leadership compared with Hanno's. Hanno's defects are no doubt too gleefully stressed by Polybius, but if he had achieved anything so far in the war it was limited: preventing the rebels from capturing Utica and Hippou Acra. Hamilcar, despite his propensity for risk-taking and occasional misjudgements, had inflicted real hurt on them. Had the troops voted the other way it is far from certain that the Carthaginians would have won the war.[10]

Hamilcar's position was significantly enhanced by this step. He was now in supreme command. Another general, Hannibal by name, was soon sent out by 'the citizens'—but he held a clearly subordinate authority and quite likely was chosen at Hamilcar's request. Barca thus took over the military and political position that Hanno had enjoyed for most of the past ten years, and with the extra advantage that there was no other general, in Sicily or anywhere else, to match him. At Carthage his interests would be looked after by his friends and associates, notably Hasdrubal. It might look as though he was now supreme politically as well as militarily—and that Hanno from now on was a mortal enemy.

This is too simple a reading of events. Hanno still had strong support at home, for some time later (probably during 238) he was not only reappointed to a generalship but, it seems, again on an equal footing with his rival. More than this, he and Hamilcar from then on 'co-operated singlemindedly' until the war was won. In other words they were still prepared to collaborate despite what had happened.

Again, if Hamilcar already had the political muscle to oust Hanno at the time they quarrelled, why use the roundabout—and risky—method of letting the troops choose between them? Of course it may be that he knew the troops were for him, while at Carthage Hanno's support equalled his. But if so, Hanno's supporters in their turn had no reason to agree to the measure, which (moreover) was unprecedented. More probably then the move was a genuine effort to cut the Gordian knot of deadlock.[11]

V

Centralized command was certainly needed now, for more disasters struck the Carthaginians. A laden supply-fleet coming up from the Emporia region was lost in a storm: a spring storm, for the year 239 should have begun by now. Even worse, their last two loyal allies, Hippou Acra and Utica, defected to the rebellion.

Polybius presents this turnaround as inexplicable ingratitude, but some of its reasons may be guessed. Hippou had been under siege from the beginning, with Mathos himself in command of the besiegers, and Utica, though relieved earlier by Hamilcar and then it seems protected by Hanno, was again exposed—probably again besieged by the enemy—when the two generals united their forces elsewhere. The paralysis of Punic effort caused by their quarrel was surely the last straw. The two cities could envisage the Carthaginians' resistance soon falling apart and themselves being easy meat for the rebels. Perhaps the pro-Carthage faction in each lost power to rivals who then led the defection.

As a result the rebels could now beleaguer the walls of Carthage herself. This was probably around the middle of 239.[12]

The city was far from defenceless. It had its large population and at least a modest navy; sea communications were open and so food and fresh mercenaries could be obtained; the king of Syracuse and the Roman republic both supplied help. Hamilcar's son-in-law, later famous as a master diplomat, may have contributed to these relations working smoothly. Hamilcar and his deputy Hannibal, too outnumbered to tackle the besiegers directly, instead harassed their communications with the rest of the country, while Naravas the Numidian continued his invaluable support. Rather like Caesar's legions outside Alesia two centuries later, the besiegers in effect became besieged.

The siege probably lasted some months. Hamilcar's attrition strategy was bound to be a slow process: his forces were not large and the small Punic navy likewise could not hope to cut off all supply by sea to the rebels. Yet the Carthaginians, masters of their seas and of much of the countryside, could afford a slow-strangulation struggle better than their foes. In these conditions, the siege was even an advantage to them.

By contrast Mathos and his colleagues no longer had much choice of strategy. To abandon the siege would be a heavy blow to morale. Besides, the only alternative would be to try to crush Hamilcar himself, and he had shown how dangerous that would be. They hung on grimly outside Carthage, with numbers no doubt thinning from sickness and desertion as Hamilcar's pressure tightened. If they kept the siege going through the winter of 239–238, the starvation their troops came to suffer is all the more readily explained. Supplies to Carthage too probably lessened, but with the return of spring they would grow again and the rebels' spirits could only sink further.

Finally they did give up the siege. All they could do now was go after their tormentor. The breakout at least allowed them to collect some new recruits, though Polybius' figure of 50,000 looks grossly inflated. Not much imagination was shown. Mathos held the rebel headquarters at Tunes while once more Spendius and Autaritus led an expeditionary force inland, now with a colleague, Mathos' fellow-Libyan Zarzas, who was probably one of the new arrivals. Once more they tried Fabian tactics in hopes of trapping the Carthaginians amid hills or in a pass. But this time Hamilcar harassed them. What was virtually a guerrilla campaign, most likely during the spring and early summer of 238, steadily whittled down their numbers. Mathos remained immobile at Tunes, which suggests that another Punic force (the garrison in Carthage?) was pinning him down. At length Hamilcar succeeded in manoeuvring the whole rebel army into an escape-proof trap at a place called The Saw, probably a razorback mountain ridge—much like the trap in which Spendius and Autaritus had once shut him up, but there was no Naravas to rescue them.

The general's later Roman detractors probably made much of what ensued. Even though we have only Polybius' friendly account, his behaviour hardly shines. Having eaten all their stores and even their prisoners and slaves, the rebels sent out ten delegates—Spendius, Autaritus and Zarzas among them— to ask for terms. Hamilcar promised to release the entire army except for ten whom he would choose. The ten delegates must have known what was coming but, heroic in their way, they accepted and of course were seized. Hamilcar did not tell the suddenly leaderless rebels what had been agreed; instead, when they sprang to arms, they were slaughtered to the last man.[13]

Hamilcar was taking the policy of frightfulness to its extreme. The murderers of Gisco did not in his view deserve civilized handling. Promises to and pacts with them need merely be manoeuvres. His harshness was not played out, either. While he and Hannibal brought most of rebel Libya back under control, Spendius and his nine confrères were kept to become a public show. At length—probably it was the middle of 238—the victorious generals marched back to Tunes, boxed Mathos' camp in between their two forces, Hannibal on the Carthage side of the position and Hamilcar on the southern, and nailed the ten rebel leaders to crosses outside Hannibal's camp, in sight of their remaining comrades.

This public gesture of how the republic punished rebellion and treachery backfired right away. The infuriated Mathos fell on Hannibal's camp, routed his men and captured the general himself, without Hamilcar on the opposite side of Tunes learning of it until too late. In grim parody of a sacrificial rite Hannibal was tortured at the foot of Spendius' cross, then nailed to it alive in place of the Campanian, while around the dead rebel leader's body thirty high-ranking Punic prisoners were slain. With Hannibal's force fled, Hamilcar found it necessary to retreat with his own troops northwards to the mouth of the Bagradas. The siege of Tunes was over.

This defeat probably came about because he and his deputy had been more concerned with making a propaganda point—punishing the rebel leaders— than with keeping proper watch on Mathos. Their forces may have been equal, or even superior, to his (an encouragement to overconfidence), but by separating them too widely Hamilcar had handed a tactical advantage to the enemy. He had not made that mistake when surrounding Spendius and company at The Saw.

All the same it was a defeat, not a disaster. Hannibal's camp had lain between Tunes and Carthage, and his army was routed but not destroyed. Much or most of it could escape to the city or else the coast beween Carthage and the Bagradas. Carthage itself had its own defenders, whom Mathos had not been able to defeat while the Punic field army was away. The most pressing needs would be to gather up Hannibal's surviving troops and prevent Mathos from fleeing to, or drawing any aid from, Utica and Hippou Acra (not that these places ever had given the rebels much help, so far as we know). This would explain why Hamilcar marched northward rather than, for example, moving to shield Carthage. Mathos had won himself some breathing-space but that was all. Hamilcar still held the strategic advantage.[14]

It did not seem so reassuring to the people in the city. Yet again the war had taken an unexpected and frightening twist. Thirty chosen senators and a force of citizen troops escorted his old colleague Hanno out to Hamilcar's camp, with a mission to persuade the two men to be reconciled and to co-operate for the sake of the state. By going with them Hanno already showed he was willing, but Hamilcar took a deal of persuading. None the less, from then on he and Hanno did co-operate smoothly to bring about final victory.

VI

Hanno had masterminded a skilful comeback, or so it might seem. Polybius specifies that when he went out to Hamilcar he was general once more; and the stress on their reconciliation and co-operation indicates that, as before, the two were equals in authority. The death of Hannibal had probably left the way open for him to win re-election, if only because there was no other leading commander available. Yet even with Hamilcar's prestige temporarily dented it would have been fatuous, not to mention perilous, to appoint to equal rank someone guaranteed to wrangle with him and oppose his plans. Obviously he did have a following among the citizens, but so did Hamilcar, whose interests were being sustained by Hasdrubal and others. And Hanno's troops would be those sent from Carthage, no serious match for Hamilcar's veterans in numbers and experience.

By going to Hamilcar with the 30 senators Hanno was not just signalling his readiness to co-operate for their country's good but, in effect, conceding the other's political superiority. At the same time he made it clear, through his equal status as general and the troops he brought with him, that he was still a force to be reckoned with. This was an arrangement that Hamilcar could accept, quite likely under advice from his son-in-law (who may even have been one of the 30), even if it took some effort—'many and varied arguments', Polybius writes—by the envoys to bring him round.

The war entered on its last stage, probably around autumn 238. As the Carthaginians could send city troops to Hamilcar, clearly as reinforcements, the rebels had probably abandoned Tunes. Certainly they neither attacked Carthage nor threatened Hamilcar after their success, and they are next heard of near Leptis Minor, in Byzacium to the south—an obvious refuge since the Punic field army barred the way northwards. No longer able to threaten Carthage or bring help to Utica and Hippou, their only hope was to try to rouse the Libyan hinterland anew.

But like Spendius and his confrères earlier in the year, they were harried relentlessly until driven to stake everything at last on a pitched battle. Polybius mentions skirmishes 'around Leptis and some other cities' and then a final calling-in, by both sides, of all available allied and garrison troops. This suggests that the campaign went on for some weeks or months. What garrison troops the rebels might still have by then is not clear—but there were some in towns in Byzacium, one of which became their last refuge—while for allies they were probably limited to some Numidian chieftains plus Utica and Hippou, none of which seems likely to have furnished many men.

Hamilcar and Hanno by contrast would have few problems maintaining or even adding to their numbers and keeping them well supplied. When the last battle came, it is no surprise that they won. The rebels who survived fled to a nearby town (we are not told its name) and then gave themselves up. Mathos, captured separately, was taken back to Carthage for a horrific death-march through its streets some time later, apparently as part of Hamilcar's and Hanno's triumphal parade.

The whole of the Libyan hinterland was now back under Punic rule. The last stage of all was forcing Hippou and Utica on the coast, Carthage's sister cities, to yield. They were fearful of surrendering because their treatment of the Carthaginians in their midst had been so merciless—but it was not long before Hanno outside one city and Barca outside the other prompted a change of mind. Quite possibly the generals offered mild terms, for Utica at any rate kept its special relationship with Carthage. Indemnities (noted by Polybius) and the handover of the rebel faction leaders can be surmised.

At some point too, perhaps when reasserting Punic control over the Libyan hinterland, the generals may have extended the boundaries of control over some of the Numidian peoples who had miscalculated which side to back in the revolt. The Carthaginians were unforgiving. One tribe, the Micatani, Diodorus mentions elsewhere: it suffered wholesale slaughters, women and children as well as menfolk. Hamilcar no doubt found Naravas an invaluable ally for this too, though (rather oddly) the young Numidian lord never reappears in our sources.

The great revolt, begun in the late months of 241, had lasted three years and about four months—so Polybius records. Early in 237, then, North Africa was again at peace. This left only Sardinia to be dealt with, and its recovery now looked all the easier: the native islanders had recently been so provoked by their mercenary occupiers that they had risen up to drive them over to Italy, whose rulers had recently shown them no sympathy at all.[15]

VII

The effects of this lengthy struggle are hard to gauge in detail. Besides the main campaigning that we hear of, there must have been many smaller conflicts and scuffles around Punic North Africa—loyal Punic groups versus rebel ones, defecting Libyan communities confronting loyal ones, deserters and brigands operating impartially at everyone's expense—not to mention the marches, countermarches, raids and skirmishes by the field armies in their excursions into the hinterland. Some regions may have remained fairly untouched, like the Syrtes coasts, or lightly affected (Byzacium, and other places well removed from Carthage's environs like Thabraca, Thugga and

Theveste). Yet losses in men, animals and goods must have been heavy on both sides. So too the money costs: as one indicator, the gold and silver coins struck by the Carthaginians and rebels during the war seem even worse debased than those of Carthage in the war with Rome.[16]

The Carthaginians had been at war, in practice, for 27 years: first with the Romans, then with their own rebels. They had lost territories, and their own countryside had been fought and refought over. They can scarcely have kept their trade and finances flourishing at the levels of 264. Across the Mediterranean they had a former enemy, even if now a friend, with might and resources much greater than in 264 and a vigorous commercial community in its own right. To avoid becoming by default a satellite of Roman power, the Punic state had to recover from its trials as fast as possible.

Recovery depended on making fullest possible use of what advantages remained. The city was essentially untouched, so far as we can tell. Trade and a small navy had operated throughout the war; and revenues, indemnities and fines could now flow in from the reconquered territories (nothing suggests that the Libyans were let off lightly). But more was surely needed to pay for restoring what had been lost and to rebuild prosperity—not to mention paying the Romans their war-indemnity, whether or not this had been suspended in the meantime. New and copious sources of wealth were needed.

Sardinia might be retaken and there were plenty more of Numidia's broad uplands that might be annexed, but the island's wealth was limited and the Numidians were not easy to hold down against their will. Hamilcar had a different project in mind, one he probably formed before the war ended but when its end was in sight: the Carthaginians' major move should be into Spain.

Spain, or Iberia to the Greeks, had long been part of their western network of trade and influence, with its Phoenician colonies stretching along the south coast to the Atlantic at Gades, and its wealth in precious metals and agriculture. Mercenaries from Spain—Iberians and Celtiberians—were important elements in Punic armies (and in the recent rebel forces). The Carthaginians' special interest in southern Spain was shown, for instance, in their second treaty with the Romans, struck around 348: not only were Romans barred from sailing along sensitive North African coasts as in the first treaty, but now they were barred too from sailing beyond 'Mastia Tarseiou'—probably if not certainly the port of Mastia in south-eastern Spain, today's Cartagena.

But the Carthaginians had never directly conquered or settled Spanish territory. An expedition to save Gades from enemy neighbours is mentioned, probably in the time of the early Magonids, but once the danger was over the force went home. Gades and other Phoenician settlements in Spain were probably allies of Carthage, but on terms looser than the ones binding the settlements in Africa (for instance they did not fight in Punic wars). Hamilcar's grand design was to transform these light and indirect relationships into direct and firm domination. What his predecessors had done in Libya—Hanno among them—he would do across the Mediterranean in southern Iberia.[17]

The benefits would be enormous. Spanish wealth could be exploited and also further developed. Carthage's trading position—damaged by the war with Rome, which for instance had effectively abolished the treaty of 348—would be strengthened. Iberians could be recruited not only as mercenaries but if necessary as conscripts, like the Libyans. The result would be a great increase in Punic military resources, a factor particularly important now when the republic, under the eyes of the entire Hellenistic world, had lost and suffered so much in its two ordeals of fire.

The benefits to Hamilcar and his group of friends and supporters would be enormous too, so long as they were given charge of the project. Whatever Hanno's recent services were, it was Hamilcar who enjoyed the lion's share of public favour as saviour of the city—deservedly. He saw no reason to include Hanno and Hanno's faction in future activity. Before the war was fully over he was busy planning the expedition to Spain and making his own faction dominant in affairs at home: a combined political and military initiative that would affect the history of the rest of the century.

IV

BARCA SUPREME

I

With the close of the Mercenaries' War, events both at home and overseas collided in yet another crisis. Preparations to recover Sardinia and invade Spain were disrupted by a totally unexpected confrontation with the Romans that ended in yet another Punic humiliation. But when Hamilcar did at last set off on his grand design, he was unmistakably the political leader of Carthage.

As we saw earlier, the time indications in the ancient accounts point to the war ending early in 237, and Hamilcar being in Spain before mid-year. This shows that events moved fast and that domestic events overlapped with foreign, which need not be a surprise. It implies too that some moves must have got under way before Hippou Acra and Utica capitulated, again no surprise since their resistance was limited to their own walls. The generals hardly needed to share the entire Punic field army, by now 30,000–40,000 strong, between them to besiege the two cities. Some troops could be detached to prepare for the retaking of Sardinia at least.

Politically Hamilcar moved to confirm his pre-eminent position. Diodorus, whose history for this era survives only in extracts and snippets but was plainly based on circumstantial sources, reports that after the war's end Hamilcar 'formed a political group of the lowest sort of men, and from this source, as well as from the spoils of war, amassed wealth'. He capitalized on the popularity won by his successes—'currying favour with the populace', in Diodorus' pained phrase—to have the people grant him 'the generalship of all Iberia for an indefinite period'. The text is faulty but this is the best interpretation of it.[1]

This was not the same episode as the one Appian records, of him being saved from a messy trial by 'the leading men'. As shown earlier, Appian's story should belong to the aftermath of the war with Rome. By 237 Hamilcar himself was the leading man, in fact was acclaimed (by many though not all) as saviour of his country. His purpose was now very different.

Punic generals were normally elected for the length of a war. When the

47

war ended, so did their command—a practice Hamilcar himself had taken advantage of in 241. On the surrender of Hippou and Utica, then, both his and Hanno's generalships would lapse. Hanno might have hoped that they would both then retreat into more discreet, elder-statesmanlike rôles, leaving centre stage to a new generation. Instead Hamilcar exploited his own popularity, and (a point worth noting) the wealth he had accrued, to win election to a new command, one effectively open-ended. Using wealth to gain office was a time-honoured aspect of Punic public life, as Aristotle had stated 100 years earlier. The note of disapproval comes from the source Diodorus followed, one friendlier to Hanno's side than to Barca's.

Who was to command the expedition—no doubt a smaller one—to retake Sardinia is unknown. Hamilcar very probably intended it to be either himself or a supporter, and Hanno's position was probably too weak to prevent this. Certainly Hamilcar was so confident of his own dominance over Punic affairs, only a few weeks or months later, that he took his popular son-in-law Hasdrubal with him. But meanwhile the recovery of Sardinia had been aborted, and the Spanish expedition made more urgent, by the confrontation that came out of the blue with Carthage's hitherto helpful ex-enemies.[2]

News arrived that not only had the mercenaries driven from Sardinia been sympathetically received now by the Romans, but these were readying their own expedition to the island. The Carthaginians reacted angrily and no doubt quickly, sending off envoys to advise their former foes of the true situation—the mercenaries were rebels, Sardinia was a Punic territory and in fact a force to bring it back under Punic authority was being readied. What came back was a thunderclap. The Senate and People had denounced the preparations at Carthage as being aimed against the Romans themselves and had gone on to declare war.

This extraordinary—and to the Carthaginians surely appalling—news was brought, it seems, by a Roman embassy. Its audience quite likely found it hard to believe their own ears. The Romans had been full of helpful concern for Carthaginian fortunes almost up to the present; had refused to accept Sardinia from the rebel mercenaries while these were actually in possession of it; but now had declared war on the basis of preposterous allegations. If they were serious—Hamilcar and the rest of the ruling élite may have wondered whether they could be serious—this had to be settled urgently and at any cost, for it was an utter impossibility that the Punic state could go to war with the Romans. The field forces, even if veteran and loyal, were at best equivalent to two consular armies, and there were few reserves. The naval forces were totally outclassed. And the moment Roman ships and troops touched land in Africa, most or all of Libya would go over to them (or so the Carthaginians could reasonably fear).

A new embassy was deputed to travel to Rome. It included, at least according to the very late writer Orosius, the ten most eminent men in the state—though there is no evidence that Hamilcar, Hasdrubal or even Hanno the Great was a member. Whether or not it was dawning on Hamilcar, Hasdrubal and their associates that the Roman accusations camouflaged a hidden agenda, they had little choice but to try to mollify the other side. The Carthaginians 'at first sought to come to an agreement on every point, expecting that they would prevail on the merits of the case'. After all it was easy to show that Sardinia had been a Punic possession from time more or less immemorial, the mercenaries there had been rebels, and the force being readied to recover it was far too small to look like a threat to the Romans or any of their allies.

The response was a switch in the Romans' accusations: now they complained about the traders arrested early in the recent war. These supposedly had been ill-treated, some even murdered; now compensation must be paid—to wit, Sardinia and 1,200 talents in cash.

This unconvincingly trivial allegation unveiled what the other side really wanted. Why they wanted it they did not say. Ancient historians fail to tell us too: Polybius simply denounces the affair as unjust while later writers, all of them of course pro-Roman, either swallow the traders story or (even worse) offer the fiction that Sardinia and its neighbour Corsica had been ceded with Sicily in 241. It is easy but misleading to suppose that the Romans had abruptly realized how strategically useful Sardinia could be to them—as though it had not figured repeatedly in their old war with Carthage—or how economically valuable its cornlands and metals, as though they had not had trade relations with the island since the time of their earliest treaty with the Carthaginians. If they wanted Sardinia now after turning it down two years earlier, something had made the Romans change their minds.

The most obvious factor was not the Punic victory over their rebels at home, for the Romans had actively supported this, but that they had done it chiefly thanks to Hamilcar Barca; more disturbingly, under his leadership they were already busying themselves with renewed expansionist projects. Parts of Numidia, now Sardinia, and a bigger scheme stood behind that. These preparations, involving ships, equipment, animals and stores (not to mention the troops), were no doubt open to view: the Carthaginians had nothing to hide. But even if Spain was mentioned as the major goal—and even if the Romans believed this—all this activity sharply revealed that the Punic state was not at death's door after all.

The Romans, it would seem, put two and two together and got five. Hamilcar, the new leader and their undefeated opponent in Sicily, stood for rebuilding Punic power and plainly his city had the ships and men to start doing it (it was easy enough for outsiders to overestimate the strength of those forces). If Sardinia was the Carthaginians' goal now, Sicily the former jewel of their empire, where Roman rule was still recent and fairly light, might well follow, with Sardinia serving as an extra strategic base for reconquest. They had no intention of losing a territory they had fought a 23-year war over. Therefore they would prevent Sardinia from becoming Punic again even if they had to use specious pretexts—and only the Carthaginians and Romans themselves, not the rest of the watching world, would know for certain how specious they were.

The Romans might overestimate Punic strength, but they could calculate (rightly enough) that it was not as great now as it would be when recovery had progressed. The time to strike therefore was now. The armament they had been readying for Sardinia did not leave port: it waited, some or all of it probably at Ostia for the Carthaginians' envoys to view on arriving from North Africa. To them the Senate presented the Roman republic's demands, that the Carthaginians not only abandon Sardinia but also pay over 1,200 talents—a bigger lump sum than had been paid in the peace of 241. The finances to pay for any central Mediterranean ventures were being confiscated.[3]

Whether the second Punic embassy was empowered to accept these terms or whether it needed to take them back to Carthage for discussion, the outcome was inevitable. A new war with the Romans was out of the question. Hamilcar could see this as plainly as anyone. He would not be the only Carthaginian to feel deep and lasting anger—though he was to dramatize it more memorably than any of them—but he too had to accept submission to the Romans' terms. Peace was declared anew, and an extra clause annexed to Lutatius' treaty which summed up the Carthaginians' capitulation in lapidary simplicity: 'the Carthaginians are to retire from Sardinia and pay a further 1,200 talents'.

The immediate loss was the money: there cannot have been much left in the Punic treasury after it was paid. But more funds could be gathered in time. A worse blow was to Punic maritime power. The prewar overseas empire had now shrunk to a few small islands like Malta, and of the former sphere of dominance only the western half remained—Ebusus, the trading stations along the African coast, and the friendly cities of south Spain. Punic prestige and self-confidence were injured, just at the moment when the Carthaginians had begun to restore them. Alarming too must have been the realization that the Romans, whatever their veneer of goodwill, could still harbour suspicions deep enough to erupt without warning into ruthless confrontation—at least if they thought their ex-enemies would hesitate to fight back.

The Spanish expedition was more vital than ever.[4]

II

Rather surprisingly Hamilcar took his son-in-law with him. Now, or less probably later, Hasdrubal was appointed trierarch, naval commander, which suggests Hamilcar was attentive to his communications with Carthage. But it suggests too that Hasdrubal was not politically indispensable at home and others could take over the job of nurturing Barca's political position in the city. They too may have been relatives by marriage or blood (these would be the strongest bonds) but we know hardly anything of such people—nothing for instance of brothers, sisters or cousins apart from a relative named Mago, whom the Romans captured in Sardinia in 215.

One of Hannibal's oldest and most durable friends was the Mago nicknamed 'the Samnite'. They enjoyed a friendly and military rivalry from their earliest years, according to Polybius. This Mago was obviously then close to the Barcid family though, to judge from Polybius' silence, not a kinsman by blood or marriage. His family must have been important among the supporters of the Barcid ascendancy in Punic politics.

In turn, speculation or imagination can play only with the Bomilcar who, if Appian is right, must have married one of Hamilcar's daughters and whom Polybius calls 'king': his real political standing remains a guess. If the ancient kingship still existed it may well have been limited to religious matters; equally Polybius may use the word to mean sufete, and he or his source need only have meant to convey that Bomilcar was sufete at the time his son is mentioned.

Apart from later officers in Punic armies or fleets like Mago the Samnite, the famous cavalry general Maharbal son of Himilco and an admiral also named Bomilcar (he may have been the brother-in-law for all we know), the only high-ranking supporters of the Barcid faction who earn any mention are a few senators. A Himilco, perhaps Maharbal's father though Livy does not say so, supposedly mocked old Hanno after news of the victory at Cannae, and the inventive poet Silius credits an even more shadowy 'Gestar' with an earlier outburst against the same target. Hanno in turn is found, in Zonaras, rebuking a war-enthusiast named Hasdrubal in 218 who may or may not have been the later well-known general, Hasdrubal son of Gisco.

That Hamilcar had many and keen supporters at Carthage, both among ordinary citizens and in the senate, can be assumed even if just who they were cannot be said. Connexions between Africa and Spain were maintained in various ways and at every level. The high officers in the army, like those already mentioned, were Carthaginians; surely too some of the lesser ones, and others might include citizens from allied states like Utica and Hippou Acra (like an officer of Hannibal's many years later). Carthaginians and others from Africa helped populate the new cities founded by Hamilcar and his successors. The Barcid generals themselves, to judge from a few items again in Hannibal's time, had senators from Carthage among their councillors. How they were chosen, whether they were rotated, and what positions they held from time to time at Carthage and in the army we do not know: but it makes sense to infer that they were important—arguably the most important—links in Hamilcar's and his successors' relations with their homeland.[5]

According to one Roman historical tradition, though, Hamilcar did not go to Spain with the ruling élite's blessing. This claim might go back to Fabius Pictor, the earliest Roman historian and a younger contemporary of

Hamilcar's—who did find things to criticize in Barca's successors—but more likely it was invented later. Polybius tells us of Fabius' strictures on Hasdrubal and Hannibal but not of any against Hamilcar. Livy, implicitly rejecting Fabius' version, presents a Barcid faction dominant in Punic affairs from Hamilcar's day till the last years of the second war with Rome. The claims of opposition between generalissimo and home authorities turn up in late writers, Appian and Zonaras. No trust can be put in them. Nor, for the same reasons, can it be believed that Hamilcar and his successors set up a Spanish principality or fiefdom virtually independent of the Carthaginian state.

Obviously Hamilcar had to work hard to keep himself and his faction in the ascendant. He and his closest collaborator, Hasdrubal, were far away, and with them his two older sons. His domestic grip had to be fuelled with more than victory bulletins, especially in a republic where money was a crucial ingredient. His biographer Nepos notes that with the spoils of his victories 'he enriched the whole of Africa'. Appian more precisely reports largesse to political supporters.

So far as we can see, the method was a success. Others besides Barcid supporters may have won offices from time to time, but not enough to upset the dominance achieved by Hamilcar: a dominance he was able to pass on first to his son-in-law and then to his eldest son. As time passed, the offices of state and the senate will have taken on a more and more Barcid-friendly cast. For the first time since the Magonid dynasty Carthage was firmly in the hands of one family and its supporters.

It would be interesting to know whether Barca's prospective son-in-law, Naravas the Numidian, went to Spain too; but no ancient writer mentions him after the African war. The marriage may well have taken place, for Hamilcar's family kept up a close connexion with Naravas'. During the next war against Rome one of (it seems) his brothers fought for the Carthaginians in Spain, and another married one of Hannibal's nieces. Naravas, though, quite likely preferred or needed to stay in Numidia, where rivalries between tribes and chieftains, and pro- and anti-Punic groupings, kept the North African uplands unstable; his energy and resourcefulness would be valuable to his own people.[6]

III

With the general and trierarch went the general's eldest son. Hannibal was nine years old. Hamilcar must have been an absentee father for much of the boy's life—only during his retirement from public office from mid-241 to mid-240 can he have lived at home—but his impact on his sons was deep. All three followed in his footsteps to become generals and leaders, none of course more memorably than the eldest.

Even at nine Hannibal was strongly attached to his father, for whom no doubt he felt a blend of love, admiration and awe. A famous episode took place just before Hamilcar set out for Spain. He performed sacrifice to Ba'al Hammon (or Ba'al Shamim) for divine favour, and when the omens proved favourable 'he ordered the others who were attending the sacrifice to withdraw to a slight distance and calling Hannibal to him asked him kindly if he wished to accompany him on the expedition'. The boy accepted eagerly: whereupon his father made him lay his hand on the sacrificial victim and swear an oath 'never to bear goodwill to the Romans'. Hamilcar himself told the story to King Antiochus III 44 years later, as an assurance that his attitude was unchanged.

It has been disbelieved from time to time, on the arguments that it smells of a historical novel rather than history, or comes from supposedly tainted sources—Hannibal himself, anxious to win the royal trust with an inventive lie, or imaginative Roman writers prone to dramatize everything they could about his life—or because it would make sense only if Hamilcar were seeking to bind a son he was leaving behind. But the story has no blatantly false features. The oath as Hannibal reported it, 'never to bear goodwill to the Romans', was so limited that later Roman tradition had to sharpen it for drama's sake and make him swear to become their enemy. Hannibal himself, if he were inventing it, might well have phrased it the same way—after all King Antiochus was at the time close to war with the Romans, and the exile from Carthage was trying to win his favour.[7]

The story as he told it did convince Antiochus, an experienced and successful ruler. Nor does it require a parting between father and son to be convincing. Whichever Punic god was involved, he was one of the city's principal deities (Nepos translates him into 'Jupiter best and greatest', the supreme one at Rome) and it was during a peculiarly meaningful rite, initiating a wholly new venture by Carthage and its general. And the venture was made all the more necessary by the Romans' sudden and opportunistic betrayal of the goodwill they had previously shown.

If true, the episode casts light on both father and son. Hamilcar had the Romans much on his mind at this time, and the oath he made his son swear reflects his bitterness. As his city's supreme general he had shared personally in the frustration and humiliation of the Sardinia crisis. The Romans had shown that their seeming goodwill of recent times had been a sham: beneath it still lurked the ill-will of the war years, now compounded by treacherous amorality. No Carthaginian could ever again feel well disposed towards them. To bind his eldest son by such an oath, in turn, was a public as well as personal gesture. Hamilcar was telling his family, followers and fellow-countrymen both of his own present feelings and also that the price of renewing Carthaginian greatness was perpetual watchfulness against their former (who might seek to become their future) enemies.

Obviously the oath made a lasting psychological impact on the boy who took it: it would still be meaningful to him more than four decades later. He was already devoted to his father, as his keenness to go with him shows. The oath (negative and limited though it was) strengthened the bond between them—no doubt more because of its solemnity and the trust being ceremoniously placed on him, than because Hannibal at nine could have any clear idea of who or where the Romans were. Ancient writers emphasize his lasting enthusiasm and loyalty to his father's guidance. From that day on he was never far from Hamilcar's side.[8]

V

HAMILCAR IN SPAIN

I

The army Hamilcar took to Spain cannot have been very large. For one thing, given the costs of the African war and the new indemnity over Sardinia, the Carthaginians could hardly afford to keep under arms all the 30,000–40,000 troops they probably had in the field by late 238. For another, Hamilcar had to leave some forces at home to maintain order and security: not all Numidians were allies or subjects, and there was no certainty what the Romans might try next. When facing a war with them two decades later, his son would station some 16,000 troops in Africa. In a season of peace, guarded though it was, 10,000 or so might do.

In Spain ten years later, after economic recovery and much power-building, Punic forces totalled 56,000 according to Diodorus. On a reasonable estimate Hamilcar's expeditionary force in 237 can be put at around 20,000, 2,000 or 3,000 of them cavalry, and no doubt a corps of elephants. This was sizeable enough for the purpose, and he could expect to recruit Spanish mercenaries and allies before long.

As soon as the crisis over Sardinia ended he embarked for Spain, as Diodorus reports, sailing along the African coast to the straits of Gibraltar and then crossing to Gades. The transport ships were available—especially as there was now to be no expedition to Sardinia—and the trading-stations along the coast would provide stops for rest and resupply. It is very unlikely that Diodorus is wrong and that he marched by land along the coast to the straits. That would have taken far longer, would have worn down his forces to no appreciable benefit, and by the time they reached Spain he would have lost most of his first campaigning season.[1]

Spain was a busy jumble of towns (including the many Phoenician and Greek colonies along its southern and eastern coasts) and rural cantons. Many were prosperous or even rich, especially in the south across the broad fertile basin of the river Baetis, now the modern Guadalquivir, and along the Levant coast from Cape de la Nao to the Pyrenees. Tougher terrain and lifestyles prevailed farther inland and along the north-western coasts.

Some relatively sophisticated communities were republics of varying forms, with regularly chosen officials and senate-like councils: for instance not only Gades and probably the other foreign colonies, but also an Iberian city like Saguntum. Even such places were probably run in practice by their small local élites. In other communities the oligarchic, even feudal element would be still more dominant, often with 'kings' at the top.

Political structures more extensive than the individual community were loose and changeable. Outsiders like the Greeks and Romans, and probably the Carthaginians, did identify major groupings of peoples—Iberians across the south and east, Celtiberians on the plateaux and uplands beyond the river Tagus, Lusitanians over in the west, Cantabrians and Gallaecians and others in the mountainous far north. These they subdivided into various smaller regional 'tribes', for instance Turdetanians in the Baetis valley, Vaccaei around the river Durius (today's Duero), Bastetani in the south-west corner of the peninsula, Contestani and Edetani along the east coast.

Religious practices, dialect and old traditions may well explain such groupings. But in political and military affairs the individual communities were their own masters. Some might form alliances, or be united under a successful leader for a time. In the dim past the region north-west of Gades had formed a kingdom of some kind, called Tartessus by the Greeks (and possibly Tarshish in the Old Testament), but little is known of it apart from the exaggeratedly fabulous wealth of its silver mines in the Río Tinto area, and by Hamilcar's time it was three centuries gone.

The disunion and quarrelsomeness of peninsular states made them relatively easy targets for a determined Punic expansionist. Their high cultural level (visible still in pottery, architecture and surviving sculpture like the fourth-century 'Lady of Elche'), widespread natural wealth and well-developed military prowess were, in turn, powerful attractions to such an expansionist. Hamilcar could count on the Phoenician towns of the south coast as allies, supply-bases and anchors for his communications with home. Some Iberian states too may already have been well disposed: with warfare so endemic in the peninsula, he needed only to assure the ones whose alliance he wanted that he would back them against their enemies.[2]

II

A paragraph of Diodorus and generalities in other writers are all we have on Barca's doings in Spain. Diodorus is coherent and plainly well informed, but only a few events in the nine-year saga are described. The first is Hamilcar confronting a coalition of the Iberians and 'Tartessians', together 'with Istolatius, general of the Celts, and his brother'.

The realm of Tartessus no longer existed but, if 'Tartessians' is not just a cloudy misunderstanding, the term should mean people in south-western Spain and Portugal: that is, northerly neighbours of Gades. In later times most communities of that region were covered by the general names Turduli and Baeturii. It is much less plausible that Diodorus, or the source he used, really meant Turdetani—the later broad term for virtually all the Spaniards in the Baetis valley and the mountains north and south of it. Rather these, and probably only some of these, were the 'Iberians' in the hostile alliance.

For the newly arrived Hamilcar to be confronted by an anti-Punic coalition is not surprising. A veteran army landing in the richest region of Spain would look like nothing but trouble to peoples not already allied with the invaders or disposed to submit to them. Gades itself probably had a number of regional enemies (just as when the Magonids had intervened in the distant past); they would be very alarmed at Hamilcar's coming, and so would other communities.

More than that, the 'Tartessians' give a clue to Hamilcar's opening strategy. The wealth of ancient Tartessus lay in its silver and copper mines in the country along the river now called Río Tinto, only 60 miles (100 kilometres) or so north-west of Gades. These remained productive, as they would into modern times. They were an obvious—and pressing—attraction to a Punic conquistador. Other sources of precious metal existed, but were farther off to the east and needed development; not so the long-established Tartessian workings. Nor could Hamilcar afford to wait, either financially or strategically.

This first coalition against him may have been fairly limited. Communities in the eastern half of today's Andalusia would be worried about Punic intentions, but would not be likely to risk sending forces far to the west in aid of the peoples there. They rarely tried such co-operation even in the next century during the Roman conquest. Perhaps too not all the communities in Hamilcar's area of operations chose to resist; as mentioned earlier, some may even have been willing to collaborate.

Those who did resist had the help of the Celtic chieftain Istolatius and his unnamed brother. Diodorus' phrasing strongly implies that these two were, in effect, mercenary condottieri—no doubt leading a contingent of Celtic warriors. This can be believed, for a branch of Celtiberians, called Celtici by later writers, dwelt in the south-west between the Sierra Morena, the river Anas (the Guadiana) and the Atlantic coastline. Celtiberian war-bands, like Iberian ones, are found on other occasions serving for pay outside their home territories, including in Carthaginian armies. On this occasion it looks, too, as though the two Celtic chieftains were given command of the allied forces.

A different excerpt in Diodorus plays up the boastful overconfidence of the Celts and how much they outnumbered the Punic forces. Whether this is accurate reporting or exaggeration for effect is impossible to tell. If Hamilcar was outnumbered, one reason may be that he had stationed part of his army elsewhere—for instance to protect Gades or new and hesitant allies in the lower Baetis valley, a job he could leave to Hasdrubal. He himself smashed the enemy allies in a bloody battle. The two Celtic generals and 'other very distinguished leaders' were among the dead. Three thousand of the defeated army were promptly enrolled in his own. This not only added to his military strength but was useful propaganda: a general both humane and, when it came to judging military worth, impartial would greatly impress the Spaniards.

The results of the victory are not stated, but quite likely it brought under his control the territory Barca aimed at, stretching from Gades to the Tartessian mines along with some of the lower Baetis valley—districts conquered in the campaign or within a few days' march of his Gaditane headquarters. Gades soon began issuing a new, high-quality silver coinage. He could now direct his energies to the rest of the Baetis valley and its neighbouring highlands.[3]

The Baetis valley stretches over 250 miles (400 kilometres) from the Atlantic coast to the edge of the vast mountain- and plateau-lands of south-eastern Spain. Fertile and well populated, it had the potential for stiff resistance to the Carthaginians if enough of its towns and peoples held together. To the Carthaginians the same endowments were a powerful attraction, and more powerful still the silver workings in the mountains north of the river: the Mons Marianus of Roman times, today's Sierra Morena, and the even richer ones to the east around the important town of Castulo.

In Diodorus' account Hamilcar next confronted a leader named Indortes. This chieftain's connexions are not described but must have been extensive: the army he commanded is given as 50,000 strong. If Hamilcar was now ranging eastwards, up the Baetis, Indortes' resistance probably drew on the communities of the central and eastern districts of the valley. After all, they were next in the path of the lightning.

Yet Indortes' army and campaign collapsed before he could fight a battle. Diodorus fails to explain why, but one obvious possibility is desertion. Barca may have enticed some of the large but heterogeneous Spanish force to join him, or at least to go home. Indortes judged retreat the best option with the troops still loyal to him. Diodorus describes him as routed, but since he was able to concentrate his remaining force on a hilltop a rout seems exaggerated. All the same, Indortes only postponed destruction. Once again, rather like the African rebels at The Saw, Hamilcar succeeded in surrounding an enemy army. This time they tried to break out, only to be slaughtered or captured.

One of the prisoners was Indortes himself. Hamilcar made a ruthless example of him. The Iberian leader was blinded and mutilated—probably much as the African rebels had treated Gisco and their other Punic prisoners, cutting off hands, feet and private parts—then crucified. Yet the ordinary prisoners, no fewer than 10,000, were set free. Hamilcar plainly meant Indortes' fate to carry a warning to other Spanish leaders who might be considering resistance, and that of the ordinary prisoners to reassure their peoples.[4]

Diodorus' extracts give no chronology for these campaigns, and any estimates of time based on Punic Spanish coin-series are guesswork. But it would be surprising if the fighting against Istolatius and then Indortes lasted beyond 236 or at latest 235. After that Hamilcar fought further campaigns and scored diplomatic successes, but Diodorus offers no details. He simply affirms that the general, partly through diplomacy and partly by fighting, brought 'many cities throughout Iberia' under his power. Still, as the last drama in Barca's life was played somewhere in the south-east, we can infer that from about 235 on his activities, military and civil, spread across the Baetis lands including the silver-rich Sierra Morena. With Hasdrubal a reliable deputy and their military strength growing, expansion and consolidation could take place together. The proceeds of conquest that began to accrue—some of it sent over to Africa—were phenomenal: horses, weapons, men and money, writes Nepos. Strabo tells a story of Hamilcar's expedition finding that the Turdetani used feed-troughs and wine-jars of silver, not a literal but a proverbial way of highlighting the mineral wealth of southern Spain.

Of course Punic rule in some of the more difficult mountain or desert regions, for instance the Sierra Nevada, the neighbouring Alpujarras and the semidesert region inland from modern Almería, may not have been much more than nominal. Such places were hard to get at and there were few mineral riches to attract sustained attention. Equally difficult was much of the south-east's interior, where the Sierra Morena range meets the complex massifs that separate the Baetis valley from the coastal plains of Murcia and Alicante. Hamilcar, as we shall see, perished while campaigning to bring these under control for strategic reasons.[5]

III

At some stage the general was distracted by news from Africa. The Numidians, or many of them, had risen against Carthage (again). The résumé in Diodorus gives no reason. After the drubbing many had suffered for backing the losers in the African revolt, the cause must have been specially pressing. The drubbing itself may have been the cause—we saw earlier that Hamilcar and Hanno had not been mild. As generalissimo of the republic Hamilcar was responsible for Africa as well as Spain. How seriously he viewed the situation is shown by his reaction: he sent Hasdrubal his son-in-law to take command.

Hasdrubal had probably added to his military experience through the recent Spanish campaigns (he had not had much opportunity before). In his war with the Numidians Naravas' people, the Massyli, may well have been allies again, for the prince's family continued to rule their region of the country and be loyal to Carthage until late in the Second Punic War. Certainly Hasdrubal must have had efficient cavalry, and therefore local auxiliaries. He succeeded in bringing the hostile Numidians to a decisive battle, in which 8,000 of them were killed and 2,000 captured, and the revolt was over.

The subdued Numidians were firmly treated. 'The rest were made slaves and liable to tribute', Diodorus rather contradictorily puts it. Enslavement of all the defeated tribes and clans is more than unlikely, so it is better taken as a rhetorical touch which the mention of tribute then more mundanely explains. Reprisals after the earlier war may have involved fines and levies rather than tribute, or else their new tribute was heavier than the old.

How Hasdrubal's arrangements related to the later known situation in Numidia can only be surmised. The rebel territory was obviously too large, and not productive enough, to annex—and too risky to give to the Massyli. When the region earns more detailed mention 20 or so years later, the pro-Carthaginian Massyli in its east are balanced by the larger (but probably not more populous) kingdom of the Masaesyli in the west under Syphax. This uneasy consolidation of Numidian territory into two realms may have been Hasdrubal's doing, possibly too the installation of Syphax or his father as the western king. Certainly the Masaesyli make their appearance only after this time. They, like the Massyli, furnished Carthage with troops in 218, but Syphax's attitude to the Carthaginians was variable—hostile enough some years later for these to arrange with the Massyli to attack him, yet after a time he became their ally again. In the circumstances Hasdrubal did reasonably well, for both kingdoms remained true to Carthage for the next two decades.[6]

His success surely reinforced the Barcid group's prestige and popularity at home too. The impact of Spanish victories and wealth could easily have been blunted (or worse) by a serious continuing threat to Carthage's territories in Africa. Hasdrubal averted the risk, and a stay—even a short one—in the city must have enabled him to strengthen his and Hamilcar's grip on domestic politics. When he reported to his father-in-law on returning to Spain, the general would be well satisfied.

IV

During all these years of expansion Hamilcar not only had to nourish his power-base at home—successfully, as we have seen—but to keep an eye on the Romans. After their chicanery over Sardinia, he might well feel wary. They traded with North Africa and the eastern parts of Spain too, so that care was always needed in handling their merchants in Punic territories. Hamilcar would not have forgotten the dispute over these in the early days of the African revolt and the use that the Romans afterwards made of this in the Sardinia affair. Some new unpredictable coup against Carthage, or directly against his growing empire in Spain, could never be ruled out.

As it happens, one or two late Roman writers tell stories of repeated confrontations between the Romans and the Carthaginians in the later 230s, which if true would reveal almost a cold-war climate in the western Mediterranean. But in fact the stories are either confused repeats of the Sardinia crisis—misdating it to 236 or 235—or grotesque misrepresentations of other events. The Roman statesman Q. Fabius Maximus (for instance) is reported as sending an ultimatum to the Carthaginians when consul in 233, commanding them to choose between war and peace. This tale was obviously concocted from the famous ultimatum on war and peace presented at Carthage in 218 by another Fabius, then a Roman envoy. Again, in an episode Zonaras dates to 230 the Romans are represented as marching to fight the Ligurians (of northern Italy) via Punic North Africa; a charitable excuse might be that somewhere along the line a copyist wrote Carthaginians where he should have written, for example, Boii—a Gallic people of north Italy— but incompetently inventive malevolence by some propagandist might be the explanation instead.

Another story directly involves Hamilcar. In 231, again according to Dio, the Romans sent over envoys to see what he was up to in Spain. Hamilcar received them cordially and explained that he was seeking the means to pay the indemnity imposed by Lutatius' peace. The envoys, Dio affirms, could not find anything to criticize in this. The tale is hardly the stuff of high drama (Zonaras did not think it worth including in his précis of Dio) but basically is another confrontation story from the same source as the others. It arouses suspicion. No other writer knows it, and the nub of it is one side making a neat response when pressured by the other—just as in the other confrontations. Dio concedes that the Romans had previously had no interest in Barca's doings and implies that they left him alone again after this. In sum, the embassy story is no more believable than the other confrontations.

The Romans no doubt knew about Hamilcar's expansion. Not only did they trade with Spanish ports as well as North African, they were on good terms too with Massilia, which had its own wide-ranging trading network. Even if their embassy to Hamilcar had taken place it would have been the only recorded official contact between the two powers after 237 and before 225—that is, in a dozen years. This does not square with sustained or anxious suspicion. Rather, the Romans were prepared to let their ex-enemies do as they wished in their quarter of the world, so long as they themselves could get on with doing as they wished in and around Italy.[7]

Some Romans even then may have admired Hamilcar, as we know Cato the Censor (a younger contemporary of his son) did later. But after a time— maybe even within Hannibal's lifetime, once the story of his boyhood oath became known—Romans and Greeks came to believe that Hamilcar's doings were the start of a carefully worked-out scheme for a fresh war against Rome. Infuriated by the defeat of 241 and then by the rape of Sardinia, he and his countrymen supposedly built their new empire in Spain for this purpose, with the war finally being launched by Hannibal. Polybius states this as a fact and nearly all other ancient sources follow suit.[8]

This was not the predominant view among the Romans at the time. Certainly the Sardinia crisis had shown that concern about Punic moves might flare if these looked like coming close to Italy and Sicily, and no doubt some members of the Roman Senate did feel a continuing antipathy for their ex-enemies. The same thing was to happen in 225, as we shall see. No doubt too critics of Barcid activity and Roman unconcern made themselves heard from time to time. But the Romans' general inattention to Barcid affairs and to Carthage for nearly 20 years until 220—only the brief business of the 'Ebro treaty' in 225 was to punctuate it—reveals that any such criticisms failed to affect Roman policy-making.

Fabius Pictor, the Barcids' senatorial contemporary, blamed the war in general terms on ambition and greed in Hasdrubal and Hannibal his protégé, not on a war-scheme handed on from Hamilcar. One line of thought, surfacing in Appian's history, even limited the blame to Hannibal himself, as a device for turning the tables on his hereditary enemies at home—though how far back that idea went we cannot say.[9]

Hamilcar surely had little liking for his old enemies, as the oath he administered to Hannibal shows. He may well have believed too that, one day, another war would come. But his programme was to rebuild Punic strength and wealth, a pragmatic and defensive aim. If the Romans should choose to bring on some new confrontation, a possibility no Carthaginian leader could dismiss, the Punic state had to be able to stand up to them as it had not been over Sardinia. But that was quite a different aim from a revenge-war.

Another war would call for large resources to match those of the Romans, and also a set of alliances with states around Italy, either to support the war-effort or at least to distract the Romans. Of course Hannibal was to invade Italy with a small army and few allies—but no long-term planner would rationally aim at waging war on those terms. Hamilcar made no such alliances. Nor did his successor Hasdrubal; and Hannibal was to seek them, with the Gauls of north Italy, only on the eve of war itself.

Planning a new war would also require readying a fleet. True, neither Hamilcar after 244 nor his successors showed any enthusiasm for naval warfare. But even negatively a fleet was a plain necessity, for the Romans could be counted on to launch their own powerful navy for invading North Africa and Spain as soon as war came. Arguably, of course, building one might invite as hostile a Roman reaction as preparing to retake Sardinia had done, and this might explain the Barcids' avoidance of it. But if they were seriously bent on war it was a necessary risk.

In any case suspicion could be disarmed by putting off the actual fleet-building until the war was fairly near. It had taken the Romans only a few months to construct their first-class war-fleet, 200 quinqueremes strong, in 243 or 242. So we could expect Hannibal to start laying down keels at any rate during 220 or 219, when a clash over Saguntum became predictable. Some naval craft should already have been available: the warships used during the African war plus any built (as some surely were) for the aborted Sardinian expedition afterwards. Yet the Punic war-effort at the start of 218 had available only 105 quinqueremes and a few smaller ships, with just 87 of the quinqueremes properly equipped. Their enemies launched 220.

It could hardly be that the Carthaginians had defective information about

Roman naval strength. When the Romans warred on the Illyrians across the Adriatic in 229 they equipped 200 ships, and the second Illyrian war ten years later (again involving both consuls with fleet and army) no doubt saw a similar armament. Anyone intending to bring on a new war against them had to count on a Roman navy of some such size and aim to counter it. Hamilcar did not. After him Hasdrubal—despite having been his father-in-law's naval commander—did not; nor again did Hannibal. The only persuasive inference is that their plans never included a Roman war.[10]

V

Hamilcar's next reported measure was to found a city, a very large one according to Diodorus. He does not state where it was but its name was Acra Leuce, meaning 'White Fort' or 'White Cape'. The Carthaginians had founded a few colonies in past times, like the one on the island of Ebusus off the east coast of Spain, but founding cities had not been a habit of past Punic leaders, not even the Magonids. On the other hand it was a notable characteristic of monarchs of Hamilcar's own era, starting with Alexander the Great himself whose most famous creation, Alexandria in Egypt, stood on Africa's Mediterranean coast like Carthage itself. The Roman republic too was a notable city-founder within Italy, its Latin and citizen colonies planted at strategic locations on the coasts and in the countryside of the peninsula.

Hamilcar, generalissimo and chief executive of a republic, founded a centre with resemblances to both types. Unlike Hellenistic rulers with their Alexandrias and Antiochs, it did not perpetuate his own name. Like their foundations and Roman ones, it held a site important strategically and economically. Unlike Roman creations, it advertised the success and the promise of his political mastery of Carthage, and no doubt others would have followed had he lived.

Archaeological finds starting from the later half of the third century show towns, especially in the upper Baetis region, improving many of their features—both private homes and public structures like walls and sacred shrines. Hamilcar and his successors quite likely encouraged these upgrades. Better amenities could claim to advertise the new prosperity and security under Punic rule. Improved urbanization in turn could help to make that rule more effective, at any rate so long as the dominant levels of Spanish society were won over. Hamilcar, who achieved much using diplomatic tactics as well as military, would not find that difficult to do.[11]

Acra Leuce is generally identified as the south-eastern coastal city which the Romans called Lucentum, today's Alicante. Rising over this is an imposing headland of bare rock, a natural (and long-used) citadel. If the identification is correct, Acra Leuce formed a new power-centre on the eastern side of Carthage's new province, to balance—and even outshine—old Gades on the western.

This identification has been disputed. No Punic remains have been unearthed at Alicante, though there was a Phoenician trading-post at nearby Tossal de Manises. That the Roman name Lucentum derives from the verb for showing light, *lucere*, has been questioned—and thus any connexion with Acra Leuce.

These objections are not compelling. Archaeological finds at, or rather under, existing cities are erratic, all the more so if the Punic character of a place lasted three or four decades at best: and 30 years later Acra Leuce was in a Roman province. At New Carthage (as the Romans were to call it), founded later on by Barca's son-in-law farther down the coast, Hasdrubal built a splendid hilltop palace for himself which Polybius saw, but of which no trace now survives.

The Greek name Acra Leuce described the site, according to Diodorus— wherever it was. It does not suggest that a Greek colony or trading-station already stood there. True, Massilia in Gaul had founded three very small colonies on Spain's east coast, but Strabo the geographer, who tells us so, also implies that they lay between Cape de la Nao and the river Sucro, today's Júcar. That zone lay well north of any district Hamilcar can have reached.

The Greek name may simply translate the Punic one, just as the Punic may have translated a native one. Hamilcar himself may well have encouraged both the Punic and Greek forms. Hippou Acra is the Greek name of a North African port whose Punic name may have been Hippo Zarytos. In turn Roman Lucentum might conceivably derive not from the Latin for light but from Leuce, with a Latinized ending.[12]

There are more objections. Hasdrubal's more southerly creation, the modern Cartagena, stands on a harbour much better than Alicante's and had a rich hinterland including silver mines. That Hamilcar should ignore the advantages of such a site in favour of lesser ones farther north may seem too much to swallow. On this argument, since he did not site his city at Cartagena he cannot have sited it at Alicante, and we should look elsewhere for it.

All this is close to a non-sequitur. Hamilcar may well have had reasons for preferring the more northerly position, even if we discount mere oversight of the site of Cartagena. The Alicante site has a good harbour and would give a shorter run to and from the island of Ebusus, a prosperous Punic colony with busy connexions to Carthage. Again, the Cartagena site housed or at any rate belonged to the people of Mastia, mentioned as long ago as 348 (in the second Punic treaty with Rome) as being within Punic-protected waters. They would contribute a contingent to the Punic war-effort in 218. Hamilcar may not have judged it politic to force an old Spanish ally to give up its rich territory and harbour to new residents (even if Hasdrubal later did). Nor of course need we imagine that to found New Carthage Hasdrubal would have had to give up Acra Leuce, were this at Alicante, and the territory in between—another objection offered.[13]

Another alleged difficulty is linked with how Hamilcar eventually died. He was besieging a city Diodorus calls Helice; with winter coming on he sent away the bulk of his forces, elephants included, to winter-quarters at Acra Leuce—a fatal move, as it turned out. Helice is generally identified with the Roman Ilici, today's Elche famous for its fourth-century BC Iberian noble-woman's statue and equally for its broad palm-groves, the most extensive in Europe, that surround the city. But Elche is only 13 miles (21 kilometres) south-west of Alicante. It is hard to believe that Hamilcar could safely found a major city in the farthest region of his new province with a powerful hostile centre standing so near—blocking, in fact, direct land-communication with the rest of Punic Spain. Elche incidentally has warmer winters than Alicante.

These arguments might suggest that Acra Leuce really lay somewhere else in Hamilcar's province—closer to the heartland or close to the inland fron-tier. Livy names a site, seemingly near Castulo in the eastern Sierra Morena, as the place where Hamilcar died, and its generally supposed name Castrum Album ('White Fort') could obviously mean much the same as Acra Leuce if this meant 'White Citadel'. This might seem to clinch the matter: Hamilcar's city would be not on the coast at all, but at a strategic strongpoint in silver-mining territory and pointing the expansionist way to the plains of La Mancha and central Spain.

But Hamilcar did not die at Acra Leuce. Diodorus' account shows him cut off from there as he retreated from Helice. And the argument from Livy turns out to be circular. In all Livian manuscripts the name is Castrum Altum, 'High Fort'. Text-editors supposed a connexion with Acra Leuce and changed Altum to Album—even though Acra Leuce was identified with Ali-cante while Livy is plainly narrating events inland. In other words 'Castrum Album' is only a mistaken inference from Acra Leuce and cannot be used as evidence for it. What Livy does imply is that Hamilcar's Helice is not Elche but some place farther off, as we shall see.[14]

Acra Leuce, then, can remain identified with Lucentum and Alicante. Its foundation should date to the last years of the 230s: Hamilcar would have taken time to come round to that region, very likely via the coast, and his next recorded move was into the inland mountains of the south-east.

The settlers probably were a mixture: loyal natives, people from Gades and other Phoenician towns, a sprinkling of outsiders (for instance from Ebusus), and no doubt an element of Carthaginians in the governing élite. The town's position at the eastern end of the Punic province, and its use as a base for further operations, suggest that Hamilcar had only recently con-quered the area. It protected the productive south-eastern coastlands and, with Gades, Malaca, Abdera, Mastia and the other Phoenician or allied Iberian ports, completed a semicircular chain of secure points around the province. And with the interior of the south-east a harsh tangle of moun-tains and valleys and even some deserts, Acra Leuce was an anchor for the vital coastal roadway that linked the south-east to the rest of Punic territory.

VI

It is not certain that Hamilcar treated Acra Leuce as a new capital for Punic Spain, but likely enough. Gades was a very small town on an offshore island and the Gaditanes, though allies, were an independent state; besides, Gades lay inconveniently far off in Spain from Carthage itself. His new city had none of these drawbacks. This then was probably where he and his two eldest sons were based in the last years of his life, although he, his son-in-law and eventually the boys must have spent much of every year on the move around their territories, campaigning and administering.

Hamilcar's second son Hasdrubal came to Spain before his father's death. It is economical to suppose that the boy came with his brother-in-law and namesake after the older Hasdrubal put down the rebellion in Numidia. Young Hasdrubal had been born around 244, if a late writer is correct in making him three years younger than Hannibal; so he would have been ten or eleven when his namesake came to Africa to deal with the Numidians. Hamilcar had had his eldest son by him from the age of nine, and judged the years of older childhood, merging into early youth, as the right ones to start training each boy in warfare and leadership. At any rate Polybius describes his youngest son Mago as 'trained from boyhood in military matters'. Mago, born around 241 or 240, will have come to Spain just before or not long after his father's death.

By 218 the younger Hasdrubal was experienced enough, and respected enough, for his elder brother to deputise him to govern Punic Spain while Hannibal was away. Mago, in his early twenties at most, marched with Hannibal and was given crucial tasks like commanding the ambush corps at the battle of the Trebia. Hamilcar obviously meant all three to qualify for high position in Punic Spain and at home. This was a normal enough ambition in any aristocratic leader, and all the more then to be expected in Hamilcar. After all he was now—so long as victories continued and Spain's riches kept flowing—supreme in the state and the focus of political enthusiasms both at Carthage and in his expanding province. (The story that he claimed he was rearing lion-cubs to ruin the Romans belongs, on the other hand, to the revenge-war legend.)[15]

Grooming for high position meant training in war primarily, as Polybius writes of Mago. Skill on horseback and with weapons, and in commanding formations large and small, had to be gained, and by the end of 229 both Hannibal and Hasdrubal were campaigning with their father. But literacy and a knowledge of the world, present and past, were equally necessary. Nor could this education be limited to purely Punic matters or be put in purely Punic terms, important though these—like the Barcids' Punic religion— remained. A good grasp of the Greek language had been desirable or essential to a Carthaginian aristocrat for a long time, given their city's links in peace and war with the Greek world, Sicily above all. With that world revolutionized by Alexander the Great and his successors and imitators both eastern and western, the need for Carthaginians to understand Hellenistic civilization had become at least as great as its attractions already were.

Hannibal was taught Greek by a Spartan named Sosylus. He seems to have become fluent in the language, so Sosylus probably arrived in Hamilcar's time. Sparta was no longer the officious military state of older times but Spartan expatriates were well regarded abroad—for instance Xanthippus, the professional soldier who had saved the Carthaginians from Regulus. Sosylus may have known something of war too, to judge from the one surviving fragment of his history of the Second Punic War. He became a devoted friend of his pupil, went with him on his epic quest against Rome, remained with Hannibal 'as long as fortune allowed' (Nepos writes) and then wrote his history, which irritated Polybius but was still read 200 years later.

At some date Hannibal's circle was joined by another notable Greek. Silenus, of Cale Acte in Sicily, also followed him 'while fortune allowed'. Later he too wrote an influential account of the war against Rome, though neither it nor Sosylus' survives. The two men's association with the Barcid family illustrates the family's Greek connexions and interests. Hannibal in later years would deal with Greeks, in Italy and Asia Minor, easily and on the same cultural level; his military talents and methods matched Alexander's. Even so the connexions need not be overestimated. Greece was still producing mercenary officers, not just soldiers, but though Punic armies continued to hire the soldiers no Greek (not even a Spartan) ever held a high command again.[16]

VII

Hamilcar next struck into the hinterland of Acra Leuce. It was late 229 or very early in 228, since Polybius writes that he spent nearly nine years in Spain and perished ten years before the outbreak of the Second Punic War in 218; and Diodorus shows that his death took place in winter. Polybius and Livy also attest that his successor Hasdrubal held power for eight years before being assassinated late in 221. Hamilcar met his end probably not long into the winter of 229–228, as we shall see.

His sons Hannibal and Hasdrubal accompanied him while his son-in-law held a separate command elsewhere. As Diodorus tells it, he laid the town of Helice under siege but then sent the bulk of his army and the elephants to winter-quarters at Acra Leuce. With the remaining Punic forces thus weakened, a new danger arose. The 'king of the Orissi' arrived with an army, feigning a wish for friendship and alliance with the Carthaginians but in fact aiming to help the besieged. At the right moment he attacked Hamilcar's troops and put them to flight.

Barca saved his sons and his friends by sending them off on one road while he took a different one to draw off the pursuit. As the enemy, led by their king, were about to overtake him he plunged on horseback into a broad flooding river to perish. But Hannibal and his brother escaped to Acra Leuce, where their brother-in-law Hasdrubal soon joined them with other troops.

'Helice', the town Hamilcar was besieging, can hardly have been Ilici, the modern Elche: as mentioned earlier, this lay only 12 miles (20 kilometres) or so south-west of Acra Leuce and astride the road to the rest of Punic Spain. It would have been strange, and hard, for Hamilcar to found his city if a strong hostile centre stood so near. Nor was there much need for winter-quarters in those parts, a district where Europe's biggest palm-forest has flourished for a millennium, or much difference between the climates of the two towns. Again, if Ilici had submitted at first to Punic domination but now revolted, it was acting in dangerous isolation. The only help came from the Orissi, in Roman times called Oretani, whose territory lay on the plateau of La Mancha and in the eastern Sierra Morena over 100 miles (160 kilometres) distant in a straight line—and in reality a much longer and more difficult route, across the mountains.[17]

Hamilcar's target was probably a different 'Helice' inland. The trouble is that there is no place known by that name. Ilucia, a stronghold of the Oretani themselves according to Livy (in a later context), does not suit. Diodorus implies, if anything, that 'Helice' was not Oretanian—and if it was, the Ore-tanian king would hardly turn up to help one of his own towns only when a siege was well under way. Nor would he have then been able to put Hamilcar so completely off his guard.

Less likely still is it that 'Helice' stood somewhere near the river Iber (the Ebro) far to the north—although the Byzantine versifier Tzetzes so names the river that claimed Barca. Tzetzes is just guessing wrongly. The Ebro valley lay beyond the Carthaginians' attested areas of action until the end of the 220s, not to mention lying even further from Oretanian territory than Ilici did. In turn it would be incomprehensible that Hamilcar should choose to send the bulk of his forces (elephants included) all the way back to Acra Leuce and maroon himself with the rest hundreds of miles away in hostile country. For the same reason we must rule out Alce, a Celtiberian stronghold about halfway between the upper reaches of the rivers Anas and Tagus, north of the Oretani.[18]

As it happens, there is a second Elche in the south-east: the small town of Elche de la Sierra, in dramatically wild terrain in the heart of the mountains, about 65 miles (115 kilometres) west of the first and only 3 miles north of the river Segura, the ancient Tader. There are drawbacks: its ancient name is unknown (even assuming the town existed then) and the region gives no good access westwards. But only 20 miles (32 kilometres) to the east, today's Hellín is probably ancient Ilunum, on the route southwards from Saltigi (Chinchilla near Albacete) to the coast—later to be a Roman road. This inland route linked up at Saltigi with an east–west one, another Roman road-to-be, giving access to the plain of La Mancha and the upper reaches of the river Anas. Tobarra, on the same road a few miles north, was very likely the Turbola listed by the geographer Ptolemy among the Bastetani of south-eastern Spain; and the town of Cieza, on the road 30 miles (50 kilometres) south across rough but low-lying country, may have been ancient Segisa, another Bastetanian centre.

Ptolemy also lists two places called Arcilacis, giving one to the Turduli and the other to the Bastetani. He is probably repeating one and the same place. It cannot be located with any exactness, but the name is noteworthy. Greek and Roman writers rendered Spanish place-names in varying ways (especially the obscurer ones): as an example, the towns of Aurinx and Orongis that Livy mentions in different passages were probably identical—and may in fact have really been Aurgi, modern Jaén. 'Helice' could well be a different form of Arcilacis; or else Diodorus' source mistakenly supposed that Arcilacis and Ilici were the same.[19]

Livy, as noted earlier, names the place where Hamilcar died as Castrum Altum. Some distance away was a Mons Victoriae or 'Victory Mountain', though that need not have been named from his defeat. The names point to mountainous terrain for Hamilcar's end. Livy's own context is military operations in the south-east in the Second Punic War. These operations afterwards involved the towns of Castulo in the eastern Sierra Morena, Iliturgi on the Baetis not far from Castulo, and Bigerra, identified either as a place not far east of Castulo and Iliturgi or as one in the mountains west of Ilunum and north-west of Elche de la Sierra. The campaign itself is debatable but it seems, all the same, that Livy's source used actual topographical names. They indicate that the upper Baetis valley was strategically accessible from the region where Barca met his death.[20]

'Helice' then may well have stood somewhere in the rugged country south or south-west of Saltigi, whether or not Elche de la Sierra marks the site. It would have been a strongpoint—not necessarily the only one—from which the local tribe dominated the route between the coast and the inland plains, or at least their refuge when things went badly.

Barca's strategic plan can be reasonably inferred. He meant to subdue the hinterland of Acra Leuce, moving through the high country to the eastern reaches of the river Anas. Since his first campaign had brought the lands around the lower Anas into his power, the final goal of this new drive may have been to round off control of the entire river north of the Sierra Morena.

Access from beyond that range to the ore-rich areas around Castulo was (until quite modern times) chiefly by the pass of Despeñaperros, 30 miles (50 kilometres) or so north of Castulo. Mastery of the Anas riverlands would safeguard Punic possession of the silver-bearing mountains on their northern side. Equally it would mean a convenient start-line for further annexations, if and when they were wanted. Hamilcar surely saw no need to stop his empire-building at the Anas—or even at the Tagus. Central and north-eastern Spain was the homeland of the warlike Celtiberians, valuable as allies and dangerous if hostile. To their west on the plains around the river Durius (now the Duero), the Vettones and Vaccaei grew plentiful harvests of grain.

With all of these the Carthaginians would have had long-standing contact through trade and mercenary-recruiting. Before 229, too, Barca may well have sought closer links with communities north of the Sierra Morena. Almost certainly the town of Castulo, in the heart of the silver-lands of that range and an Oretanian city according to later writers, was within the Punic area of dominance by then—otherwise his activities over on the east side of Spain, with so glaring a gap in his control of the Baetis heartland, are inexplicable. Larger or stronger towns within a Spanish tribal region did act fairly independently (Numantia in Celtiberia is an obvious later case) but, if Punic hegemony had now spread to their southern kinsmen, the Oretani-Orissi beyond the Sierra Morena too may well have struck up a friendship or alliance with Hamilcar. This would help explain why he was taken in by their king when that person arrived offering military support against the enemy at 'Helice'.

But not every Spanish leader or people welcomed being under Punic domination, however mild. The people of 'Helice' did not; nor did the Oretani-Orissi, who faced the prospect of firmer control or even ultimate conversion from allies into tribute-paying subjects.

Significantly, the siege of 'Helice' was still on when winter caught up with the Carthaginians. If campaigning had begun in spring 229 as usual, Hamilcar must have reached the town only after working through other areas— starving out or storming places like Segisa, Ilunum and Turbola one after the other. Plainly 'Helice' was both well sited and held by a fairly small though hardy force. This would account for Hamilcar deciding to send most of his army back to the coast even though the town was holding out. He did not expect to overwhelm it by weight of numbers but would let a winter-blockade do the work. Sending off the bulk of the army, including the elephant corps, eased his own problems of supply and was done probably at the start of winter, late in 229, for to leave it until well into the season would have been undesirable (especially for the animals). Diodorus moreover implies a certain amount of time between the ensuing disaster and Hasdrubal's vengeance on the Orissi, which was the new general's first military move in 228.

Despite his reduced strength Barca can hardly have thought there was much danger, for he kept both sons with him. The arrival of the Orissi with their king did not alarm him: had he been expecting their support and thus felt able to send away so many of his own force? At all events he accepted their supposed help, to his own destruction.

Later writers tell an elaborate tale of oxen being yoked to blazing wagons and sent charging against his panic-stricken troops, and Hamilcar being killed in the battle that followed. It is not easy to accept this alongside Diodorus' differing and matter-of-fact report. Nor is Nepos' naming his attackers as Vettones (who dwelt far to the north between the Tagus and Durius) any more believable. But we can accept that in December 229 or January 228, in a swollen stream—probably the Segura—in the uplands of today's province of Albacete, the founder of Barcid supremacy found his end. He was 50 or 51.[21]

VIII

Hamilcar's achievement was great. He had not only saved the Carthaginian republic but rebuilt it as a first-class power. The new mines and tribute-revenues from Spain brought new prosperity; some of it may have trickled across to allies like Utica and their Libyan subjects too, if it is true that the conquests enriched 'all Africa', while Punic Spain opened up fresh opportunities for citizens prepared to venture there. Over his home country Hamilcar skilfully set up and maintained a political dominance not seen since the time of the earlier Hanno the Great—or even the Magonids—and left it secure enough to be passed on first to his son-in-law and next to his son.

Ancient observers found him both attractive and enigmatic. Naravas was impressed enough by his fame to become his ally and kinsman; Polybius, rather exaggeratedly, sees him as the best general on either side in the war with Rome, admires his leadership in the African revolt and in Spain, and—again admiringly rather than in hostility—judges him the ultimate inspirer of the Second Punic War. In Diodorus he is both the saviour of his country and the practitioner of dirty politics. Romans judged him variously: Cato put him on a par with Pericles, Epaminondas, Themistocles and the Roman hero Dentatus, and in Nepos' short biography he is a mighty figure; then as the notion spread of his ultimate responsibility for Hannibal's war, for Livy he is a great-souled leader driven by anger against the Romans, and for the later poet Silius a grim patriarch likewise typified by resentment against them, even as a spirit among the dead.[22]

There were less splendid aspects of Barca too. He was ruthless whenever he felt it suitable: with mutinous troops in Sicily in 247, towards captured rebels in the later stages of the African war, in his treatment of Indortes. His generalship could be ill judged, careless or both—the unprofitable years on the heights of Heircte and Eryx come to mind, so too his narrow escape (thanks to Naravas) from Spendius and Autaritus' encirclement, his other set-backs from the rebels, and the miscalculation at 'Helice' which led to his death. He did not always feel it necessary to be over-scrupulous or avoid chicanery: he made promises to his mercenaries in Sicily and then left others to cope with them, and he liquidated the rebels at The Saw by—at best—questionable dealing.

Hamilcar, rather like Philip II of Macedon a century earlier, built a power-structure—domestic and imperial—that his son and successor would exploit.

His achievement was not as enduring as Philip's because the war his son launched was finally lost, and with it the Barcid empire. Yet in establishing a foreign dominion in Spain, levying tribute and exploiting natural and human resources, cultivating natives as allies as well as subjects, and founding a city, he not only made Carthage an imperialist power in the mould of those in the Hellenistic east but created a provincial system that could be taken over and developed by (ironically) the Romans in their turn.

He was not and probably never intended to be a king, though in Spain he held virtually monarchic power (as Roman proconsuls would in their provinces). His position rested on an elected command, and so did that of his successors in it. The historian Fabius Pictor would criticize Hasdrubal, not him, for supposedly monarchic pretensions and evil influence on Hannibal. As noted already, their younger contemporary Cato—not normally pro-Carthaginian in his views—ranged Hamilcar with great Greek and Roman republican leaders in favourable contrast to kings. Rather like Athens under Pericles, Barcid Carthage could be described as a republic ruled in fact by its first citizen.

Whether Hamilcar and the other Barcid generalissimos are portrayed in regal style on the fine series of coins from their Spanish mints is still, and no doubt will always be, disputed. Probably not: none offers even an initial to tell a user that it depicts a Barcid ruler; the supposed 'Hamilcar' and 'Hannibal' portraits bear the symbolic club of Hercules who was identified with Carthage's city-god Melqart; other Barcid coins portray female divinities as Carthaginian coins had done for generations. But the coinage, Hellenistic in style and associations, advertised the financial and cultural dynamism of the Barcid province. It fits in with the other Hellenistic associations cultivated by Hamilcar's family, all of them put to use to serve the Punic republic and its *de facto* rulers.[23]

In Hamilcar the Carthaginians found the right man for their times. He gave them both leadership and vision. Within ten years after the two most draining wars in their history they had returned to wealth, prestige and power, travelling an expansionist path very different from Carthage's old island-bound and trade-based hegemony, and on a par militarily and territorially with the other great Mediterranean powers. Where the path was to lead, probably even Hamilcar did not know, though likely enough he expected all of Spain to be conquered in due course. Likely enough too, considering his attitude to the Romans, he judged it highly possible that one day they would again intervene somewhere against Carthage's interests: if so, the Carthaginians must be as strong as possible so as to deter the threat or else defeat it, while meanwhile keeping on amicable or at least respectful terms with their ex-enemies to allow Punic strength to develop. Polybius reports just such advice from him to his successors, though misinterpreting it as part of the supposed master-plan for a war of revenge.[24]

VI

HASDRUBAL'S
CONSOLIDATION

I

Hasdrubal had not accompanied Hamilcar against 'Helice', nor was he at Acra Leuce. He was commanding another force somewhere in the province, for Diodorus writes that as soon as he learned of the disaster he 'broke camp' and hurried to join Hannibal and his brother. Most likely he had been watching over the province while Hamilcar operated on its fringes, and gathering extra forces: for Diodorus adds that he brought 100 elephants with him, giving him 200 altogether in his first campaign as the new general—one of the largest elephant corps on record. The town of Lascuta east of Gades, the only Spanish town to put an elephant on its Punic-era coins, may have housed the elephant corps and was centrally enough sited to keep watch over all four quarters of Punic Spain. From there Hasdrubal could take the coast road via Malaca and Abdera to Acra Leuce. Some reinforcements were later sent from Africa too, if Appian can be trusted.

There were certain things to do before Hasdrubal could retrieve the disaster to Hamilcar—above all, ensure Barcid continuity. Hamilcar had of course not expected to die in his prime and may well have planned on being replaced as generalissimo, when the time came, by a mature eldest son. But war by definition is unpredictable and in 228 Hannibal was still in his teens. Now aged around 40, Hasdrubal was the obvious choice.[1]

According to Diodorus he was 'acclaimed general by both the army and the Carthaginians'. This adds valuable detail to Polybius' statement that 'the Carthaginians entrusted the generalship' to him, which Appian more or less echoes. The soldiers making the decision were probably—as in the army vote on Hanno and Hamilcar during the African war—the citizen officers and troops, not the mercenaries and levies (Libyan and Spanish) as well. Their numbers may not have been large but that was irrelevant.

Hasdrubal had no trouble making the arrangements, as it was still winter and plainly the Orissi and the men of 'Helice' did not follow up their success. To judge by Diodorus' wording and Hannibal's later election, the army in Spain made its decision first, then (in the spring) referred it on to the citizen

73

body at Carthage for ratification. Hamilcar's victories and the shock of his loss guaranteed Hasdrubal's confirmation, even though Hanno and other opponents surely argued against installing, in effect, a dynasty over the Punic republic. To prove the voters—and the army—right in confirming him, though, Hasdrubal had to avenge his father-in-law as well as continue his policies. A visit in due course to Carthage would not come amiss either, especially if he had not been there since the Numidian rebellion five or six years earlier.[2]

The Orissi were soon brought to heel. With part or all of an army of 50,000 infantry, 6,000 cavalry and the 200 elephants Hasdrubal marched into the land around the upper Anas and 'killed all who had been responsible for Hamilcar's rout. He acquired,' Diodorus continues, 'their twelve cities and all the cities of Iberia.' The first part of this blend of precision and vagueness may be correct—the geographer Ptolemy credited the Oretani with 14 towns four centuries later, one of them Castulo—though obviously not the second, which reads at best like an exaggerated summing-up of his whole career. Given their treachery to Hamilcar, the Orissi were most likely made tributary subjects rather than being left as allies, no doubt after condign slaughter, sackings and enslavements. So the avenging of Hamilcar usefully extended the north-eastern reaches of the province to the lands of the upper Anas.[3]

II

Avenging Hamilcar had been not merely a family duty but a political necessity. It retrieved the blow to Punic and Barcid prestige and showed that the new general was as decisive a leader as his predecessor. But Hasdrubal was not just a carbon-copy continuator. Younger, originally a popular politician, he was more assertive and publicity-conscious and he took a rather different approach to ruling Spain.

According to Diodorus it was after wreaking vengeance on the Orissi that the new general took an Iberian king's daughter as his wife, then was acclaimed by 'all the Iberians' as 'general with supreme power' (Diodorus uses the Greek term *strategos autokrator*). Diodorus' text—nothing more than a set of often clumsily made excerpts from two Byzantine collections—is thus tantalizingly silent on context, calculations and even names. Hasdrubal may or may not have been a widower by now, for Carthaginians were monogamous; even if not, he might well put *raison d'état* ahead of custom, like the elder Dionysius of Syracuse and Philip of Macedon in the previous century. A royal Spanish wife created a closer link with (at least) the communities in his province who counted as allies. She symbolized a commitment to the lands he ruled, a relationship more appealing than the plain exploitation which is all we know for Hamilcar. The same symbolism recurred some years later when Hannibal in his turn took a Spanish wife.

Hasdrubal's next move reinforced the bond between Punic general and Iberian peoples. How he arranged to be acclaimed supreme general 'by all the

Iberians', and just who these were, again can only be surmised. One suggestion is that he summoned a congress of representatives from the peoples under Punic rule and prompted them to elect him. Or perhaps he arranged for the Spanish contingents in his army to make the acclamation. They would be varied enough to allow a propaganda claim that 'all the Iberians' had acted, and for the native troops to do so paralleled suitably his earlier election as Carthage's general by the Punic soldiery.

As often pointed out, this was a gesture immediately recognizable beyond Spain too, and for more than one reason. Syracusan leaders had often been elected *strategos autokrator:* Dionysius the Elder, Dion the liberator, Agathocles and probably Hiero had all been. Obviously Hasdrubal would not use the Greek term officially but will have styled himself 'supreme general' (or leader) or the like in Punic, Iberian and the other languages of his territories. On the other hand when writing in Greek he may well have used the term, and historians after him could follow suit, like the pro-Barcid Silenus and Sosylus.[4]

Election or acclamation as leader by an alliance was also common in the Hellenistic world. Alexander the Great had been leader, *hegemon,* of the League of Corinth against Persia a century earlier; Pyrrhus seems to have been leader of the Sicilian Greeks against the Carthaginians before getting himself acclaimed their king; and the continuing use of both these Greek terms in Hasdrubal's day is shown by the Macedonian king Antigonus Doson's election in 224 as *hegemon* of the Achaean League around the time that the Achaean statesman Aratus had been appointed its *strategos autokrator.*

Hasdrubal's signals were both to his own political world, in Spain and North Africa, and to the world outside: he was the leader of two peoples— Carthaginians and Spaniards—with the interests of both at heart; and was the chief of a major state, a power on a level with the other major powers and with a similar coalition of dependent allies and subjects. Of course to the allies and subjects this remained essentially a gesture. The high command of the army and even of Carthage's thinned-out fleet continued to be exclusively Carthaginian. Like Hannibal after him, Hasdrubal no doubt had senators from Carthage in his advisory council along with his chief officers. The reality of dominance was much the same as that which the Romans and the kings of Macedon enforced over their own hegemonies.[5]

III

Political considerations also prompted the new general, it seems, to visit Carthage soon after. For this we have only a report by the unfriendly Fabius Pictor relayed by Polybius.

Hasdrubal, 'after acquiring great power in the Spanish lands', travelled to North Africa, in a move to overturn the laws of Carthage and transform its political system into 'monarchy'. If Polybius relays Pictor correctly the wording suggests that the visit followed the new general's opening measures in Spain, including his acclamation as the Spaniards' *strategos autokrator*—but not a long time later, since Pictor also implied that he went on ruling Spain for quite some while afterwards. As for his supposed goal at Carthage, the Greek word *monarchia* need not mean actual kingship but, literally, one-man rule: Pictor's obvious point was that Hasdrubal wanted autocratic power over the republic.

But 'the leading men in the state, foreseeing his scheme, got together and opposed him; Hasdrubal, feeling suspicious, departed from Africa and thereafter governed Spain according to his own judgement, paying no attention to the Carthaginian senate'. Pictor blamed Hasdrubal, too, for passing on his acquisitiveness and arrogance to Hannibal, with the Second Punic War the result of these vices.[6]

Polybius may overcompress this report but he does not deny Hasdrubal's trip to Carthage (his interest is in denying Pictor's claim that the Carthaginians at home were hostile to Hannibal). How Hasdrubal meant to carry out his supposed coup, and who its opponents were, Polybius does not state, although Fabius Pictor himself may have offered fuller details. Worth notice, though, is the comment about the general 'feeling suspicious', presumably of his opponents. It implies a scenario of intrigue and uncertainty, suitable enough to the story. Certainly Hasdrubal would not have arrived in Carthage trumpeting a plan to overturn the existing constitution and make himself legally the autocrat of the state. At most he would urge fair-sounding reforms, even if he had a hidden agenda. Nor could opposition to his supposed scheme have been overt if it simply roused his suspicion.

In other words, Pictor knew of some sort of muffled political contest between the new general and anti-Barcid interests, and inflated it into a supposed coup-attempt on the model of Peisistratus or Dionysius the Elder. A more plausible picture can cautiously be drawn.

Hasdrubal sailed over to Carthage late in 228 (staying for the winter, maybe, as campaigning in Spain would be in recess) or else during 227. Later than 227 is not likely, both for the reasons already mentioned and because on returning to Spain he launched his biggest project, a new city-foundation which was well under way by 226. Essentially the purpose of his visit home must have been to confirm his political grip there, so it was not one he would make until he had an opening military victory—the avenging of Hamilcar, at that—to his credit. But he may well have had some domestic measures that he wished to enact too, measures political enough to prompt Pictor's notion that he was aiming at 'monarchy'.

It is hardly likely that Hasdrubal was forced to abandon them, though Pictor obviously suggested this, and retreat in dudgeon to a quasi-kingdom effectively divorced from his mother city. Hannibal's smooth succession in 221 at Carthage as in Spain is the best token of the Barcids' continuing grip on the state. On all the evidence, both of Hamilcar's successors were the elected supreme generals of the republic, governing lands and waging wars and making treaties on its behalf just as Punic generals had done down the ages.

Thus Hasdrubal's proposals probably did not include adding to the powers of the generalship. Nor do the functions of the Punic senate seem impaired in the glimpses we get of it over the next quarter of a century, so it is unlikely that Hasdrubal mooted any measure affecting it either. Any proposals he had would aim elsewhere.

Polybius writes (disapprovingly) that by 218 'among the Carthaginians the people had already acquired the most power in deliberations'. Since there is no evidence of this in reality, arguably he viewed the elected and popular Barcid supremacy as embodying popular supremacy. But arguably again there was rather more to it. Not a full-blown democratic revolution as sometimes claimed for 237 but, at some date before 218, adjustments to the working of the citizen assembly (greater freedom over its own agenda, for instance) or indeed to the citizen-body itself. It could be attractive, for example, to make Punic citizenship more accessible to deserving foreigners, especially ones sponsored by the supreme general. The Roman poet Ennius not many decades later portrayed Hannibal promising his men that whoever showed valour would for him be a Carthaginian, whatever his origin, and Livy very similarly reports the promise of citizenship just before his first battle in Italy. In other words, citizenship was something likely to appeal to non-Carthaginians in Carthage's service, and could be a valuable patronage tool to a political leader.[7]

One other institution might well attract Hasdrubal's attentions. The tribunal of One Hundred and Four existed to scrutinize how generals had behaved at war, and Hamilcar quite possibly had risked being prosecuted before it in 241. But after that nothing is ever heard of this function. When the unlucky general Hasdrubal, son of Gisco, fell foul of his countrymen in 203 or 202 he had a death sentence decreed—and afterwards repealed—by the people, or so it seems in our only source, Appian; and according to Appian again the hapless man was later on hunted down and murdered by citizens after a tumultuous assembly-meeting.

Livy does record the power and arrogance of an 'order of judges' dominating the Punic state by 196—a period when the republic, now shorn of practically all war-making capacity, would have had minimal work for the Hundred and Four in their original rôle. As remarked earlier, it is an obvious though tentative inference that the tribunal still existed in 196, was still powerful (especially after the disaster that Hannibal's war inflicted on Barcid interests), but by then judged non-military issues. Already by Aristotle's time it may have widened its functions, but the loss of its supervision of generals must have come later.

To Hasdrubal, the Hundred and Four could seem potentially irksome even if they had no power to investigate him until—if ever—he stepped down from command. Many of them would have joined the tribunal before 237 and even some of the recent entrants need not have been too submissive to Barcid blandishments. Unlike other senators, who still had careers to pursue and so had to stay on Hasdrubal's sunny side, the Hundred and Four as a body could afford to be relatively independent, just as Livy portrays them in 196.

So Hasdrubal might have sponsored, for instance, a scheme to take away their jurisdiction over generals. His opponents and unfriendly Romans, in turn, could easily paint such a proposal as overturning the laws and pointing to one-man rule. But abolishing this rôle would surely have sparked opposition too overt to make him merely suspicious of his opponents. There were other ways of bringing the tribunal safely to heel: for instance a measure that would stack it with Barcid supporters, or one to widen its competence in administrative areas and so deflect its focus from politics.[8]

The first seems less plausible than the second, for a court progressively stacked with supporters over the next quarter-century should not have been that hostile to Hannibal in 196. By contrast, widening its competence could be presented as a good thing. The return of prosperity and the growth of the empire must have increased judicial activity, whereas there was no prospect of the Hundred and Four investigating the current general's doings for a long while at best. If such a modification seemed reasonable to most Carthaginians and not just the Barcid faction, its opponents would certainly be as circumspect as Fabius Pictor implied, working behind the scenes rather than publicly attacking it.

Fabius implied or stated that Hasdrubal failed to get his proposals through. Yet, as noted earlier, nothing suggests that Barcid dominance at Carthage was dented. So Fabius may simply be wrong, just as he is wrong to imply that Hasdrubal was independent of the Punic state. Or maybe the general did decide that the time was not ripe and shelved his proposals—only to revive and enact them quietly later on. Either way, critics could later misrepresent him as suffering a defeat and retreating to Spain to act in virtual independence.

That sophistry meant in turn that the sole blame for the Second Punic War could be laid on his successor and imitator in wilfulness, exonerating the rest of the Punic oligarchy. According to Livy these began blaming Hannibal even before the war was over: the same view that Fabius was to urge on his readers. Fabius' source was very probably Carthaginian and maybe not all that far from the circle around Hanno the Great. Hanno's basic attitude to any proposal put up by Hasdrubal does not have to be guessed.[9]

IV

Hasdrubal, his political supremacy at home confirmed, sailed back to his province, likely enough in spring or summer 227. He had another important project to carry out in the service of its development and the Barcids' glory. Like Hamilcar he founded a city.

This was 'a city by the sea', Diodorus writes, 'which he named New Carthage': today's Cartagena, 60 miles (100 kilometres) south of Alicante. This was the site, as noted above, of an earlier Iberian town called Mastia. New Carthage was in reality the Greek and Roman version of the name, and here Polybius is more informative: it was 'called by some Carthage, by others New City' (he normally uses this second version himself). In Punic 'New City' was a single word—Qart-hadasht. Hasdrubal's new city was in fact another Carthage.[10]

This might look like a challenge to old Carthage, or a declaration of independence from it. Some at the time probably did see it so: we remember Fabius Pictor's later claim that after returning from North Africa Hasdrubal 'governed Spain according to his own judgement, paying no attention to the Carthaginian senate'. Some modern historians see it in the same light—the visible evidence of a virtually separate Barcid kingdom, Hasdrubal's more or less private domain.[11]

The inference is not warranted, even though the governmental palace that Hasdrubal built there did strike some at the time as betraying royal ambitions. We have seen that like his predecessor he kept a firm grip on affairs in North Africa as well as Spain—and as Carthage's generalissimo, not as king. Equally we cannot read too much into his new city's name. A new Carthage it certainly was: but it was not the only Qart-hadasht in old Carthage's territories. Fifty miles (80 kilometres) by air from Carthage, just north of the gulf of Hammamet, stood the coastal town of Neapolis (Nabeul today), a Greek name which in Punic can have been no other than Qart-hadasht again. On the coast to the south lay another town called Neapolis by Greeks, then known in Roman times as Macomades, a Phoenician name (Maqom-hadasht) meaning very similarly 'new place'—no doubt its original name persisting.

Nor was this the only Macomades in the region; there was another in Numidia and a third to the east of the famous city of Lepcis Magna, halfway between Carthage and Egypt. Lepcis Magna itself was also called Neapolis according to various Greek geographers, including one in the fourth century BC. The geographer Ptolemy even mentions an 'old Carthage', which would be yet another Phoenician or Punic 'new city', in north-eastern Spain, in the land of the Ilercavones around the mouth of the river Ebro.

Ptolemy's item must be a mistake or misunderstanding: it was probably a town that Strabo records as Cartalia. But names like New City and New Place are typical enough for colonies. The Phoenicians had so named the town in Cyprus afterwards called Citium. We recall that Aristotle in the fourth century reported the Carthaginians periodically sending out citizen colonists. They went normally to an existing centre, but their numbers and dominance might sometimes prompt a renaming (formal or informal). At Carthage itself a new quarter existed by the fourth century which Diodorus names Neapolis, another 'New City'. The Carthaginians presumably called it Qart-hadasht too, or else Maqom-hadasht. Obviously the duplication or near-duplication did not bother them.[12]

Hasdrubal's reason, then, for naming his new foundation after his home city was not a declaration of independence but a natural enough, almost a traditional, choice. An alternative would have been to keep the old name Mastia, but this surely had little resonance for Carthaginians. Calling it Qart-hadasht had extra propaganda value, symbolizing the Barcids' linking of Spain with Africa and the strength of the Carthaginians' stake in their new province. More subtly it advertised to a suitably impressed world the renewed power of Carthage: not one but two strong and rich Qart-hadashts would sustain and reinforce it. The people Hasdrubal most wanted to impress were surely the Romans. He succeeded.[13]

New Carthage was impressive from the start. It stood on four hills dominating a safe southward-facing harbour at the head of a deep gulf of the Mediterranean, just short of Cape de los Palos where the Spanish coast turns northwards. The westernmost hill was crowned by Hasdrubal's citadel and palace. On its north side lay a broad lagoon, linked to the sea by a canal that protected the city's western flank. An ideal site for commerce and fisheries, its wealth was multiplied by the rich silver deposits in the hills to the east. Communications with the rest of the Punic province were rather shorter than Acra Leuce's, and those with North Africa and Ebusus not much lengthier. Altogether it was an inspired choice as the site for a capital.[14]

According to Diodorus, Hasdrubal founded another city too, though he does not give its name. The early Byzantine geographer Stephanus lists an otherwise unknown city called Accabicon Teichos, or Fort Accabicon, which he claims the Carthaginians founded by the straits of Gibraltar; this has been suggested as Hasdrubal's other creation. But such very late evidence is obviously dubious when no other trace of the supposed city exists. Even if genuine, 'Accabicum' may have been a Punic epithet for a known city.[15]

Diodorus' words do not rule out an addition to an existing town—rather as New Carthage itself seemingly was to old Mastia—though this time the old name might have persisted. Hasdrubal may have chosen a site inland, for instance to reinforce his control in the Baetis valley. Or, another possibility, he was the founder or refounder of the small town of Tiar or Thiar, known to have stood near the coast between New Carthage and Ilici to its north.

Tiar seems unusual as an Iberian name-form, but instead could be similar to the names Gadir, the Phoenician and Punic form of Gades, and Tharros, a Phoenician (or Punic) colony in Sardinia. If so, Hasdrubal's aim would have been to protect New Carthage's communications up the coast to Acra Leuce, now that the eastern side of his province was growing in population and wealth. The notable salt-marshes of Torrevieja and La Mata, valuable for fisheries and 30–40 miles (50–60 kilometres) north of New Carthage, may have been another attraction.[16]

V

These creations, of course the new Carthage above all, impressed Spaniards and non-Spaniards with Barcid achievements to date and ambitions for the future. The Romans paid particular notice. According to Polybius, it was because of the new city and Hasdrubal's powerful military forces that they 'made haste to busy themselves with the affairs of Spain' which they had hitherto ignored.

They had other worries which reinforced their concern. Their activities in the north of the Italian peninsula had upset the Gauls of the Po river-lands, dangerous warriors whose ancestors had sacked Rome itself a century and a half before. As the year 225 approached, a massive Gallic army gathered to invade Italy. As a result, along with their military preparations the Romans sent an embassy to Hasdrubal, very likely early in 225.[17]

Polybius does not fully explain why a looming northern invasion of Italy should prompt an approach to the Carthaginian generalissimo in Spain. He certainly implies that, without the invasion, the Romans themselves would have imposed demands or even made war on Hasdrubal; but he claims that instead they decided on 'petting and conciliating' him. Logically, if they had simply decided not to make demands or war they need not have approached Hasdrubal at all, so Polybius fails to account properly for why they did. His thinking has to be inferred from what he claims later: that not only did the Barcid generals plan a revenge-war against the Romans but (by implication) the Romans suspected so. If they did, it would be natural to try to conciliate Hasdrubal in such a critical moment.

We saw earlier that not only is there nothing to suggest a real Barcid war-plan, but nothing points to Romans at the time believing there was one. Still, Polybius did not jump to a simply unwarranted inference about the Romans' anxieties. Besides readying troops against the Gauls in the north and to protect the City itself, they sent substantial forces—four legions altogether—to Tarentum, Sicily and Sardinia. The only sensible explanation for this dispersal of strength must be that they aimed at deterring misbehaviour from the Illyrians across the Adriatic (whom the Romans had recently warred on) and from the Carthaginians.

As events between 241 and 237 had shown, the Romans paid their ex-foes real attention only when unusual happenings cropped up. The rape of Sardinia suggests too that they had been worried lest the victorious Carthaginians be tempted, at some stage, to recover their lost Sicilian ground. The military arrangements in 225, plus the military promise they coaxed from Hasdrubal, point to a similar type of worry: that the Carthaginians (and Illyrians) might try to take advantage of the Gallic distraction.

In Carthage's case this could mean having a go at Sardinia and Sicily, but there was another calculation bothering the Romans. In the accord he made with them Hasdrubal guaranteed that he would not move militarily north of the Ebro river. This points to them feeling concern that he might lead an expedition, not just into north-eastern Spain (which from their strategic viewpoint in 225 was neither here nor there) but into the south of Gaul or even into north Italy, which the Romans called Cisalpine Gaul. Not specifically as an ally of the Gauls; there is no evidence that he had any Gallic contacts, and even in 218 the Romans were not aware—until too late—that Hannibal had just developed some.

But should the Gauls bring chaos down on Roman Italy, who could prevent an ambitious Punic leader from moving to take advantage—either as self-imposed peacemaker and arbiter or simply as opportune exploiter? Looked at coldly, of course, the odds on any such event were small to vanishing. But the Romans, viewing their chances against the Gauls alone as balanced on a knife-edge, were scarcely disposed to look at the odds coldly. At all events they judged it worthwhile to send envoys to sound out the Carthaginian commander-in-chief in a friendly manner.[18]

Hasdrubal surely found this gratifying. By sending the envoys to him in Spain, and not to the authorities at Carthage, the Romans were plainly recognizing his pre-eminence over Punic affairs. This in turn could only enhance his pre-eminence, especially if he struck a successful agreement with his visitors. Since he obviously harboured none of the schemes they seemed to fear, an agreement was easy to make. All he had to do, in fact, was promise that 'the Carthaginians are not to cross the river called Iber in warfare'.

Why the Ebro and not, rather, the Pyrenees which were a much more obvious barrier? Perhaps because it was precisely southern Gaul, on the other side of those mountains, that the Romans wished him to abstain from. Moreover they were probably already friends with the little Greek port of Emporiae in north-eastern Spain, a potentially useful observation post, and wanted to preserve it from Punic hegemony. At the same time the Ebro at its nearest was more than 220 miles (350 kilometres) from his new city and there was plenty of intervening Spain to occupy him. Hasdrubal had no trouble agreeing.

The envoys promptly left for home; and in due course—and the nick of time—the consul sent to Sardinia sailed back with his legions and helped his colleague entrap the Gauls into annihilation in Etruria.

Both sides could congratulate themselves on an accord well made. The Romans had been relieved of their Punic worries: Hasdrubal, attractive in personality and subtle in diplomacy, no doubt contributed greatly to this in his talks with the envoys. He in turn had Roman acquiescence in treating the great bulk of Spain as free range for further expansion: for the accord plainly implied—and the envoys surely discussed this face to face with him too—that the Romans would complain only if he were 'to cross the river called Iber in warfare'. Given their intermittent sensitivity to potential Punic initiatives, it was an implication worth having. They in turn could feel reassured that Carthage was under sensible government, with no inclination to get involved in Rome's regional affairs, while he could feel not only correspondingly reassured over Spain but also domestically strengthened thanks to this proof of Roman recognition and respect.

Neither side paid the other diplomatic attention after this. The Romans went on to conquer Cisalpine Gaul, Hasdrubal to consolidate the Punic dominion in southern Spain. They had no more dealings with each other during his lifetime.[19]

VI

According to Appian, Hasdrubal conquered Spain 'up to the river Iber, which divides Iberia more or less through the middle, five days' journey from the Pyrenees, and flows to the northern ocean'. This Appianic mélange of precision and confusion suggests that he really means the Tagus but—either by his own effort or thanks to his source—has worked in a careless recollection of the Ebro, which does lie about five days' distance (on foot) from the Pyrenees and, as we have just seen, did mark the limit of Hasdrubal's potential expansion after 225. That the Tagus was the furthest north of Punic control under the second Barcid is confirmed by Hannibal's campaign of 220, launched into the lands beyond its middle reaches.

Just what such a frontier meant is a rather different question. Hasdrubal left behind a reputation as both a military man and, even more emphatically, a supple and appealing diplomat. Just as Hamilcar had done, but apparently more often, he used persuasion and alliances in lieu of armed might to extend Punic dominance. Such links would be most prevalent in the outer reaches of his province, though not there alone. The Tagus then would not be a patrolled border strictly marking off Punic from non-Punic territory, but rather would mark the furthest zone (so far) of communities friendly with— or in some cases firmly subjected to—the Carthaginians.

Punic dominance extended across southern Lusitania to the Atlantic coast. Hamilcar had secured the lower reaches of the river Anas, and during the Second Punic War we find Punic armies wintering comfortably among the Conii in the Algarve and by the mouth of the Tagus. The gold washed down in some Lusitanian rivers, notably again the Tagus, may also have drawn Punic notice.[20]

East of the Toletum district the Tagus flows from the north-east, rising as it does in the mountains of the Cordillera Ibérica or ancient Mons Idubeda. In these upper Tagus lands—the nearer parts of Celtiberian Spain— Hasdrubal may well have enjoyed friendly relations with what communities there were, but nothing suggests Punic dominance or any need, strategic or commercial, for it. The Carpetani, who dwelt on the plains by the Tagus with Toletum as their strongest town, may have maintained friendly or at least correct relations, but were outside any real control, as they showed in 220 and still later. In Polybius' roster of subject or allied troops under Hannibal's command at the start of 218, the most northerly contingents (apart from the pro-Punic Ilergetes beyond the Ebro) are Oretani and Olcades, both certainly or probably dwelling south of the river. And though Hannibal campaigned across central Spain in 220 and in theory imposed control up to the Ebro and Duero, many Celtiberian communities switched support to the Romans during the Second Punic War. Those who served in the Punic army did so, it seems, for pay as professional mercenaries.

But friendly contacts and commerce did not stop in central Spain. The accord with Rome had no bearing on these. The little Greek colony of Emporiae on the coast well beyond the Ebro used a Punic standard for its coins although, as noted earlier, it was very probably on good terms with Rome too. The Ilergetes in the middle Ebro region not only had a small contingent in Hannibal's forces at the start of 218 but fought against the Romans in most stages of the ensuing war (even after Punic Spain itself had been overrun). They, and especially their energetic chieftains the brothers Indibilis and Mandonius, must have formed strong bonds with Barcid Spain a good while before Hannibal took command.[21]

On the east coast the Saguntines, at least, had a different view. Small but prosperous, their town traded with the Punic province as with other regions, but in diplomacy and policy they stayed at arm's length. At some date—hardly earlier than 225—they in fact struck up friendly contacts with the Romans. This link was one-sided in practice. The Saguntines every so often sent word to Rome about developments in Punic Spain, obviously with an eye to their own interests, but were paid no attention apart from (presumably) a polite acknowledgement. Not that they were in any danger, for Polybius indicates that down to 220 the Carthaginians maintained peaceable relations. Nor did Punic dominance otherwise extend as far as the Ebro before 220, as Polybius also makes clear. On the other hand the Saguntines did have disputatious neighbours (as we shall see) and, on the principle that your enemies' enemies or potential enemies may as well be your own friends, these very likely kept up good relations with New Carthage. When they became Punic subjects is not clear, though Hannibal described them as such in late 220: probably during 221 or 220 when with torrential speed he spread his hegemony across Spain up to the Duero and Ebro.[22]

The northern bounds of Hasdrubal's province, then, stretched seemingly along the Tagus to about the centre of Spain, and from there roughly along the ranges separating the middle Tagus and upper Anas; next eastwards across the southern plains of La Mancha, either to the lower reaches of the river Sucro and along this to the coast, or else turning south-eastwards to meet the coast around Cape de la Nao. He may not have directly controlled the eastern regions of the Tagus (the Toletum district was independent-minded Carpetanian territory, as mentioned earlier, and beyond it the river-line turned to the north-east), but Hasdrubal thus had a grip on the routes from the south and south-east into the interior. Only the east coast up to the Ebro remained outside his control.

Expansion in that direction could wait, or so he might reckon. By 221 he had charge of nearly half the Iberian peninsula: on a rough estimate, over 90,000 square miles (or 240,000 square kilometres). This was an area greater than Punic territory at home, even including the subject Libyans. Administration, exploitation and political relations—between the inhabitants and the Carthaginians, and no doubt among the variegated communities themselves—needed constant attention. Mineral exploitation continued, not only in the area of New Carthage but in other districts like the Sierra Morena. Hannibal pushed it forward energetically, according to Pliny the Elder. Pliny adds that the great mine of Baebelo—its shafts running up to a Roman mile and a half into the mountain—yielded 300 pounds of silver a day to Hannibal, the one such statistic surviving from Barcid times. Despite Pliny, this mine was probably not first opened during Hannibal's governorship, which in Spain lasted only two and a half years. It more likely dated from Hasdrubal's time, though Hannibal may well have improved it to that impressive level.[23]

Affairs at Carthage needed supervision too, though in detail they could be left to Barcid kinsmen and allies to look after. Steady progress in Spain and the successful accord with the Romans can only have enhanced Hasdrubal's dominant position over both these allies and the republic as a whole. Such criticism as there was came, as usual, from Hanno the Great and his friends, but their influence was now at a nadir. Livy tells a story of Hasdrubal sending to Carthage in 224 for a 'hardly yet adult' Hannibal, and Hanno opposing it on the moral ground that Hasdrubal had the same homosexual designs on his brother-in-law that Hamilcar allegedly had once had on him, and the political ground that Hannibal was being groomed for virtual monarchy. In reality Hannibal had been in Spain since 237 and in any case was a man of 23 by 224. At some stage Hasdrubal appointed him commander of the cavalry, and effectively his deputy: this quite likely happened in 224. The kernel of truth in Livy's tale then may be that Hanno objected emphatically to the promotion and claimed that the republic was becoming a *de facto* monarchy. True as this might be, it would hardly be news to his hearers. The Hannonites remained mired in impotence.[24]

VII

In Spain, whatever Hasdrubal's later reputation as a lover of peaceful solutions, warfare did not fully cease. There may have been less fighting than in Hamilcar's time, but Hasdrubal's military strength grew. From 50,000 infantry and 6,000 cavalry in 228, he commanded 60,000 and 8,000 respectively during his later years according to Diodorus, and the 200-strong corps of elephants continued in service at least for a time. Hannibal's appointment to be cavalry commander was a far from ornamental post, as Livy's glowing description of his military prowess shows, not to mention Appian's remark that 'where force was needed he [Hasdrubal] made use of the young man'.

Polybius confirms the picture obliquely: he mentions how Hannibal and his friend Mago each captured cities in Spain (never together, to avoid disputes over booty), and given Hannibal's age this can only point to exploits in Hasdrubal's time. Again, as soon as Hannibal became general late in 221 he launched and won a lightning war against a hostile Spanish people—showing that Hasdrubal's military machine was in first-class condition, perhaps too that the Olcades had been the murdered leader's next war-target.

Nor was Hasdrubal's treatment of his Spanish followers always mild. He had shown his harsh side in dealing with Hamilcar's slayers (not to mention the rebel Numidians years earlier). The poet Silius may not just be inventing that he wished to be feared, even if Silius overdoes it into caricature. In 221 a particular act of sternness rebounded fatally. He put to death a Spanish chieftain for some offence, only for one of the man's loyal followers to break into his quarters and murder him in his sleep. This may have happened in the palace at New Carthage, or a country villa since Appian has it done on a hunting expedition.

Hasdrubal had been general for nearly eight years. The season was autumn 221, for Hannibal on becoming general still had time for a first campaign. In southern Spain, warfare could run until quite late in the year, as Hamilcar's last campaign showed; if Hannibal spent six to eight weeks on his fighting and ended it sometime in November or even early December, we can put Hasdrubal's death in September or October. He was probably still in his forties.[25]

The Carthaginian state and empire that he left behind was at least as strong and rich as it had been in 264—in some ways stronger and richer. At home Punic territory had been enlarged, and relations with the Numidian princes seem to have been more peaceable than for a long while past. Overseas, for the first time in the republic's history it controlled sizeable continental territories, whose tribute and trade very likely outclassed the returns garnered before 264 from Punic trading-stations and island possessions. The still uncertain Punic predominance over southern Spain in 229 had become firmly established by 221, while trade with other lands no doubt continued as before, including Italy and Sicily and probably even Africa's Atlantic coastlands.

Finally, the republic had large, highly trained armed forces, whose use of cavalry and resulting mobility—tactical and strategic—were superior to virtually any other Mediterranean military establishment, a corps of officers who, as the future would show, were probably the ablest of any army of that age, and leadership of the same order. In sum, what Hamilcar had aimed at, Hasdrubal achieved. The Carthaginians were again a first-class power whom no one could browbeat or victimize, not even the Romans. The new general and leader would put this regained strength to its utmost test.

VII

HANNIBAL IN SPAIN

I

The same procedure for replacing Hasdrubal was followed as for Hamilcar. 'The forces' in Spain—Polybius assures us, and so do later sources—unanimously chose Hannibal as their new general. As before, this choice was most likely made by the Carthaginian troops and officers, under arrangements equally unknown. Then, when the events in Spain were reported at Carthage, the citizen assembly ratified the appointment. Of course there was no question of other candidates or any competition. Thus a third Barcid took control of the city and the empire, confirming the de facto monarchy into which the republic had evolved. If Hanno the Great protested this time, it went unrecorded.

Livy draws a famous and biased character portrayal of the new leader, supposedly at the time he became Hasdrubal's subordinate. Hannibal's vividly described warlike qualities are convincing enough, partly because they fit many of his recorded doings. To the old soldiers (Livy writes) he recalled his father Hamilcar in looks and energy, he showed superb qualities of leadership, bravery and endurance, and yet—the Roman historian insists—he was a tissue of cruelty, treachery and atheism. The alleged vices are briefly listed and generalized, nor does Livy mention a failing that Polybius later stresses, greed for money. Even at this point to accuse Hannibal of atheism reads oddly when, just a couple of chapters earlier, the historian has told the story of his boyhood oath and plainly means us to take it seriously. A few pages later he then tells how the general went to Gades to make vows at the temple of Hercules, meaning Melqart, in preparation for his expedition to Italy. The vices in the portrayal obviously owe more to Roman tradition than to accurate reportage, even though there is no reason to imagine that Hannibal was a saint.[1]

Hannibal in a real sense was entering on his inheritance. Having accompanied his father and brother-in-law to Spain he had seen every stage in the development of Punic power there and had contributed to much of it. What his long-range aims were at this point, if he had any, is not reliably recorded. Fabius Pictor, then Polybius, and afterwards other writers, stressed how deeply the new general had been conditioned by his predecessors: to equal either Hasdrubal's supposed level of arrogance and acquisitiveness (as Pictor claimed) or, as Polybius and later writers saw it, Hamilcar's determination to revenge on the Romans all the wrongs they had done to Carthage. But these notions were formed in hindsight and prompted by the war of 218.

Hannibal's expectations in 221 were probably different. By now he had a Spanish wife, a girl from Castulo, the silver-mining town in the Sierra Morena. Silius the later epic poet names her Imilce, claims noble birth for her, and avers that during 220 she bore him a son—items that may all be true though Imilce is actually a Carthaginian name; but where Silius got them from is unknown. Like Hasdrubal's marriage in 228, this would strengthen Barcid ties with their Spanish subjects and allies. It might even suggest that Hannibal expected to continue a mainly Spanish rôle, like his predecessors. For when his plans changed and he marched for Italy, neither his wife nor his son (if the child existed) went with him.

With him in Spain he had both his brothers, Hasdrubal the younger and Mago, and (if Appian is right) an already adult nephew named Hanno—all of them holding high rank in the army. This concentration of family strength is striking, all the more as we know of no kinsmen at Carthage apart from another Mago, who does not seem all that prominent. But the Barcid generals had built up a broad network of political alliances at home, as the impotence of Hanno the Great's group shows, and Hannibal very likely had other relatives or relatives-in-law there helping to keep the family's grip firm: Bomilcar his brother-in-law for instance. Among political allies we might guess at Himilco, the father of his cavalry officer Maharbal, if he still lived. His close friend and lieutenant Mago the Samnite surely had family connexions at home too that were important to Barcid dominance, and so too a tough officer and friend also named Hannibal with the sobriquet Monomachus, or Gladiator. Gisco, a senior officer mentioned only at Cannae, Plutarch terms 'equal in status' to the general—an unexplained but striking description that again suggests more than just military importance.[2]

Hannibal probably had a particular need for vigorous political aides and allies at Carthage. Like his brother-in-law and father, he had never held a civil magistracy there. But unlike them he had spent no time there as an adult, so his knowledge of and dealings with his fellow-countrymen were at long range and at second hand. This was not a crippling disadvantage. Barcid dominance rested on military success and imperial profits, and was institutionalized in the office of general and the military posts subordinate to this, all of them in safe hands. So long as success and its profits continued, so would the dominance. Again, Hannibal may well have meant to visit his home city after a while—as Hasdrubal had done early in his command—to strengthen his ties with important individuals, the institutions of state, and his fellow-citizens overall. Meanwhile, though, he would be very reliant on the Barcids' leading supporters there.

As a result, on some matters he may have been readier than either pre-decessor to follow their advice: for instance about constructing the city's famous artificial ports. These, the rectangular outer one for merchant ship-ping and the circular inner one for warships very possibly date to the period from 218. Though Appian (probably following Polybius) describes them in the context of the Third Punic War, and archaeological remains earlier than 200 are very scarce, after 201 the Carthaginians neither needed nor were allowed to have a navy. Nor did they have a significant one between 241 and 218 as we have seen—in 218 Punic naval strength in Spain and Africa together amounted to fewer than 100 ships ready for service. By contrast, once they had to wage the new war with the Romans they needed and did develop large naval forces (not that these ever performed impressively). But Hannibal by 218 was busy with land campaigning and anyway, like his pre-decessors, rarely showed much commitment to sea-power. A project like the double port was more likely the brainchild of supporters at Carthage, who saw the need both to strengthen Punic naval efforts and also to protect Punic commercial shipping against Roman raids.

Hannibal never in fact got to Carthage while the war lasted, and keeping in touch with Africa from Italy must have posed as much of a problem as with Spain. Inevitably he would have to leave a good deal of local decision-making to the city authorities, even though the overall direction of the war remained with him. Now and then bigger responsibilities too may have been taken on by the authorities there: in 215 the Mighty Ones sent orders to his brother in Spain to march with reinforcements to him in Italy, while later that year the new king of Syracuse, with the general's obvious encouragement, sent envoys to Carthage for an alliance. This might be convenient enough—as long as the home authorities continued to be Barcid supporters. But as more years passed and both victories and benefits receded, this crucial aspect might well weaken.[3]

II

Hannibal's first move as general was a new campaign. Polybius records this after giving details of how the citizen body at Carthage ratified his election in Spain, but that may be simply for neatness' sake. If Hannibal waited until he learned of the ratification he would lose anything up to a month (depending on winds and waves) of what was left of the campaigning year. As Hasdrubal's deputy, and at all events general-designate, he was surely free to act.

He attacked and stormed the Olcades' strongest centre, Althia, which was enough to prompt the rest of them to surrender. His swift and sharp offen-sive suggests advance preparation: as was noted earlier, the Olcades may already have been in Hasdrubal's sights. They were relatively affluent, for he was able to garner booty and funds, but they are unknown after Barcid times.

Their territory probably lay not on the coastlands just beyond Acra Leuce—that would have made them far too vulnerable to be independent as late as 221—but in the interior, for when in the next year he campaigned towards the Duero, the Carpetani by the Tagus let him go by but then were persuaded by Olcades fugitives (among others) to attack him on his return. This points to the Olcades being not too far from the Carpetani, and to their south since the Vaccaei lived to the north. So it is plausible that the Olcades dwelt on the northern La Mancha plains, between the Oretani and the Carpetani: they may have been related to these latter and lost their separate identity later. It is at least interesting that a town named Alce, or Alces, stood in that area in Roman times.[4]

Subduing the Olcades brought Punic power close to or up to the middle Tagus. It may also have brought the nearby region up to the Cordillera Ibérica under Hannibal's influence, which reached the Ebro by the end of 220 though his campaign that year was against the Vaccaei in the west.

This second campaign was not a mere outgrowth of the first. Not only were the Olcades and Carpetani warlike and therefore better within his military establishment than outside, but the mountains beyond them were rich in iron and the Celtiberians there skilled ironworkers. Even if conceivably the Olcades had provoked attack in some way, the move against the Vaccaei was simple aggression and, as with the Olcades, produced booty and glory—both of which he needed.[5]

Aged 25, a virtual stranger to Carthaginians at home, and appointed to his post arguably for no reason but family ties, Hannibal had to prove himself to everyone: to his fellow citizens, his soldiers, Carthage's Spanish allies and subjects—many of them led by warrior princes—and even the Spaniards outside his province. The one way to do so fast and effectively was by warfare, and this was also where his best talents lay.

The Vaccaei were masters of cornlands and livestock on the broad plains spreading up to the middle Duero. Whatever their past relations with Punic Spain, war had not featured. Between them and the Tagus dwelt the Carpetani and, further west, the Vettones, neither of whom were ruled from New Carthage though they may have passed for its friends. So if Hannibal used a pretext, it might be that the Vaccaei had been intimidating these peoples. The Carpetani, who did not bother him on his outward march, were hardly sorry to see him going to teach their neighbours a lesson.[6]

He stormed two Vaccaean strongholds, Helmantice—in Livy, Hermandica (the later Salamanca)—and Arbucala, which has been identified as the town of Toro on the river Duero. A dubious later tale, not in Polybius or even Livy, has him tricked by the women of Hermandica when the town surrendered: they walked out with weapons under their clothes to rearm their menfolk, who then fell on Hannibal's plundering troops. So impressed was he by their courage that he gave them back their town and goods. This does not square with him taking both towns by force, as Polybius and Livy record, amassing booty as Livy affirms, or prompting a flood of aggrieved fugitives from Hermandica to join those from the Olcades in pressing the Carpetani to turn against him.[7]

These successes were enough for him: he then set out homewards. Yet Hermandica and Arbucala were not the only important Vaccaean centres—so too were Pallantia and Intercatia, both north of the Duero, which in the next century were to give the Romans much trouble. Maybe these two avoided trouble now by a timely submission, though nothing like it is mentioned. More likely the general decided he had done enough for one year's campaigning. Though Hermandica had been captured in one go, Arbucala had held out and cost him time and no doubt lives. He may have decided that it was time to declare victory and go home, or that further efforts against the Vaccaei must wait until next season.

The Carpetani, 'and likewise the neighbouring peoples gathered together with these', now turned on him. The arguments used by the fugitive Olcades and Hermandicans to instigate them to do this are not mentioned, but the most obvious one would be the danger to Carpetanian freedom from a too-successful Punic expansion. The allied forces pursued the Punic army to a crossing of the Tagus, presumably near Toledo—but were crushingly beaten.

Hannibal in this his first major battle showed his tactical skills. Having crossed the river southwards, he turned and marched back to its banks so as to tempt his pursuers to cross for battle; then once they began crossing—thus dividing their strength—he fell on them. Exploiting similar tactics, the Greek leader Timoleon with inferior forces had smashed an army of Carthage in Sicily 120 years before. But Timoleon's opportunity had come almost by accident. Hannibal made his own. Now he could march untroubled back to New Carthage for the winter.[8]

Up to a point the successes of his first two campaigns were striking: towns stormed, booty and captives gathered, and now 'none of the peoples south of the Ebro ventured lightly to confront the Carthaginians, except the Saguntines'. Closer study might modify the picture a little. The town-captures in both campaigns relied on direct assault, single or repeated—for in contrast to his genius with armies, Hannibal's siege-skills would always be limited. The Vaccaei had not been annexed, indeed may not even have been forced into dependence. The Carpetani and their allies were no doubt taught a lesson; but they had not been hostile before 220 so, in effect, Hannibal had simply restored the status quo with them. And the operations in 220—two towns stormed and one battle won—are surprisingly few for a whole campaign year: a hint that they were not the blitzkrieg that Polybius' and Livy's brief reports might suggest. It looks as though the Vaccaei, even apart from Hermandica and Arbucala, put up some serious resistance, and may even have foiled a completer success.

The booty and fame, though, and the intimidation of northern central Spain were valuable for reinforcing his authority as new Punic leader. Hannibal may have intended to return in 219 in greater strength to impose more thorough control. But his exploits had other and fateful repercussions.

The antagonistic neighbours of the Saguntines, probably the Turitani at the town of Turis, a few miles down the east coast, now if not earlier entered under Punic tutelage along with the rest of 'the peoples south of the Ebro'. And the Saguntines themselves, who for some time had been informing the Romans of Barcid activities, were finally rewarded with a pair of Roman ambassadors being sent to look over the situation and meet the new general. When he returned to spend the winter at New Carthage, he found the two waiting for him.[9]

III

Probably deliberately, Roman historical tradition afterwards distorted the facts about this embassy. This was to give the impression that during the next year's long siege of Saguntum the Romans did not leave their Spanish protégés entirely in the lurch. Supposedly (so Livy tells it) they voted the embassy in 220, but Hannibal launched the siege too quickly and the envoys had to travel to his camp outside the town—only to be turned away. This story gathered increasingly implausible features as it went on, including a band of Saguntine envoys able to get out of and back into their town at will. The versifier Silius economically then blends this 'siege-embassy' with the war-embassy of 218. Only Polybius has the persuasive version: envoys arriving in late 220 to interview the new Punic leader. But Roman tradition is probably right about their names: P. Valerius Flaccus, very likely the one who had been consul in 227, and Q. Baebius Tamphilus who may have been an ex-praetor.[10]

These were weighty envoys, and the first from Rome in five and a half years. Hannibal must have heard of their arrival before he reached New Carthage. He probably had no trouble working out why they had come. He surely knew of the Saguntines' various earlier messages to Rome and he now also had their fractious neighbours under a Punic wing. With the Romans aware that his influence—either firm or fluctuating—now reached to the river Ebro, they might well want to discuss the future of Hasdrubal's five-year-old agreement. Maybe the future of Saguntum too, small, independent and now surrounded by Punic subjects or dependants. The Romans wanted, he might reckon, to establish a working relationship on these and other matters with the clearly energetic successor to their old negotiating partner.

Now from Hannibal's point of view the Ebro and Saguntum were ticklish topics. Once he finished nailing down Punic dominance over Spain beyond the Tagus, and that would take only another campaign or two, the obvious ground for further conquests lay over the Ebro and up to the Pyrenees. After all, the only alternatives were the harsh mountain-lands of Spain's north-west or the North African hinterland of Carthage—or for Hannibal, less than two years after assuming command, to give up warfare and turn his leadership into purely peaceful and civilian paths, something not even Hasdrubal had done. None of these choices, it is clear, appealed to him, least of all the third, which would have brought to a stop the momentum and charisma fuelling Barcid supremacy at home and in Spain. So the Ebro line would have to be reviewed.

As for the Saguntines, they had never come up in Punic–Roman relations before. But plainly they had a friendly link with the Romans. Not only were they sending them regular messages on Spanish affairs, but recently— probably just a few weeks earlier—they had invited in Roman arbitrators to settle a bout of domestic political strife, arbitrators who were probably these same envoys or companions of theirs. These had entrenched the diehard pro-independence Saguntine faction in power—putting to death several of their opponents to do so. Those opponents had more than likely favoured bringing Saguntum into the Punic empire as subordinate allies, like so many other Spanish communities, whereas the arbitrators found the faction refusing any accommodation with the Carthaginians more to their taste.

This outcome was not as foregone a conclusion as often thought. The Romans would not have been accepted as arbiters if one Saguntine side had seen them as its enemies. Nor had they hitherto shown any interest in Saguntine affairs, even though the town had shown itself aloof and suspicious towards Barcid expansion for quite some time—in other words even though the pro-independence faction had been running its affairs for some time. To come down now so firmly on this faction's side (even if it was what most Saguntines wanted) marked a shift in Roman attitudes.[11]

From Hannibal's point of view, a worrying shift. It suggested that the Romans had decided to keep Saguntum apart from—and not well disposed to—Punic rule in Spain. Moreover by bloodily confirming the pro-independence party in power they bound it and Saguntum into dependence on themselves, a move both ironic and dangerous. It signalled, or it seemed to signal, that the Roman republic was tying itself more closely to the Saguntines just as the escalating dispute with their neighbours was threatening to lead them into a confrontation with New Carthage. Hannibal seems, in fact, to have inferred that the Saguntines had become Roman allies. He may also have inferred that the Romans had now decided to take a hand in the affairs of Spain. That would colour his attitude to the envoys waiting for him at New Carthage.

IV

As a boy Hannibal had no doubt often heard of how the Romans' decision to get involved in Sicily in 264 had led to Carthage's most disastrous war. He himself had seen how their out-of-the-blue move to take a hand in Sardinia in 237 had precipitated a crisis costly and humiliating to his people. Even in

225 the agreement with his brother-in-law had been, in effect, a one-sided Roman initiative prompted by Roman self-interest. To be faced now with what looked like a fresh bout of unprovoked intervention—Polybius emphasizes that up to now Hannibal had avoided any confrontation with the Saguntines—could understandably arouse both irritation and suspicion.

Nor did the envoys Valerius and Baebius behave ingratiatingly: a contrast to their predecessors in 225 whose job had been 'petting and conciliating' Hasdrubal. The present ones 'solemnly called on', or in a different translation 'emphatically warned', the new general to do two things: keep clear of the Saguntines, 'for these lay in their [the Romans'] trust', and keep firm to Hasdrubal's promise not to cross the Ebro. [12]

Polybius does not elaborate, but by their very nature neither of the two demands was flexible or conciliatory. Why the Romans took this line needs to be surmised. It had not been forced on them by circumstances. Saguntum had been of no interest to them hitherto and the Ebro was not much more meaningful, from a standpoint in Italy, than the Pyrenees. If they had wanted to cement friendly relations with the Barcid régime and the new Barcid general, they could have asked (for instance) whether he wished to renew Hasdrubal's agreement or else discuss a replacement for it, and if he was willing to give a safety-assurance to the Saguntines—in return, say, for an amicable settlement of their dispute with the Turitani. Even if in fact they had expected Hannibal to be hostile on both counts, it would have done no damage to make a show of supposed Roman reasonableness.

To level two non-negotiable demands on such immediately relevant issues, at this first meeting between spokesmen for the Roman state and the new leader of the Carthaginians, points to quite a different motive. Not to provoke war (as sometimes thought), for when Hannibal did offer his own provocation by attacking Saguntum the Romans did nothing about it; but instead to ensure that the new leader was as willing as his predecessors to accommodate Roman concerns. The démarche was most likely meant not to challenge Hannibal to a new confrontation, but to put him and his state in their proper place—independent, indeed, but confined. Then the Romans could go about their affairs in northern Italy, the Adriatic and neighbouring lands without having to keep an eye out for possible Iberian difficulties.

But their demands concerned his own region of operations, not regions of possible mutual interest further away like southern Gaul or Liguria. If he agreed to them, he would certainly relieve the Romans of concern about Spain, but would be granting them—in effect—the right to curb what the Punic state did in its own part of the world. A right which, of course, the Romans would never have dreamt of conceding in reverse to the Carthaginians. Had he or Hasdrubal sent over demands about the future of Syracuse (where King Hiero was nearing 90) or about Roman campaigning north of the river Po, the people on the Tiber would have been seriously offended; indeed might have judged it a deliberate provocation.

But the Carthaginians had been defeated in war once, had been forced to surrender territory twice, and a few years ago had agreed to soothe Roman concern about Spain and Gaul. The Romans no longer saw them as on a completely equal footing with themselves, any more than they so saw (or would in future see) other defeated states inside or outside Italy. It was quite in order to put demands to them to satisfy Roman convenience.[13]

Nor does Polybius' term for the ambassadors' manner suggest a friendly delivery or any effort to mollify the import of their démarche. To two senior senators, a general not yet out of his twenties in command of a bi-continental empire may have seemed just the sort of Hellenistic virtual king who had to be spoken to firmly and made to recognize his duties. Hannibal quite clearly found both their message and their manner offensive.

But to him the envoys' manner was probably the lesser evil. It must have been at this interview that he concluded that the Romans were aiming to destabilize Punic Spain or even provoke a war.

Nothing they had done previously suggested such a goal—even as recently as Hasdrubal's murder they had not tried to sow mischief—but this only strengthened the abruptness of what he took to be their volte-face. Here were the Romans, who in previous years had sponsored contentious friends to Carthage's hurt—Mamertines in 264 and mercenaries in 237—and who had laid down for Hasdrubal a military *ne plus ultra* to spare themselves worry, seeking to entrap him in the same way. To him that would explain both the sudden championship of the Saguntines whose leaders they had now firmly re-established in control, and the suddenly renewed line of the Ebro, a line whose original significance for them was long past.

Though the Barcid generals had never planned a Roman war it was always, after 237, a contingency which they had to bear in mind. Now, so far as we can tell, Hannibal judged that the contingency was real and his duty lay in confronting it. No surprise then if he was angry and showed it. Still, to confront envoys who had come on a limited if imperious mission, the first in half a decade, with the accusation that their state was seeking to provoke war would have been wildly impolitic. Nor would Polybius' suggestion, that he should have complained about the events of 237, have been any more suitable. (For Polybius, of course, Hannibal was planning a justified revenge-war, the Romans knew it, and the envoys' interview with him merely confirmed that he would launch it: none of which is plausible.)

Instead the general 'affected to be guarding the interests of the Saguntines' and complained that in the recent arbitration the Romans had unjustly executed leading men of Saguntum and 'these treacherously treated men he would not overlook, for it was an ancestral principle of the Carthaginians to overlook no one who had been unjustly treated'. This was unmistakably a dig at the Roman claim that the Saguntines 'lay in their trust', their *fides*, a virtue that was one cornerstone of their revered *mos maiorum* or 'ancestral principles'. It was a bitter dig, for *fides* had been invoked to justify their helping the

Mamertines, and maybe the Sardinia mercenaries too. Hannibal was turning a Roman shibboleth against its users.[14]

More ominously, he thus openly signalled that he meant to intervene in Saguntine affairs to champion the supposedly victimized faction. In itself this may not have been a spur-of-the-moment decision. From the time the Turitani came under his sway he must have seen a showdown with Saguntum as likely, and what he learned of the Roman arbitration would only confirm this. But the envoys' demand obviously crystallized his thinking. He signalled to them that he would act and, a few months later, act he did.

On the other hand, though he may indeed have been angry he was not mindlessly so—contrary to Polybius' notion. He did not mention the Ebro at all. Not only was it plain there would be no Roman negotiating over that, but as an issue it had just lost its primacy to Saguntum. And his one accusation against the Romans was that they had abused their trust as arbiters, not (as sometimes supposed) that they had no right to arbitrate at all or had violated some treaty in doing it; still less that their actions amounted somehow to anti-Carthaginian aggression.

He thus laid down a limited challenge. He would impose Punic hegemony on Saguntum now that the place had clearly become a problem. By implication, if the Romans chose to support it they would ignite a new Roman–Punic war—one which, plainly, he judged himself and Carthage capable of waging victoriously. At the same time he may have reckoned that a policy so abruptly begun at Rome might be just as abruptly reversed if resolutely confronted: another reason for letting his anger show impressively.

Saguntum was small, surrounded by Punic territory and (he may have reckoned too) not harder to subdue than earlier strongpoints like Althia and Hermandica. A vigorous stroke could neutralize it before the Romans could intervene militarily, and then conceivably they might decide that it was futile to fight over a faraway ex-protégé of which most Romans knew nothing. If they did want war, at all events he would thus gain the strategic advantage.

V

The Roman ambassadors must have been dismayed at the reception their straightforward demands about Saguntum and the Ebro aroused. A furious generalissimo virtually promised to annex Saguntum and totally ignored the Ebro. Later on they may well have convinced themselves that Hannibal's outburst had made it clear 'there must be war' between Rome and Carthage. But though Polybius has them thinking so at the time, this is not likely, for what followed in 219 shows that the Romans were not in fact inclined to fight. On the other hand the outburst told Valerius and Baebius that, instead of achieving a simple confirmation of the diplomatic status quo between the two republics, they had tapped an unforeseen vein of resentment. This was obviously going to lead to complications: if nothing else, an imminent attack on Saguntum.

Valerius and Baebius had no leeway to negotiate, even if they had wanted to. The Senate had sent them to put simple requests to the general and accept his compliance. Failing to get this they could only take their leave.

They sailed, not back to Rome, but over to Carthage in Africa, 'wishing', Polybius writes, 'to put the same demands' (or 'warnings') there. Without a doubt their ship from Spain to Africa was paced or outpaced by a courier-craft from Hannibal to the home authorities. Polybius does not tell what answer they were given at Carthage but almost certainly it was non-committal (had the sufetes thrown a Hannibalic tantrum or disclaimed all responsibility for their general, this would surely have got a mention). There was no gain in having the Punic state officially repeat what Hannibal had forecast about Saguntum: far better to leave the other side guessing. This must have been nearly as unsatisfactory to Valerius and Baebius, who had to travel home with their mission effectively in ruins.

Hannibal had sent home another message too, this one surely for public attention, as its language shows. The Saguntines, 'relying on their alliance with the Romans', were harming Punic subjects (the fractious neighbours in other words) and he wanted instructions on what to do. Now a Punic general did not have to ask for guidance on how to treat provincial aggressors. Nothing suggests that he or Hasdrubal had waited for orders before dealing with, for instance, the Orissi or the Olcades. This message was to alert his fellow-citizens to a confrontation potentially very different: a signal (probably the first) that the new affair could involve great-power politics.[15]

Naturally he was given a free hand by the authorities. These messages back and forth must have taken place while sailing was still practicable, and so in the autumn of 220. Appian's report of him then making a pretended offer of arbitration in his turn, this one to sort out the quarrel between the Saguntines and their neighbours, may be correct: he had the winter to do it in, and some show of justification was desirable before he launched his attack on the town in the spring of 219.

The Saguntines were predictably immune to either cajolements or threats. Very possibly they sent word to Rome about his offer too, as Appian states (though in winter the messengers would have had to travel by land), but after what had happened at New Carthage it must have been all-but-expected news. What is more striking—and less expected—is that when news of the attack itself arrived the Romans did nothing. And over the eight months that it progressed, they went on doing nothing.[16]

VIII

THE INVASION OF ITALY

I

Hannibal besieged Saguntum from about May 219 to the end of the year or the start of 218. This can be worked out from the rather sparse time-details in Polybius. Hannibal moved at the start of the campaigning season and 'when summer already had begun', and spent eight months on the siege. So the town fell during the winter following. The Romans reacted as promptly as was practicable, sending an ultimatum to Carthage virtually as soon as the envoys could sail.[1]

The siege did not show Hannibal's military skills in the best light. Eight months was a long time to beset a small and friendless city, however strong its hilltop site and defences—even longer than Alexander the Great had taken to capture Tyre, a city on an island. Polybius limits himself to a general picture of the general's leadership and bravery, and stresses the 'hardship and anxiety' of the siege. Livy tells a stirring story of assaults and counter-assaults, Punic siege-engines and Saguntine heroism; and (even if embellished by Roman historical tradition) something of the sort must have occurred across the eight months.

Early on, again according to Livy, Hannibal was badly wounded by a javelin in the thigh, and later he was called away to put down restiveness among the recently conquered Oretani and Carpetani, leaving his vigorous officer Maharbal, son of Himilco, to maintain the siege. If accurate, these details only illustrate the dangerous frustrations of a long and fixed commitment. Against resolute resistance, the Carthaginians had only attrition to use.[2]

Whether or not the Saguntines themselves got a message out to Rome, the Romans certainly heard about the siege. Yet, while month after month the town that Valerius and Baebius had warned Hannibal not to attack kept fighting off Hannibal's attacks, they did nothing to help. This inactivity was covered up by later Roman tradition in inventive ways. For instance, as noted earlier, Valerius' and Baebius' mission was redated to 219 and during the siege. A different excuse is Polybius' claim that a new Illyrian war launched by the Romans during 219 prevented them intervening in Spain. This might be true up to a point but hardly as a complete excuse, given that the war was over by late summer and—in any case—some of the Roman forces could have been released early for tasks elsewhere.

The likeliest reason why nothing was done for Saguntum was that the Roman Senate was deadlocked over whether to act. Glimpses of inconclusive debate are given by more than one writer drawing on Roman historical traditions, not only Livy but also Silius and Appian, all of them firmly placing the debate in 219. Dio, later than any of these, is not to be believed when he transfers debate to 218 when Hannibal was on his march to Italy: he may be following a chronicler who wanted to have the Romans discuss peace or war with Carthage at a more dramatic moment.

On the other hand Dio may be right that the most forceful speaker for intervention was L. Cornelius Lentulus, for Silius' pro-intervention spokesman is called Lentulus too—probably the Lentulus who had been consul in 237 when Sardinia was seized. And like Silius again, Dio's spokesman for restraint and caution is named Fabius, though probably not the famous and equally cautious Q. Fabius Maximus who later campaigned against Hannibal.[3]

Opponents of intervention in Spain need not have been all that many so long as they included ex-consuls of high standing and influence, for the Senate worked by consensus whenever possible—especially on major issues like peace and war. Arguments against intervening would include how recent the Romans' link with Saguntum was and how unclear Hannibal's intentions were. Maybe too Fabius the spokesman alleged that relations between New Carthage and old Carthage were rocky—this was what the historian Fabius Pictor, a senator at the time, was to claim—and that a restrained reaction from Rome now could split the two and enable the Romans to tackle Hannibal on his own soon. Events would show that there was no basis for such a conceit but, just as Pictor held to his view of antagonism at Carthage versus the Barcids, so too it may well have been held by others in 219 with a hope that something could be made of it to Rome's advantage. When it turned out false, the easy explanation was that Hannibal had dragged the leaders of Carthage all unwilling into his war.[4]

Saguntum's long resistance must have been an unpleasing surprise to the Punic commander. There had been nothing like it in Barcid Spanish warfare before. It wore down men, equipment, supplies and money. Nor could he be sure, at first anyway, that he was safe from a Roman expeditionary force arriving to help the besieged. Not sending one was a serious missed opportunity for them, as he could appreciate better than most. They could have caught his army immobilized around a fiercely resisting stronghold, with little freedom to manoeuvre, and could have mauled him badly with Saguntine help before he got free; or could have landed somewhere else in Spain to make mischief in his absence.

On the other hand, the longer no help arrived the more secure he must have felt, especially after learning of both consuls' departure for Illyria; nor can he have missed hearing of the Romans' debate or debates over Saguntum. In the end the town fell when part of its walls collapsed under battering-ram attack. Many Saguntines, unyielding as ever, destroyed as much of their possessions as they could and then killed themselves and their families. By then it was long past any chance for the Romans to intervene.

II

How these would react to the loss of their supposed protégés neither Hannibal nor his fellow-citizens could be certain, but his measures over the following winter and spring show he presupposed war.

The booty from Saguntum, large in spite of the destructive efforts of some Saguntines, was shared out—Hannibal keeping for his treasury the money garnered from the town and from sales of plunder, rewarding his officers and men with enslaved townsfolk, and sending further goods and valuables to Carthage to sharpen support there. The troops were then given a well-earned winter rest, while he set about preparing for what was likely to happen in 218.[5]

First his brother Hasdrubal was appointed, in effect, his deputy and empowered to take over command in Spain 'if he himself were to be somewhere else'. Presumably Hannibal had done without a second-in-command for his first two years as general. Next he arranged some transfers of troops: some 16,000 Spanish soldiers to Africa including Carthage, and some 15,000 from Africa to Spain, the idea being that this would bind the two lands more effectively. Carthage too received a garrison of 4,000 other African troops. These could march there as soon as their muster-rolls were complete, but the transfers across water very likely waited until it was safe again to sail, in February or March 218.

Hasdrubal was also assigned 21 elephants, while for his own expedition Hannibal earmarked 37. This seems all that still existed of their brother-in-law's great 200-elephant corps; given its size and the nature of the warfare in rugged Spain, it looks as though downsizing had taken place. Hasdrubal took charge too of what passed for the Barcid navy in Spain: 32 quinqueremes and five triremes, all properly manned, plus 18 quinqueremes (and a couple of quadriremes) that lacked full crews. At Carthage naval strength was a little better, since a few months later 55 warships were available for failed missions to Sicily and Italy. Very likely, orders for fresh shipbuilding went out about this same time or not long after, for any war with the Romans would need far more than 100-odd vessels. The Romans, in fact, already had 220 quinqueremes in commission.[6]

Hannibal's third measure points most clearly of all to him expecting a Roman war. He sent agents into the western Alps and north Italy to sound out the Gallic peoples there about him passing with an army through their territories, and to win their agreement 'promised everything' (writes Polybius). This was not a move to be put off until he knew for certain that war existed, but equally there was no point in it if he was not fairly sure that war was coming. The general was already well informed about the people and resources in north Italy and (Polybius expressly adds) about how much the region's Gauls loathed the Romans who had made victorious war on them only four or five years earlier. His agents now reported back that the Gauls were keen to join him if he came.

These soundings must be decisive against the idea that he began 218 aiming only at subduing Spain beyond the Ebro, but changed his plan to invading Italy when he learned of the Romans declaring war. Yet Hannibal did nothing after Saguntum to provoke them or bring on hostilities. He sent his troops into winter-quarters or (the Spanish ones) to their home towns for rest and relaxation; and reassembled them at New Carthage for a military review only after hearing from Carthage that a Roman embassy had declared war. Even then his next move was to dismiss them again—presumably back to their encampment—with orders to be ready to march on a fixed date.[7]

All this deliberateness confirms that he had meant the sack of Saguntum as a challenge to the Romans, which they could choose to take up or ignore. Of course he expected them to take it up—and, in any case, as a responsible leader he had to be ready if they did. In other words he had to have a war-plan.

This in turn was dictated by strategic, logistic and above all political realities. Standing his ground and fighting in Spain was not a serious consideration. No doubt he would defeat any Roman invasion, but meanwhile there might also be a Roman invasion of Punic Africa. No amount of victories in Spain would compensate for Carthage being blockaded and starved into surrender. And even if the Romans were to concentrate all their efforts against Spain, defeating them would not end the war: he would still have to carry it to them to achieve that.

The earlier war had told the world how all but inexhaustible were Roman resources of manpower and munitions. Although every attack on every sector of Carthage's dominions might be beaten back, that would only mean fresh attacks before long. Even if in the end the Carthaginians won through, the price could (or must) be exhaustion. No less worrying, such a war—long, costly and draining—risked undermining the position of the faction that had brought it on. Barcid control, in other words, might not survive a war of attrition.

Everything thus pointed to his invading Italy. Pretty certainly Hannibal was well informed on affairs there: travellers, traders, Carthaginians with Roman guest-friends, and Silenus the Sicilian his own close friend could all supply facts. Even though the other Italian states had shown their loyalty to the hegemonic Roman republic throughout the first war with Carthage and had stood shoulder to shoulder with it against the great Gallic invasion of 225, this alliance system had originally been imposed by Roman military might and it was still relatively new to some areas. For instance the grandfathers of the warlike Samnites of the central southern mountain-lands had been at war with the Romans until 290 while the Greeks in the south had come under Roman domination only after 280. At least a few members of the ruling élite of Capua, the wealthy chief city of Campania, felt that Capua rather than Rome ought to enjoy Italian predominance: something Hannibal may or may not have known.

Certainly he reckoned that a successful invasion would disrupt the Romans' alliance system and at the same time enable him to build a Punic one. This was the policy he followed as soon as he reached Italy. Victories over Roman forces under the Romans' and their allies' own eyes, combined with benign treatment of allied land and prisoners, must prompt defections, and the defectors would have no choice but to join his side. His military and political strength would wax as the Romans' strength waned, with his brother Hasdrubal joining him with fresh forces at a convenient time and other reinforcements coming over from Africa. In the end, a definitive peace settlement would not merely reverse the verdict of 241 but establish a new Punic-dominated alignment of power across the western Mediterranean—one dominated, in turn, by the Barcids and their friends.[8]

III

That would be the grand strategy. More immediate were the needs of ordinary strategy: above all, how to reach Italy in fighting trim when seaborne transport was out of the question. A large army and a high level of resourcefulness were required (and, fortunately, both were available). But it was just as important to calculate the enemy's possible moves. Hannibal had to expect either simultaneous offensives against North Africa and Spain, or else a concentrated assault on Spain with a smaller push against Africa. His planning probably or certainly depended on finding out which alternative it would be.

This helps account for features of his own movements in 218 that puzzle historians. Although the Romans declared war at Carthage in March and he received word of this 'early in the spring', probably around 1 April, he did not march from New Carthage until late May or even early June. In other words he set out surprisingly late. Then after crossing the Ebro three or four weeks later, he spent a rather long time in north-east Spain between the Ebro and Pyrenees—some two months, subduing some fairly obscure peoples who fought hard but whose military importance was scarcely high. He did not leave for Italy until late August or early September.

Yet the north-east was hardly of prime strategic value to his expedition, given that he and his men were abandoning Spain and any supplies from there to live off the land *en route* to Italy. If urgency was supposedly the keynote of their march, it is surprising too that he fought this preliminary campaign himself. If the region were strategically or economically important to his brother's defence of Punic Spain, the conquest could have been left to him, or a lieutenant like Hanno whom Hannibal then put in charge of the territory with a corps of 11,000 from the grand army. But even a defensive importance is to be doubted. No move was made against Emporiae on the coast, the Greek port allied to the Romans, a potential bridgehead into Spain as any general could foresee—and one duly used a few months later by the arriving Roman forces of Cn. Scipio.[9]

Various explanations have been offered for all this: the Spanish rivers needing to subside from their spring flooding, the army having to wait until enough food and fodder were available *en route*, the north-eastern conquests having to be organized and the army reconsolidated, or a wish to lull the Romans into a false sense of security. Some of these features may well have contributed. Rivers may have been in flood that winter (we can recall how Hamilcar died in winter 229–228) and certainly food and fodder needed to be available in quantity, since the expedition could not be reliably supplied by sea. But if those were the chief factors, late August or early September—or even a month or so earlier, on other calculations of the chronology—is unconvincingly late for marching from Spain. Rather it looks as though Hannibal was deliberately taking his time about leaving.

Early in the new consular year, in other words after 15 March, the consul P. Cornelius Scipio, Cn. Scipio's brother and superior, had been commissioned to take an army and fleet to Spain—only to be delayed by the Gauls in north Italy rebelling—and his colleague Sempronius to ready an invasion of Africa from Sicily. The preparation and indeed destinations of these forces could scarcely be hidden. Probably in June or July the consul Sempronius set out for Sicily, but Scipio got going only in August or early September. And Hannibal himself started for the Pyrenees and Italy around the same time, for two months later he descended into north Italy.[10]

Marching through southern Gaul he used the coastal route as far as the Rhône, the same route that Scipio was heading for in the opposite direction. Nor did he press his troops unduly, if the pace Polybius records for a late stage of the march across Gaul—800 *stadia*, or 90 miles, in ten days—applies more or less to the whole of the march until they reached the Alps, as has been inferred. Roman imperial armies, fully equipped, averaged up to 15 miles (23 kilometres) daily on good terrain, and southern Gaul was easy enough going. By the stage Polybius mentions, Hannibal knew that the Romans under Scipio were no longer pursuing him and so may have allowed his men a more relaxed pace before they moved into the Alps; but, on the evidence, they had not moved with any urgency even between the Pyrenees and the Rhône.[11]

Why these late departures and relatively unhurried movements? The likeliest explanation is that Hannibal first waited to learn of the Romans' general military dispositions. If both consuls were sent against him and he destroyed their armies, preferably in southern Gaul away from his own territories, and then invaded Italy, the impact on the Romans and their allies would be gigantic. If only one consul came, he could either handle him similarly or let him reach Spain—where Hasdrubal could deal with the intruder while he himself still fell on Italy. In either case the shock could prompt the Romans to abort any plans for attacking North Africa, lower their morale and achieve a Carthaginian victory more swiftly.

By contrast, if the enemy learned too early that he was moving on Italy, they might well stand on the defensive and, worse still, raise even larger forces than usual in the hope of overwhelming him. Any such reactions would make his own task a good deal harder and slower—and, most dangerous of all, Carthage itself could be strangled by a Roman expedition while he was still campaigning in Italy. His expedition itself, which transferred the bulk of Punic military strength from Punic territory into the militarily more or less unknown reaches of Gaul and beyond, needed to win successes both swift and smashing to maintain his fellow-citizens' morale. It had to be nicely timed.

A less likely suggestion is that he meant to await the consul P. Scipio in north-eastern Spain, crush him there and then invade Italy, but that on learning of the Gallic revolt (to which Scipio's original forces were diverted) he decided the Romans would not come after all and so began his own march. If that were true, he must have remained unaware of Scipio levying a fresh army for Spain until he himself was marching through southern Gaul. But this is implausible, for trade between different regions would not have dried up with the declaration of war and the Carthaginians had at least one spy even at Rome (the one detected in 217 after two years' activity).[12]

He fairly soon must have learned that Scipio was to invade Spain and Sempronius North Africa; then, not long after, that Scipio had been held up by the Gallic revolt in Cisalpine Gaul (prompted, ironically enough, by Hannibal's agents earlier). Once he knew the Romans' initial expeditionary destinations, he could march north from New Carthage; then he paused in the north-east, even after subduing it, because Scipio had been held up in Italy. With one and not two consuls to confront, he could afford to cut the size of his army—by over 20,000, or more than one quarter after its losses in the north-east—to improve flexibility in movement and supply. North Africa would be defended against Sempronius by the forces he had sent, plus any further levies the home authorities made.

Finally, when he calculated or learned that Scipio's expedition was soon to start he marched into Gaul, arguably to waylay the advancing consular army (so there was no need for an urgent advance), destroy it and so both assure Spain's security and clear his road to Italy. But although his departure from Spain was late, he then made it as far as crossing the Rhône before the consul even drew near. By then autumn was drawing near too; his army's numbers had fallen, the Boii and their neighbours the Insubres were successfully in arms, and the Alps were still to be crossed. There was a skirmish between reconnoitering Numidian and Roman cavalry—which his men lost, allowing the Romans to ride briefly up to his camp—but he had to recalculate. If he waited to cross swords now with Scipio's army he might not reach Italy until the following spring, even if he won. Much might happen before then, including in North Africa.

Arguably, therefore, Hannibal now abandoned the plan to intercept Scipio; instead he swung north away from him and struck out for Italy. An echo of the discussion that led to this decision may survive in Livy's report of how the general hesitated over the two alternatives and was persuaded to head for Italy by the Boian and other chieftains who had crossed the mountains to meet him. But he marched north for only four days more before halting in friendly territory for some time to rest and refit, even though Scipio's army was in pursuit for all he knew. So he may have been hoping that he might still succeed in enticing the consul after him in search of a battle. In fact Scipio did march fast to reach the Carthaginians' crossing-place over the Rhône three days later and only then turned away.

Hannibal will have learned of this while resting his troops. There would be no battle in Gaul, but neither would he be dogged by the Romans as he crossed the mountains into Italy. Scipio he expected to return there too, Polybius writes, but not at any speed. He would continue to hold the military initiative.[13]

IV

Invading Italy was an immensely bold venture which in the 23 years of the previous war the Carthaginians had never tried. But they did have an old tradition of taking war to their enemies. Their earliest warlord, Malchus, supposedly had led expeditions to Sicily and Sardinia; and down the centuries Punic armies had several times moved against Syracuse and other Sicilian Greek cities. Hamilcar's expedition to Spain had fitted the same vigorous tradition. Where Hannibal's was unprecedented was in the great distance he had to travel and the vast resources of his foes. But he could be encouraged by the century-old precedent of Alexander the Great, who with fewer than 50,000 troops had overthrown the Persian empire in three great battles and replaced Persian mastery over the east with Macedon's.

Ironically enough, in this new war the Carthaginians—hitherto renowned for mastery at sea—would be inferior navally to the Romans, who less than half a century earlier had not rated at sea at all. This Roman naval superiority was a drawback, but the Barcids themselves had always been land generals. All the same, the Carthaginians during the next few years did again build up their sea-going forces, so as suggested above Hannibal may now have sent around orders for fresh shipbuilding, as well as for properly manning all the ships already available. He may also have backed the scheme for building the artificial ports in the southern quarter of the city, if these do date to the period from 218.[14]

His own concern was the army he was leading to Italy. Made up of infantry from Africa (no doubt mostly subject Libyan conscripts with Carthaginian officers) and Spain, and cavalry partly Spanish and partly Numidian—Numidian horses and their practised riders were arguably the best light cavalry in the world at that time—it numbered 90,000 foot and 12,000 horse according to Polybius and Livy. But as often pointed out, not only are these figures implausibly huge in themselves but they clash with others that the same historians offer. Thus Hannibal reportedly crossed the Pyrenees with 50,000 foot and 9,000 horse, then the Rhône with 38,000 and 8,000 respectively, finally arriving in Italy with 20,000 and 6,000. Polybius drew at least these last figures from Hannibal's later inscriptional record in the temple of Hera at Cape Lacinium, just as he did his detailed breakdown of the forces transferred between North Africa and Spain, so it is likely that the other totals have the same origin.

Therefore if the original strength is correct too, the general's forces must have fallen by 43,000 men—over 40 per cent—even before he reached the Pyrenees, which is extraordinary. True, he suffered 'great losses' in subduing north-eastern Spain and then he left his officer Hanno with 10,000 foot and 1,000 horse to hold the region, while another 10,000 disillusioned Celtiberians were allowed to go home. But that would mean his fighting losses in the north-east were great indeed, over 20,000 men—more than his coming losses at the Trebia, Lake Trasimene and Cannae. This is not very plausible.

Polybius may have drawn, and in his inscription Hannibal may have chosen to give, the wrong impression about the starting total. For although 102,000 as the grand army's original strength is hard to account for if it actually left Spain numbering only 59,000, such a figure fits fairly well if the 15,000 troops entrusted to Hasdrubal to hold Spain are counted in and if the general lost about 7,000 men subduing the north-east. These plus the 21,000 sent home or left with Hanno add up to 43,000, which would leave Hannibal his 59,000 to lead into Gaul. The only difficulty is with the cavalry, whose various attested figures—Hasdrubal's 2,500, Hanno's 1,000 and Hannibal's 9,000—add up to rather more than 12,000, with at least some hundreds more lost in the campaign beyond the Ebro. But the discrepancy is probably only about 1,000, and some rounding-off of totals (even by Hannibal) can be surmised.[15]

In other words the original total more likely shows the full military strength that the Carthaginians had in Spain by mid-year. Hannibal himself then probably marched from New Carthage at the head of 87,000 men, including about 10,000 cavalry. He may have chosen to blur this in his Cape Lacinium record to impress readers with both the vastness of his original resources and, contrastingly, the smallness of the army he actually brought into Italy and with which he wrought such monumental havoc on the Romans. All the same, 87,000 was a massive force: bigger than his brother-in-law Hasdrubal's largest reported armed strength, twice as large as two full consular armies, larger than either of the armies that the kings of Syria and Egypt would put into the field when they met in battle the year after. Together with the 20,000 troops holding North Africa and Carthage, it means that to confront the Romans in this new war the Punic republic under its Barcid leadership had mobilized 122,000 men on land alone. The Romans with their six legions and allied contingents, some 71,000 all told, were in fact outnumbered in 218.[16]

V

As winter gave way to spring 218 the Punic generalissimo learned at New Carthage of the Roman embassy to old Carthage and its theatrical declaration of war. With Saguntum captured around the end of 219, the earliest that the Romans could send envoys overseas (short of risking their lives and, more important, their mission) was March. This helps explain why two of the envoys were the consuls of the previous year: they left office on 15 March. The embassy's mission was to demand 'compensation' over Saguntum—not help or recompense for the Saguntines, who no longer counted, but that the Carthaginians hand over Hannibal and his senatorial councillors for punishment. When predictably the senate at Carthage rejected this, the leader of the embassy symbolically let fall war from a fold of his toga. Many senators shouted their acceptance: no doubt Barcid kinsmen and supporters especially, but even senators outside the ruling faction might well be antagonized by the Romans' non-negotiable stance.

This outcome to the ultimatum was no doubt expected on both sides. Already Hannibal's military preparations, and his soundings in Gaul, the Alps and north Italy, were well under way. He had ceremonially visited the ancient temple of Melqart, Carthage's patron god, on the island where Gades stood, to fulfil old vows and swear new ones in hope of future success (so much for Roman claims of his irreligion). Already too the Romans had authorized Scipio and Sempronius to levy armies and fleets for Spain and Africa. But Hannibal had neatly got them to bring on the war in formal terms, and to do it so gracelessly that even wavering Carthaginian citizens must see their country as a victim of aggression. This plus the wealth from Saguntum united his fellow-countrymen behind him, all at any rate save Hanno the Great and his thinned-out political circle.[17]

All the same, for the reasons suggested above he did not launch his expedition until almost mid-year and even then did not cross the Pyrenees for another two months or so. No one in his council was under illusions about the risks of the invasion. Polybius even tells a story of how at one meeting the officer Hannibal Monomachus declared that the only way they would make it was to live off human flesh (prisoners', presumably), though Hannibal refused to consider this. He certainly had to face the possibility of some opposition *en route* even though his agents had striven to conciliate the peoples between the Pyrenees and north Italy, and also the dangers of poor supply and—even worse—of desertions.

Both Hannibal's sense of mission and his overall confidence are shown in his visit to Melqart's temple during the winter and then by his famous dream, recorded by his friend and historian Silenus. On the march up the east coast towards the Ebro, at a place Livy calls Onusa, the general dreamt he was summoned to a council of the gods, whose chief gave him a divine guide for the road to Italy. Bidden to follow the guide without looking back, he nevertheless disobeyed and saw a monstrous serpent ravaging the land. This, he was told, was the fate of Italy. The chief of the gods, naturally called Jupiter in the Roman versions, must have been Ba'al Hammon: so Hannibal could be confident, and could assure his officers and men, that the expedition was blessed by both the supreme deities of Carthage.[18]

VI

Beyond the Ebro the peoples brought into subjection, according to Polybius, were the otherwise unknown Aerenosii and Andosini, the pro-Roman but just as obscure Bargusii, and the 'Ilurgetes'. Of these Livy gives only the last two and adds the rather better-known Ausetani and Lacetani—who later on that year reappear as Punic allies instead. These two were probably mistaken guesses by a source of Livy's, baffled by the genuine but unrecognized tribes' names. As for the Ilergetes, the well-known people whose chief town was Ilerda, modern Lleida or Lérida in Aragon, they were almost certainly on the Carthaginians' side already, for their powerful leader Indibilis had 'always' been strongly pro-Punic (so Polybius affirms elsewhere) and he dominated nearby peoples too, including the Lacetani. Hannibal's conquest may have been another, smaller community of Ilergetes, perhaps a breakaway branch, attested on the coast between the later cities of Tarraco and Barcino.

These may all have put up a fierce resistance and cost him men, but as was noted earlier they cannot be the main reason why he chose to fight them himself and took so long to move into Gaul. As for the 11,000 troops he left behind under Hanno, they were not enough to cope with a consular army but—again as argued earlier—Hannibal himself was expecting to meet and destroy Scipio somewhere in Gaul. In any case it was open to the commanders left behind (Hasdrubal included) to call on allied Spanish communities for auxiliary corps and, of course, to levy further forces from Carthage's Spanish subjects. The 10,000 disgruntled Carpetani and others whom he released from service may well have found conscription-agents looking for them after a year or two.[19]

To Hanno he also entrusted all the heavy baggage that the grand army had brought along from New Carthage. With it now more streamlined though smaller, and reckoning that the Roman consul was close to setting out for

Spain, the general marched in three columns through the Pyrenees and into Gaul on the true start of his epic venture.

Not everything was or could be planned for a certainty. The Gauls along the route had not agreed in advance to let the army pass, so he had to placate an armed and suspicious warrior assembly gathered at Ruscino (today's Perpignan) with reassurances sweetened by gifts to their chieftains. Why he had not done this earlier, when he was sending agents to Cisalpine Gaul, is hard to understand. According to Livy he had, though it still needed to be followed up with gold; but if he did seek their agreement earlier he cannot have been very successful, and Polybius in fact mentions him forcing some of them *en route* to concede it.

Rather than a mere oversight, the failure to conciliate the Gauls in advance may have been due to his strategic plan as suggested above. Fighting the Romans in Gallic territory, even if he won the Gauls as allies or kept them neutral, was not a scheme likely to please people whose lands would bear the brunt. Even if he had claimed that he meant to march directly to Italy, they could not be sure the Romans would let him. Only the fresh reassurances, and gifts, at Ruscino won him passage.[20]

The same suspicions explain why the Volcae on the lower Rhône opposed him crossing their river though they were no more inclined to the Roman side than to his. Hannibal had to disperse them by skilful use of a detached cavalry column under his nephew Hanno, which crossed higher up and struck the Gauls in the rear. Interestingly the Volcae made no other effort against the Carthaginians: news that Scipio was now only a few days' march away conceivably prompted them to leave the field clear to the two armies to fight it out. But it was at this stage, as argued earlier, that the general changed his strategy.

Polybius gives the army's size at the Rhône as 38,000 infantry and 8,000 cavalry. If correct, this means that in his largely unopposed march across southern Gaul Hannibal had somehow lost 12,000 foot and 1,000 horse, yet no ancient source mentions how. One obvious-looking explanation has been suggested: garrisoned strongpoints along the Gallic route. But none is ever mentioned, though if they existed they ought to have given some trouble both to Cn. Scipio awhile later, when his brother the consul sent him with part of the Roman army on to Spain, and again to P. Scipio himself the following year. This service would have been even more vital in 211 and 210 when Roman reinforcements were sent over to retrieve the disaster that had befallen the Scipio brothers.

Of course these expeditions went by sea, but ancient ships could not avoid putting in to land every two or three days. Besides, the mere presence of enemy units along the line of communications between Italy and Spain should have aroused Roman concern and some sort of counteraction, but again none is heard of. Nor did the hypothetical garrisons achieve anything positive, for instance like channelling reinforcements to Hannibal in Italy as the war went on. His only recorded reinforcements came from Africa by sea. In sum, if he did station troops in southern Gaul it was a complete waste of men. But the theory should be dismissed.[21]

Desertion better accounts for the shrinkage of the army. Already at the crossing of the Pyrenees Hannibal had had to send home a large contingent. As the army left Spain further and further behind, pressing on with meagre belongings and living off the land, disenchantment was bound to grow in some of the men. To some, too, the attractions of life in the future Langue-doc and Provence might outmatch the doubtful prospects of warring in a hostile Italy. This sort of wastage was not unique. In another famous invasion, in 1812, Napoleon's main army fell from 450,000 in June to some 185,000 by mid-August as it marched across western Russia, with half or more of the rest left behind sick or deserted, and this before it had done any serious fighting.[22]

Four days north of the crossing-point over the Rhône, Hannibal intervened to settle a kingship struggle among the people of a fertile district Polybius calls 'the Island', and by winning their friendship was able to rest his men and refit them with food, weapons and footwear. Another ten days' march brought them east to the foothills of the Alps and into real danger, in the shape of the hostile Allobroges who held the region. Repeated attacks by these and then by warriors farther into the mountains were driven off, but the cost was nearly as heavy to the Punic side as to the Gallic.

The danger from humans ended as the army, nine days into its painful ascent, crested the pass—the identity of which remains, and probably will always remain, debated. But the descent was steep and seriously broken in places, and with old snow already covering the ground fresh snowfalls made the going even more treacherous. As a result, Polybius claims, the army suffered losses nearly as heavy as before and the men's spirits were badly battered—even after the famous moment when Hannibal gathered them (or a lot of them) at the top of the pass and pointed out the plains of Italy spread out below.[23]

When the general reviewed his badly shaken forces in the fertile countryside of northern Italy some days later, they amounted to 20,000 foot and 6,000 horse (he recorded these figures himself), plus the elephant corps and his Balearic slingers, specialist irregulars who turn up in his ensuing battles but by now would number only some hundreds. The African infantry contingent was now much larger than the Spanish (12,000 to 8,000): a disproportion that probably had not existed when the army left Spain and probably again reflects the impact of desertion, for it was obviously even harder for a disenchanted African than for a Spaniard to consider deserting either for home or for safe parts of Europe.

Polybius, apparently still citing the Cape Lacinium inscription, implies that this tally of forces took place not directly after the army came down from the Alps but when it reached the territory of the Insubres on the plains—their capital was Mediolanum, modern Milan—after crushing the Insubres' foes the Taurini, around modern Turin nearly 60 miles (100 kilometres) to the west. Desertions during these early days in Italy are not to be ruled out. They may have been low during the Alpine crossing itself, for getting safely out of the mountains would be a problem, but quite a few men must have been tempted as soon as the army reached the amiable terrain below. Only rest, recuperation and then some swift successes could transform the men's attitude.[24]

The Taurini, slaughtered in a brutal three-day operation for refusing to become friends, were the first such needed success. Neighbouring peoples hastened to submit and Hannibal pressed on eastwards looking for the Roman forces in north Italy.[25]

VII

Crossing the Alps remains the most famous and mistakenly emblematic of his feats. The stunning victories that followed give a sheen of paradoxical brilliance to this opening venture, enhanced by the exotic image of elephants from the world of the tropics battling their way through snow-covered passes and gorges. The heroism and endurance of general and troops were no doubt underlined in Silenus' and Sosylus' histories, and grudgingly or admiringly outlined by Fabius Pictor, Cincius Alimentus and their successors. In reality, not only was the march close to a disaster but its outcome may have cost Carthage the war.

As the ancients knew, it was ordinarily no great task for an army to cross the Alps. The Gallic peoples in Cisalpine Gaul had migrated there—armed warriors, their families, wagons and animals—two centuries before. Seven years earlier an army from Gaul, the Gaesati, had crossed to help the Boii and Insubres in their southward onslaught on Italy. Eleven years later, Hannibal's brother was to march unruffled from Spain without loss. Hasdrubal perhaps managed this because of the lesson Hannibal had taught the locals (though they had seen nothing of Carthaginians since) or because he bought them off. But Hannibal himself had supposedly made arrangements with them through his agents for safe passage. The agents must have been too optimistic, or misleading, when they reported back to him—unless he had originally planned a different route, more to the south in line with his initial strategic plan, and so had conciliated what turned out to be the wrong Alpine folk.

Even so, the losses in the Alps were only one part of the total strength lost. To judge from Polybius' account most of the missing 33,000 went between the Pyrenees and the Rhône or on the descent from the pass. As we have seen, desertion was probably the chief cause rather than battle-casualties (or falls from heights). Those who remained at the end were indeed troops of proven quality and loyalty, one of the finest armies in history; but the quality of the grand army that crossed the Pyrenees had been high too, according to Polybius. Hannibal realized the impact of the losses. For the next 11 years he looked and hoped for reinforcements, from his brother in Spain or from Africa—reinforcements which in effect would bring his Spanish and Libyan forces more or less back to the strength of the original grand army.

With what remained of that army and with his new Gallic allies he won huge victories, detached half of Italy from its allegiance to Rome and hemmed the Romans in with enemies at home and abroad: and yet failed in the end. Had he reached Italy with the army largely undamaged, he might not have failed.[26]

This suggests some limitations to Hannibal's leadership in 218. He did not succeed in inspiring enough commitment in all, or even most, of his troops to see them through to Italy; and his preparations for the expedition turned out to be deficient. Just why the Allobroges and the other mountain folk were so hostile is not clear: presumably they suspected the army's true intentions or resented its intrusion into their territories. Even so it might have been possible to bargain with them—had he had the time. Instead he pressed forward into their lands with no recorded effort at negotiating. It was already autumn, snowfalls threatened to block the passes, and he must have thought he could push through by simple fear or force.

There was another, related flaw in carrying out the venture. By setting out when he did, first from New Carthage and then over the Pyrenees, Hannibal added to the risk and dangers that the expedition faced from the seasons. The delay was dictated, as argued earlier, by his original plan to destroy the consul's expeditionary force in Gaul and so safeguard Spain while clearing the way to Italy. With his timing thus dependent on Scipio's movements, the consul's own lateness in turn contributed indirectly to the damage that the Punic army suffered. P. Scipio the elder therefore helped to bring about Hannibal's ultimate failure, even before any fighting had occurred between the two armies.

Scipio's unwitting service partly mitigates the miscalculation he and the Romans went on to commit. On learning that the Carthaginian army was heading for Italy over the Alps, Scipio decided to go back to confront it himself—but still sent most of his army on its mission to Spain, with his brother Cn. Scipio as commander. He himself took over the legions sent to north Italy against the Gauls. The Senate at Rome, in turn, recalled the other consul Sempronius Longus from Sicily in haste, so that both consuls and two consular armies could confront the invasion. Carthage and North Africa in other words were spared immediate attack, an outcome Hannibal himself no doubt much appreciated.

This in reality meant favouring a secondary priority over the primary. Of course Spain was important: the Romans worried about Hannibal drawing reinforcements from there, and steps had to be taken to block any. But Roman forces loose in North Africa, endangering—worse, besieging—

Carthage could have been catastrophic for him. Regulus 40 years before and Agathocles of Syracuse still earlier had brought the Carthaginians to desperation, and in Regulus' case almost to terms. Sempronius Longus, true, proved no match for Hannibal in battle, but the Carthaginians had no other Hannibals available. It is striking that when Punic Spain was lost in 205 Hannibal and his fellow-countrymen carried on with the war in Italy, even though his own fortunes were plainly sinking—but once Scipio the younger invaded Africa and put direct pressure on the Carthaginians at home, Hannibal was recalled.[27]

Once Sempronius' expedition was aborted it was not revived for 14 years. Various raids on the African coast were made between 217 and 205 but had little discernible impact on the Carthaginians' war-effort. Yet most raids met little serious resistance, some garnered notable booty, and they showed how vulnerable the Punic heartland was. Instead the Romans were fixated on Spain: the brothers Scipio operated there for years and did thwart Hasdrubal's planned march to Italy in 215 by defeating him in battle. But in the end, seven years later, he broke out, even though by then his Roman opponent was the famous Scipio, Hannibal's own nemesis.[28]

Had as much attention from the start been paid to Africa as to Spain—or, arguably, more attention—the war might well have been shorter and Punic defeat have come sooner. Instead, Hannibal's war would bring untold disasters on the Romans.

IX

THREE GREAT VICTORIES

I

A sharp cavalry skirmish at the river Ticinus, west of Mediolanum, was Hannibal's first victory over the Romans. The consul Scipio, badly wounded, pulled back south of the river Po to await his colleague, but the doubling of Roman forces that resulted when Sempronius' army arrived did them no good. On a freezing snow-driven morning in late December, beside the river Trebia a little south-west of Placentia, the 40,000-strong Roman army was largely destroyed by Hannibal's 40,000.

The victory was due to the classic encirclement tactics which have made the Punic general famous among military theorists. His cavalry cleared the enemy cavalry off the field while his infantry battled the enemy infantry, then victory was clinched by a rear-and-flank attack on these—first by his youngest brother Mago from an ambush site, then by the returning cavalry plus skirmishers. The elephants also took part, though this was their swan-song as all but one perished in the inhospitable winter following. The only Romans to get away were those who broke head-on through the Gallic infantry they were charging. Hannibal's losses were thus suffered mostly by the Gauls.

With north Italy his, the general could rest his forces over the winter while planning his next move. After the Trebia he developed his liberation propaganda-line, freeing his Italian prisoners without ransom and sending them home with a message which he obviously thought would strike a chord: he had come to free the Italians from Roman rule and (a neat appeal to past grievances) to win back for them the lands they had lost to the Romans. He had been encouraged in his hopes, even before the battle, by the defection of a Brundisine commander who handed over the town and grain-depôt of Clastidium, for Brundisium was not just an Italian ally of Rome but was a Latin colony, one of the 30 privileged city-states that enjoyed a special relationship with Rome and contributed vitally to Roman war-power.

But just as the North Italian Gauls had given him support only after he reached their own territories, equally he could not expect any Italian states to join him unless he came nearer—and came as an assured victor. So he had to march south, seek out whatever armies the Romans next produced, and defeat them.

This was what his existing allies the Gauls expected too. For them, invading the peninsula meant booty while staying put meant facing new Roman attacks at home. The Gallic warriors who joined up with him during the winter cannot have expected a mere defensive campaign. Nor had they ideological or emotional ties to the newcomers from Africa and Spain. The self-interest linking the two sides began to fray over the winter lull, if the story in Polybius and others of Hannibal repeatedly donning varied disguises to evade Gallic attempts on his life has any basis (it may exaggerate one such stratagem). But even less hostile expressions of disenchantment, like desertion, would do his cause no good. Invading the peninsula was the obvious move in any case, for to stay in Gallic Italy would achieve nothing and the Romans would certainly counterattack. In late spring 217, with 50,000–60,000 men, he moved south.[1]

II

The invasion of Etruria began badly all the same, with the army forced to march—or wade—for days and nights through the flood-swollen marshes of the middle Arno river to avoid the more obvious open routes, and suffering losses as a result, notably among the Gallic contingents. Even if Polybius and Livy overdramatize the rigours of the marshes, these did take some toll of the men and animals: the most famous casualty being Hannibal himself, who suffered a severe attack of ophthalmia that damaged (if it did not fully destroy) the sight of his right eye.[2]

But stunning success followed. By arriving in central Etruria he drew the consul Flaminius in pursuit, then ambushed him on a mist-laden June morning as the Roman army marched eastwards along the narrow northern shore of Lake Trasimene. In spite of desperate resistance by the strung-out column, Flaminius and 15,000 of his men were killed, the bulk of the survivors taken prisoner. A few days later the cavalry commander Maharbal in turn defeated and captured a powerful cavalry corps that the other consul, Servilius, had sent over from Picenum to join Flaminius. In half a week the Romans lost nearly 30,000 men dead or captive, much the same number as at the Trebia half a year earlier. The Punic losses were under 2,000 men, mostly Gauls again. With Servilius still in the north, nothing stood between Hannibal and Rome.[3]

Earlier in the year he must have been able to send messengers off to Carthage. It was important to let his countrymen know of his victories in north Italy, to encourage morale; but his despatches probably dealt with other matters too. Some time in June, a strong fleet of 70 warships sailed from Carthage via Sardinia to the Etruscan coast at Pisae hoping to meet his army, a rendezvous surely prearranged. If Polybius is right that Hannibal was able to communicate by sea with his home city only when he reached the Adriatic coast after Trasimene, an earlier missive can have got there only via the overland journey to Spain and then on by sea. If so it must have been sent quite some time earlier, while he was planning his move southwards.

Polybius connects the launching of the fleet with Hasdrubal's recent defeat in Spain, but Spain was not its destination even after it left Italian waters. Nor would it have known where to look for Hannibal without being instructed beforehand. A scheme for the army to link up with a fleet suggests that his original strategy for 217 was not just to invade the peninsula but, more specifically, to do so in a combined operation. Such a bold course could have only one goal: the city of Rome.

But when the fleet arrived off Pisae it found no sign of Hannibal. He had marched east to the Adriatic instead of west to the Tyrrhenian coast. After destroying Flaminius' army, even though he soon rearmed his African infantry with captured—and presumably superior—Roman weapons, yet 'having become very confident about the total situation he decided', Polybius writes, 'for the time being against marching towards Rome'.

Polybius neither explains why nor mentions the fleet in this context. His phrasing is noteworthy all the same, for it implies both that a march on Rome had been envisaged by Hannibal and that he was still leaving the option open for the fairly near future. These are less likely to be just Polybius' inferences (for one thing, he knew that Hannibal did not actually march on Rome until 211, and then only as a feint) than to reflect one or more of his Hannibalic sources. Whether Sosylus or Silenus was any more forthcoming about the decision cannot be said. It would be interesting to know whether either of them thought it sound.

If Hannibal had been able to link up with the fleet and move fast, while the other consul's army—shorn of cavalry and cut off from Rome—struggled to find out what was going on, the Carthaginians could have blockaded the city by land and sea. That would have severely hampered, if not prevented, the Roman authorities from organizing fresh forces and concerting further resistance and might have changed the direction of the war. But he may have learned that the Romans had 110 ships available to oppose the Punic fleet, or concluded that his army was too battered for a combined operation to succeed. Yet the substitute decision to march eastwards meant, arguably, a great opportunity missed.[4]

Polybius certainly emphasizes the army's battered state as well as its rapid restoration to health, both men and horses, once they reached the prosperous dales by the Adriatic. On the way there they plundered and ravaged the countryside, while 'the order was issued to slaughter those of adult age who fell into their hands': plundering, and presumably killing, that continued when they marched south to Apulia. This was normal practice for an invading army, and besides Hannibal needed to reward his much-stressed troops and no doubt replenish his own military treasury. He also aimed to provoke the

Romans to battle again, confident, as Polybius implies, that a further decisive defeat in battle would make them give in. Slaughtering all adults met with *en route*, though, was an ill-judged policy even if limited to adult men. It was at odds with his freeing of Italian allied prisoners of war, for he was moving through not just Roman but also Italian allies' lands and an essential ingredient of his war- and postwar plans was to win over as many Italians as possible.

The general soon found his confidence frustrated. The new Roman supreme commander, the dictator Q. Fabius Maximus, refused to fight a pitched battle and instead stalked the Punic army around southern Italy in the classic style of harassment-warfare, cutting off stragglers and threatening the Carthaginians' gathering of supplies. Farmers in districts approached by the Punic army were ordered to destroy their buildings and crops and then leave the area. Unfamiliar and unpopular though this Fabian strategy was with many Romans, including Fabius' own deputy the master of horse Minucius, it can only have alarmed Hannibal. If he could neither acquire Italian support nor threaten Rome effectively with Fabius' four legions constantly shadowing him, nor secure reliable contact and replenishment from Africa or Spain, the expedition was in a strategic and political limbo. To stay in it for long would be in effect the kiss of death for him and for Punic prospects—all the more because (as he probably had heard by now) things were not going well in Spain.[5]

His manoeuvrings in the second half of 217 sought to break this dangerous stalemate. To force on a battle, and at the same time sweep up fresh plunder and provisions for the coming winter, he moved across the mountains and valleys of Samnium and into northern Campania, where his vast garnerings of booty suggest that the dictator's edict had been poorly obeyed. According to Livy he furthermore had the hope, from three aristocratic Campanians captured and freed after Trasimene, that towns in the region would defect to him. Such defections would have been the first in the peninsula, but none in fact happened.

Fabius followed along high ground, did not interfere, and then—when the booty-laden Punic army moved to leave Campania for Apulia—so neatly blocked its intended route through a pass in the hills that it could neither advance nor safely retreat. For once the tables had been turned: but only for a moment. Hannibal used a simple but well-executed night ruse (a herd of cattle with burning faggots tied to their horns and shepherded by some light troops) to divert the Romans' attention in another direction and achieve an unopposed exit. But he still could not shake off Fabius' frustrating companionship on the march back to Apulia.

There, operations centred on the small town of Gerunium which Hannibal took by storm in the usual style, massacring its uncompliant residents, and for a while he seemed to have fresh opportunity to annihilate an enemy army. Minucius the master of horse, buoyed by a skirmishing success that brought him unprecedented codictatorial status because of Roman irritation with Fabius' delays, let his forces be enticed into a Hannibalic encirclement. But he got out of it thanks to Fabius' prompt intervention with the rest of the Roman army, after which the war settled into further stalemate.

III

Irritating as this again was to the Romans, potentially it was a disaster for the invaders. That they had serious problems getting supplies during late 217 and early 216 can be believed: the army stayed at Gerunium till mid-year, though Hannibal then eased its discomforts by capturing a large Roman depôt at Cannae, in Apulia. Had the Romans persisted in Fabius' admittedly thankless methods till the next winter, Hannibal could not have avoided crises in his army—the Gauls would hardly have clung to him indefinitely and by mid-216 there were even rumours of the Spanish mercenaries plotting to desert—as well as politically, at home and in Spain. It cannot have been easy to get word out regularly to Carthage, nor would the word be very cheering if he did. Besides, his brother Hasdrubal was roundly defeated at the Ebro's mouth in the spring by Cn. Scipio, so much so that the Romans were emboldened to send Gnaeus' brother P. Scipio thither with fresh forces. Not only critics of the Barcids like old Hanno the Great, but any Carthaginians who doubted the wisdom of a militarily unsupported expedition into Italy, would feel confirmed in their pessimism about the progress of the war.

The Romans came to his rescue. Confident in their manpower reserves, angry and anxious at his menace in their midst, they created for the consuls of 216, L. Aemilius Paullus and C. Terentius Varro, an army greater than any seen before—over 80,000 strong—and sought battle. The Punic general offered it in August with 40,000 foot and 10,000 horse, on an open plain beside the river Aufidus in Apulia, near the hill-town of Cannae. The force arrayed before them troubled some of his own men, and one senior officer named Gisco pointed out its astonishing mass to him as they surveyed the scene from a knoll before battle. Hannibal commented seriously that he had missed something more astonishing still: 'in all that many, not one of them is called Gisco'. The Carthaginians went laughing into battle.

Facing foes lacking in virtually all tactical manoeuvrability except the forward charge, he met their massive infantry centre with his Spaniards and Gauls while on the wings his Spanish, Gallic and Numidian cavalry between them fought and drove off the opposing horse. The enemy centre, over 50,000 men, pushed back the heavily outnumbered Spanish and Gallic infantry for some distance and even broke their ranks; but then Hannibal's African infantry—stationed on either side of the Punic centre but till now held back—swung in to take the Romans in flank. As the densely ranked legionaries struggled to cope with this new assault, Hannibal's Spanish and Gallic cavalry in turn left pursuing the routed enemy horse to the Numidians and closed in on the legions' rear.

What at daybreak had been the most confident and impressive Roman army ever to take the field was by evening a massacred wreck. The garrison left in its nearby camp surrendered. Whether the dead numbered over 70,000 as Polybius claims, or Livy's more plausible 47,200 (with 19,000 or so survivors taken prisoner), the army had ceased to exist except for some thousands of fugitives scattered over the Apulian countryside. One of the consuls, L. Aemilius Paullus, was dead and so were 29 of the army's 48 military tribunes, its senior officers; 80 senators and ex-magistrates; and enough Roman cavalrymen, distinguished by their gold rings, to give Hannibal's brother Mago a bushelful of rings to pour out over the floor of the Punic senate-house at Carthage a few weeks later. Punic losses were under 6,000, 4,000 of them Gauls.[7]

Once again nothing, or almost nothing, stood between Hannibal and Rome. When the news reached the city, the people there expected him to march directly against it. But he was 250 miles (400 kilometres) away— further away than at Trasimene—a march of three weeks even if unopposed; the army was weary from its strenuous fighting and colossal slaughtering; Rome was massively fortified, and he knew or could surmise that it would be defended—it had a potential reserve in the fleet based at Ostia and could raise levies from its own and nearby residents. He decided not to march.

IV

Like the Romans, some of his men expected otherwise. Livy tells of Maharbal the cavalry commander urging him on: let Maharbal go ahead with the cavalry, follow behind and 'in five days you shall banquet on the Capitol'—then, when the general insisted on putting off a decision, a biting comment, 'You know how to win a victory, Hannibal; not how to make use of one.' Maharbal's proposal, though not the pithy epigram, goes back at least to their contemporary Cato the Elder, writing 50 years or so later, who may have got it from a pro-Carthaginian source. It may not be strictly true as told: for one thing, Hannibal could not march from Apulia to Rome in five days (though he might have from Trasimene). But it illustrates a point of view that at least some of his officers surely held. Even if Maharbal actually said his say after Trasimene, the point was still more relevant after Cannae and it need be no surprise if Maharbal or others put it to the general once again.[8]

Modern as opposed to ancient historians mostly commend Hannibal's decision. Various justifications are mentioned: he could not provision his army along the way; it lacked siege equipment and anyway he and it were not adept at sieges; he realized that once in place before the city he would risk being trapped between it and fresh Roman forces raised outside; he expected that the southern Italian allies would defect more readily if he stayed in their midst.[9]

Yet all such points, impressive at first glance, fail to convince. True, Maharbal's proposal might sound overenthusiastic: how could a cavalry corps hope to capture a major fortified city? But Maharbal cannot have proposed using his troopers' weaponry or siege-skill. Cavalry's strategic virtue lay in speed—and therefore surprise. The idea clearly was to reach Rome ahead of or along with any friendlier messengers, and seize the city as disbelief and panic boiled up inside as well as outside.

Thirteen years later this happened at Cirta, capital of the Numidian king Syphax, following his defeat and capture by his rival Masinissa and the Roman commander Laelius. Masinissa galloped ahead with his own Numidian cavalry, appeared outside the walls with his prisoner and achieved instant surrender, though Cirta stood on one of the most defensible natural sites in the ancient world. Rome's residents had been frightened enough at the thought of Hannibal coming down after Trasimene, and five years on he produced great alarm when he did make a march from Campania to its outskirts—even though there were troops within the walls, more on the way, and other Roman armies all over Italy. On the day after Cannae there was no regular army at all left in the peninsula except for the troops with the fleet at Ostia and (maybe) two legions of new recruits at Rome. The only other army nearer than Spain was in north Italy where the Gauls would annihilate it later in the year.[10]

Nor did sending Maharbal on ahead have to be Hannibal's only option for approaching Rome. If it seemed safer to keep the cavalry with the rest of the army, nevertheless the army could have reached the city in three weeks or—given that this could be the most vital move of the whole war—even sooner by forced marches. It was high summer and the necessary supplies in Italy's heartland were available to his foragers, as in 217. Certainly the Romans would have had some time to launch defence measures: at the news of Cannae the praetor Marcellus, commanding the fleet at Ostia, sent 1,500 naval troops up to the city and a legion of them to Teanum in Campania (to try to bar the routes from there northward), and then the new dictator M. Junius Pera began levying fresh recruits. Yet this was no complete answer. Siege equipment could have been manufactured from the woodlands of Latium and Etruria, the extensive city walls could not have been strongly manned, the legion at Teanum was perilously isolated over 90 miles (150 kilometres) to the south-east, and the advance of 40,000-odd enemy troops would have driven refugees from all around its path into Rome—cramming extra mouths to feed into a besieged town was a standard method of war.[11]

Hannibal may not have been good at sieges and Rome may have been far too large for one anyway, but a blockade was practicable enough. With one in place, efforts by magistrates in the countryside (including the surviving consul Varro in Apulia) to organize fresh resistance would have been hampered by the sealing-off of the political centre. Nor is it certain that Rome would have been immune to treachery, for along with the Roman population there were other residents—Italians, foreigners and slaves (the dictator recruited 8,000 of these for army service), not all of whom need have been totally committed to the Roman side. Late in 217 two dozen slaves had been put to death for a plot of some sort: Livy does not state what sort, but their comrade and betrayer was generously rewarded. It did not call for more than a few resolute partners to betray a city gate, as 13 did at Tarentum only a few years later.[12]

Blockading and starving out Rome would have been still more effective if the Punic fleet joined in. That Hannibal, or at any rate his supporters at Carthage, recognized the fleet's value had been shown after Trasimene, though to no great avail. It could have been summoned again: he was able to send his brother Mago to Carthage by sea not long after Cannae, with his bushel of Roman gold rings and a request for reinforcements and supplies. With the Roman fleet at Ostia weakened by Marcellus despatching thousands of its marines inland, it could have been worthwhile to try running its gauntlet to land the reinforcements and supplies somewhere on the Latin coast (rather than at Locri as was finally done). Failing the fleet, Hannibal's army could have cut Rome off from waterborne help with some straightforward barriers across the Tiber like chained booms or sunken barges.

In turn, Hannibal encamped around Rome and paralysing the Roman war-effort would scarcely discourage wavering southern Italian allies from defecting (as is sometimes argued) even if the city held out. More likely, even more allies—in north and central Italy as well as in the south, and conceivably even some of the Latins—would have come over. In Spain the currently successful brothers Scipio would have found themselves cut off and practically irrelevant. Nor is it likely that the Macedonian king Philip V's interest in a Punic alliance would have waned if Hannibal stood outside Rome instead of in Apulia.

The result of a march on Rome would very probably have been a monumental change to the history of the Mediterranean world. Livy's verdict, then, should stand. 'That day's delay is well judged to have been the salvation of the city and its empire.'[13]

X

HANNIBAL'S ITALIAN LEAGUE

I

After Cannae, some of the Romans' south Italian allies at last thought the time had come to change sides. Several Apulian towns declared for Carthage—for instance Salapia, Arpi and Herdonea—then many of the Lucanians. Some weeks later the Bruttians far to the south defected when Hannibal's brother Mago came among them with a division of the Punic army. Hannibal himself marched into Samnium where two of the three cantons followed suit, the Hirpini and Caudini; only the Pentri stood firm for the enemy. And on the Punic army's advance into Campania in the autumn he won the greatest prize of all: Capua, the second city of Italy.

Like other Campanian towns, Capua held a limited Roman citizenship. Its leader in 216, Pacuvius Calavius, and many other aristocrats had formed links of marriage or friendship with leading Roman families. But the disasters suffered for the Roman cause since 218 and the prospect of taking over as dominatrix of Italy were too much for Capua's loyalty. The year before, Hannibal's tentative hope of winning it over had failed but now the Capuans, prompted by Calavius and another leading man, Vibius Virrius, welcomed him in and struck a treaty with him.[1]

The terms were very good for the Capuans—and contrastingly of limited value to the general. In effect he struck a friendship-agreement with no obligations. The Capuans were guaranteed their self-government and freedom from compulsory military or other services. It was obviously implicit that they would support the Carthaginian side in the war, but nothing was specified, not even a proviso about aiding each other in peace and war (unlike the Punic pact later on with Locri in the south). Nor were there any commitments about supplying Hannibal with munitions or money gratis.

In effect what he gained was Capuan neutrality in the war, as likewise that of satellite towns like Atella and Calatia. According to Livy he promptly broke the treaty by arresting a Capuan critic of the city's defection, Decius Magius, and sending him off to Carthage. If true, it was probably a gesture of intimidation and may not have gone down well. He never repeated it, and never got much voluntary help from Capua either. The city may have supplied him with goods and provisions over the next few years (there is not much evidence) but he no doubt had to pay good money for them.[2]

When the Greek city of Locri on the south coast of Italy came over in summer 215, it struck a rather different pact. As at Capua, Locrian autonomy was affirmed, but more explicit provisos were stated too: the Carthaginians were assured of access to the town (in whose citadel they installed a garrison, then or later), the Locrians kept control of the harbour (important for their trade and their links with Greece), and each side was to help the other 'in peace and war'. With Roman-held Rhegium and Sicily uncomfortably close, it was probably the Locrians who were keen to have this last proviso written in.

Some of Hannibal's other pacts may well have had such a clause too, to judge from scattered but suggestive items. In 215 his new Samnite allies complained that he was not protecting them against Roman attacks even though he had taken their young men to serve in his army. The pro-Punic Bruttians and Lucanians figured in operations outside as well as in their own territories—for instance in 214 an army mostly of their troops, under a Punic general, was marching to join Hannibal when defeated by the Romans at the river Calor near Beneventum, and in 209 a Bruttian force was the main part of the garrison at Tarentum. On the whole, though, separate allied forces figured little in major operations, and Italian manpower—we shall see—was mainly useful to Hannibal as recruits into his own army.[3]

According to Livy and some others, Hannibal's appeal to some sections of the Italian population was not just as a champion of freedom from Roman mastery but as a champion of democracy against local oligarchies. 'A single disease so to speak had overtaken all the states of Italy', Livy comments with obvious distate, 'so that the common people were at odds with the aristocrats, the [local] senate sided with the Romans, the commons moved over to the Carthaginians.' In fact his own narrative contradicts his facile generalization over and over: Capua's defection, though instigated by the popular boss Pacuvius Calavius (an aristocrat himself), had plenty of aristocrats wholeheartedly behind it, something still truer at Locri where—according to Livy himself—'the masses were betrayed [to Punic control] by the leading men', and at Tarentum whose defection in 212 was engineered by a baker's dozen of young noblemen. At Arpi when the Romans broke in once again, in 213, the ordinary citizens were quickly able to convince them that it was local aristocrats who had sold them out to Hannibal. Indeed practically no recorded defection took place without one or more local notables leading it, and would-be defectors who cropped up unsuccessfully, in places like Nola or (late in the war) Etruria, were the same.

Nothing suggests, either, that the general was democratically inclined. At home Barcid dominance did rest on a carefully cosseted popularity, but as noted earlier there was no democratic revolution at Carthage under Hamilcar or Hasdrubal—still less any coup against the aristocracy, to which the Barcids themselves belonged. In Spain Punic and Barcid rule was authoritarian, indeed military. What mattered in Italy, in turn, was having a city or canton as an ally: how that was brought about and how it was maintained were practical questions, not ideological ones.[4]

<h1 style="text-align:center">II</h1>

Hannibal needed to spread defection as widely as he could and, where defection did not occur, he tried force or guile—starving out towns like Petelia in Bruttium and Casilinum, Nuceria and Acerrae in Campania, subduing Consentia in Bruttium, using his agents at Syracuse to steer first its ruler Hieronymus and then (after the boy-king's murder) the new Syracusan republic into the Punic camp. The strategic and economic importance of Campania led him to make repeated but thwarted efforts to subdue its other leading centres like Naples, Cumae, Puteoli—all of them seaports—and the stronghold of Nola. Likewise he sought to win over Tarentum, first in late 214 and then successfully early in 212, a success that brought over other Greek cities on that coast—Metapontum, Thurii and Heraclea.[5]

The stir aroused by his invasion and victories had spread abroad too. In 217 a peace conference in Greece was warned by a delegate that those 'clouds gathering in the west' might one day settle on Greece; and the young King Philip V of Macedon, one of the conference-participants, was already taking an interest since he had ambitions coveting the Roman-dominated coastlands of Illyria. Cannae prompted him to the friendliest feelings for Hannibal. Though his envoys were afterwards captured by the Romans, the king and the general struck a treaty in summer 215.

At Syracuse too Cannae was an earthquake. Though the 90-year-old Hiero II remained loyal to the Roman alliance, dissatisfaction with it had reportedly spread even to his son and heir Gelo. Gelo and then his father died in the months after Cannae but Hiero's 15-year-old grandson Hieronymus, on the throne early in 215, quickly made it clear that Syracuse was changing its alignment to what it saw as the winning side. Like Philip V, this was in the hope of direct profit: control over the eastern half of Sicily, if not the whole island. Envoys were sent over to Hannibal, who naturally spoke encouraging words and sent them home in the company of an officer of his—Polybius terms him the general's trierarch—also named Hannibal (quite possibly his friend Monomachus), along with two Syracusan brothers of part-Carthaginian ancestry. A Syracusan embassy to Carthage then resulted in a treaty of alliance against the Romans.[6]

Hannibal had probably not planned such broad international activity back in 218. His strategy then had been to strike into Italy, shatter the Romans' military effort and their alliance, and establish peace on Carthage's (and Barcid) terms. Though he had sent envoys into Cisalpine Gaul before he marched, he had sent none to Macedon. But when Cannae brought victory seemingly within his reach and attracted new friends, he readily expanded the scope of his thinking. As we have seen, he was pretty clearly looking ahead to the post-war containment of the Roman republic as much as to its early capitulation.

III

Immediately after Cannae he did expect a fairly prompt peace. As well as releasing all his Italian prisoners once again, he spoke amicably to the Roman ones for the first time (those from earlier battles he had simply sold as slaves), assuring them, Livy writes, that this was a war not to the death but for honour and power. More mundanely, he allowed them to send delegates to Rome to ask for ransom, and they were accompanied by an envoy of his own, an aristocrat named Carthalo, to see if the Romans were now disposed to peace and to offer terms if they were. There is little point in supposing Carthalo's mission a later Roman fiction to illustrate the Senate's firmness in the face of disaster. His brief was not to make peace-overtures but to put his general's terms if the Romans made them.

Hannibal's battle-methods were original but he relied on his opponents to be conventional, and not only in war. Crushing victories normally led to the losers asking for terms or being forced to ask. Alexander the Great's father had become master of Greece with his triumph at Chaeronea five generations earlier; Alexander had become lord of Asia with his three victories over the Persians; the ambitions of his most powerful successors Antigonus and Demetrius had been shattered at Ipsus. Carthaginian war-efforts had sometimes suffered the same fate, as in Sicily both in 480 at Himera and again in 341 at the river Crimisus—not to mention the naval catastrophe off the Aegates islands that lost them the First Punic War. Now it was surely the Romans' turn.[7]

True, Hannibal very likely knew that they had seldom obeyed this convention. Repeated disasters against Pyrrhus and in the First Punic War had not brought them to terms. After Cannae they repeated this inflexibility. They refused to let Carthalo stay in Roman territory, far less talk of terms; refused even to ransom their captive citizens. On the other hand, as Hannibal also may have known, they had actually negotiated with Pyrrhus after two heavy defeats, and he could reckon that their situation now was unprecedentedly desperate—massive human losses, ally after ally defecting, nearby foreign states wavering or hostile. Many or most outside observers probably gave them little chance of holding out for long. His own treaty with Philip V shows that in 215 he was expecting them to come to terms: his terms.

Polybius' verbatim quotation of this treaty-text, with the oath to it sworn by Hannibal and his Carthaginian councillors and troops, is the one piece of writing by the general that survives, at any rate in a Greek version. The treaty bound not just the expeditionary army in Italy but the Punic state and its allies, with a matching obligation on Philip, the Macedonians and their allies. It declared mutual friendship and enmities, stipulated that Philip would give military aid to the Carthaginians if asked, laid down that 'if the Romans ask us to come to terms of peace' specific territorial benefits in the Illyrian region would flow Philip's way, and promised that 'if ever the Romans make war on you or on us, we will help each other in the war as may be required on either side'.

In practice the treaty was never more than a paper statement, for Philip was never asked for help and peace on Punic terms was never signed. Macedon was to pay heavily in a later age for this empty flirtation with the invader of Italy. What was really significant was that it occurred at all. The king's tentative naval intervention in Illyrian waters the previous year had dissolved in panic at the arrival of just ten Roman warships: now he was ready to declare himself their enemy's ally and make military promises against them. More vividly even than the defection of half southern Italy and Campania, his move shows how convincing was the impression after Cannae that the power of Rome was broken and the time of Carthage had arrived.[8]

The treaty also hints how its makers envisaged the postwar position of the Roman republic. It would have to give up its area of hegemony across the Adriatic but, far from being destroyed, would remain able to make war against a major foreign state. This chimes with the attitude Hannibal showed to the Romans after Cannae: he was fighting them not to the death but 'for honour and power', in other words the honour and prestige of the Carthaginian state—not to mention its Barcid leadership—and its hegemony over the lands at issue. Both aims were perfectly acceptable to the Mediterranean world of his time, just as in other eras.[9]

But if the Roman republic stayed in being, and especially if it stayed capable of fresh war-making, it had to be constrained. Otherwise the whole expedition, the Alps and the Trebia, Trasimene and Cannae, would have been for nothing.

This was to be the crucial rôle of Hannibal's new alliances within and beyond Italy. They were not just for winning the war but—more important—for maintaining his peace. The postwar provisions of the treaty with Philip V show this feature plainly and so does the logic of the situation. A lasting Punic alliance-system in Italy would deprive the Romans of the massive manpower that underpinned their military might, would hem them in geographically, and would immediately give the Carthaginians the strategic upper hand if a new war broke out.

Just how all this would work in practice was never of course tried, nor was the question explored while the war was on. The vagueness was convenient and necessary, for Hannibal's new Italian friends—some of them anyway—had expectations rather different from this. Livy reports the Capuan leader Vibius Virrius assuring his countrymen that 'once the war was finished and Hannibal departed victorious to Africa and removed his army', they would be left as masters of Italy. Hannibal himself (again according to Livy) confirmed this to the Capuan senate. Quite possibly he did encourage the Capuans in this bracing notion—though Capuan hegemony was hardly a scenario to appeal to Bruttians, Samnites or Tarentines.

Some Italians thought the new situation ideal for settling scores. The Bruttians fell first on their own kinsmen of Petelia who refused to defect, then on Greek Croton which was an old foe, and they were prevented from sacking Locri only by its timely defection to the Carthaginians. No doubt particular defector-states looked for particular benefits from a postwar Italy, but overall they probably expected the sort of Italy that had preceded Roman hegemony—in effect a cheerful anarchy.

None of this would suit the Carthaginians. Quarrelsome disunited Italians left to themselves would be a power-vacuum guaranteed to entice and revive Roman power, or else attract into Italy a third force like Philip V. Hannibal himself need not have intended to stay on indefinitely, but his and Carthage's interests plainly required some continuing Punic presence in the peninsula. It would make sense for him to leave forces there to protect his allies from both the enmity of the Romans and the dangerous friendship of Philip.[10]

Just possibly he meant to annex some Italian territory as a Carthaginian possession. Not only is there a Roman tradition that he promised to reward his soldiers with Carthaginian citizenship, but another tradition represented him as claiming all of Italy in right of victory. Polybius reports him promising this to his army a couple of days before Cannae, Livy and Zonaras set it out in distorted versions of the treaty with Philip, and Livy depicts the defeated consul Varro forecasting Italy as a province ruled from Carthage. Strikingly too, Livy has Hannibal make a detailed list of promises to his army (and affirm them with a religious rite) in autumn 218 just before the skirmish at the Ticinus—citizenship, land in Italy, Africa or Spain, money in lieu of land if preferred, even rewards for loyal slaves.

Much of this would be Roman propaganda, and the promise made before Cannae might be just Hannibal's way of enthusing his men, but these varied items all share the theme of direct annexation. Conceivably they draw on a kernel of fact: conceivably, for example, he meant to acquire a stretch or stretches of Italian land centred on ports in easy communication with North Africa, Sicily and Sardinia, paying some sort of taxes and settled with veterans as well as, no doubt, civilians from Carthage and its other provinces. Livy's Varro finds the thought repulsive, but it would simply have been an extension to the Italian peninsula of Barcid methods of governance. If Punic forces and a Punic general were to be left in peacetime Italy, basing them in Punic-governed territory with at least some local funding made ample sense.[11]

IV

To bring about all these aims, military, political and diplomatic, a strong army-in-being was essential. And the more so as time passed and made it clear that the Romans were far from giving in despite all their disasters.

How Hannibal kept up his military strength is another debated question. Every battle imposed some losses, though they were low compared to Roman losses and—down to 216 anyway—fell mostly on his Gauls. Wounds, illnesses, desertions and mishaps must have taken further tolls. After Cannae he called for reinforcements from Carthage and 4,000 Numidian cavalry and 40 elephants, plus large funds, were sent over in 215 under an officer named Bomilcar. But the 13,500 infantry and cavalry, 20 elephants and further funds that were to follow these went instead to Spain, to offset a big Roman victory over his brother Hasdrubal, and a similarly strong force was voted for Sardinia to support the rebellion there. Their other brother Mago was sent to Spain to raise fresh troops for Italy, but none actually went. Bomilcar's corps was the only reinforcement Hannibal ever had from abroad.[12]

Yet the general obviously kept a powerful army in being. He attacked major towns like Neapolis, Nola, Nuceria and Tarentum—not to mention marching on Rome itself in 211—and fought big battles, like those around Nola in 216–214 and at Herdonea and Numistro in 210. From 216 to around 211 he could divide his field forces into a main northern army under himself and a smaller southern command led first by his brother Mago and then by Hanno, whom Appian calls his nephew. More than that, he installed garrisons at many allied towns, not just Capua: Arpi reportedly housed 5,000 Punic troops in 213, Salapia 500 Numidians in 210, and a couple of Samnite towns were garrisoned by 3,000 men that same year; at Tarentum a year later there was a garrison partly of Bruttians and partly of 'Carthaginians', probably meaning non-Italian troops. A passing comment in Livy implies that even as late as 207 Lucanian, and presumably other Punic-allied, towns normally had Punic garrisons, and at Locri in 205 a Punic force was holding the citadel when the Romans recaptured the town.

To judge from all this, the Carthaginians' total forces in Italy from 215 to at least 207 must have been sizeable, even if they lessened as years went by and Punic fortunes gradually waned. Between 216 and 211, when two field armies as well as garrisons were operating, Hannibal overall may have had as many as 60,000–70,000 troops in arms between Campania and Bruttium. Yet his reinforcements from abroad were minuscule.

The answer must be that he replaced losses among his original troops with mostly Italian recruits. Mercenaries from abroad may have made their way to him too but cannot have been all that numerous, while for Italians in the Punic army there is a fair amount of evidence. As mentioned earlier, Samnite spokesmen as early as 215 put it to him that all their young men were serving with him (no doubt an exaggeration). In 214 his lieutenant in the south, Hanno, had 17,000 largely Bruttian and Lucanian infantry and 'a few Italians' in his 1,200 cavalry, when the proconsul Ti. Sempronius Gracchus badly defeated him at the river Calor near Beneventum. This was not Hannibal's own army but it suggests that he too could recruit locally. By 207, when his area of control had shrunk to little more than Lucania and Bruttium, he is in fact recorded sending Hanno, still in harness, to raise fresh levies from the Bruttians.[13]

Nor is that the end. At his departure from Italy in 203, hostile Roman tradition claimed, he massacred Italian troops who refused to sail with him—20,000 according to a credulous Diodorus. If this atrocity tale is based on anything, it may be that he did put to death some recalcitrants (who would count as mutineers); at all events the story presupposes he had Italian troops to punish. Then Livy describes his reserve corps at the battle of Zama—the veterans from Italy—as mostly Bruttians. Polybius more carefully calls them 'the ones who came over with him from Italy'. Though he has Hannibal make them a speech recalling their past glories as far back as the Trebia, the corps was most likely made up not just of the survivors of that and the other battles but of later, mainly Italian recruits as well, and these were probably the majority. Like any well-knit army they would have taken on the *esprit* and traditions of their older comrades. Appian, for what his word is worth, stresses their military quality.

The population of the Italian defector-states, then, probably did supply manpower to Hannibal's army, not in separate allied contingents but as volunteers under direct Punic command. This surely suited him much better, for otherwise he would have had to cajole semi-autonomous contingents out of his allies, with the inevitable headaches that that would have entailed. Like the Spanish and African infantry, Numidian cavalry and Balearic slingers, his Italian troops were probably organized in regional units, for instance the Bruttian force at Tarentum.

Overall, the part played by Italian troops in his operations from 216 on is not to be underestimated. Although Hannibal called for reinforcements from home directly after Cannae, this was at a stage before such recruiting can seriously have begun. By mid-215 it was probably well established, since the further reinforcements being readied for him at Carthage were diverted to Spain without any known protest from him or noticeable damage to his own campaigning. In the first half-decade or so after Cannae his areas of recruitment would have been widest, which explains how he could afford so many garrisons and—strikingly—could maintain both a northern and a southern field army for some years. In the last years, by contrast, his range of both operations and recruiting shrank: as a result so did his forces, even if he kept them well-trained and tough enough to be the mainstay of his army at Zama.[14]

V

Italian recruitment to Hannibal's forces explains why the Carthaginians used their other military resources as they did. In 215, as noted, the much larger army due to follow Bomilcar's initial cavalry reinforcement to Italy was rerouted to Spain instead. Another army, just as large, was sent to Sardinia to help the rebellion there. Two years later 25,000 infantry, 3,000 cavalry and 12 elephants (forces larger than Hannibal had brought to north Italy in 218) arrived in Sicily to support the Syracusans in their new Roman war. In Spain strong Punic armies regularly operated down to 206.

This was not because Hannibal had lost control of the Carthaginian war-effort, still less because a hostile or suspicious home government starved him of forces. If he could recruit enough troops for his own army where he was, he could let other forces be deployed where they could be useful—not that they always proved to be so, notably in Sardinia and Sicily. Polybius emphasizes not only how he kept overall direction of the war but the obvious point that many of the other commanders were relatives, like his brothers Hasdrubal and Mago, or officers of his like the half-Carthaginian Syracusan Hippocrates, who with his brother Epicydes brought Syracuse over in 213, and Mottones of Hippou Acra who later on operated in Sicily too (only to let Hannibal down).[15]

The terrific successes of the first three years of war in Italy cannot have weakened Barcid political dominance at Carthage, even if things were going less well in Spain. There is no reason to visualize the Mighty Ones, magistracies and official boards as packed wholesale with Barcid nominees, for other aristocratic families and interests still existed, like Hanno the Great's, even if his was the only one overtly critical. But 20 years of victory and wealth can only have produced a large pro-Barcid majority, in which relatives and friends no doubt enjoyed prime status. It must as always have meant supporters winning offices and—just as important—other office-winning and place-holding aristocrats continuing to see it in their own interest to give support too. The first years of the new Roman war probably brought this dominance to its zenith.

Livy's picture of the Punic senate joyfully receiving Mago's account of Cannae—with only Hanno the Great like a wise but tiresome old owl counselling caution and indeed peace—may be embroidered but can hardly be far from the truth. Like the general himself, everyone expected 'that the war would soon be ended if they were willing to make a small extra effort'. Solidarity on the home front was strengthened by the tasks that Hannibal gave the authorities to do: for instance, preparing reinforcements and funds for the war-effort overseas.

Such delegation of tasks was probably well established by now. As mentioned earlier, Hannibal from the start may have listened to suggestions by Barcid supporters at Carthage, for instance on questions like the city's ports and fleets. Naval operations too from North Africa must have been organized, and presumably were authorized, at Carthage. Once Hannibal had accepted that such operations had a rôle to play, this arrangement made sense, even after he was able to re-establish regular contact with home from southern Italy. So too with other theatres of war. As long as loyal men were in charge at home, it made sense to leave many tasks to them, though under direction from him if he chose to exert it.

So too with the generals in other theatres. Some were members of the Barcid group by definition, including Hannibal's brothers Hasdrubal and Mago, and subordinates of his in Italy like Maharbal and nephew Hanno; others, during the early and middle years of the war anyway, were probably either members of the group too or else allies—a distinction that may not have been too sharp in some cases. Notable among them were Hasdrubal (nicknamed 'the Bald', for reasons perhaps obvious at the time), sent to Sardinia in 215, and Himilco and Hanno the successive commanders in Sicily in 213 and 212. Probably an ally—a leading figure with his own independent connexions—rather than a group member was Hasdrubal son of Gisco, as we shall see in a while, but he too was part of the war-effort led by the Barcids at Carthage and supervised by Hannibal.[16]

On the other hand, as just noted, Hannibal sensibly left theatre operations to the local commanders and intervened rarely, just as he left to the authorities at Carthage tasks best performed there. Thus most obviously the dealings with Hieronymus of Syracuse. These began with Syracusan envoys being sent to Hannibal in Italy. He then despatched his trierarch Hannibal to Syracuse, and this officer in turn accompanied new Syracusan envoys over to Carthage to negotiate an alliance. In 213, with Syracuse now under the pro-Carthaginian brothers Hippocrates and Epicydes and the Romans preparing to move against the city, a letter from Hannibal seconded a call for military support from the brothers, prompting despatch of the already-mentioned army from North Africa to Sicily. In 212, trying to rescue the situation after the Romans captured Syracuse, the Carthaginians sent over a new general, yet another Hanno, while from Italy Hannibal transferred his able cavalryman Mottones, of Hippou Acra, to serve under him. These two eventually fell out and Mottones went over to the Romans, but his initial appointment shows how Hannibal could intervene as he thought fit. Hanno's appointment was made at Carthage no doubt because a general officer could not be spared from the army in Italy, and quite possibly it was with Hannibal's agreement. There is no point seeing him as a latent anti-Barcid: though he despised the non-Carthaginian Mottones, Epicydes—another trusted agent of Hannibal's—stayed with him throughout.[17]

Already mentioned too was the scheme that Hasdrubal should march from Spain to join his brother, a prospect the Romans were worrying about as early as 217. Early in 215 the senate at Carthage reportedly sent Hasdrubal his marching orders, and reiterated them over his objection that it was too risky to leave Spain (as it turned out, the brothers Scipio prevented him anyway). It is very unlikely that the Mighty Ones were dealing with so critical a strategic issue on their own. If they sent Hasdrubal orders to join his brother, almost certainly they were doing so at his brother's behest; besides, it was much more practical for Hannibal in south Italy to communicate with Spain via Carthage than to try doing so direct. Livy or his source may not have appreciated these details—or else, conceivably, Hasdrubal's ensuing disastrous defeat at Hibera prompted writers like Sosylus and Silenus later to play down the ultimate origin of the marching orders.[18]

VI

By the end of 215 Hannibal had created an alliance-system covering the bulk of southern Italy. The only exclusions were the Greek cities along the south-eastern coast (save Croton, conquered by the Bruttians, and Locri), Rhegium at the straits, and the Latin colonies of Beneventum and Luceria in Samnium, Venusia in Apulia, and Brundisium and Paestum on the coasts. At the other end of the peninsula, Cisalpine Gaul was out of Roman control even if Hannibal did not have regular contact with it. At the end of 216 the Roman army there and the newly elected consul who led it were wiped out in an ambush, yet another catastrophe for the enemy. If a fresh Punic army arrived from Spain—something he and his brother Hasdrubal were already thinking about—the region could serve as a resupply-base as it had in 218. With Macedon too on his side and Syracuse wavering, and even the Sardinians staging a rebellion, he had the Romans virtually surrounded. It was a situation all but unprecedented in their history. It was natural to expect that sooner rather than later they would ask for terms.[19]

Yet his new alliance system was a flawed mosaic. Important members of it, and maybe some others, had to be won over by guarantees which made them only a passive asset—no longer in the Roman alliance but not contributing positively to the Punic one either. Hannibal in no way held the sort of commanding leadership over his miscellany of allies that Philip II of Macedon and Alexander the Great, or the Athenian state before them, had held over theirs. To the Italians he was paradoxically both necessary and an irritant. Only he could preserve them in their new-found freedom, but he made demands on them (for supplies even if he paid for these, and for recruits even if these were for his own army) and their association with him brought Roman reprisals on their heads. Not surprisingly there is little evidence of real enthusiasm among the defecting Italians for their Punic alliance. At some places pro-Roman factions continued to exist—Arpi, for instance, and Salapia where the pro-Romans would take the city back into the Roman fold in 210.

Hannibal found himself in a dilemma with the Italians rather similar to theirs with him. Passive or not, he needed them; but in turn he had to support them against their old hegemon—a disadvantage rather than an asset. The strategic situation would have been easier had the defectors formed a solid block of ground from coast to coast, but instead they were parcelled out over southern Italy with enemy strongholds scattered among them. The Romans continued to hold Nola, Neapolis, Puteoli and the strategic mountain-height of Castra Claudiana between Nola and Capua, Pentrian territory in Samnium, all the Latin colonies, and (till 212) many of the Greek cities on the coasts.

This meant that Hannibal's alliance had little territorial cohesion and not much chance of—or interest in—concerted action or even mutual support.[20]

By contrast, with all 30 Latin allies, the Etruscans, and the other central and north Italian states continuing to stand with them, the Romans kept a superiority in resources and a solid and productive mass of territory from which to fight. They reverted to Fabius Maximus' strategy of avoiding pitched battles with Hannibal and concentrated instead on wearing down his allies. From 215 on, Roman armies operating in several simultaneous theatres around southern Italy laid waste to croplands and villages, attacked towns and generally made the defectors' lives miserable—as the Samnites appealing to Hannibal pointed out. They even began winning back some centres, like Casilinum (which he had captured in 215) as early as 214 and in the following year Arpi, which had defected after Cannae.[21]

Hannibal could neither intervene in every quarter nor divide up his forces into enough detachments to cope. Yet the success of his whole venture depended not only on protecting his new allies but, even more importantly, on nurturing their belief that they would do better under his leadership than they had under the Romans. This conundrum was to dog all his remaining years in Italy.

XI

INDECISIVE WAR

I

The ambitiously energetic Barcid strategy in the years after Cannae was on a scale greater than anything in past Punic history. It marked the zenith of Hannibal's military and diplomatic power, with the Romans confronted not only in Italy but across the western Mediterranean—in Cisalpine Gaul, Spain, Sardinia, the Adriatic and finally Sicily. But an ever-widening ring of confrontation could not by itself bring victory. The confrontations had to be pressed and be successful. At this crucial level, his and the Carthaginians' impetus stalled.

In one region after another—Spain, then Sardinia, next the Adriatic and even Sicily—the Romans won the upper hand again. In Spain Cn. Scipio's naval victory in 217 near the Ebro was followed two years later by the rout of Hasdrubal's army at Hibera, again near the mouth of the Ebro, and then by years of stalemate which strategically was more in their favour than in the Carthaginians'. In Sardinia not only was the local revolt, encouraged from Carthage, a total failure in 215 but the army sent to help was delayed by storms and then met total defeat: even its commander was captured. The Macedonian intervention in the Adriatic fared ingloriously in its turn—Philip V's operations in Illyria in 214 were wrecked when the Romans made a surprise attack on his camp and then forced him to burn his ships and retreat home. This was not the end of operations in Illyria but it was the end of Philip's usefulness as an ally.

In Sicily too, the Romans checked their enemies' opening successes. Despite joining the Punic side twice, first under Hieronymus and later when Hippocrates and Epicydes won control, the Syracusans found themselves besieged by the unrelenting M. Claudius Marcellus. Nor did the powerful Punic army sent to their rescue manage to do anything but perish in an epidemic along with its commander.[1]

Hannibal's own progress in Italy, apart from recruiting new allies, was hardly different. He spent 215 and 214 moving between Campania and Apulia, concentrating most of his energies on trying to take enemy strongholds and ports

134

in Campania. He succeeded with Casilinum, Nuceria and Acerrae, but failed at the more important Neapolis, Nola, Cumae, Puteoli and Tarentum—and before long the Romans retook Casilinum. His various encounters with Roman armies outside Nola under the tireless Marcellus equally failed to repeat Trebia, Trasimene or Cannae (even if they were not the victories by Marcellus that Roman tradition later claimed). With the Romans grimly continuing their resistance, the momentum built up by Cannae and its immediate aftermath was plainly running down. Indeed campaigning in the year 213 was more or less at a standstill: its one noteworthy event was Arpi in Apulia going back over to the Romans, a coup by Fabius' son and namesake.

By contrast, every now and then the Romans won successes where Hannibal was absent. Fabius Maximus the Delayer reconquered places in rebel Samnium in 214, including the important town of Compsa, then Aecae in Apulia. The energetic Ti. Sempronius Gracchus in 215 pounced on a Campanian force at Hamae near Cumae, and at the river Calor near Beneventum in 214 he routed the strong secondary army of Bruttians and Lucanians marching under Hanno's command to join Hannibal in Campania. Then in 213 Arpi rejoined the Romans.

Even the general's own army was not immune from ennui: in 215 about 300 Numidian and Spanish cavalry decamped to the enemy outside Nola, in 213 nearly 1,000 Spaniards in the Arpi garrison did (on condition that the rest of the Punic force went free), and Bruttian deserters over time formed a sizeable body that the Romans were to use in 209.[2]

Still, even after these frustrations Hannibal was able to score some more successes. The most important was Tarentum defecting to him early in 212—though the Romans kept hold of its citadel—quickly followed by Metapontum, Thurii and Heraclea. In the same year the rest of the Lucanian communities deserted the Roman side too. Now he controlled virtually all the coast of the Tarentine gulf and the Ionian Sea, with their hinterlands: this strengthened his grip on what supply-producing areas there were in southern Italy and also made communicating with Carthage easier than before.

And he still won some successes in the field. In 212 if Livy's report is correct, and again in 210 more crushingly, he defeated Roman armies at Herdonea in Apulia. Smaller victories in the south were won—according to Livy again—by Hanno in 213 and Hannibal himself in 212, 209 and 208 against various corps of Romans or Roman allies operating independently. His battle with Marcellus at Numistro in 210 was another victory or at least a draw, and the following year he dealt the same commander heavy losses in an indecisive tussle outside Canusium. There was even a small naval victory in 210, when a Tarentine flotilla defeated a Roman squadron trying to bring supplies to the Roman-held citadel at Tarentum.[3]

The half-decade after Cannae, in sum, brought both the high point of the expedition to Italy and yet a strategic stalemate. The Romans could not defeat him, but neither could he break them. Successes on the one side were matched by successes on the other. He maintained the strength of his armies and garrisons, but the Romans increased theirs until by 212 they had no fewer than 25 legions under arms, four times as many as at the start of the war, and 14 of them in Italy where ten operated in Campania and the south.[4]

II

From 212, in fact, the tide began to turn in Italy, if slowly. Although that was the year Hannibal won over Tarentum and other south-coast cities, it was also the year when the Romans with six legions put Capua under siege and Marcellus in Sicily completed his siege of Syracuse by capturing the hitherto impregnable city. Nothing the Carthaginians did could deflect the besiegers at either place. In Sicily Himilco's army, sent over from Carthage in 213, did no damage to them and in 212 perished thanks to an epidemic; and then a powerful fleet, the most powerful sent out by the Carthaginians during the war, managed to achieve nothing at all—in the end sailing away rather than battle an outnumbered Roman force off Cape Pachynus.

In Italy, the hapless Hanno, trying to get provisions into Capua before the legions closed in, lost his camp (again near Beneventum) and all the provisions to a Roman assault. Hannibal's foray later in 212 into Apulia and victory at First Herdonea did nothing for the Capuans, though he had probably hoped otherwise; in 211 he tried to break the siege and failed, then led his troops on the famous—and again fruitless—march to the outskirts of Rome itself, provoking much alarm but no wavering either there or among Capua's besiegers; and just as ineffectual was his extraordinary return march, not back to Capua but down the entire length of southern Italy to Rhegium in the (predictably futile) hope of capturing that.[5]

These strange manoeuvres virtually symbolize the general's activity from 212 on: bold and risky moves, impressive-looking coups, even some victories, yet little impact on how the war was really developing. His successes in these years were very different from those that had climaxed at Cannae. The value of Tarentum was impaired by the continuing Roman occupation of its citadel, which dominated the city's harbour. And with several enemy armies operating in Italy at the same time, beating one or other had a distinctly limited impact—even when, as at the two Herdonea battles, he smashed his opponents. Once Capua surrendered and the Campanian front collapsed, his war-effort was effectively confined to the regions further south, and after the Samnites in their turn gave up the fight in 210 and 209 only Lucania, Apulia and Bruttium remained for campaigning.

All his campaigning was now defensive, as indeed it had been since Capua went under siege. His approach to the walls of Rome in 211 (even if it left the Romans with an imperishable memory of danger and alarm, and the proverbial cry 'Hannibal at the gates!') would remain the only time he ever sighted his enemies' city, a futile gesture five, if not six, years too late.

More and more the Romans were waging the war as though Hannibal was not really there, or was there only as a nuisance—like a buzzing wasp—to be ignored or deflected. It still cost them dearly at times, notably in the battles fought in 210, 209 and 208; and yet Hannibal failed to capitalize on the momentary advantages he thus won. Second Herdonea and the death of the proconsul Fulvius Centumalus simply prevented the Romans from taking that town as they had hoped, while the ensuing drawn battle of Numistro against Marcellus merely gave Hannibal the opportunity to retreat out of Lucania into Apulia.

These battles were really defensive and reactive: it was the enemy who were now usually taking the initiative and the Carthaginian general who largely had to stand on guard to repel their unending thrusts and slashes at what was left of pro-Punic allied Italy. Likewise his semi-success at Canusium in 209, against Marcellus again, merely gave him the opportunity to march from there into Bruttium to save Caulonia from attack by the Sicilian and Bruttian irregulars—and the upshot was that Fabius the Delayer meantime retook Tarentum. Intentionally or not, the Romans had diverted the general from the main game: he had not been so outmanoeuvred since Fabius had trapped him in Campania in 217. Nor did success attend his ruse to entice the Delayer into moving out from Tarentum against Metapontum or, as we shall see, his stratagem in 208 to recover Salapia nearby.[6]

Ironically (and he may have been aware of the irony) the man who had effectively launched the entire war was in danger of becoming irrelevant to it. By the end of 208 his one hope of regaining the upper hand in Italy, and with it a last chance for overall victory, rested on his brother Hasdrubal's long-delayed but now-begun march to Italy with a new army.

III

Hasdrubal had become the general in command of the Spanish territories once Hannibal crossed the Pyrenees. He stayed in command for ten years, until leaving for Italy at the end of 208, the longest Spanish tenure of any of the Barcids. The other generals operating with him—Hanno in 218, and later his brother Mago and Hasdrubal son of Gisco—must then have been subordinate to him even though in practice they sometimes acted separately.

Polybius offers a glowing assessment of the middle Barcid brother: brave, resourceful, prudent, and throughout his life worthy of his father. But in various situations he emerges less ideally. Notably, he was not good at imposing his supposedly superior authority on his lieutenants. Some years later he reached the point where he could not get on even with his own younger brother Mago (and in his final battle he was completely unable to control his contingent of Gauls). And already in 218 strategic liaison with Hanno, the officer in charge north of the Ebro, was unsatisfactory.

When Cn. Scipio arrived with the army sent on by his brother the consul, the Romans were able to land at Emporiae, make their presence felt as far as the Ebro—180 coastal miles (290 kilometres) to the south—and defeat and capture Hanno at Cissis near Tarraco. Only then did his superior arrive from the south. Unless his information-gathering methods were much more inefficient than his brother's, it is hard to imagine that Hasdrubal had had no inkling of the approaching invaders while they moved along the south coast of Gaul, and that word of their arrival at Emporiae fell on him like a bolt from the blue. He would know that Hanno's 11,000 men were bound to be outnumbered, and he could have joined him from New Carthage in just a few weeks. It looks as though Hasdrubal had suffered dangerous complacency.[7]

Nor did he show himself a first-class commander the following year, when he decided to take on Scipio by sea and land only to have his fleet soundly beaten at the mouth of the Ebro. The catastrophe seemingly cancelled his interest in fighting on land as well: another strategic mistake, since Cn. Scipio was soon joined by his brother with reinforcements. This confirmed the Roman grip on Spain-beyond-Ebro and exacerbated the danger to the Punic position across the peninsula. Then, when in early 215 Hasdrubal received some reinforcements from Africa and again moved north, he was even more soundly defeated on land, at the battle of Hibera near the Ebro again.

If nothing else, he was proving that he was no master of warfare like his brother. More important, if Livy is right that he had been under orders from Carthage to lead an army to Italy, then Italy was saved.[8]

Hasdrubal suffered—or gave himself—trouble too in his treatment of Carthage's Spanish allies and subjects. The Celtiberians, between the Tagus and the Ebro, were not effectively under Punic control at all and any effect from Hannibal's lightning campaign of 220 had worn off; reportedly they or some of them turned hostile in 217 and distracted Hasdrubal from his Roman foes for the rest of that year. Nor could he reimpose respect afterwards, even though from 214 to 212 he had the time to try: they were later on happy to sign up—if only temporarily—with the Scipios instead. Again, he so harshly criticized the Spanish captains of the ships captured by Cn. Scipio at the Ebro in 217 that (according to Livy) they deserted and sparked a rising among the 'Tartessians' in 216 serious enough to delay his advance against the Scipios; in fact it lasted into 214. Later still, early in 209, Hasdrubal is found campaigning against the Carpetani, so relations with them too had definitely turned negative.

Not all of this need have been his fault. If a general could not rebuke his underlings for slack performance in combat, his rôle was compromised. The Carpetani had not relished being crushed by Hannibal in 220 or having a large force of warriors dragged off in 218 to fight outside Spain (these had had to be sent home). With the Romans actually in the country, service abroad no doubt had poor appeal to many other Spaniards too, as Livy attests at the time of the battle of Hibera. Again, when in 209 the northern Spanish lords Indibilis and Mandonius, after a decade or more of enthusiastic loyalty, were provoked into defection by Punic high-handedness, the culprit was not the governor of Spain but his lieutenant Hasdrubal son of Gisco, who had gone so far as to seize their womenfolk as hostages.[9]

Even so, these thorny and at times fractious relations with such a variety of Spaniards stand in contrast to how the earlier Hasdrubal, in particular, had handled affairs only a decade before. Nor was it a good sign that in so important a matter as dealing with Mandonius and Indibilis—who contributed greatly to the destruction of the Scipio brothers in 211—he could or would not control a subordinate. As for the Tartessians, if the name in Livy is correct these had been Hamilcar's first conquest: a quarter of a century's Punic rule plainly had not won them over and, on a reasonable guess, their revolt now may well have been due to Punic demands for money and men, something for which the governor again was ultimately responsible.

It is striking too that, with the war intensifying in 217 and 216, Hasdrubal called for and was sent reinforcements from Africa, first a body of 4,500 and then an army under one Himilco. In 215 yet another army was sent under the third Barcid brother Mago: all this even though Spain itself was supposed to be a reservoir of first-class fighting men. This supports Livy's notices about the Celtiberians turning hostile and the Carthaginians having to combat provincial rebels too. Plainly Hasdrubal's leadership left something to be desired.

Given these stresses in Spain, it is risky to trust Appian's unsupported claim that Hasdrubal was called back with part of his forces to North Africa to fight the newly hostile western Numidian king Syphax. Syphax's enmity developed in 213 (fostered by the Scipios, who even sent him an army officer to train his troops) but Appian or his source probably confused Hasdrubal the Barcid with another Hasdrubal: perhaps the son of Gisco.[10]

IV

The Roman invasion thus soon began to have damaging impact on the structure and security of Punic rule in Spain, even if Livy's account of the Scipio brothers' campaigns offers too many suspect Roman victories and Carthaginian setbacks. As the case of the disgraced ships' captains and the Tartessians illustrates, and then later episodes like Hasdrubal's war in Carpetania, the Roman war shook (predictably enough) the old yet still not very old Punic hegemony, much of which had been imposed by force or the threat of force. And as Punic hegemony faltered so did Hasdrubal's political authority—to judge from Hasdrubal son of Gisco's actions and the ensuing bad blood between him, his nominal boss and the latter's own brother Mago. This all flowed from Hasdrubal's early failure to repel the Roman invasion.

The Scipios' main achievements were to bar him from Italy and weaken Punic control in Spain. Just how they did it is hard to follow, since Livy's details of marches, sieges and battles all over southern Spain are too often questionable—for instance a claimed advance to the Castulo region in 217 after Cn. Scipio's naval victory, and a sweeping campaign all over the Baetis valley supposedly in 214. Advancing to the Castulo region makes no strategic sense in 217, and according to Polybius the Ebro was first crossed by both brothers together, later that year. Other reports of fighting in 215 and 214 have aroused doubts too, and only Livy's account of the brothers' destruction in 211 has been generally accepted (even then, his date of 212 has to be corrected).[11]

Scepticism may go to excess. Even the impact of the battle of Hibera in 215 is occasionally but needlessly doubted, and the brothers' rescue in late 217 of the Carthaginians' Spanish hostages from Saguntum—thanks to a resourceful Spanish chief who tricked the city's Punic commandant into sending them away—is circumstantially reported by Polybius as well as Livy and can be believed. Even the account of their southern Spanish campaign in (supposedly) 214 offers some plausible-sounding topographical details—for instance Castrum Altum, identified as the site of Hamilcar's death, Castulo as the hometown of Hannibal's wife, and Iliturgi nearby—and Appian reports the pair wintering around Castulo. Very likely Livy's source misdated this campaign from 212, for he adds that the Scipios re-established the surviving Saguntines in their town and that this was seven years after Hannibal had taken it. Besides, Appian has the brothers campaign successfully in the south in 212 before wintering there. Probably they had sought to break the stalemate of 214–213 with an ambitious drive into the Punic–Spanish heartland.[12]

But after initial successes their momentum faltered. Instead, in 211 Hasdrubal and his confrères scored stunning successes. First P. and then Cn. Scipio and their separated armies were overwhelmed—Hasdrubal's first and, as it proved, only major victory over Romans—with the sterling aid of the northerner Indibilis and the Numidian prince Masinissa. Yet Hasdrubal's limitations as general and governor now saved the enemy from total annihilation. The remnants of the Scipios' forces were able to retreat all the way north, cross the Ebro and regroup; even if Hasdrubal eventually marched northwards in pursuit, as Livy and others claim with decorative fictions about Roman victories, quite plainly the surviving Roman troops were not dislodged from Spain-beyond-Ebro. More than that, reinforcements arrived from Italy: first under C. Claudius Nero and then more in 210 with his replacement P. Scipio, son and youthful namesake of the late proconsul.[13]

One reason for Punic inattention may have been that the enemy no longer seemed a threat; another, mentioned earlier, was that Hasdrubal and his lieutenants—his brother Mago, and Hasdrubal son of Gisco—quarrelled furiously after victory and each went his own way. These were hardly adequate excuses. Both reveal a surprising level of miscalculation and irresponsibility. Worse still, they fatally compromised Punic and Barcid fortunes in Spain.

XII

THE DEFEAT OF HASDRUBAL

I

The Second Punic War most plainly reached stalemate in 211. In Spain, Hasdrubal destroyed the Romans' invasion of the south and killed the Scipio brothers. In Italy, Capua surrendered to the consuls Claudius and Fulvius, and Campania fell out of Hannibal's orbit. Syracuse had already been taken by Marcellus; Macedon was no threat to the Romans or help to Hannibal. The Romans maintained 21 legions and 100 or more warships. Stalemate dragged on in 210: Hannibal won at Second Herdonea and effectively at Numistro, but neither was decisive and the strategic reality stayed the same. The Romans might not be able to crush him, but he could no longer threaten them, or even safeguard all his remaining allies from them. Hasdrubal in Spain let the Roman forces keep their coastal footing beyond the Ebro, though they had no strength for wider ventures. Observers of the war might well suppose that it would drag on for a very long time, even a quarter-century like its predecessor.

What impact this had at Carthage can only be estimated, but by 210 the war must have stopped looking hopeful. Hannibal no longer won smashing victories; Hasdrubal failed to follow up his defeat of the Scipios. Finances must have been under pressure: there can have been little benefit any more from captives or booty, though a raid on Sardinia in 210 garnered some. At the same time costs were surely higher than ever: troops had to be levied and fitted out in North Africa for expeditions overseas, some to Spain, others to Sardinia and Sicily; funds had to be sent too.

Again, by these middle years of the war large and therefore expensive Punic fleets existed. As many as 155 warships operated under Bomilcar's command outside Syracuse in 212 and later that year 130 sailed to Sicily and Tarentum. True, most other Punic fleets recorded were half this size or less, but they still cost money and no fleet achieved great success. Nor did the Carthaginians even manage to ward off repeated Roman raids on their coasts yearly from 217 to 215 (though in the first two they did inflict some losses when the Romans landed) or fresh attacks from 211 on, which according to Livy inflicted much damage.[1]

If these unpromising conditions weakened Barcid political dominance at Carthage, it would be no surprise. Hardly anything is known of domestic alignments in these years but it is not plausible that Hannibal and his supporters continued to dominate affairs as easily as before. Other figures, with their own interests, had to be taken into account—Hasdrubal son of Gisco being the most notable.

As we saw earlier, he (not Hannibal's brother) was probably the general sent against the western Numidian king Syphax in 213. He then went to Spain, probably late in 213 or at the start of 212, as a lieutenant of his Barcid namesake, and no doubt as an ally of the Barcids: he would hardly have been sent otherwise. On the other hand, as already noted, he was plainly an independent-minded officer whom the Barcid Hasdrubal found hard to discipline. He must already have held both seniority and prestige, for after Hasdrubal left for Italy in 208 the son of Gisco and not the Barcid brother Mago took over the Spanish command. Livy describes him in Spain as the most distinguished Punic general apart from the Barcids, and in North Africa later as 'the first man in the state by far'.

By 205, in fact, Hasdrubal son of Gisco probably commanded a backing at Carthage equal to the Barcids'. Besides Livy's description of his eminence the poet Silius, borrowing this or using other information, describes him frankly as the man in charge there. Again, when he commanded in North Africa from 205, he had no known Barcid lieutenants (notwithstanding an officer named Hanno son of Hamilcar) and acted very much as his own man. Then in 204 he was to win the newly reconciled Syphax, who by then had made himself master of all Numidia, as husband for his daughter, the famous and accomplished Sophoniba.

Rather than being a follower or protégé of the Barcid group, Hasdrubal looks very much like a high-ranking Carthaginian aristocrat—no less high than Hanno the Great, for example—with his own following and resources. Originally no doubt he had allied with the Barcids for patriotic and personal reasons, but even as early as 211 he had begun to assert his independence. If he could be the prime figure at Carthage after losing Spain, his political position must have been remarkably strong; it would no doubt have been stronger without his unfortunate talent for incurring defeat at Scipio's hands. A good deal of his support probably came from men who had hitherto backed the Barcids but were growing disenchanted with the war's progress.

The war-effort outside Italy had always had to be left to the local commanders for practical reasons, even if Hannibal remained the final authority, and when the Romans invaded Punic North Africa it was hardly possible for him in Italy to try to direct the defence of the homeland. Hasdrubal son of Gisco, resilient and energetic despite his setbacks, was the obvious one to take charge. He thus became the local man of destiny—briefly. It was his misfortune that, after helping the Barcids to destroy the Scipio brothers in Spain in 211, all his tireless energy never won him another victory over the Romans.

Nothing suggests that he and the Barcids were at loggerheads, even if he was not part of their faction. As just noted, they collaborated in Spain. In Africa, after Scipio the younger destroyed his and Syphax's armies in their camps in 203, he and the Barcid faction together were to rally the Carthaginians to a new effort, including the recall of Hannibal from Italy. True, according to Appian even when Hannibal returned Hasdrubal continued to operate on his own until he met an untimely death: but quite apart from the fact that independent operations do not prove antagonism, Appian's details of the war in North Africa need to be treated very cautiously, as we shall see.[2]

Another hint to a weakening of Barcid dominance at home is the rise in political power of the 'order of judges': probably meaning, as we saw earlier, the tribunal of One Hundred and Four. By 196 the 'judges' were, Livy reports, the dominant element in the republic—and an arrogant and corrupt element at that. Of course they had always been important (and doubtless arrogant and corrupt too), but this had not prevented the Barcids from controlling Punic affairs since Hamilcar's time. Many members of the Hundred and Four by 211 owed their position to Barcid support; some surely were kinsmen or close allies of Hannibal; and many other 'judges' had no doubt found advantage in being aligned with the Barcids. But Barcid dominance relied on success and its profits and prestige, all of them declining assets after 210.

As the war went on, the bulk of the Hundred and Four—all of them senators, and no doubt the senators with most influence and status—probably needed Barcid support less and less. More and more, by contrast, the Barcids would need to bargain to gain support from the Hundred and Four. Hasdrubal son of Gisco looks like the strongest of their allies, and it may be more accurate to see Punic affairs, by 208 if not earlier, as being run not by Hannibal's family and supporters alone, but by a coalition of Hannibal's group and Hasdrubal's.[3]

II

For in 209 the fortunes of war turned against the family and Carthage. After four years on the Punic side, Tarentum in Italy was recaptured by the Romans under Fabius the Delayer thanks to a lovesick Bruttian captain changing sides—a stratagem quite in Hannibal's own class, and compounded by the Romans' success in luring him away beforehand into Bruttium. In Spain the three discordant Punic generals had betaken themselves to widely separate locales in the centre and west of the peninsula; they thus allowed an improbable new Roman leader—26 years old, with no previous experience of high office or independent command, notable only for being the son and namesake of the dead proconsul P. Scipio—to lead a bold thrust down the coast from the Ebro and capture no less a prize than New Carthage the day after he arrived outside its walls.

Hasdrubal and his colleagues had managed yet another misjudgement. They must have heard of young Scipio's appointment to Spain or else his arrival at Tarraco—not to mention the 11,000 fresh troops he brought with him—but they failed to send even a detachment to keep an eye on the Ebro line and left barely 1,000 troops as garrison at New Carthage. To unjustified strategic complacency, in other words, they added a disastrous misestimate of the new general. Maybe they had viewed the appointment of another Scipio to Spain in quasi-Barcid terms—as a political move to ensure the loyalty of Spain-beyond-Ebro that his father and uncle had won, but with his youth and inexperience posing no serious military problems for them. That young Scipio should match the Barcid model militarily too, by proving himself a better general than his father and as much a master of the unconventional as Hannibal, must have come as a shock—including to Hannibal over in Italy.[4]

Not only was Scipio's booty from New Carthage colossal but, at a stroke, he effectively cleared the Carthaginians from eastern Spain, threw them onto the defensive and won over a growing number of Spanish peoples and princes. Even the Ilergetans Indibilis and Mandonius, veteran enthusiasts for Carthage though they had been, now decided on a policy reversal. This series of misfortunes paralysed the Carthaginian leaders' judgement. They not only waited in the south for Scipio's next onslaught, though he had withdrawn to Tarraco for the winter, but also—because of their continuing antagonisms, according to Polybius—failed to unite their armies or even bring them into supporting distance of one another.

As a result, in 208 Hasdrubal confronted the enemy by himself and with inferior numbers. Once he had taken up a hilltop position at Baecula near Castulo, he showed no tactical flexibility (except for extricating part of his army after defeat): Scipio pinned him down frontally and then shattered both his flanks. But the Roman did not pursue the defeated troops as they retired northwards because he would risk attack from the other Punic armies too. This is a damning implication for what the three Carthaginians might have achieved had they co-operated closely against him from the start.[5]

Even before Baecula, if the sources are correct, the Carthaginians had revived the scheme of Hasdrubal marching from Spain to Italy to reinforce his brother. This had first been mooted in 216–215, only to be quashed by the Scipio brothers' victory of Hibera. The reason for reviving it now was drastically different—no longer to strengthen a victorious Hannibal as he moved to force their foes to peace, but to bring him help in a last effort to retilt the military balance and stave off final Roman victory. Scipio let Hasdrubal go, confident that the 12 legions in Cisalpine Gaul and Italy would cope with the new invader and intent on prising the rest of Barcid Spain from the Carthaginians' grasp. His confidence was sound.[6]

III

By now Hannibal could manage only negative wins. In the same year 208 he mauled, but failed to destroy, a Roman corps marching against Locri. Then an ambush on a hill in Lucania killed Marcellus, again consul, and mortally wounded his colleague Crispinus, but the coup gained little: Crispinus alerted allied communities against deceptive use of Marcellus' signet ring and Hannibal's try at capturing Salapia backfired badly. The locals let in his advance body only to shut the gates and slaughter the men. The incident may even have cheated him of a victory over the consuls' combined armies, for they reportedly had been keen on a battle—one that, judging by past form, he might well have won. If so, Hannibal had defeated himself. Crispinus now took care to avoid fighting.

The general did succeed, by a classic speed-march, in sweeping away a Roman force besieging Locri where his friend Mago the Samnite was commandant, another negative win. In effect he was down merely to defending his status quo in south Italy. Plutarch reports that after the loss of Tarentum he had told his lieutenants there was no longer any possibility of conquering Italy: in other words of winning the war. The report may be true, even if the general spoke in a moment of atypical gloom. As noted earlier, Hannibal was in danger of becoming irrelevant to his own war.[7]

Hasdrubal's approach therefore offered the last hope for regaining strategic dominance and, with it, final victory. Moreover victory had to be won, and be seen to be won, in Italy. Not only was it virtually impossible to force the Romans to peace through winning in Spain (the events of 211 had shown that); but success in Spain under Hasdrubal son of Gisco, counterbalanced by defeat—or just stalemate—in Italy, would see the Barcids' already fragile primacy at Carthage collapse. The political and dynastic achievements of Hamilcar, his son-in-law and Hannibal himself were at stake.

By contrast, if Hannibal could combine his veteran army with his brother's new forces he could revive the possibilities of 216 and 215, with better prospects. Forty or fifty thousand trained and experienced troops—plus whatever Gallic contingents Hasdrubal might recruit on the way—would enable him to force battle on the legions that dogged his path yet refused to fight, or open the way to Rome and the blockade that he ought to have mounted after Cannae. It might encourage Philip V to re-enter active warfare against the Romans. The blow to Roman morale and resources, after so many years of struggle, could be terminal.

The Romans recognized this well enough. Six legions guarded northern Italy, seven were spread across the south from Capua to Bruttium and two waited in reserve at Rome. For the new consuls of 207 they turned not to well-used veterans like Fabius Maximus, Q. Fulvius Flaccus or M. Valerius Laevinus, but to a surprising combination recommended by the Senate. Along with the competent if unspectacular C. Claudius Nero, who had commanded in Spain before young Scipio's arrival and more recently had served under Marcellus in southern Italy, they elected the oddest choice of the whole war— M. Livius Salinator, consul in 219 but afterwards convicted of embezzling booty, and since then a total outsider to affairs. The combination was all the odder because the two men thoroughly disliked each other. What prompted Livius' fellow-citizens into appointing the two of them to cope with the crisis can only be guessed, but the wily old Fabius Maximus, who through the Senate prevailed on them to accept reconciliation, plainly saw potential.[8]

Hasdrubal had left Spain during 208 with a rebuilt army, wintered comfortably in southern Gaul and marched for the Alps in spring 207. He crossed these, reportedly by the same route as his brother but without any losses, arrived in Cisalpine Gaul earlier than his foes expected, and added large numbers of Gallic and Ligurian warriors to his forces. This was a textbook example of efficient achievement, very unlike Hannibal's messy experience 11 years before.

Hasdrubal was a skilful general as long as he was not facing opponents. Once on hostile ground he began to make mistakes, his first being an unnecessary siege of the Roman stronghold Placentia on the river Po. His aim was to impress the region's Gauls, but this backfired since he failed to take it. Worse, it lost him the momentum he had won by his early arrival in Italy. The new consuls had time to join their armies: Livius in the north, Nero watching Hannibal near Tarentum. Hasdrubal gave up the futile siege and moved south-eastwards to the Adriatic coast. Everything now hung in the balance. The fortune and future of Carthage depended on his joining up with Hannibal.[9]

IV

Hannibal knew he was coming. Locri, Metapontum and other ports still gave contact with Carthage, while new prisoners and deserters could tell of the Romans' plans and anxieties. If he were to stay in Apulia or Lucania, Hasdrubal would have to march most of the length of the Italian peninsula, 250–300 miles (400–500 kilometres), to join him—all the while fending off Livius and the other Roman forces that would swarm to block his path. It would make eminent good sense instead for Hannibal, whose knowledge of the terrain was now unrivalled, to move northwards to link up with the newcomers in or near Cisalpine Gaul. How fast he could move even in these times he had shown in 211 with the march on Rome, followed by the extraordinary lunge down to Rhegium, and again in 208 in his lightning thrust to raise the siege of Locri. As senior general it was his responsibility, too, to fix the arrangements with his brother, if only in broad terms initially while leaving greater precision to when the armies came closer.[10]

Hannibal did little of either. Livy's account has some oddities and maybe a textual error, but plainly shows him prowling restlessly around Apulia, shadowed by Nero and his watchful subordinates and unable to break away. This from the general who had pounced out of the mist on Flaminius and broken free of a trap laid by no less a foe than Fabius. He could not even get messengers or officers through to his brother to concert plans—or he did not try. It was left to Hasdrubal the newcomer to send off half a dozen riders, Numidians and Gauls at that, southwards in search of the Punic army of Italy. They carried a despatch asking Hannibal to link up with his brother's army in Umbria. Surprisingly enough they did penetrate all the way to Metapontum, where Hannibal had last been reported. But they found him gone—and as they doubled back searching for him they fell into the enemy's hands. Had Hasdrubal sent Roman or Italian deserters, this setback might have been avoided.[11]

Hannibal's behaviour almost gives the impression that he had decided to leave it entirely up to his brother to try to make contact and to propose how to join their armies. Since he sent no messengers to Hasdrubal—or even if he did—he had to expect that Hasdrubal would seek to send some to him; but he left no guides or escorts in any of the allied centres (like Metapontum) where such messengers might come looking for him. He moved around southern Italy, apparently seeking to break away from the Romans but in effect going about in circles.

Livy first has him marching from near Larinum in Apulia towards the Sallentine peninsula, the heel of Italy, before the consul Nero's arrival in the region. 'Larinum' may be a textual mistake for Tarentum, but such a manoeuvre looks pointless anyway; if it was a decoy force which later Roman historians misunderstood, the decoy-attempt failed after a collision with a Roman propraetor. Next—wherever he himself had really been—the general swung away south to Bruttium, gathered reinforcements and moved north into Lucania; he fought scrappily with Nero at Grumentum, went on to Venusia and another scrappy encounter, then southwards to Metapontum for more troops (recruited in Bruttium by Hanno). After that he moved once again to Venusia and came finally to rest near Canusium in northern Apulia.

Some of these marches and battles may well be Roman exaggerations, as Hannibal's alleged losses surely are, or else doublets (for instance the double set of Bruttian reinforcements). If all his movements are reliably reported, he must have covered at least as much ground as in a march from Bruttium to Umbria. In any case the outcome is clear. He advanced no further north than to Canusium, and there he came to a stop.[12]

One view is that, all along, Canusium was where he intended Hasdrubal to join him, contrary to his brother's call for them to meet in Umbria nearly 200 miles (300 kilometres) farther north, but this is hardly plausible. He may have had a high estimate of Hasdrubal's abilities, but it would have been asking too much: even supposing the latter could fight his way down the length of Italy he would have arrived with an army shrunken and devastated. Nor can Hannibal have notified his brother of any such intention, seeing that Hasdrubal was expecting him to come north—yet not to notify him would have been unbelievable folly. Much more likely, the halt at Canusium was meant to give messengers from his brother a chance to find him so that, at last, they could concert their moves.

The idea that Hasdrubal's despatch about Umbria was a deliberate red herring, meant to mislead the Romans, is hardly plausible either. It would mean that Hasdrubal sent off no genuine message at all or, if he did get one through, that it had no effect (for it is quite unlikely that a genuine message would tell Hannibal simply to stay quiet in Apulia while his brother fought his way down). Claudius Nero took the despatch with deadly seriousness. He warned the Senate at Rome to station the urban legions at Narnia and himself took an action that changed history.

Hasdrubal's proposal for a junction in Umbria was asking a lot of his brother, but no more than the task Hasdrubal himself had undertaken. Both were facing powerful enemy forces with limited numbers. Umbria was nearer Cisalpine Gaul than Apulia, but Hasdrubal had crossed over from Spain and now had to make his contested way from the Cisalpine plains through unfamiliar hills, dales and mountains. Hannibal knew the country and had proved to the world his skills in moving swiftly and in eluding foes. If they could join up, Umbria offered a notable strategic advantage: the fertile Tiber valley and the major new road from Ariminum to Rome, the Via Flaminia.

This is a clue to Hasdrubal's thinking, which may well have been his brother's too if they had been in touch, via Carthage, before the younger Barcid left Spain or while he was *en route*: the joint armies should make Rome their objective. A vigorous redirection of the war-effort, breaking free from the frustrating cul-de-sac of Apulia and Bruttium, would be a bold move quite in Hannibal's style. It would not mean abandoning the pro-Punic Italians of the south to Roman mercies. The towns were garrisoned, his indefatigable nephew Hanno could be left with a mobile army once more and, if Hannibal and Hasdrubal did join forces and menace Rome, the bulk of enemy forces in the south would more or less inevitably be drawn northward too.[13]

Beyond that we can only guess at the brothers' hopes. To move against Rome would have to mean first defeating the swarms of Roman forces that would gather against them. Hannibal, eager for another and more conclusive Trasimene or Cannae, would be ready for that. A big victory or series of victories in the north might bring over some of the Etruscan cities, wavering and unhappy in their loyalty to the Romans and already a worry to the consul Livius. In fact the Romans knew or at least suspected that some Etruscan help had already reached Hasdrubal: later on a commission was set up to investigate how much and by whom. More Gauls would surely flock from Cisalpina to join the Barcid standards. Hannibal had probably heard too how, in 209, 12 of the 30 Latin colonies had declined to supply further levies for Roman armies, claiming physical exhaustion—a refusal they were still persisting in. Three of the recalcitrants lay in Umbria and Etruria: a major victory there might entice even them to change sides, and that might draw in others as well. Everything would build pressure on the Romans to concede peace at last. And even if that took time to happen, at Carthage meanwhile the insecure dominance by the Barcids and their friends would be immeasurably fortified.[14]

<h2 style="text-align:center">V</h2>

Whatever the possibilities they envisaged, the brothers' failure to keep in touch—or even to try very hard at keeping in touch—was a planning disaster second only to the costly crossing from Spain to Italy 11 years before. Hasdrubal's mistake in making only one effort at contact was outdone by Hannibal's failures, first to make any contact-effort at all and then, far too early in the campaigning season, to give up trying to move nearer the northern theatre of operations. Whether he thought there was still plenty of time—or came to despair of being able to achieve a junction—he thereby made effective nonsense of his brother's coming to Italy.

His inactivity stands in glaring contrast to the consul Nero's reaction once Hasdrubal's captured despatch was interpreted. After alerting the authorities at Rome and ordering the urban legions to Narnia, he selected 7,000 men from his army (1,000 of them cavalry), left a subordinate in charge of the rest, and led the select corps by forced marches to join his colleague Livius. Provisioned by the communities along the route and joined by many volunteers, his force swiftly reached Livius' army near Sena Gallica without Hannibal realizing where he had gone or even that he had gone.

Hasdrubal did notice that Livius was reinforced (despite the consuls' efforts to hide it) but was brought to battle beside the river Metaurus on 22 June. As usual he displayed no great generalship; by contrast, Claudius Nero again did. Prevented by an intervening hill from clashing with the enemy wing opposite, he marched some of his troops round behind Livius' heavily engaged forces to take Hasdrubal's Spaniards in flank and rear and roll up the Punic army. Hasdrubal had no flanking cavalry and his elephants proved useless. With the battle and the whole expedition lost, he spurred into the mêlée for an honourable death.[15]

This self-immolation aroused admiration in Polybius and Livy, and many others since, but arguably was another act of ill-judgement. Not all his army was destroyed and the surviving troops—anything between 5,000 and 15,000—managed to get away as a body, though it seems they afterwards dispersed. Had Hasdrubal survived to rally them in retreat he might have maintained a resistance in Cisalpine Gaul to distract the Romans and then to reinforce his brother Mago when the latter landed in northern Italy two years later. He would have enjoyed much support: much of Cisalpine Gaul was furiously anti-Roman and even after Hannibal's war ended fighting went on there, some of it led by a Carthaginian officer who had been there since 205 or even 207. At the least he would have denied the Romans a grisly propaganda coup. Nero bore the dead man's head back to Apulia and flung it at the feet of a Punic outpost, to be taken to Hannibal.[16]

Hannibal had sought Flaminius' body after Trasimene to give it proper burial, and had honourably buried the slain Aemilius Paullus after Cannae and Marcellus the year before this. But it was not for some generations yet that the Romans' hatred and fear of their invader would change to a grudging admiration. Hasdrubal was the first Carthaginian general in the war to fall in battle against them, in contrast to three consuls and three proconsuls since 217; besides, in the Romans' eyes he with his brothers had brought on this whole calamitous war. Nero's barbarism is comprehensible though not laudable.[17]

Hannibal recognized the import of the gift: he saw in it (Livy makes him say) 'the fortune of Carthage'. He could not win the war in Italy any more. Now it had always been obvious that defeat for his brother would mean this: which makes it all the more extraordinary how completely he had been outgeneralled by the Romans. Not only had Nero brought him to a stop at Canusium, but the general then let himself be cajoled into remaining there while the consul vanished with a sizeable contingent. Nero supposedly gave out that he was leaving to subdue a still-hostile Lucanian town and its Punic garrison. If this item of disinformation crossed to Hannibal it at least told him that the Romans were dividing their forces right in front of him, and that a nearby stronghold of his was in danger. If he did not hear it, he might at least have noticed afterwards that the enemy forces facing him were fewer and have received some reports or rumours of Nero's vigorous dash for the north.

True, Livy implies that march, battle and return march all took a mere 12 or 15 days, but even that would have given time enough to take advantage of the situation. In any case modern scholars plausibly urge that so short an interval is hardly believable, for Livius' army and the Metaurus were a good 300 miles (400 kilometres) from Canusium. The longer Nero really was absent, the less can Hannibal be absolved from the error of culpable inactivity. It was his last chance to exploit Hasdrubal's arrival in Italy: either to strike at the remaining Roman forces in turn (the rest of Nero's army under an untried subordinate, Q. Catius, and the propraetor Fulvius Flaccus in Lucania) or indeed to imitate Nero and lead a flying column north to join Hasdrubal (Hanno could replace him in the south). The latter move would have been more like the Hannibal of the early days—and would probably have brought about a different outcome at the Metaurus.[18]

Instead he paid the price for waiting on events. He abandoned Lucania, abandoned even Metapontum—forcing its citizens to follow him—and withdrew into Bruttium, with Croton, Caulonia and Locri his seaports. Roman armies followed, watchful as usual but uninterested in battle. Too weak to break out, too strong to be attacked, Hannibal and his men would spend the last four years of the epic expedition virtually under open siege in this corner of Italy, while the fortunes of the Carthaginian state went from one disaster to another.

XIII

AFRICA INVADED

I

After the Metaurus Hannibal made no further military moves apart from guarding his south Italian turf—not always successfully even there, for the rich prize of Locri would fall to the enemy in 205. To judge from his actions, or lack of them, he had decided to wage only a holding action with the forces left to him. He would hold on as long as possible, to distract the enemy from fresh thoughts of invading Africa—though it was being raided almost every year—while hoping that Hasdrubal son of Gisco might somehow turn the tables on young Scipio in Spain, as the dead Hasdrubal had done against Scipio's elders.

This was not much of a hope, for the son of Gisco had shown (and would show) as little aptitude for defeating Romans as Hasdrubal the Barcid had. Nor would the prospect be all that pleasing if he did. Mago was with him, but any lustre he might win would be secondary. A successful son of Gisco would pose nearly as great a danger to the Barcids as would defeats, for it would mean an independent gaining victories while Hannibal could not.

This decision for holding tight was a strange one. The Carthaginians' war-effort was far from exhausted. A new general and new army had been sent to Spain late in 208 or early in 207 and fresh forces were raised among the Celtiberians—even though Livy reports Scipio's subordinate Silanus as swiftly defeating Mago and the new general and taking the latter prisoner. But Hasdrubal son of Gisco once more raised a powerful army to confront him in battle in 206, an army of colossal strength according to Polybius' figures— 70,000 infantry and 4,000 cavalry, almost the size of the mighty Roman army of Cannae. Whatever the right figure, the Carthaginians plainly still had enough resources as well as energy to achieve an armament which they hoped would finally crush the invader.

Of course Scipio put an end to that hope at Ilipa and by the end of 206 Punic rule had ended throughout Spain. Hasdrubal betook himself back to Africa, leaving Mago to fight whatever rearguard actions he wished. The youngest Barcid was ruthless—when Gades showed itself fickle, he seized and crucified its chief magistrates as a payback—and energetic, as in his effort *en route* to the Balearic islands to repeat Scipio's coup of capturing New Carthage, but no more successful than the son of Gisco in delaying the total loss of his father's empire.[1]

Yet Punic resourcefulness was not finished. When Scipio sailed across to Syphax's coastal stronghold Siga to try winning over the Numidian (it would have been a major coup if he had), he found Hasdrubal son of Gisco a fellow-guest of the king, and Hasdrubal secured Syphax for Carthage despite Scipio's charm. Hasdrubal could offer a unique inducement—his daughter Sophoniba as Syphax's new wife—but more than romance was surely needed to bind the Numidian's loyalty. He must have reckoned that in Africa at least the Carthaginians' prospects still looked better than a Roman invader's.

Syphax before long improved his and his new allies' position by making himself master of all Numidia. Originally he was lord of the Masaesyli of western Numidia, and it was Naravas' brother Gaia who as lord of the Massyli held the east. He had been firmly loyal to the Carthaginians' and the Barcids' cause, and his son Masinissa had rendered years of sterling service in Spain. On Gaia's death in 206 the old king's brother and successor Oezalces married a young niece of Hannibal's—one of his sisters' daughters—thus carrying on the tradition of Barcid links to Numidian royalty.

Hannibal, as head of the family, must have approved the marriage and very likely had initiated it, to ensure that the Massylian alliance would continue in spite of recent Punic disasters. With Syphax on friendly terms too, thanks to Hasdrubal son of Gisco, it meant that all Numidia should be secure against Roman blandishments. But Oezalces' early death, and contacts between Masinissa and the Romans, brought trouble. Oezalces' elder son and successor soon fell to the machinations of another ambitious lord, Mazaetullus, who forcibly put the younger brother in place of the elder, became the power behind the new throne and took Hannibal's widowed niece as his own wife in hope of Carthaginian support—another token of the Barcid group's continuing potency. Hannibal may have acquiesced in this coup (at any rate Mazaetullus and his puppet king were afterwards allowed refuge in Punic territory), but Masinissa now ousted the ousters to make himself master of the Massyli. Syphax, prompted by his new father-in-law, then ousted him in turn and united the whole of Numidia under his own rule.

Hasdrubal's political strength at home can only have profited from the success of his son-in-law. Nor was Masinissa's overthrow a blow against Barcid interests: his enemy Mazaetullus had won Punic favour by marrying Hannibal's niece, whereas his own contacts with the Romans were suspected or known by now at Carthage. The Numidians united under a pro-Punic king were plainly preferable to a Numidia divided and its eastern folk under a dubious or even hostile ruler.[2]

Mago meanwhile was given command of a new expedition from the Balearic islands to Italy, this time by sea with 14,000 troops, including about

2,000 cavalry. After seizing Genua (today's Genoa) on the Ligurian coast in 205, he received nearly 7,000 more men and even a few elephants, not to mention substantial funds for hiring extra troops. This again points to collaboration between the Barcids and Hasdrubal son of Gisco: the forces and funds committed were substantial, the military move plainly serious—in fact it was the Carthaginians' last overseas effort.

On the other hand, Mago's landing in Liguria, 550 miles (900 kilometres) or so from his brother at the opposite end of Italy, was only the latest peculiarity in the war-effort. Had he tried for Bruttium and had just some of his troops got through with or without him, they would have contributed more to Hannibal than the whole force did when deposited in Liguria, too few in number to dent the Romans' north Italian array and too far away to be any use to the general. No doubt Bruttium would have been a hazardous attempt, with Roman fleets patrolling, but ancient fleets always had difficulties doing this—and in any case in 206 the Roman fleet in Sicily had been cut from 100 warships to 30. In 203 Hannibal would take himself and at least some troops over to Africa quite safely.[3]

Moreover the Carthaginians still had warships even if no fleet after 211 numbered as many as 100. Despite Roman naval might, in 209 and again in 207 a Punic fleet operated in western Greek waters, intending to support Philip of Macedon's campaigns in Greece—though it failed in this and its absence from south Italian waters in 209 aided Fabius' recovery of Tarentum. True, in 208 Valerius Laevinus won a victory (the biggest of the war) over the 80 ships that tried to stop him raiding North Africa. But more ships could have been built and may have been—to judge from the naval activities in following years and seeing that, when peace was made in 201, Scipio had large numbers of war-vessels to burn. In other words, the Carthaginians in these years still had significant naval resources, but used them poorly.[4]

Now operational matters were still Hannibal's to direct. This is shown not just by Polybius' insistence but by such evidence as there is. For instance the expedition to Liguria: it is hard to imagine why an anti-Barcid faction, if it now held power at Carthage, would choose their enemy's brother as commander. Not only was Mago chosen but he was later reinforced and supplied with copious funds. Hannibal surely had to be consulted at least, and quite probably he was the initiator. Again, on his own return to Africa in 203 he continued in supreme command: Hasdrubal son of Gisco, hitherto in inglorious charge of home defence, had been sacked and his interim replacement was—according to Appian—Hanno son of Bomilcar, who sounds like Hannibal's nephew (and, if Appian can be believed, it was Hannibal who saved Hasdrubal from vengeful prosecution at Carthage).

Obviously the general did not and could not direct operations in detail in other lands and at sea, any more than a Roman emperor did in later times. Details were the business of the commanders *in situ*. In the same way he had to leave it to the authorities at Carthage to administer Punic North Africa, gather and embark troops and supplies for abroad, and organize defence against raids or invasion. But ultimate responsibility for major initiatives had to be his. Nothing suggests that he had to impose his wishes on a reluctant home government or was thwarted at times by one—even if later on the Carthaginians chose to claim so. Had he opposed the fleets being sent to Greece, it is hard to imagine they would still have gone. Had he directed the home authorities to send him regular supplies and money, they would have made the effort, as in fact they did in 205. And had he wished Mago's fleet and the later reinforcements to sail for southern Italy, that would at least have been tried.

But on naval matters Hannibal had always been a landlubber. As was suggested earlier, most naval initiatives stemmed probably from Barcid kinsmen or supporters at Carthage, where the main fleets remained based. Even where he probably had originated an initiative—for instance sending a fleet into Etruscan waters in 217, and the fleet that sailed to Tarentum in 211 to prevent enemy ships from resupplying the citadel—he still had to rely on others to carry it out. This was a bad handicap when the quality of Punic naval commanders was unimpressive. Bomilcar, the most active of them, had been energetic but largely unsuccessful and is not heard of after 211 anyway.

It may well have seemed attractive, even rational, to send fleets over to Greece in hopes of encouraging Philip V. It may have seemed more sensible too for Mago to head for a part of Italy where he was totally unexpected, avoiding the perils of being intercepted or being confronted by Roman forces as soon as he landed. That such initiatives could only indirectly affect the real war-effort, while spreading around resources that would have better been focussed on south Italy, was a fact that obviously failed to affect the planning.

In other words the naval advice offered to Hannibal in these later years, and any naval moves he himself devised, were second-rate—to term it mildly. Opportunities were not taken, bold though risky efforts not even (it seems) considered, and instead available resources were ineptly used. This ineptness, compounded with his own caution on land, reduced his strategic rôle during these years to a nullity.[5]

The energy and resourcefulness that had once typified him now showed itself instead in the Romans: the consul Nero in 207, and more lastingly P. Scipio the younger in Spain. Scipio, though frustrated in south Spain by Hasdrubal son of Gisco in 207, reinvaded the following year and overthrew the Carthaginians in a mighty battle at Ilipa near either Hispalis (modern Seville) or more likely Castulo. He won by putting his legions on either wing through an involved but skilful manoeuvre which outdid in subtlety anything Hannibal had ever tried and which was too much for the son of Gisco. It must have confirmed to Hannibal that the Romans had produced a commander who could equal him. He surely reckoned it was only a matter of time till they met.[6]

Scipio's efficient follow-up to his victory drove Hasdrubal over to North Africa and Mago to the Balearic islands, though Mago did make some last-ditch efforts to keep a foothold on the mainland. Once Gades had surrendered, Carthaginian rule in Spain—created by Hamilcar Barca, consolidated by Hasdrubal his son-in-law and extended furthest by Hannibal—was over. Apart from Hannibal's cramped zone in Italy beside the Ionian sea, Carthaginian territory now was limited to North Africa itself. The Romans' next target was obvious.

II

It would be easy to blame the Barcids' enemies at home for wrecking Hannibal's prospects, and their own country's, through failing to send help to him in Italy and showing greater devotion to the war-effort in Spain. Livy offers the latter claim at just this stage and he and other ancient writers have Hannibal complain in 203 about being denied resources and left in the lurch—thanks to Hanno the Great, Livy has him add. Many moderns agree: Hannibal was let down by the home authorities. The truth, though, looks more complex.[7]

No doubt Hannibal's and his supporters' position at home suffered, probably badly, after the Metaurus. Eleven years after leading the Punic state into war he was holed up in a corner of Italy, and the Spanish empire—the Barcids' greatest gift to their fellow-Carthaginians—was close to collapse. Hasdrubal son of Gisco had become its prime defender and he, as suggested earlier, was an independent leader in his own right though allied with the Barcids: an alliance probably due to patriotism and expediency rather than any personal or family closeness.

Yet this cannot mean that Hannibal's and his supporters' influence in affairs collapsed. Livy's and others' claims that he lacked home support simply continue the litany dating back to Fabius Pictor (and probably Fabius' Carthaginian contacts) who blamed the entire war on the Barcids to exonerate the rest of the aristocracy. Even if the home authorities had turned hostile, there was no profit for them or their city in trying to make Hannibal's life miserable. Were his position to become untenable or he to be destroyed, it would simply free the Romans to unleash their fury on North Africa. In any case the historical record does not support the notion. Least of all did old Hanno the Great and his friends benefit from Barcid misfortunes.

The Carthaginians in reality remained full of fight. When C. Laelius raided North Africa in 205 they certainly suffered alarm and fear, but Livy then attests them taking energetic and wide-ranging defensive measures—raising troops, gathering munitions, readying the fleet. With Hasdrubal son of Gisco back home by then and effectively in charge, this vigorously practical reaction is explicable. Livy's picture of the Carthaginans' gloomy spirits, even if he based it on comments in an informed source, is at best overdrawn and certainly is no pointer to anti-war feeling. They were to remain pugnacious even amid disaster in 203, as their spirited reaction to Scipio's destruction of Hasdrubal's and Syphax's camps and armies would make clear; and so did their dealings with Scipio later in 203, as we shall see, even though by then Hasdrubal's repeated defeats had eclipsed him politically.

Even after Zama in 202 a prominent senator urged them to fight on, and when Hannibal unceremoniously shut him up the rest of the Mighty Ones, far from approving, were so annoyed that the general had to apologize. When peace was finally made in 201 a younger leader of the dogged Hanno the Great's anti-Barcid circle—yet another Hasdrubal, obscurely nicknamed 'the Kid'—assured the Roman Senate that even though he and Hanno had long been urging peace on the Carthaginians, they had been ignored.[8]

Interestingly enough, after the Metaurus and Ilipa no one at Carthage seems to have suggested that the time had come to make peace-overtures. In 255 when hard pressed by the invading Regulus, the Carthaginians had offered to talk, and report or legend had it that some years later they sent the same man, now their prisoner, to urge peace at Rome. Arguably it would now be in their own best interests to see whether they could reach some sort of compromise settlement—even if it meant sacrificing Spain. But had any overture been made we should have heard of it, for Roman annalists would hardly let such a sign of weakness slip by unmentioned.

Perhaps Hannibal, Hasdrubal and their countrymen felt that the Romans, who had refused to negotiate after Cannae, would take nothing less than unconditional surrender (an opinion almost certainly wrong, as Scipio's terms in both 203 and 202 were to show). Perhaps they felt too that even now the situation might change if only Hannibal held on. More of the Romans' exhausted allies might withhold men and munitions, as several had from 209 on; the general might yet win a big victory in the south; in Spain, till 206, or afterwards in Liguria, the other Punic commanders might pull off a lifesaving success; Philip V might somehow master Greece and be able to lend help; Numidia unified under Syphax could help make Africa unconquerable by invaders and that in turn might prompt the enemy to offer terms.

Barcid pride and self-interest would contribute as well. Appian tells a story set during the siege of Capua in 211 in which Hannibal refuses to relieve the city because, he says, if the war were to end he would lose his generalship. This looks like an invention or, if based on fact, like an ironic Hannibalic joke put into the wrong context: it would better illustrate his position and his worries around 206. Returning home under a compromise, after all the expectations of victory, would be not just humiliating but politically perilous. It would certainly end his supreme command, and with it what was left of Barcid primacy in the state.[9]

But refusing to consider offering terms was not just Hannibal's personal attitude. As mentioned above, his fellow-Carthaginians, senators and ordinary citizens, were ready to fight on. The very fact that their homeland and city were now liable to be invaded no doubt strengthened their resolve—just as the invasion of Italy in 218 had strengthened the Romans'. Politically the danger may well have buttressed Hannibal's own authority despite his set-backs and strategic isolation. After all, as war-leader they had no ready alternative: Hasdrubal son of Gisco, however formidable he had become in domestic affairs, still had no aura of victory against the Romans, though he would keep trying.

Thus the Carthaginians' overall commitment to the war meant continuing to support the Barcids in practice—and any others who also devoted them-selves to it, the son of Gisco most obviously. By now Barcid political primacy can have rested only on the qualified consent of other leading aristocrats, notably the son of Gisco and his supporters, and so on a great deal of bar-gaining, compromise and give-and-take; plus the fact (as it seems) that no one wanted to give the primacy to Hanno the Great and his anti-war circle. Whether much enthusiasm continued for Barcid political primacy may be doubted. After 207 all the factors that had brought Hamilcar and his succes-sors their mastery of the state had dwindled: charismatic leadership (with Hasdrubal dead and Hannibal becalmed), continual victories, territorial expansion and regular widely shared booty. All that the Carthaginians had left was the darkening war, and memories.

The élite tribunal of One Hundred and Four, in particular, need not have felt that it or the republic owed all that much any more to Hannibal and his family and friends. There was no question of attacking him in the midst of the war, or even of attacking him at all (it did not happen after the war ended). But equally there was no need for sentiment. If he could yet save something from the wreck of Punic fortunes, there would continue to be room for him and his followers at the highest levels of public life. If he could not, he and they need not expect to play a major rôle in Carthage's future. Many other aristocrats, no doubt including former friends and protégés of the Barcids themselves, were ready to take on that rôle—especially members of the Hundred and Four.

In other words, during these years the dominance of the 'order of judges', as Livy terms them, was very likely emerging, or more accurately re-emerging after decades of Barcid overshadowing.[10]

III

In 205 P. Scipio, barely 30 and now consul, took command of Roman forces in Sicily with a commission to prepare the invasion of Africa. The opponents of this project, led by the old and cautious Fabius the Delayer, demanded total concentration on Hannibal first: 'let there be peace in Italy before there is war in Africa', says Fabius in the speech Livy gives him. Not only would invasion mean a new army outside Italy for the hard-hit Roman treasury to maintain, but the thought of what Hannibal might yet do while their best general was overseas was worrying to many Romans (in Livy, Fabius frets that he might even march on the city again). Even though the opponents of invasion were outvoted, their worry was clearly shared by others, for Scipio was not allowed to conscript troops but only to accept volunteers, as well as using the forces already in Sicily—the survivors of Cannae and other disasters, some of them already in their twelfth year of service. This gave him some four legions, though he also had a fleet. Hannibal in south Italy was still watched by as many as seven.

The sharp anxiety felt by so many Romans about Scipio's project testifies to the fear that Hannibal still caused. This even though he was doing almost nothing in his region: in 206 he gave the consuls a fright in a gorge near Consentia, then let them bring Lucania back to heel while he stayed quiet in Bruttium. He spent some of his time composing the record of his military career which, the year after, he set up as an inscription in both Punic and Greek in the temple of Hera at Cape Lacinium (now Capo Colonna, the name commemorating its ruins) near Croton. In the far north he had a brother equally cautious or sluggish. Had he shown greater energy and a spark of his old inventiveness, he could well have excited such fresh alarm at Rome that Fabius' side would have won the debate against Scipio's. That was surely now a major part of his mission in Italy—to keep Africa free of invasion. Instead of trying to fulfil it, the general busied himself with his memoirs, a discouraging sign.

During the year, though, he did come near to a confrontation with his new rival. Locri went over to the enemy but one of its two citadels remained Punic-occupied. The standoff drew both Hannibal southwards from his cantonment and Scipio from Messana in Sicily. The Romans under Scipio made a sortie as Hannibal's army moved up to the assault—and Hannibal withdrew, followed at night by his Locri garrison. It was a performance neither glorious—Scipio beat him to the city and kept his prize—nor particularly skilful, but fateful. Scipio with a few thousand Roman troops at Locri was surely outnumbered even if Hannibal came south with only part of his army. Destroying him would have prevented Zama and so, even now, have changed history.

No further opportunity offered itself. Instead an epidemic of some kind struck the region, damaging both the Roman forces there and—more severely—Hannibal's, which Livy reports as also short of food. Livy avers elsewhere that the general controlled too little territory to guarantee enough local produce for his men, but since he then seems to have had no food trouble in 204 and 203 maybe the harvest was poor in 205. His shortage would have been eased had a supply fleet from Carthage, 80 strong, made it to his coast but—in yet another lacklustre Punic naval performance—this was blown wildly off-course into Sardinian waters and taken by the Romans.[11]

In 204 Scipio sailed from Lilybaeum in Sicily to Africa, landing at Utica, 30 miles (50 kilometres) north of Carthage. Although he had only 40 warships to escort his transports, the Carthaginians' fleet completely but predictably failed to intercept him or fall on him as he disembarked; and although they had known for a year that he planned to come, they had no proper forces in hand to confront him. This hardly reflects well on Hasdrubal son of Gisco's leadership in Africa. Instead the city suffered a ferment of alarm and feverish preparation—exactly as one year earlier when Laelius raided—while the Roman army set about establishing itself on Carthaginian soil and was joined by the exiled Masinissa. The first Punic efforts against it were left to small cavalry forces with predictably disastrous results. Then by the time Hasdrubal and his son-in-law Syphax mobilized proper armies, it was winter and—even though they had Scipio cooped up on a narrow peninsula, with his fleet beached and communications overseas seasonally impossible—they were content to set up their camps not far inland from his. Syphax, encouraged by Hasdrubal, even began negotiations with him about a compromise end to the war.

Hannibal's priorities amid all this are a puzzle. During the same year he scrapped inconclusively in Bruttium with the Romans and lost still more strongpoints, including Consentia and Clampetia—probably his last footholds on the western side of Bruttium. The following year's campaigning was yet more inconclusive (Livy merely repeats some of the events of 204 without noticing the doublets) until he was recalled home. All this while Punic Africa was invaded by the enemy's foremost general, who threatened Carthage with direct attack and in 203 was to win one victory after another.

It is hard to see what prevented Hannibal from returning in 204 rather than waiting, as he did, until his countrymen had suffered these devastations and defeats. Arguably the Romans might have intercepted him at sea *en route*, but the risk was still there in 203 when he did cross successfully. The squadron guarding the Italian coasts was only 50 strong in 204 (though it fell to 40 in 203); in fact the Romans' overall naval strength in the earlier year was less than in the later one. Returning in 204 would have put at his disposal the resources and armaments, including the Numidian allied forces, with which Hasdrubal confronted Scipio in 204 and 203—disastrously as usual—and to them Hannibal would have added his veterans from Italy.[12]

The reason for staying where he was more likely political than military. As was noted earlier, the leading Carthaginian in North Africa by 204 was the son of Gisco: an independent partner now, with his own friends and following. By 204 Hannibal and his supporters could run Carthaginian affairs only in coalition with such an ally, and this would require allowing Hasdrubal scope to exercise authority. If so, the command in Punic Africa, whatever his actual title and official relation to Hannibal, was Hasdrubal's price for supporting the Barcids politically.

So too with the negotiations over winter 204–203 between him and Syphax on one side and Scipio on the other. Syphax played (or Scipio led him to believe he was playing) the mediator's part, while it was Hasdrubal who spoke for the Carthaginians. No doubt, for political reasons, any agreement would have had to gain Hannibal's approval, but nothing suggests that Hannibal was consulted or even kept informed as the talks proceeded—something the winter would have made difficult anyway.

All the same, the terms that Syphax proffered with Hasdrubal's blessing, and that Scipio for a time professed to find agreeable, were ones that Hannibal surely would approve at this bleak stage of the war. The Romans should evacuate Africa, the Carthaginians Italy, and each side should keep 'the positions in between' that they currently held. This effectively meant ceding Spain too to the Romans, even if it was not expressly mentioned: in other words, sacrificing what the Barcids had built. But Hannibal, though he might grieve at the sacrifice, was certainly realistic enough to face what had to be done to achieve peace. He was, it seems, willing to offer much the same a year later when he met Scipio before Zama.[13]

IV

Scipio, it turned out, was using the long-drawn-out talks to lull his opponents' alertness and spy out their two camps. He finally told them that while he liked the terms, his counsellors did not, and left them to infer that the talks were over. Yet the terms were essentially those he offered later in 203, and close to those he imposed after the battle of Zama in 202, after more battles and vastly more bloodshed. True, these later terms had extra clauses, notably a heavy indemnity and limitations on the Carthaginians' war-making capacity. By contrast the implication in Syphax's terms, so far as we have them, was peace on the status quo alone. Did Scipio decide it was worth continuing the war to squeeze those extra concessions out of the Carthaginians, as a way of reducing the Carthaginian state to impotence?

That is possible: yet then it is puzzling why even the final terms were not more sweeping. In the peace of 201 Punic Africa was not bound tightly to Roman dominance, for instance by making Carthage and other cities like Utica and Hippou dependent Roman allies, even by annexing some Punic territory. Hannibal himself was left unmolested and free to hold further office—conceivably even a fresh generalship. True, by then Numidia was under the rule of Masinissa, who in the following decades would prove a thorn in the Carthaginians' side, but this was hardly foreseeable in 201. Masinissa had had close Carthaginian ties before and his notorious episode with Hasdrubal son of Gisco's daughter Sophoniba in 203 might be a warning that such ties could easily be resumed. Plainly such possibilities did not trouble the Roman peacemaker.

Did Scipio have much larger aims initially, say the total dismemberment of the Carthaginian state, and so break off the talks to achieve them—only to find the ensuing campaigns, including the one in 202 against Hannibal, so arduous that he had to scale his aims down to the terms finally imposed? It is unlikely, for the victories he won were not all that costly to him (even Zama cost only some 1,500 Roman casualties) and after Zama the Carthaginians lay at his mercy. Nor was the notion of dismembering the Punic state ever raised, any more than the idea of sacking and destroying Carthage itself.

Did he, then, break off the talks so as to chase military glory against Hasdrubal and inevitably Hannibal? He was running the dual risks of being defeated in battle or being replaced by another ambitious commander who fancied his own abilities (as more than one consul did in the coming years). But if he was anywhere near as confident in his own genius as Polybius, other ancient writers and many moderns believe, these were risks he would judge worth taking for the sake of imperishable renown. He may even have hoped that the surprise destruction of Syphax's and Hasdrubal's camps and armies might liquidate those leaders too, putting Carthage with one stroke at his mercy.[14]

If so he was disappointed, but the survival of both men did them little lasting good. While Hannibal prowled around his virtual cage in Bruttium under the watchful eyes of the usual Roman armies, Hasdrubal energetically as usual—within 30 days if Polybius' figure is right, but more probably within 50—raised fresh troops from the city and countryside, made a rendezvous on the Great Plains 75 miles (120 kilometres) inland with a new Numidian army likewise put together by Syphax, was also joined by some Celtiberian mercenaries just arrived from Spain, and then with them and Syphax was shatteringly defeated by Scipio all over again. Only the doomed valour of the Celtiberians allowed Hasdrubal and his local forces to escape. Syphax, pursued all the way back to his own land, was soon beaten and captured by Masinissa and Scipio's lieutenant Laelius, a prize which led his capital, Cirta, to surrender. This brought much of the Numidian kingdom into Masinissa's hands, with Scipio's blessing once the new king got rid of Syphax's wife with whom he had rashly fallen in love, Hasdrubal's beautiful daughter Sophoniba.[15]

At the same time the fleet at Carthage bungled an attack against Scipio's ships at anchor near Utica, an attack that might have done something to redress his land victory if the fleet commanders had fully exploited Scipio's absence inland. Instead they waited until his return march took him to Tunes, from where he could see their ships put out to sea. They then took overnight to reach the Romans' roadstead, allowing him to get by land to his encampment and organize defence. As a result the Punic attack was beaten off with limited Roman losses. This last action in the war by the navy of Carthage lived up to the ineptitude it had shown more or less consistently since 218.

Hasdrubal son of Gisco now disappears from Polybius' and Livy's narratives. Appian may be right that his infuriated fellow-citizens removed him from his generalship, even voted his death—a common penalty in pre-Barcid times for military failure. Much more dubiously, Appian has him raise a rough-and-ready force on his own account, including slaves, and carry on resistance to the Romans for a time (a friendly tradition may have invented this). During 202, according to Appian, he died—forced to kill himself to avoid being lynched by an angry mob in the city. Dead in any case was his pre-eminence in the state. If his faction did not completely disintegrate, at least many of its members must have betaken themselves elsewhere. With few of them likely to gravitate to Hanno the Great's peace-group, the biggest beneficiaries of his ruin were probably the Barcids.

If Appian is right, the new general by land was Hanno son of Bomilcar, who as noted earlier may be Hannibal's nephew, last heard of in Bruttium in 207: if so Hannibal must have sent him back to Carthage. But whoever did take over the command plainly could do little except await the enemy's next move, and press Hannibal to come home.[16]

XIV

DEFEAT

With their only ally Syphax fallen, Hasdrubal's generalship discredited, the countryside open to the invader—and already inclined to rebellion, Polybius claims, because of heavy war-taxation—and Scipio preparing to blockade their city, the Carthaginians had only two real alternatives: seek terms from the enemy, or carry on the fight and recall Hannibal and Mago from their useless footholds in Italy. Dispirited yet still pugnacious, the Punic senate promptly did both.

This was not due to a compromise between peace-inclined doves and warlike hawks in the aristocracy. Not only was the most obvious peace-group, Hanno the Great and his friends, sidelined as before but such a combination of peace-moves and war-moves was not so much a compromise as a self-contradiction. Everyone had to be aware that at some stage—not too distant—the Carthaginians would have to choose one course or the other and stick to it. Even if a faction of doves did push the senate into seeking terms, they could have got their way only with support from a majority of senate and citizens: the same senate and citizens who equally supported recalling the Barcid brothers. But though doves there surely were at Carthage (Hanno the Great's circle at least) they probably played little part in 203. When the time to choose came later that year, the great majority chose war and there is no evidence of opposition from any doves.

More likely the decision to seek peace-terms and simultaneously send for Hannibal and Mago was pushed through by the same men: the battered but still vigorous Barcid group of kinsmen and supporters, now probably enlarged by ex-supporters of the fallen Hasdrubal, maybe led by the new Punic field commander Hanno if this was Hannibal's nephew, and in collaboration with other bellicose senators. This coalition could command a majority in the senate and its inner 'sacred council', and hold the support of the tribunal of One Hundred and Four and of the citizen body generally. Hannibal and his supporters thus had one last chance to restore Barcid dominance enduringly—so long as they won the war or, at the very least, did not lose the peace.[1]

Seeking terms and simultaneously sending for the brothers now became official decisions of the Carthaginian state, decreed by its senate and backed by its citizens. The Romans could scarcely see them in any other light and the Carthaginians never denied it. There was in other words an element of insincerity, if not duplicity, built into the approach they made to Scipio. This makes sense only as a calculated risk. The most that the Carthaginians could now hope for from peace-terms was to keep Punic North Africa intact while giving up everything else, and even this they could not count on. Far harsher Roman demands were conceivable: not only a heavy indemnity but territorial cessions, the destruction of the navy and the ports, even the surrender of Carthage itself to Roman occupation like so many other cities in the war. The only bargaining-chips left were Hannibal, Mago and their armies.

Yet for bargaining purposes the brothers were useless in Italy. The Romans had their measure. That summer Mago was defeated and seriously wounded in Cisalpine Gaul, putting an effective end to his expedition and making his brother's even more questionable. Plainly not even a new march on Rome (even were it feasible, as Fabius Maximus reportedly feared) would deflect Scipio in Africa. If things continued this way, the last three fading foci of Punic power—Hannibal's army, Mago's, and Carthage itself—would merely wither separately into ultimate surrender.

But if all three could join forces, there was still a chance of ending the war on less than disastrous terms. The fighting spirit at Carthage would be reinforced, Scipio would face the risks of battle against the greatest general of the age and might prefer to compromise on moderate terms, and if warfare did drag on there might yet be pressure at Rome to end it on such terms. There was, too, the possibility of Scipio being replaced by another commander—who more than likely would be easier prey for Hannibal. From the Carthaginians' point of view it was not just sensible but even essential to recall the Barcids at the same time as they sought peace, and what looked sensible at Carthage cannot have looked otherwise in Bruttium.

It cannot be supposed that Hannibal was ignorant of the peace-talks that now opened with Scipio, or disapproved of them. He may even have known (from prisoners or traders, for instance) that by now, in the greatest irony of the war, the Roman Senate was anxious to keep him and Mago in Italy and had ordered the consuls to see to it, obviously to prevent the brothers from complicating Scipio's life. But it would take time to organize transport to Africa and, if hostilities there were pressed meanwhile, his countrymen— already suffering hunger under the Roman blockade—might yet be forced into capitulation. Peace negotiations made military sense.

The same calculations would be obvious to Scipio. But he took a calculated risk too: that if strong enough pressure was put on the Carthaginians before the Barcid brothers could leave Italy, he could force a victorious end to the war. It is much less likely that he wanted a pause merely so that Hannibal could return and be defeated by him. Not only was any battle's outcome unpredictable, as Regulus had found in 255, but at least one consul in 203 was keen to supplant him in Africa so as to win that glory for himself, and Scipio had no guarantee that the next year's pair would leave him alone either. According to Livy, his trusted lieutenant Laelius in person made it clear to the Senate that Scipio did not want Hannibal and Mago back in Africa until peace was made: a comment distorted in Livy's telling, as we shall see, but in itself probable enough.

If peace was made the Barcids would still have to come home, of course—but peaceably. Even after Zama, Scipio was uninterested in capturing or humiliating Hannibal. Had lasting peace been made in 203, he would no doubt have been satisfied with the brothers returning and entering civil life and their armies being disbanded. In sum, an early peace was attractive to him too, so long as it made the Romans' victory clear. Thus both he and the Carthaginians, for quite opposite reasons, had reason to press on with talks.[2]

II

The talks were not lengthy. The thirty senators of the 'sacred council' went to Scipio at Tunes and prostrated themselves Persian-style before him and his war-council—quite possibly an exaggerated flattery for the Romans' benefit, since prostration is not otherwise known among Carthaginians and, a Polybian excerpt reports, the envoys even kissed the Romans' feet. This certainly riveted the Romans' attention.

According to Livy the envoys proceeded to lay all the blame for the war on Hannibal and ask for fair terms. Polybius' account does not survive but, in seeming contrast, the later excerpt has a Roman spokesman remind the Carthaginians that their envoys had accepted all the blame—obviously in the name of the Punic state. Even so this does not disprove Livy's report. Hannibal was the elected generalissimo of the state, acting in its name and sanctioned by senate and citizenry. Even if they sought to blame him for devising the war, they could not deny that the republic had agreed to it (and had told the Roman envoys so in 218). At worst Livy is guilty of focussing on the envoys' blame of Hannibal to the exclusion of any broader admission by them. Roman historical tradition, moralizing and cantankerous towards foes, was partial to such an individual focus. As for the envoys, blaming the absent general was a predictable rhetorical and diplomatic ploy which Scipio did not take seriously (his terms for peace said nothing about war-guilt). Later, though, some Romans were to prove credulous, like the historian Fabius Pictor.[3]

What is noteworthy is Hannibal's uninvolvement in the negotiations, both now and later at Rome. The sources narrate him and his doings as though these were an entirely separate affair, and none records him being consulted on the transactions or even being told of them. This is hard to believe, given that the Romans were aware of his relevance and given that he was the generalissimo of Carthage. As suggested earlier, he must in fact have approved of negotiating to gain time. In turn, once negotiations began it was important for him and Mago to reach Africa as soon as possible.

This left a critical contradiction at the heart of the ensuing peace agreement. As noted just now, it was obviously necessary for this to require the Barcid brothers to leave Italy but, no less obviously, the Romans expected them to take their armies back for demobilization. After all it would be nonsensical to make peace on condition that the enemy's overseas forces be brought back but be allowed to continue making war. This inference surely seemed too obvious to need spelling out.

But there was no formula in the agreement imposing demobilization. Very oddly, as noted above, our sources in practice treat Hannibal and his men, and Mago's, as virtually outside the talks and the terms. Even Polybius (but his account does survive only in extracts) seems to view Hannibal as an autonomous player on his return. How this could legally have been so is hard to see, but in practical terms everyone seems to have viewed him as such. Scipio seems to have taken it for granted: he did not call on the Carthaginians or Hannibal himself to make the returned forces obey the terms, or complain that they were not doing so, but instead treated the war as under way once again. By then the Carthaginians had given him other, more overt grounds for doing this, but it was implicit from the moment Hannibal and his army landed from Italy and did not lay down their arms.

When in mid-203 the dominant figures at Carthage—the Barcid group and whoever else now gave them support—sought to negotiate, they surely saw these possibilities. So could Scipio; for him the key to achieving peace was to achieve it quickly, so that Hannibal on returning would find a *fait accompli*. His terms were therefore clear-cut. They were along the lines of Lutatius' in 241, but of course harsher: Roman prisoners, deserters and runaway slaves to be handed over; the Barcids to evacuate Italy; Spain and all the islands between Italy and Africa (essentially meaning the Balearics and Ebusus) to be renounced, an indemnity paid, and the Roman forces in Africa meanwhile provisioned with substantial quantities of wheat and barley. And, the starkest proof of all that Carthage was beaten and would stay beaten, the navy was to have no more than twenty warships. He gave the Carthaginians three days to accept or refuse his terms.

Of course they accepted. An armistice was called, with (it seems) oaths being exchanged to observe it, and envoys were sent off to Rome under escort by a Roman officer.[4]

III

The Punic envoys arrived there some time after Laelius had presented the fallen Syphax to the Senate and news had come in of Mago's and Hannibal's departures. As Syphax had been captured late in June, the envoys reached Rome probably in August or September 203.

Both Polybius and a short papyrus fragment of another second-century Greek account make it clear that the Roman Senate and People approved Scipio's terms. Livy by contrast turns the Punic envoys' reception by the Senate into burlesque. They ask the Romans to renew the peace-terms of 241, not to ratify Scipio's—which nobody discusses at all—and are shouted down. Then, following other senators' sharp comments, Laelius opines that the whole thing is a trick to buy time and that Scipio had counted on the Barcid brothers not leaving Italy; since in Livy's account the brothers have already left, the plain implication is that Laelius now opposes peace. The Senate finally sends the envoys home empty-handed and authorizes Scipio to prosecute the war vigorously.

This rejection is hardly believable, nor is it to be saved by drawing on Appian's version of events. He has the Punic envoys go to Rome without any terms from Scipio at all, and so the Senate sends over senators to work out terms with him; then, once Scipio announces these—with some extra clauses not in either Polybius or Livy—the peace treaty is agreed. This account matches neither Livy's nor Polybius': like Livy it claims that the Senate did not at once ratify Scipio's terms, but it gives this a different cause (no terms to ratify); from some other source it imports the otherwise unattested senatorial commission sent to Africa, and adds extra clauses to the ensuing terms; then it confirms, as Polybius does, that peace was ratified. Rather than an independently trustworthy narrative this is normal Appianic confusion, due to compiling a single narrative out of several incompatible (and imperfectly understood) sources—including ones used by Polybius and the historical fragment, plus another which added extra provisos to the peace-terms. Yet even Appian has a peace treaty agreed on, unlike Livy.

Dio in his turn has 'the Romans' (plainly meaning the Senate) refuse to receive the Punic envoys until the Barcid brothers leave Italy; wrangles then follow over whether or not to ratify Scipio's terms—which Dio has not bothered to detail—till finally their ratification is voted. The wrangling may be authentic (Scipio did not have only admirers among his fellow-senators), but Livy's report that earlier the Senate ordered the consuls to keep the Barcid brothers from returning to Africa and that, according to Laelius, Scipio agreed with this, make more sense. It was not convincingly relevant, even if Dio thinks it is, that King Pyrrhus' offer of talks 75 years earlier had been turned down because he was an enemy on Italian soil: the Romans had had no troops on Pyrrhus' soil, so the strategic situations were quite different. Nothing suggests that the Senate in 203 would prefer upholding a recently minted 'tradition' to exploiting realities. Dio quite possibly took the claim from the source Livy was following, but otherwise his account basically conforms with the dominant version of events—that the Romans ratified Scipio's peace.[5]

Livy's version of what happened at Rome can only be following a peculiarly tendentious narrative which would not accept that a peace had been agreed on as early as 203. But even if he was drawing on Coelius Antipater or Valerius Antias, regular sources of his, it does not follow that this version was purely Roman-inspired. As often pointed out, it would have pleased Roman historical tradition much more if the Carthaginians did agree to peace-terms only to break them soon after (confirming the Roman image of 'Punic faith'). By contrast, to claim that the Romans refused after all to make peace was a line more likely to appeal to pro-Carthaginian writers, for it would explain and justify Hannibal's continuation of hostilities in Africa. Besides, pro-Carthaginian accounts did not cover up the armistice with Scipio and the Punic embassy to Rome—these are in all our surviving sources, with no hint of a different tradition—so they would certainly need to lay the alleged failure of the peace at the Romans' door.

Livy's claim may thus reach back to a pro-Carthaginian account, though he gives it a pro-Roman angle. On the other hand he surely acquired from a Roman writer the supposed details of how individual senior senators reacted to the Punic envoys. Yet what he reports of those senators' comments, even Laelius', is not totally hostile to the Carthaginians and not totally improbable. Quite possibly the acerbic Livius Salinator did complain about peace-terms being discussed in the absence of both consuls (he was ignored) and possibly too Scipio's friend Q. Metellus did urge the Senate to accept what the proconsul decided. Possibly again Valerius Laevinus did grumble that the envoys were just spies and ought to be deported; genuine or distorted, his comments in Livy provide a transition to Laelius'.

Laelius avers that Scipio had expected Hannibal and Mago to stay in Italy, and that the Carthaginians would stoop to any trick to drag out talks until the brothers returned home to renew the war. This way of reporting him suits Livy's claim that the brothers had already gone: in reality they had probably not yet left Italy and the alleged early departure may be another distortion to help along the notion of Punic ill-faith. But in any case it was natural enough for someone to warn against extended negotiations lest these tempt the Carthaginians into recalling the brothers and renewing the war—particularly if Scipio was keen for a swift peace. So Laelius might well state that 'Scipio had placed his hope of peace on Hannibal and Mago not being recalled' and obliquely warn the envoys against trying to prolong the talks (for instance by haggling over terms). Later on these comments could easily be turned into the form Livy gives them.[6]

Similarly with the Punic envoys' alleged demand for Lutatius' treaty to be renewed. Quite possibly they did mention that treaty in their opening statement to the Senate, for it was after all the only previous peace settlement between the two republics and it had not curtailed Carthage's great-power status. Besides, it had been followed by some years of friendly relations between the two, a useful point to put now. Later on, though, it would be an easy and cheap ploy to represent any such remarks as just a demand for Lutatius' treaty to be renewed.

A Roman writer with access to details of the discussion in the Senate, but anxious to claim that the senators had rejected treacherous Punic overtures, would thus have little trouble adapting such items to the goal of claiming that the Senate had rejected peace. This was—it seems—a writer who could not believe that the wise Senate of those days would be taken in by Punic deviousness and judged his disbelief confirmed by the pro-Carthaginian source who denied (or ignored) Senate approval of Scipio's terms. When the Carthaginians seized the Roman food convoy afterwards, the writer could report Scipio complaining that they had broken not the allegedly rejected peace but the armistice and the law of nations—as Livy does, in contrast to Polybius who reports the proconsul specifically referring to a violation of the newly ratified peace.

Livy himself probably did not originate the alleged non-ratification, for that would mean he found all his sources—Greek and Roman, pro- and anti-Carthaginian—unanimous that the terms had been ratified and yet he decided to contradict them. Such a procedure would be unique in his history and it is hard to see why he would want to do it here. By contrast, if he found the story in a respected enough predecessor (or predecessors) he could feel that he was justified in preferring this version to the one in Polybius.

At least one of his Roman predecessors is known to have consulted a pro-Carthaginian source, Hannibal's friend Silenus in fact, as well as Roman ones. This was Coelius Antipater, an author happy to invent dramatic details elsewhere in his history of the war. But he was not the only pre-Livian historian prone at times to distortion and invention (Valerius Antias was the notorious example), and other Roman historians too may have consulted non-Roman sources. If Livy himself chose to look up such non-Roman sources, he might feel further reassured about the Senate rejecting Scipio's terms. But wherever the story came from, it is not one to believe.[7]

IV

By the time the Punic envoys returned from Rome, Hannibal and his army had sailed from Italy and landed in Africa (Polybius makes this clear). According to Livy and Appian he had built transports in anticipation of recall, while a naval escort was provided by a squadron under Hasdrubal the admiral. Most of the veterans cannot have been very good as shipwrights, but men from Croton and other coastal towns could have done the work once the soldiers had felled enough trees. All the same, this would mean that the Roman armies were content to look on, throughout the year, while Hannibal's men went about obviously readying themselves for departure—a move the Roman commanders were under orders to prevent, and one too that would make a Roman offensive harder for him and his preoccupied troops to resist.

Nor did the Romans make naval efforts to raid or harass his ports while a transport-fleet was supposedly taking shape. On balance it is likelier that, even if Hannibal gathered or built some craft locally, most of the transports were sent over with the escort from Carthage, taking the Romans enough by surprise to prevent them interfering with the evacuation.

Even so, it may have taken the Carthaginians some time to collect the necessary shipping. The recall to Hannibal was sent soon after they had news of Syphax's capture, thus probably at the end of May; but he crossed to Africa only in autumn, late September or early October at the earliest. How many ships he needed is not known, but if he took 10,000–15,000 men to Africa he would have to have a fair number. Scipio with about 30,000 troops, plus 2,000-odd horses, had needed 400 transports the year before. After years of war-spending and ship-losses, with shipping and trade surely damaged by Roman raids and Scipio's devastations, and with Mago's forces to bring back as well, the Carthaginians cannot have found it easy or cheap to gather the craft needed.

Hannibal also had to take care not to provoke the Roman armies around him into trying to throw his evacuation into chaos. That may have meant waiting for word that the Senate and People had agreed to the peace-terms, which required the brothers to depart. If Livy is right that the Senate was displeased when he did sail, the reason quite likely was that he had not made clear that he accepted the peace.[8]

Anti-Barcid tradition told lurid stories about his departure: how he sent Hasdrubal the admiral around the towns he still controlled to loot them, and massacred soldiers unwilling to serve in Africa. For Diodorus these numbered no fewer than 20,000, while Livy does not state a figure but puts the slaughter in the hallowed temple of Hera at Cape Lacinium. The town-lootings may be genuine (Appian adds the detail that Hasdrubal let the inhabitants leave first) for the general himself might see them as legitimate plunder for his troops: if they did not take it the incoming Romans would. He also may have wanted to gather whatever proceeds he could for the coming campaign in Africa, to lighten the impact on Carthage's own diminished resources. The alleged massacre is another matter.

The tale's genesis seems to have been the reportedly large number of animals slaughtered, including 3,000 horses according to Diodorus, on the eve of departure because there was no room for them aboard ship—an item supported by the fact that Hannibal had to look for fresh cavalry when he reached Africa. Maybe, too, some troops did mutiny at the prospect of leaving Italy and were duly punished with death: hardly a large number all the same, since the rest of his troops (mostly Italians as we saw earlier) would remain the most solidly loyal corps in his army at Zama. Besides, Polybius insists that throughout the Italian years Hannibal never had to face a mutiny, polyglot though his army was. A major mutiny would have made this claim ridiculous, but the historian might ignore a small one.[9]

V

The army of Italy landed at Leptis Minor near Hadrumetum a good way south-east of Carthage, and at some stage was joined by Mago's returned force. But not by Mago himself. He had died on the voyage from Italy, another casualty of the disastrous war his eldest brother had launched in 218. Of Hamilcar's three warrior sons only Hannibal was left.[10]

Hannibal reached Africa before the Carthaginian envoys returned from Rome with the Senate's approval of the peace-terms. Scipio had thus effectively lost his gamble that peace would have been ratified by now. For even though Hannibal made no offensive move now or during the winter that followed, his military preparations were a plain sign that he meant to fight on. Scipio kept to his camp outside Utica, perhaps unwilling to act until he was resupplied and still hoping that ratification would go through once Hannibal had seen the state of affairs for himself.

As suggested earlier, Hannibal returned to a homeland still committed to fighting on under the leadership of his family and its political supporters, with peace-inclined Carthaginians a disregarded minority. Hasdrubal, son of Gisco's eclipse, may even have enlarged the Barcid group into a sort of coalition of national resolve. As usual, though, other leading Barcid associates get no mention in our records and even Hanno son of Bomilcar disappears, presumably becoming one of the returned general's subordinates. But for the Barcids this had to be the last throw of the dice. Hannibal had come home to atone for six years of calamities, and had nothing to offer but hope. Many leading men—even many long-established Barcid supporters—can have been willing to continue their support only in return for victory over Scipio and a tolerable peace. So the general was able to build up his forces by levying troops locally and hiring mercenaries, which means he could draw supplies and funds from Carthage and its territory (what he brought from Italy cannot have been enough). But some strain in his relations with the ever more anxious Carthaginians in the city can be glimpsed in their urgings to him to confront Scipio, and his testy reply that he would do so when he and not they judged it right.

Outside Punic territory, the Barcids' old links with Numidian princes remained valuable too. True, Masinissa was in the process of imposing his rule over the whole country, nor is anything more heard of Hannibal's unnamed niece, Oezalces' widow and Mazaetullus' wife, but during 202 the Carthaginian army was reinforced by cavalry under one Tychaeus, a relative of Syphax. Appian names the reinforcer 'Mesotylus', probably another Appianic confusion since the real Mazaetullus had surrendered to Masinissa and earns no mention now in Polybius' and Livy's more detailed accounts—but all the same this suggests a link between Tychaeus and Masinissa's enemy. The Barcid–Numidian tie that stretched back to the days of Naravas thus revived, in modified form, for the last throw of the dice.[11]

Before long the war began again. First of all, Roman cargo ships bearing food-supplies were driven by contrary winds to shore, some on the western coast of Cape Bon and others at the island of Aegimurus—now Zembra—a few miles west of the cape and about 30 from Carthage. The hungry citizens pressured the Punic senate to send out Hasdrubal the admiral (now back from Italy) to seize the laden and deserted ships. Then when Scipio sent envoys by sea to the city to complain, these not only were sent away unanswered and insulted but, on the return trip to his camp, were ambushed offshore by some Punic warships and barely managed to reach safety. Scipio marched into the countryside, capturing towns and ravaging fields, while the harried authorities at Carthage sent messages to their returned but inactive general imploring him to take the field.[12]

The timings of these events are not clear in our sources. Hannibal and presumably Mago's forces arrived in autumn 203, but it is not likely that the ensuing events happened soon afterwards. Most modern historians agree that the provision fleet must have been sent in spring 202, and certainly for the Romans to send a large supply-fleet during the treacherous winter months from October to March would have been foolish and potentially disastrous. Nor should it have been necessary, for Scipio's army had been well provisioned by the Carthaginians. By the start of spring, on the other hand, he would be needing fresh supplies. That he had them sent from Italy means in turn he could not replace them locally—another sign that relations with the Carthaginians had turned chilly.

The picture is consistent, had always been predictable—we saw Laelius warning against it—and Polybius makes it clear: once the armies from Italy landed along with Carthage's undefeated supreme commander, a further trial of arms became preferable to a treaty that finished Carthage as a great power.

Polybius writes that most leading Carthaginians and senators saw the treaty as too harsh. As noted earlier, they had surely felt this from the start: the armies' return cannot have wrought sudden enlightenment. Nor, as we also noted, does anything suggest that at this point a 'war'-faction wrested power back from a 'peace'-faction: rather, with the military situation restored the Carthaginians' real attitude could appear. Plainly enough, most ordinary citizens felt this way—so much so that one tradition, in Diodorus and Appian and with a hint in Livy too, could distort it into bellicose Punic commons versus pacific senate. This tradition (not necessarily Roman-originated) reminds us of Fabius Pictor's anti-Barcid propaganda, which all but certainly drew on anti-Barcid apologetics in postwar Carthage.

The Carthaginians maybe reckoned that since peace had not yet been formally ratified, by them anyway, they were not breaking faith: likely enough, as the Polybian-era historical fragment implies, the requisite oaths were yet to be exchanged. Scipio's protest at the seizure of his supplies, that they had violated 'the oaths and the agreement', must have meant either the armistice, if this was secured by oaths as the fragment implies, or else preliminary oaths sworn at Rome by the Punic ambassadors whom the Senate had heard. Instead of acknowledging this, the Carthaginians refused to give his envoys a reply and, as the fragment puts it, 'sent out men bearing war instead of peace'—quite likely an epitomised allusion to the attack on the Roman envoys' ship.[13]

That this attack was a fiction of Scipio's, or of later Roman tradition, to justify his renewing hostilities is implausible. There was no need. The seizure of his supply ships and the Carthaginians' refusal to answer his protest, still less offer apology or compensation, amounted to unfriendly acts at the very least and could reasonably be judged hostile ones. Not to mention Hannibal's armed presence in the south-east, the steps he was taking not to demobilize but to build up his forces, and his continuing total silence about accepting or even acknowledging the recent peace. Attacking the envoys on the other hand brought no gain to the Punic state itself: it was most likely a hotheaded folly by the admiral Hasdrubal, with or without prompting from diehards in the city.

Even without it, Scipio had little choice but to renew hostilities, and he had the right. While Polybius stresses the anger he felt at the enemy's recent behaviour, and no doubt it was genuine, Scipio was not reacting merely out of emotion. The Carthaginians might feel, as is sometimes suggested, that they were entitled to seize Roman supply-ships because this was not expressly forbidden in the peace-terms: but merely to put the point shows its frivolity (trying to sink ambassadors was not forbidden them either, but that scarcely made it allowable).

Another suggestion is that they refused to answer his protest over the seizure because they had not yet heard what their envoys returning from Rome had to report—an odd line of argument in itself, and all the more if it is taken to imply that Scipio was somehow obligated to grant them more time. In any case the Carthaginians, having plundered his goods, were scarcely entitled to expect him still to refrain from plundering theirs. Their action posed a military threat too: it deprived Scipio of needed munitions and strengthened the city of Carthage's resources, just when Carthaginian forces were being rebuilt by Hannibal—who, it bears reiterating, was not in practice a party to the recent peace and yet was neither disciplined nor disavowed.[14]

Even now the Roman commander avoided confronting him. Instead he traversed the countryside, spreading damage and terror widely. This might be seen as an effort to draw his opponent away from the coast and onto terrain—deep in the interior, as at the Great Plains earlier in 203—where Scipio conceivably felt more comfortable about fighting and was closer to his ally Masinissa. But in fact Hannibal did not react for months. The climactic battle was not fought until autumn 202, seven or eight months after the supply-ships affair and at the far end of the new campaigning season. Throughout that time Scipio continued to avoid confrontation.[15]

He probably had other reasons for harrying the countryside. First, the

Roman army needed further supplies since (thanks to the Carthaginians) less than half those sent from Italy had come in, and the arrival of spring and then summer made supplies available locally. Another calculation may have been even weightier. Hannibal's stillness and the Punic authorities' silence over the Roman protest were not friendly acts, but equally they did not close off the possibility that the Carthaginians might yet steel themselves to peace. What—arguably—was needed to bring them round was some unsubtle physical pressure. So the Romans looted and ravaged the hinterland and enslaved all who fell into their hands. The more the destruction and disruption, the clearer they made it to the Carthaginians and their general how bleak their future was, and how unwise Hannibal was to keep the war going, for even if he won a battle it would merely mean a new invasion and new wreckage.

This strategy was obviously risky. As summer wore on without any decisive result, hindsight might suggest to Scipio that he would have done better to attack Hannibal directly the latter arrived from Italy. Then the Punic forces had been fewer, cavalry lacking and the Romans relatively fresh from their dual triumphs over Hasdrubal son of Gisco and Syphax. Now, operating in the interior, Scipio was leaving his bridgehead near Utica vulnerable to attack, when a possible combined thrust by Hannibal and the Punic fleet (stationed near Utica) might cut him off from Italy. This concern may be one reason why his war-fleet was strengthened from 40 in 203 to 70 early in 202, and why the Senate then authorized one of the new consuls to take 50 more to Africa (though he never got there).

Of course Hannibal's past military career showed that he could probably be relied on not to think about a combined land and sea operation. Scipio obviously felt he could risk striking inland. Even then, had Hannibal chosen to force an early confrontation with the Roman army Scipio would have been in a critical position again, for at some stage in 202 the Punic general was able to win the already-mentioned support from the Numidian Tychaeus—2,000 cavalry reputed to be the best in Africa. Scipio was trying to coax Masinissa to rejoin him with auxiliary horse and foot, but the king was busy imposing his rule on recalcitrant parts of Syphax's Numidia and delayed coming. It was not until autumn that he at last arrived with 4,000 cavalry as well as 6,000 infantry to give Scipio confidence about fighting.[16]

Hannibal's inaction was probably caused partly by his need to recruit and train extra troops, both foreign mercenaries and Carthaginian levies, and partly by caution. He was going to fight the one Roman who had won a series of spectacular victories against the Carthaginians, each in a different way and all of them with dazzling resourcefulness. Like Hannibal himself, Scipio had never lost a battle. A too hasty move against him might only add the crowning victory to his record. All the same this caution may have been excessive. Had Hannibal managed to bring on a battle after Tychaeus' arrival but before Masinissa's, a Roman disaster would have been much likelier.[17]

VI

The conclusive battle of the Second Punic War, somewhere in the region of Zama about 66 miles (110 kilometres) south-west of Carthage, was preceded by a face-to-face meeting between the generals. This was sought by Hannibal, reportedly after Scipio caught some spies of his and, instead of killing them, showed them round his camp and then sent them back, an act of bravado that prompted Hannibal's admiration. In reality it was a stratagem in his own best style. Masinissa, with his infantry and all-important cavalry, did not join the Romans until two or three days later: in other words Scipio was hoping to make these reinforcements an unpleasant surprise for his opponent when battle came.[18]

Hannibal was not taken in so readily. His tactics at Zama a few days later seemingly included sacrificing his own cavalry so as to draw the enemy's off the battlefield, and if so it implies that he realized Scipio's cavalry was now superior. But their interview meanwhile went ahead. There is no strong reason for doubting it, unusual though it was for opposing commanders to meet before battle. To suppose it was invented in imitation of other classic encounters—Solon and Croesus, for instance, or Alexander the Great and the philosopher Diogenes—overlooks that none of these involved two opposing generals just before combat. Nor, in Polybius' account especially, do Hannibal and Scipio exchange pithy comments or one of them teach the other some sententious lesson, as Solon famously does with Croesus. Instead they discuss the immediately relevant issues of war and peace, even if the writers' device of giving each man one fairly extensive speech is a literary touch and the original interview probably took a more varied form.[19]

Hannibal in effect offered Scipio peace on the status quo. The Romans should keep Spain and its attendant islands along with their old possessions Sicily and Sardinia, with the implicit corollary that the Carthaginians would keep their African territory. He said nothing about paying an indemnity or giving up most of the navy (other provisos in Scipio's now-nullified treaty), but maybe he assumed such matters could be brought up once fresh talks were agreed to. After all he made no reference to restoring Roman prisoners and deserters either, yet this would be an expected proviso too as Scipio's original terms had shown. Scipio in his turn made it clear that he had not come to Africa and won his victories simply to accept peace on anyone else's terms; rather, his opponent's only hope of peace without a battle was to accept the terms already agreed to, which of course were his terms.

Plainly Hannibal was not minded to do this, and the interview ended.

Did Hannibal seriously think they could achieve peace without a battle? It might seem surprising, when he was facing an enemy whose homeland, power and even existence he had menaced for a decade and a half. The bulk of Scipio's army was made up of the long-suffering survivors of Cannae, who had their own score to settle. Yet, as it turned out, Scipio's ultimate terms of peace would include virtually what Hannibal suggested: in essence the Carthaginians would surrender their empire, becoming a purely North African state, and the Romans would make no African annexations. If Hannibal was also prepared to negotiate on other matters, indemnity, fleet and so on—he did not say so, but that does not rule it out—then Scipio might have got his peace without the cost of 20,000-odd more lives, if also without the glory of a victory over the greatest general of the age.

Scipio's reply in effect demanded a *deditio*, an unconditional surrender: 'either put yourselves and your country at our mercy or fight and conquer us'. This was much more sweeping than his earlier terms or even those he would offer after Zama: yet after Zama Hannibal and the Carthaginian state were bereft of their army, their allies, their resources, and hope. Arguably Scipio was concerned by then that if Carthage held out he might yet be superseded by another Roman commander, and so he ruled out demanding *deditio* again. But he would have had much the same worry just before Zama: so why put this harshest of all demands to his opponent—an opponent at the head of a fresh and sizeable army?

The answer must be that he had no further interest in negotiation, that with Masinissa's reinforcements he was totally sure of victory. He had come to the interview at Hannibal's request and maybe because he too was interested in meeting his famous foe, but what he wanted now was a military decision. This need not have been due purely to craving personal glory, agreeable though the glory would be. Hardheadedly he could also reckon that, given the recent negotiating fiasco, no lasting settlement could be relied on if the Carthaginians and Hannibal remained able to fight—least of all once the Romans evacuated North Africa, as inevitably they must. A decisive victory on the other hand would finish the war and secure the peace; and of victory Scipio was now so confident that he confronted his opponent deep in the Punic countryside, far from his coastal bridgehead and from any chance of rescue if he lost.[20]

The battle of Zama was not a foregone conclusion, all the same. Rather surprisingly, both generals avoided complex manoeuvres such as had characterized so many of their previous victories: no doubt each was wary of exposing himself to some unforeseeable coup by the other. Scipio, who had beaten four previous Punic armies in four differently inventive ways, accepted a brutal slogging-match while letting Laelius and Masinissa rout Hannibal's cavalry and gambling that they would then bring their horsemen back—the same kind of risk, though not using exactly the same tactics, that Hannibal had accepted at Cannae. Hannibal, deploying a large elephant corps for the first time, saw them neutralized by a simple tactical device of Scipio's, and then committed each of his three infantry corps in turn against the enemy in static linear fashion. This sequence prolonged the fight to little tactical benefit when, arguably, he could have exploited the sacrifice of his first two lines (the mercenaries and the Carthaginian levies) to gain time for his powerful third corps, the veterans of Italy, to swing out and fall on Scipio's unprotected infantry flanks in a variant of Cannae or Ilipa.

The veterans when their turn came fought long and hard but, unprotected on flanks and rear, suffered their own Cannae once Laelius, Masinissa and their cavalry returned. It is surprising that, after losing his own cavalry, Hannibal had taken no steps at all to organize some sort of protective screen for his remaining troops—had all his elephants disappeared from the field entirely, not to mention all survivors of his first and second lines after each was cut up by the Romans? Scipio's deliberate slowness in launching his attack on the veterans of Italy almost dared Hannibal to take such a step, and victory, or a draw, would still have been achievable had Hannibal been able to hold off Laelius and Masinissa.

Maybe Hannibal knew he had met his match. He left the fighting to his men—Appian's picture of the two generals fighting hand-to-hand is romantic fantasy—only to see the last army of Carthage cut to pieces by the survivors of Cannae. After defeat he galloped in two days and nights back to the coast at Hadrumetum, over 120 miles (200 kilometres) away, leaving the survivors of his army to the mercy of the countryside and the Romans. He obviously had no mind to imitate his brother Hasdrubal's self-sacrifice at enemy hands. Nor indeed any wish to continue the war: though he reportedly pulled together what troops he could—6,500 according to Appian—even Appian admits he knew the war had to end.

Within days of the disaster, without opposition from their beaten general, the authorities at Carthage once more sent 30 envoys to Scipio, and when the victor's new peace-terms were brought back Hannibal himself—now at long last in the city he had not seen for nearly 36 years—pulled down from the senate's rostrum a diehard named Gisco who spoke against them. It would be appropriate if this Gisco was brother (or father) to Hasdrubal son of Gisco whose own will to fight had never faltered, even if his ungrateful fellow-citizens had finally turned on him and driven him to suicide.[21]

The silencing of Gisco was met by mutters of disapproval from other senators and plainly none of approval, for Hannibal at once felt he had to apologize. After 36 years away from home, he said, he was unused to the ways of the senate but certain that it must accept the terms. This relatively graceful *mea culpa* was successful and was remembered; less noticed but more important is that Carthaginian senators, even now, were not so cowed by defeat as to share his impatience with someone who talked of fighting on.

They had to recognize he was right in insisting on peace but they and the republic owed him nothing more. He was the leader under whom they had waged a losing war for 16 years, for whom they had recently thrown off Scipio's peace, and who had then led their last army to destruction. Just as Hasdrubal son of Gisco's influence had most likely collapsed after his defeat at the Great Plains, so too almost certainly did the Barcids' in the weeks after Zama.[22] The dice had been thrown, and the era of Barcid supremacy was over.

XV

POSTWAR ECLIPSE

I

The authorities at Carthage sent 30 envoys to Scipio when he marched back to Tunes, not to negotiate but to listen to his terms and beg for mercy. As it turned out, Scipio's second peace was not strikingly more vengeful than the first; but its immediate penalties were heavier. The war-indemnity was doubled to 10,000 talents—payable over 50 years but starting at once—and the entire Punic navy save for ten ships had to be surrendered, plus all the war-elephants. The Carthaginians also had to give compensation for 'all the injustices' committed during the previous truce: Scipio had not forgotten or forgiven the plunder of his supply-ships.

Prisoners of war, and deserters, were of course to be given up. Other provisos confirmed Carthage's demotion to geopolitical insignificance: the Carthaginians must never again wage war outside Africa, and could do so in Africa only if the Romans permitted; they must no longer recruit Celtic or Ligurian mercenaries; and they had to restore to Masinissa whatever property and territory he or his ancestors had once held in their lands—a requirement ominous for the future integrity of their state even if, at the time, meant as no more than a passing concession to the Romans' new friend. But the city was not occupied, and the Punic republic kept its independence, its home territories and its historic allies like Utica.

It was pretty well the best settlement the Carthaginians could have hoped for in their helpless position. The alternative would have been a siege and starvation, and probable destruction in the end. For the settlement they could thank not only Scipio's concern, real as it was, about being replaced by another general (one of the new consuls of 201 was soon making strenuous efforts to take over) but no doubt too their own strong walls, which had frustrated the besieging rebels four decades before and, half a century later, would hold the Romans themselves at bay for three years. One other factor may have deterred Scipio from trying a siege—Hannibal's presence within the walls, the obvious leader of a desperate resistance. If so it was one final service the general rendered his homeland before laying down his command.[1]

Appian depicts the common people even now rejecting Scipio's terms after days of debate, howling at their erstwhile hero Hannibal when he urged acceptance, and forcing many of the leading men to flee the city. But this lurid scenario is another in the sequence of foolishly fickle Punic mob versus wise, moderate and essentially peace-loving Punic aristocracy—with the general now conscripted into its ranks—which is probably Roman-inspired and has nothing to recommend it, even if it makes use of a genuine detail or two like Hannibal supporting peace.

Once the terms were ratified at Rome, early in 201, Scipio towed the warships out to sea, 500 altogether, and burned them in sight of the city. We can well believe that the Carthaginians were heart-stricken, as Livy reports. They would stay free and self-governing, but the blazing hulks of their navy sinking beneath the waters symbolized the end of Punic seaborne power and of the greatest era in their history.[2]

Before he left for Rome, Scipio also worked out the boundaries of Punic North Africa. Appian claims that he fixed them at 'the Phoenician Trenches' (having put the same proviso into his version of the earlier peace) but he fails to explain this term and the claim is dubious. A surviving excerpt from Eumachus of Neapolis and a mention in the Elder Pliny might seem to confirm that the 'Trenches' did exist, but no other writer has them in the peace and they certainly did not embrace the Emporia region in the south which still remained under Punic rule.

In reality Pliny is writing about a boundary delimited in 146—by Scipio Aemilianus after his sack of Carthage—between the new Roman province and Numidia, and later called the 'royal trench', *fossa regia*. Eumachus meantime, not in his Hannibalic history but in a geographical work, was telling a tale of the Carthaginians finding huge bodies in coffins 'while digging a trench around their territory', with no date or site: he might be referring to a much earlier, semi-legendary era and so to a trench much nearer to Carthage. Even if he did mean what Appian calls the 'Phoenician Trenches', the latter or his source quite conceivably inferred—wrongly if so—that these constituted the *fossa regia* and that it was Scipio in 201 who made them the boundary. For even though the Third Punic War arose from later clashes between the Carthaginians and Masinissa, Appian mentions neither the 'Trenches' in his account of those events nor the younger Scipio's delimitation afterwards. If these 'Trenches' did exist they most probably had no part in the treaty or Scipio Aemilianus' ensuing delimitation.[3]

Ten thousand talents' indemnity over half a century amounted to 200 a year, a tidy sum (12 million *asses* or 1,200,000 *denarii*) but less than the 220 the Carthaginians had had to pay yearly under Lutatius' treaty—and that after an initial lump sum of another 1,000. Livy tells another Hannibal-story: amid his fellow-senators' loud laments over having to pay the first instalment he was seen to be laughing, and, reproved by his enemy Hasdrubal the Kid for laughing at misery which he himself had caused, he in turn reproved the

Carthaginians. 'Then was the proper time to weep, when our arms were taken from us, our ships burnt and foreign wars forbidden. Now because you have to collect payment from private resources, you mourn as though at a public funeral.'

But unlike the earlier story of the silencing of Gisco, this one looks like a fiction. Likely enough, to be sure, the ravaging of the countryside carried out by Scipio had reduced both public and personal revenues. This anecdote, though, has a similar shape to the earlier one—Hannibal again upsetting his peers with unorthodox but realistic frankness and uttering truths they would prefer not to hear—while its moralizing and pro-Hannibalic message is much more gratuitous. Besides, though he tells it under the date 201 Livy later claims the first indemnity-payment was made in 199. More likely then the tale goes back to an imaginative Sosylus or Silenus.[4]

II

Hannibal's position after peace returned is not entirely clear. With the war over and any Punic war-making improbable for the foreseeable future, there was no lasting place for the generalship or for him as its holder. Nepos all the same reports that after Zama he levied fresh forces and, even with peace made, continued to campaign—along with Mago—until in 200 the Romans complained about it to a fresh Carthaginian embassy and got him recalled to Carthage.

This story is hardly believable as Nepos tells it. Not only was warfare even in Africa a breach of the new treaty unless the Romans gave prior consent, but there was effectively no one to war against: definitely not Masinissa, and to the south lay desert, to the east the Ptolemies. The late Roman writer Aurelius Victor's story of Hannibal having his soldiers plant olive-trees all over Africa is no support for Nepos either, for Victor expressly states that it was done to keep the men busy in peacetime.

In reality the Romans themselves sent an embassy over to Carthage in 200, to complain about a renegade officer in Cisalpine Gaul named Hamilcar—apparently a leftover from Hasdrubal's expedition or Mago's who was stirring up unrest in those parts—and the Carthaginians promptly declared him an outlaw and confiscated his property. This is very likely the origin of Nepos' story: a confusion between a little-known officer and well-known general, with resulting adjustments to details. The confusion in fact goes deeper, for Nepos' Punic envoys also ask the Romans to release their Carthaginian captives—a request actually made, at any rate for high-ranking prisoners and with success, by the Punic peace-envoys in 201.[5]

Yet there could be a small nugget of fact behind Nepos' tale, and one compatible with Victor's (who was North African himself and may draw on local tradition). Some troops escaped death or captivity at Zama, and there were other units still existing too—the stubborn garrison in Utica, for instance, and no doubt others in Carthage and other cities—not to mention crews from the extinguished navy. The Carthaginians, Hannibal included, would have all too lively memories of the disastrous sequel to the previous war when the republic's unpaid mercenaries revolted and incited the oppressed Libyans to do the same: now, with the Libyans already oppressed and restive even before Scipio in 202 spread fire and terror across their countryside, the danger of a new outbreak cannot have seemed negligible even if Punic forces were much smaller than the mercenary army in 241.[6]

What was needed was to keep the surviving soldiers and crewmen busy (and with pay) at least until they could be safely discharged. No doubt too the disruption inflicted by the Roman invaders in the hinterland called for some sort of security force to restore order, and the authorities at Carthage may well have felt it necessary too to try ways of re-establishing productivity so as to placate the locals. It may have been Hannibal's own idea (as Victor implies) to plant olive-groves; it might seem appropriate too for him to stay as general until his project was completed or at least well under way, so as to maintain discipline among the men. This would account for Nepos' idea about him continuing in command, and suit Victor's report that he carried out the plantings in peacetime.

At least Nepos may get right the date for Hannibal laying down the generalship—the year 199. The biographer supposes that after 22 years of holding military command Hannibal moved straight from it to the sufeteship. In reality he became sufete 25 years after becoming general, but Nepos' numeral need not be just a mistake or a later miscopying. After the visit of the Roman embassy in 200, silent though it was about the general, the Carthaginian authorities might understandably think it preferable that he lay down his official command, especially if his troops could now be safely discharged. In any case there was no war to fight and nothing in the republic's political system required a general or generals in place at all times. Hannibal himself could hardly quarrel with that.[7]

All the same, if he did continue as general for some time after peace was made he cannot have been shorn of political influence, despite the débâcle of the war. Nor was he prosecuted for his conduct of the war or his defeat at Zama—hallowed though such vengefulness was by Punic tradition, and though Hasdrubal son of Gisco had only recently been driven to suicide even without indictment. Dio to be sure claims there was a prosecution and acquittal (on charges of not taking Rome and of keeping booty for himself) but not even Nepos knows anything of that.

In fact it is worth noting that, to judge from our sources, no one at Carthage this time cast the blame for the war on their old leader. The 30 envoys who supplicated Scipio after Zama did not; neither did the envoys sent to Rome with the terms he imposed, even though they were 'by far the first men in the state' and included—no doubt a politic gesture—Hasdrubal the Kid. The nearest even he gets in Livy to accusing the general is not in the speech to the Senate which Livy then gives him, but in a separate earlier comment blaming the war on 'the greed of a few men'. No doubt this means the Barcids and their friends: but it is a strangely muted and undeveloped dictum, and thus all the more interesting if genuine. Appian, who makes The Kid one of the envoys to Scipio at Tunes earlier, there gives him an even more rhetorical oration (very reminiscent of Livy's) which is equally silent about the last of the Barcids.[8]

It would be unwarranted to assume that the advent of peace meant the advent to power of Hasdrubal the Kid and Hanno the Great (who may still have been alive, though surely not for much longer). As we have seen, even late in 203 majority opinion at Carthage had been not defeatist but bellicose, and even after Zama not all the Mighty Ones were ready to hear of peace. Whatever interests now predominated, they pretty clearly were not concerned to mount a persecution of Hannibal or associates of his.[9]

One obvious deterrent would be if he did continue as general and commanded troops. But this cannot have been the sole factor. Had powerful elements at Carthage really wanted to attack him they could have enlisted Roman help, as his enemies were eventually to do. For instance, in 200 there arrived the Roman embassy to complain about Hamilcar the renegade in Cisalpina and also that not all Roman deserters had been surrendered as the peace treaty required; it visited Masinissa too, to wheedle a contingent of cavalry from him to serve in the Romans' new war with Philip V. The Carthaginians did their best to mollify the envoys and furthermore sent huge gifts of grain to Rome and to the legions operating in Macedonia. But nothing was said on either side about Hannibal.

III

The state of politics at Carthage from 201 on can only be surmised, but not randomly. As suggested earlier, until Zama Hannibal and his supporters had maintained a tenuous ascendancy. But by 195, as Livy tells it, the *ordo iudicum*—probably the tribunal of One Hundred and Four resurgent—was dominant, though there was plenty of resentment against it. The all too likely shipwreck of the Barcid ascendancy after 202 would allow the 'judges' to complete a process which (again as suggested earlier) had begun in the middle years of the war as Barcid fortunes waned.

Livy portrays the 'judges' lording it over the rest in serried solidarity, all for one and one for all. 'Everyone's possessions, reputation and lives lay under their authority; antagonizing a single one made enemies of them all and a prosecutor was sure to lay a charge before hostile judges.' Making allowance for some exaggeration (his account is very much on Hannibal's side) we infer that they were once again enjoying the primacy that Aristotle had attested a century and a half earlier. They were, after all, members too of the Mighty Ones, and if Hasdrubal in the 220s had broadened their judicial rôle that would add still further to their status and influence—especially once the dominant hand of a Barcid generalissimo was withdrawn.

Many if not most of the Hundred and Four in 196 must have joined the tribunal during the years of Barcid ascendancy. Some indeed would be Barcid kinsmen. So Livy's insistence on their total solidarity is probably not literally true, but on the other hand the ties that had bound most of them to the Barcids in the days of military glamour and success would have lost their strength by 201. Instead we could expect to find leading individuals and their supporters vying for office and influence, as in pre-Barcid times: including men who had previously been in the Barcid bloc or allied with it (like the late Hasdrubal son of Gisco).

Two factors perhaps limited the intensity of postwar competition among them and encouraged a measure of solidarity. First, it was important to keep Hannibal and his remaining supporters from recovering political dominance. The Barcids might be down but were hardly out: not only was Hannibal elected a popular sufete for 196 but, even after he was forced into exile, a 'Barcid faction' (in Livy's phrase) continued to exist for some years at least, and in 193 its absent leader still believed it able to regain control. Enemies— and former friends—could not afford too luxuriant a level of competitiveness among themselves after 201 if that gave Hannibal the chance to build a new coalition. He could be tolerated as an eminent figure, but nothing more. Second, the proliferation of abuses in public finance that Livy sketches, some no doubt dating back to the war-years, would prompt mutual support because the abuses benefited the 'judges' as a class (or order) while the rest of the citizenry in effect footed the bill. The last thing desirable was someone promoting any programme of reform, however modest.[10]

Not that the tribunal itself gained new legal powers. All the other institutions of government continued: the Mighty Ones, the various magistracies, and presumably the pentarchies or Boards of Five. The supremacy of the One Hundred and Four was political and social, as Livy's terminology implies: it was the *ordo* of judges that dominated, and exerted dominance through control of the courts and, likely enough, the senate. Critics were harassed, or worse, through vexatious and biased prosecutions; but not it seems struck down by arbitrary executive fiat, far less by extralegal violence.

In turn, the siphoning-off of state revenues and other forms of corruption would most readily be carried on by holding magistracies, belonging to pentarchies if these still existed, and the like. Aristotle had noted that a Carthaginian could hold more than one office at the same time, and this feature the 'judges' (like Carthaginian aristocrats of earlier eras) surely made the most of. Nor of course need the abuses have started only from 201. During the war-years opportunities for graft of every kind would have been extensive—not only direct theft of state funds but also bribery, corrupt public contracts and other profiteering. And it would be overoptimistic to suppose that the Barcids and their supporters had kept their own hands clean; or that

Barcid leaders at Carthage, concerned to maintain an increasingly fragile political ascendancy, had always been zealous about cracking down on abuses and abusers.[11]

In 199 the 200-talent payment of the war-indemnity caused a scandal at Rome because the sum, supplied in silver coin, turned out on testing to be 25 per cent short thanks to the presence of base metal. To make up the shortfall the Carthaginian envoys had to borrow money on the Roman market: to some, a vivid example of how impoverished the Punic state had become thanks to the ravages of war. But while it is true that silver coins had been badly debased during the war, falling sometimes to under 20 per cent pure, peculation of public monies is a likelier cause of the shoddy coins of 199. Not only were the new indemnity instalments smaller than those set in 241 but the Romans had found no reason to complain of the payment or payments in 201 (the compensation for the plundered supply-ships and, if this was paid then, the initial indemnity instalment). By 196, on the other hand, embezzlement of public funds was an open scandal.[12]

Besides, some economic recovery was already under way in Punic Africa, and that should have made payment in relatively sound coin more practicable. The Carthaginians, in a rather pathetic effort to show their goodwill the year after peace was made, had made large gifts of wheat (400,000 *modii* in all) to the city of Rome and the Roman armies operating in the Balkans. Possibly enough, given postwar conditions, they put themselves out to make the gift sizeable—though on later occasions far larger quantities would be given—but it was a noteworthy gesture of reviving productivity. Trade recovered, for Spain was still a market even if lost as a province, while dealings with Sicily and Italy soon revived too, as finds of Punic pottery there show, plus sizeable quantities of early second-century Campanian ware in Punic Africa. Plautus' comedy *Poenulus*, probably of the 190s, treats the ordinary Carthaginian merchant as a standard visitor to trading cities, an agreeably amusing figure with his distinctive habits of dress and speech. All this adds to the likelihood that the debased coins of 199 were chiefly not due to a struggling economy but rather to corrupt administrators.[13]

If the return of some prosperity benefited mainly the highest level of the Carthaginian community, and inevitably the *ordo* of judges in particular, discontent was likely to simmer among other citizens. Not just among the Punic poor but among others—landowners and merchants—in between as well, including at least some of the less exalted aristocracy. By 196, Livy reports, both carelessness with state revenues, and some leading men's direct peculation, had reduced these to a level that made it impossible to pay the Romans their indemnity. This would help to explain the sort of reforms Hannibal was to enact: he opened the ranks of the One Hundred and Four to yearly election, and struck at financial corruption to avert a foreshadowed new tax on all citizens, ensure that the state received all its due revenues, and pay the indemnity.

It is rather surprising that so soon after the most disastrous war in Punic history the ruling élite, or some of them, should misbehave so crassly. Livy no doubt exaggerates for dramatic effect how thoroughgoing the oligarchy's arrogance and solidarity were (his depiction may go back to a pro-Hannibalic witness like Silenus or Sosylus) but Hannibal's attested reforms confirm that serious flaws did exist and did arouse serious discontent. One cause of leading men's unprincipled attitude to public funds may well have been the damage to countryside and infrastructure inflicted, first, by the many Roman war-raids on North Africa, then—and probably much worse—by Scipio's ruthless and wide-ranging harryings from 204 to 202. It is worth noting that one of the concessions he offered for the armistice after Zama was an instant stop to devastation. Of course everyone in the Romans' way had suffered, but only the economically and politically weighty were in a position to take early steps to recover.

A further factor was doubtless the passing of Barcid dominance itself. The 'judges' may have fostered solidarity in exploiting their financial opportunities and repressing their critics, but that would hardly inhibit competitiveness among leading men for office and eminence—and competitiveness would, almost predictably, reach new heights once the overall control of a dominant group and leader had crumbled. At Carthage, as Aristotle had stressed and Polybius would reiterate, money played a crucial political rôle and bribery was a norm. The Barcids had exploited this ancient tradition, with decades of Spanish treasure to draw on. Political competitors after 201 had to fall back on other, more domestic sources. If Hannibal and his remaining supporters were seen as less tainted than rival groups, his own aversion to such methods may well have been only one reason: another might simply be that before 196, thanks to widespread aristocratic opposition, his circle was less successful in winning office with its accompanying opportunities.[14]

IV

Hannibal kept out of public life after giving up the generalship. He may have felt out of place and unpractised in civilian life after a virtual lifetime in military and administrative command (as his words to the senate had implied after silencing Gisco). Nor had he as wide a network of kinsmen and friends as 20, or even ten, years before. Some had died—his own brothers would not be the sole relatives lost—and some would turn their backs on a defeated semi-stranger, however worldwide his fame.

It would be instructive to know what became of notable wartime henchmen and subordinates like his nephew Hanno (last heard of as following the son of Gisco in the African command, if this was indeed his nephew), Hannibal's own friend Mago the Samnite who had operated in south Italy as late as 208, Maharbal the cavalry commander (last heard of in 216), Bomilcar the admiral, the cruel Hannibal Monomachus, and the energetic half-Greek

Epicydes who after the wreck of his and his brother's Syracusan venture had got away to Carthage. Several no doubt survived the war and it is unlikely they were attacked when their old general was not, but if they associated with him they quite probably were sidelined politically. Politics, though, may not have appealed to them all; while some conceivably enough found it more comfortable to fall in with one faction or other among the 'judges' and enjoy the benefits resulting. Certainly when Hannibal re-emerged into public life—and afterwards when he left for exile—no friend or relative, or wartime lieutenant, is mentioned along with him.

The scandal of the flawed indemnity in 199 did not draw him back into public life. Taking efficient charge of Barcid property in Africa, all that was left to the family now that Spain was lost, would demand much time especially in the first years of peace. So would his duties as head of what remained of the family. Nor can we simply take it for granted that the extent of public corruption and maladministration drew his ire from the start. For one thing, as suggested above, this situation may have worsened significantly only after the return of peace; for another, Hannibal himself (on the evidence of people who knew him) appreciated the value of money and the importance of acquiring it, therefore need not automatically have looked askance at other aristocrats doing so until they caused a serious problem; and for a third, with his faction in its weakened postwar state he may well have had more interest, at first anyway, in trying to build alliances with past supporters and with newcomers to politics, rather than confronting practically all vested interests straightaway.[15]

V

Over four or five years, however, things plainly changed. His first move on taking office as sufete was to initiate a clash with the *ordo iudicum*, and on winning this he turned to reform of the state finances. These were in such a mess that by 197 it was hard to raise even the funds to pay the all-important war-indemnity—and the only solution the authorities could think of was to impose a levy on all citizens. The Carthaginians as a whole, in other words, were going to be made to subsidize the misbehaviour of the currently ruling factions.

This no doubt brought discontent to a head and gave Hannibal his opening. Likely enough he himself felt the abuses had gone too far by now, especially if they threatened to jeopardize relations with the Romans. The renegade officer Hamilcar had continued stirring up trouble for them in Cisalpina (he was at length suppressed only in 197), which was bad enough. Worse, a dispute had arisen with Masinissa. We are not told what it was, only that when Roman envoys came to Carthage in 195 on their anti-Hannibal mission their pretended brief was 'to settle the disputes that the Carthaginians were having' with the king. Since all later disputes with him were over his encroachments on Punic lands, starting with an attempted grab of the Emporia region in 193, this earliest one was very probably territorial too—the king's first tentative prodding to find vulnerable soil. Though it seems to have fizzled out eventually (when Masinissa found Hannibal was the leader he would have to deal with), any trouble with the Romans' Numidian ally and protégé could prove disastrous for the Carthaginians in their financially harassed and militarily puny condition. These worries may have helped Hannibal on the hustings.

Moreover, during 197 the power of Philip V of Macedon in turn was shattered at the battle of Cynoscephalae, and the ensuing peace, dictated by the Romans, gave them the same implicit supremacy over Macedon and Greece that they already held over North Africa. The Carthaginians could neither afford to irritate their increasingly imperial ex-enemies nor risk their own state limping along in increasing financial disarray: sober self-interest demanded reform.[16]

Not only were these issues now prime concerns of Hannibal's but he probably made that clear when he sought office (for the clash was sparked by the mulish attitude towards the new sufete of an official supported by the 'judges'). In other words he was elected to the highest civil office by popular vote, against the feelings of at least a sizeable section of the dominant élite. His reforms then, according to Livy, made him wildly popular with the common people though they put him at odds with many or most of his fellow-grandees. In his early fifties, Hannibal had discovered democracy.

Or, at any rate, how to behave like a democrat. Barcid supremacy in its golden days had been based, to be sure, on popular election—but not on civil office or regular re-election. Instead it had relied on charismatic military command, while day-to-day government at Carthage had been carried on under Barcid dominance by the established authorities. Now Hannibal relied directly on the voters. The sufeteship was not normally noted for independent policy-making, nor ever before for open challenges to the senate or Hundred and Four. Using it in these ways was a move that needed sustained and strong backing from his fellow-citizens, and plainly Hannibal had it.

Certainly he must have had some supporters among the aristocracy: those who remained in the 'Barcid faction' as Livy calls it. The historian is careful to note that 'a great part' of the élite opposed the sufete, in other words he does not claim they all did (any more than he claims all were peculators). Some grandees' willingness to stick with him probably rested as much or more on personal and family loyalty as on reformist conviction, for there had been a Barcid group large or small at Carthage for nearly 50 years and—even after Hannibal's own exile—it endured under the same epithet (rather than being called the 'democratic' or 'popular' faction) for some years more. Perhaps one such supporter became the other sufete, for Hannibal met no obstruction from him.

But the only Carthaginian named in supposed association with Hannibal at this date is Mago his late brother—a fancy we owe to Nepos, who has him alive and seeking to join Hannibal in exile in 193. If Nepos confused his brother with some real Mago linked to Hannibal in the 190s, it may have been the general's old friend Mago the Samnite last heard of at Thurii in 208, or just possibly the relative whom the Romans had captured in 215 and who by now may have returned. Whoever it was, his rôle is unknown: he probably was not the other sufete, for if Nepos imagined him to be Hannibal's brother he would surely have mentioned such a combination.[17]

The sufete's enemies afterwards claimed that he had made early contact with the Seleucid Great King, Antiochus III—self-styled 'the Great'—and the two of them had been plotting a new war against the Romans. Quite likely various accusations were made against him before 196 too, but it seems clear that his sufeteship produced a crescendo. The claims were surely lies. At the most basic level, had Hannibal been in regular touch with the king he ought to have known Antiochus' whereabouts at particular seasons: but when he fled from Carthage in summer 195 he journeyed to Syria unaware that Antiochus had left there for the Aegean. Nor of course is there sound evidence that as early as 198, 197 or 196 the king was looking for a Roman war—quite the opposite, in fact. Even when the exiled Hannibal did join him, it was only as Antiochus' relations with the Romans worsened, by 193, that the king treated him as a serious adviser.[18]

As one of the great men of Carthage, maybe still its foremost citizen (so Livy describes him), Hannibal had connexions abroad as well as at home. With Numidian lords his family had ties of marriage and kinship; links with Carthage's mother-city Tyre are known and no doubt they existed with other centres. Connexions like these were important for prestige, trade matters, travel plans and up-to-date information. In the city Hannibal held regular morning levees for large numbers of people, who must have included visitors from elsewhere; like other Punic aristocrats he no doubt put on dinner-parties and other social events. Dealings with visitors, even conversations with them, could easily be misrepresented—and Phoenicia, including Tyre, belonged to Antiochus' empire. So once it became clear at Carthage that the king and the Romans were bickering, Hannibal's foes could set rumours flying.[19]

XVI

HANNIBAL SUFETE

I

Our only account of Hannibal's sufeteship is Livy's, and like most other episodes of Carthaginian history told by Greeks or Romans it is compressed and some details are unclear. Even so, it is firmly pro-Hannibal in tone, which suggests that though Livy probably drew on Polybius for it, Polybius himself may well have used the account of someone like Sosylus or Silenus. Just where Hannibal's friends' histories ended we do not know, but according to Nepos the pair were by his side 'as long as fortune permitted it'—and that would likely have lasted until his sudden flight in 195. Nor of course did separation, whenever it happened, have to mean a loss of interest in his doings.

But if instead Polybius' ultimate informant was Roman (admittedly it seems a smaller possibility) we might think of Q. Terentius Culleo, one of the three senatorial envoys sent over to Carthage that year. Culleo was acquainted with the Carthaginians because, like the annalist Cincius Alimentus, he had been their prisoner of war. Freed by Scipio in Africa in 201, his devotion to him from then on was unbounded—and Scipio strongly opposed intervening in the Carthaginians' domestic affairs six years later, and was remembered as an admirer of Hannibal. Culleo's nomination as an envoy may have been an effort by Scipio, then honorary first senator, to soften the impact of the mission, or a move by the interventionists to mollify him. Culleo himself was still active enough a quarter of a century later to go on another African embassy, so reminiscences of his could have reached Polybius, conceivably even at first hand after the latter came to Italy in 167.[1]

The year of Hannibal's sufeteship was probably 196, when at Rome L. Furius Purpureo and M. Claudius Marcellus were consuls. The Roman embassy that arrived soon after Hannibal laid down office, and prompted him into self-exile, had Marcellus as one of its three members, a task he could not have undertaken while holding office. Moreover, as mentioned earlier Hannibal then travelled to Syria expecting to meet King Antiochus, who had journeyed there from Ephesus in late 196. But early in 195 Antiochus returned to Ephesus to pursue his difficulties with the Romans, and Hannibal on reaching Syria had to follow him westwards.

All this makes 196 the likeliest date for the sufeteship—admittedly we do not know when the Punic official year began and ended—and 195 the year of his flight. True, Nepos dates the flight to Marcellus' and Purpureo's consulate and to 'the year after his praetorship', thus putting the latter in 197, but this is less plausible. His account of the postwar years has other oddities as we have seen, and after a few paragraphs he terms the year 193 'the third year' after the flight: more evidence of indecisive dating. Quite likely he has confused Marcellus as envoy with Marcellus as consul. And though Appian too has 196 as the year the exiled general joined Antiochus, his own unreliabilities in matters and events Punic make this the reverse of encouraging. Still, Nepos may be right in relative terms about Hannibal going into exile 'the year after his praetorship'. This detail again supports 196 and 195 as the years in question.[2]

II

The new magistrate's first recorded move was to summon a 'quaestor', who refused to come. This official may have been the republic's chief of finances (the usual assumption) or, rather likelier, one of its financial officials, the *mhsbm* or 'accountables', attested on inscriptions. What Hannibal wanted to discuss we do not know: maybe the financial situation overall, but Livy afterwards records him tackling the much-abused finances of the republic apparently as a separate matter. The dispute with the 'quaestor' may have had a different cause, even if connected with finance.

The latter was defiant because he would become one of the *iudices* when his magistracy ended; and Hannibal's reaction (after having him arrested) was to legislate to remove the *iudices'* lifetime tenure. So the summons may have been over some accusation of malfeasance—corruption, injustice or incompetence—which the 'quaestor' expected to be able to shrug off once he exchanged office for entry into the One Hundred and Four.[3]

Livy is careful to specify too that this official belonged to the 'opposite faction'. It is plausible enough that there was more to the clash than just a guilty magistrate dodging investigation, for plainly the sufete found it politically worthwhile to attack him. The rights and wrongs of the dispute were one thing, but Hannibal wanted a justification for an assault on the *iudices*. No doubt he chose his issue carefully, all the same: the offender had to be fairly obviously (or plausibly) guilty, and unpopular as well. The sufete haled him before a citizen-gathering—what became of him we are not told—and then carried a law reforming recruitment to the One Hundred and Four.

The connexion between a recalcitrant magistrate and reform of the tribunal is not obvious. On one interpretation the sufete overstepped (or was accused of overstepping) his powers in summoning and then arresting the recalcitrant 'quaestor', the latter appealed to the One Hundred and Four who made their attitude clear in his favour, and Hannibal then took the issue to the assembly. But Livy's account does not suggest this line of events.

Hannibal, when defied by the 'quaestor', brought the arrested man before the citizens and criticized both him and the *ordo iudicum*; and when this met with a favourable reception, 'immediately' brought forward and carried his reform law. This must have been either at the same meeting—but Livy calls it a *contio*, which at Rome anyway was a non-legislative though officially convoked gathering of citizens—or at a legislative assembly convoked very soon after.[4]

More likely then Hannibal accused the 'quaestor' of specific offences, but made it clear that there was no point in prosecuting him as things stood. True, in this era sufetes themselves could hear at least some cases, but this may not have been one of them—or else a sufete's verdict could be appealed—very probably meaning that any charge against the 'quaestor' would sooner or later go before the far from unbiased One Hundred and Four. Although this is not certain, it seems the most plausible link between Hannibal's joint attack on the 'quaestor' and the 'judges'; and as shown earlier, there are some grounds for thinking that Hasdrubal had amended the tribunal's functions back in the 220s.[5]

The sufete's tactics worked splendidly. The prospect of an arrogant offender escaping justice thanks to his connexions aroused citizens' enthusiasm for the proposal to replace lifetime membership of the One Hundred and Four with a one-year appointment, and to ban membership of two years in a row. It seems likely that the one-year judges were to be elected by the citizen assembly, like the magistrates: the voters' keenness would surely have been dampened if the existing selection-process—the Boards of Five choosing members of the senate for the tribunal—were merely to be modified into an annual event, nor would that have brought much flexibility or freshness. The senate, with its few hundred members, would have to start recycling them for the tribunal after just a few years: not much of a blow against the widely resented coterie-character of the Hundred and Four. Annual selection points to popular election.

This was a momentous move. One obvious aim was to open judges to legal scrutiny, for a judge or ex-judge accused of impropriety could no longer count on being tried before entrenched and understanding colleagues. Again, implicit in the change was a near-reversal of the relationship of tribunal to senate. Instead of being recruited from the senate, the Hundred and Four would more often than not be recruited from non-senators (though no doubt senators could seek election too). Many of these, after a term or two as judge, would surely use their improved repute to seek other offices, including magistracies and a place in the senate.

Hannibal may have calculated on other improvements too. Judges' hopes of success in this new judicio-political scheme would force them to be more open in their work, and prevent them from favouring aristocratic special interests too blatantly at ordinary citizens' expense. The senate in its turn, the Mighty Ones, would lose their too-easily-exploitable symbiosis with the highest court of the republic and, moreover, would have to be more accountable to the rest of the citizen-body: for if prosecuted on serious charges a senator would find himself facing citizen-elected judges not at all guaranteed to be friendly.[6]

Of course critics could point out more than one potential flaw in the new system. Citizens freshly elected to the tribunal might have no, or very little, judicial experience, for instance. But this objection would be of small weight in a world where, for instance, major trials at Rome were held before the citizen assembly and at Athens ordinary citizens regularly sat as juror-judges.

Arguably again, candidates might now win election on the basis of political or personal attractiveness rather than any particular fitness for the rôle. Indeed annual elections were almost guaranteed to take on factional overtones, at any rate in times when political stresses were high, and in turn this could promote bribery and misbehaviour all over again. Still, Hannibal might reply that a regular turnover of tribunal membership would at least make it easier to bring blatant offenders to book; by contrast the old system had made it almost impossible (as the clash with the 'quaestor' illustrated). Nor—he could add—was it morally impressive for defenders of a system that helped perpetuate aristocratic exploitation of public life to complain about politics still playing a part in judicial affairs after the reform. In any case money and bribes were a standard element in Punic politics, one that none of the Barcids objected to and all had made use of. What mattered was to deter or punish those who went too far and still expected to enjoy impunity.

At least it looked good in theory. And it was better than what had gone before.

Nothing suggests that Hannibal included a qualification to ensure that existing judges would be replaced under the new scheme only as each in turn passed from life. On that basis it would have taken a generation (or an epidemic) before the last of the Hundred and Four was popularly elected, and by then the new law's and the sufete's enemies would long have rallied their forces to repeal it. The law surely came into force directly—meaning that elections for the entire membership of the tribunal had to be held during the current official year, so that the new Hundred and Four could take their seats when the next year started.

With public support strongly on his side Hannibal could count on many Barcid supporters winning membership, perhaps indeed a majority, in the new Hundred and Four—at least for 195. This would give both a positive start to the reformed court and also protection to himself after he laid down his office—an important extra benefit he might reckon on needing by then. We shall see that his calculations were probably accurate. As for the hapless 'quaestor', once his term expired his fate was probably sealed, for the same reasons.[7]

III

The reforming sufete now turned his attention to the republic's woebegone finances. As we saw, these were most likely in trouble not because of any economic downturn, still less pressure from the Romans' yearly indemnity (this was a victim of the trouble, not a cause), but because too many fingers dipped into them between collection and deposit at the treasury. The obvious solution was to ensure that transmission from the one to the other became faultless—as faultless as possible in ancient conditions, at any rate. This Hannibal achieved, though no one tells how.

Livy does insist on the waste and theft by which the republic was defrauded, and the survey Hannibal made of revenue-sources and commitments. Nepos merely reports him imposing 'new taxes' that enriched the state, either misunderstanding his cleanup measures (which were themselves new) or meaning new taxes not on his fellow-Carthaginians but on their allies and subjects. A principal reason for the Carthaginians' outrage and probably the main stimulus to Hannibal's election had been the threat of a new general tax, so he had no motive to bring in one himself. Nor any need, if Livy is right to imply that simply stopping the existing leaks was enough to make the Roman indemnity easily payable. But Nepos stresses that the new taxes enabled the treasury to build up a surplus, and we shall see that this very likely did happen.[8]

As seen earlier, rough-and-ready calculation gives Hannibal's city a postwar annual revenue of 1,400–1,500 talents. The new indemnity of 200 talents a year was then well over 10 per cent of this—but a much larger percentage of what actually reached the treasury. It is not surprising then that the Carthaginians were having trouble amassing the sum in 196. Hannibal carried out a thorough investigation into state revenues and expenditures, established what they ought to be (no doubt allowing for trade fluctuations and varying agricultural output, at least to some extent) and worked out—most tellingly of all—how and where the funding-diversions occurred. It seems he announced the results, or a résumé of them, at another public assembly: at any rate he told his listeners that removing the abuses would provide plenty of funds to pay the indemnity, and he promised to remove them.

How a sufete, or even both sufetes, could take charge of finance is not known. Sufetes are nowhere recorded with finance among their responsibilities, though this may only be due to the state of our sources. Maybe Hannibal's brisk way with the 'quaestor' had prompted the other finance officials to co-operate in practice, even if they did not have to do so in law; or maybe he put his measures to the citizen assembly for ratification. Maybe both, for no amount of ratification could guarantee the success of financial reforms if the officials who had to implement them remained opposed.

It is not certain, even if sometimes claimed, that he also made the peculators disgorge all that they had taken. Livy writes that having completed his survey of income and embezzlements 'he collected all the outstanding funds and cancelled the tax on private citizens'. If 'the outstanding funds' covered embezzlements going back over years or decades, then Hannibal would indeed have wrought a social revolution as occasionally claimed. After all, most such sums would not have been kept idle in strong-boxes, so a strict inquisition would have been needed to identify goods and properties bought with the stolen money, plus other investments such as loans and trade ventures; then all these would have to be either confiscated by the state or sold off by owners, inevitably at a loss, to meet the state's claims. The whole process would have been open-ended and dangerously destabilizing not just economically but politically, even if the inquisition went back only (for instance) to the end of the recent war. It would be likely to drag in Barcid kinsmen and supporters as well as enemies, especially if it probed beyond 201. On all these grounds any such measure was surely inconceivable.[9]

Much likelier, Livy means—or is compressing a source who meant—that Hannibal succeeded in plugging the revenue-leaks so that the sums due in the current year were all received. Perhaps too he forced those who had made off with funds earlier in the year, before his reform had gone through, to repay them: that would be logical and relatively feasible.

The methods of the reform can only be surmised. Carelessness (*neglegentia*) and direct theft were behind the losses, Livy writes briefly, no doubt compressing his source again. In this context carelessness would surely mean, as a rule anyway, not physically mislaying bags of money or losing them off wagons *en route* to the treasury, but overseers' and officials' insouciance—probably often collusive insouciance—over pilfering by lesser functionaries and other persons while funds were collected; insouciance too over supervising state contracts and supplies, and (pretty inevitably) over rendering proper accounts when these fell due. The remedy was obviously to impose reliable supervision and stricter auditing, which in turn required officials whom the sufete (and future sufetes) could trust. How Hannibal achieved it is not reported, but the election of the new and more compliant One Hundred and Four may have helped, if only by reminding existing functionaries that they now risked real penalties if caught out.[10]

Preventing outright peculation may have been an easier task, again basically calling for proper supervision (which the sufete could exert himself); maybe too Hannibal was able to get reliable men elected or selected for office at least for the coming year. The reforms would be better protected if he could enact more structured supervision-methods (a board or committee chosen from among each year's One Hundred and Four, for instance): but Livy merely generalizes that 'he kept his promise' to improve the revenues.

All the same, the financial improvement survived Hannibal's sufeteship. Five years later the Romans were once more at war, this time with King Antiochus, and the Carthaginians offered to help by paying over in one lump sum their entire remaining indemnity: forty years' worth, in other words no less than 8,000 talents or 48 million *denarii*. This was equivalent to around three and a half years of the Roman republic's own average revenues—and more tellingly, more than six years of Punic revenues as estimated earlier. So from being unable in 197–196 to pay 200 talents unless a special tax were levied, the Carthaginians by 191 had accumulated funds at an average rate of 1,600 a year. At the same time they offered to donate massive quantities of wheat and barley, up to double what they had supplied in 200. The Romans for political reasons refused these Punic largesses, but plainly the offers were genuine.

This was an amazing turnaround. Indeed it seems too much even for the reformed revenues on their own. This makes Nepos' already-mentioned report of 'new taxes' noteworthy. Conceivably enough the sufete raised the Libyans' taxes (an old Punic device to improve revenues) and those of subordinate cities like Lepcis. This would win him no friends among such folk, but none had the vote at Carthage, and Hannibal was hardly a sentimentalist when it came to his own city's interests.

Carthage's economic revival, too, should have increased the intake from customs and harbour-dues and promoted other pursuits in which Carthaginians were skilled—shipbuilding, for instance, and not just for Punic customers—which might in turn be taxed one way or another. The city after all now had two safe and usable artificial ports, for, with the navy abolished, the circular inner port was as free for peacetime craft as was the outer haven. Archaeological evidence shows the inner port remained much in use, in fact was thoroughly refurbished, during the second century and this despite the absence of a war-fleet. With no navy save ten ships, no army to speak of (and few if any mercenaries), commercial and agricultural life reburgeoning, and extra tax revenues flowing in, it need not surprise that the state soon began to accumulate money.[11]

IV

Even these measures may not have been Hannibal's sole activities as sufete. Of course he had to devote much energy and time to them, for along with a probable involvement in the first election of the new-look tribunal of One Hundred and Four he had his inquest into the public finances to carry out followed by his remedies for the ailing treasury. Nor in turn could he afford to ignore the elections for the following year's magistracies and the next Hundred and Four. Continuity of policy was vital for his reforms to be effective: since he and any allies of his in office could not seek re-election, or chose not to—and an entire new tribunal of judges had to be created—it would be common sense to try to get as many fresh supporters as possible elected instead. He must have had some success, for the Barcid faction was to remain politically powerful for some years to come.

But he may have found time for other important work too, if the suggestion is correct that he initiated a major urban redevelopment which archaeologists have uncovered on the southern slopes of the Byrsa hill, datable through pottery to the early second century and so sometimes nicknamed 'Hannibal's quarter' of the city. This was a well-designed residential and commercial project that replaced an area of iron foundries: broad stepped streets and handsome apartment blocks were laid out on the hillside, notable for Hellenistic features like peristyles and bathroom facilities. The development's date and its novel and seemingly uniform plan have prompted the suggestion that it was another project of Hannibal the sufete. This may be right, for the Barcids had a tradition of city-building—even brother Mago supposedly had established a settlement in the Balearic islands in 205, today's Mahón—and Hannibal himself was later to found one or even two cities in the east for royal patrons. With the Byrsa project, though, he can have done little more than draw up the plans and view the initial stage of work, for even by mid-195 not all the funds needed can already have been available.

Whoever was responsible, the development was probably a response to the revival of prosperity and pressures for new living space. Priests and officials have been suggested as its likely beneficiaries. To them could be added the small shopkeepers and craftsmen who rented or bought premises in the new district. Some of the grand Hellenistic-style mansions discovered down by the shore may have been established at this time too: they would be city residences for members of the aristocracy, perhaps including Hannibal himself.[12]

V

When his sufeteship expired he was plainly once more the first man in the state. As noted earlier, it looks as though he and his supporters were again in the ascendancy, whoever the supporters were, even if some proved to be fair-weather friends only, and even though the senate—whose membership had not been touched—probably remained evenly balanced.

The sources' picture is consistent even if sketchy. During his sufeteship Hannibal had carried all before him and his enemies were reduced to intriguing with their friends at Rome against him. Afterwards, Livy makes clear, political feelings were high but his supporters remained many and strong. When the Roman embassy in 195 delivered a tirade against the fugitive leader in the Punic senate, no doubt via the most senior envoy Cn. Servilius Caepio, the senators simply replied that they would do whatever the Romans thought proper: there is no sign of them enthusiastically seconding the accusations, as might have been expected had Hannibal's enemies regained control by now (these after all had intrigued to have the embassy sent), nor does the ensuing proscription of him prove anything but that the senate was obeying or anticipating Roman wishes, as promised.[13]

The glimpse Livy later allows of Carthage in 193 is just as suggestive. When Hannibal's undeclared emissary Aristo of Tyre attracted notice, a debate in the senate showed opinion to be polarized: senators demanding action on Aristo were matched by those opposing it and deadlock ensued. Rather contradictorily, Livy then depicts the senate as a whole as hostile to Aristo whereas 'the leading men' are willing to meet with him, and mutual suspicions are only worsened by ordinary citizens' equally dim view of the senate. It all produces internal wrangles serious enough to encourage Masinissa to encroach meantime on Punic lands. The contrasts are over-drawn—as another example, Livy himself records Aristo as having talks with Barcid supporters only, not all the 'leading men'—but it is reasonable to con-clude from this evidence that many aristocrats were still pro-Barcid in 193 and a sizeable segment of ordinary citizens likewise, while the senate was more or less evenly divided in sympathies. Even if by then anti-Barcid sena-tors were more numerous, they were not strong enough to overbear their opponents on a controversial matter, and the resulting standoff so paralysed Punic politics that it gave Masinissa ideas.

On the other hand Aristo's circumspect behaviour at Carthage, and ulti-mate flight to avoid an inquisition, suggest that no kinsmen or friends of Hannibal were then in high office, though many no doubt were senators and in the One Hundred and Four and could hope for sufeteships and other posi-tions in future. In other words the Barcid resurgence Hannibal had achieved can still be traced, though in weaker condition, three years later.[14]

When he stepped down from office Hannibal must have been aware of his opponents' moves to have the Romans act against him. Carthaginian grandees had been writing to their guest-friends, 'the leading men of Rome' according to Livy, to press the allegations about him being in touch with the Seleucid king and to warn in vague and general terms that Hannibal in charge of Carthage was no good thing for Rome. This had been going on since the finance-reforms, so pretty certainly Hannibal too learned of it in time. But he could do little except keep himself informed and make a few prudent prepa-rations in case of emergency.

Roman reaction was held up 'for a long time' by, of all people, Hannibal's military nemesis Scipio Africanus, who plainly viewed the accusations as slan-der. That an embassy was finally decreed in 195 may have been due to prodding by one consul, the combative M. Cato (not yet away in Spain) who was no friend to Scipio and, in later years anyway, showed notorious animos-ity towards the Carthaginians. How deep in collusion the Roman authorities were with Hannibal's enemies is shown by the deceptive way the envoys introduced themselves—stating on their Punic cronies' advice only that they had come to mediate in the dispute with Masinissa. Hannibal, not to be taken in by a palpable ruse, disappeared during the night and rode to his coastal estate near Thapsus, where he had a fully equipped ship waiting to take him via the offshore isle of Cercina to Tyre and then Syria.[15]

Had he stayed at Carthage, the envoys were probably under instructions to demand he be handed over to them. Their denunciation prompted the Punic senate to send two ships after him, which hardly squared with simultaneously declaring him an exile but obeyed the envoys' implication that he ought to be punished for his actions. The demand for his handover not only had been put to his fellow-citizens by the Roman war-embassy of 218 but became a staple in Roman dealings with those who became his hosts in exile. Surrendered leaders were not treated handsomely at Rome. Kings like Syphax and in 168 the fallen Perseus of Macedon might be put into guarded villas but even then did not survive long; other leaders (most famously Masinissa's grandson Jugurtha and the Gallic hero Vercingetorix) perished at Roman executioners' hands in the squalid Tullianum prison at the foot of the Capitol. Hannibal was wise not to risk it.[16]

The denunciations which the envoys supposedly then unleashed against him in the Punic senate bear the coarse stamp of annalistic hindsight. As Livy tells it, they accused him of stirring up both Antiochus III and the Aetolian League in Greece to make war on the Romans, and scheming to bring Carthage into the same plot, not to mention planning to involve the entire world in war. But although Roman relations with the king had soured by 195, at that period the Aetolians were still Roman allies—discontented ones to be sure, but they were not to break with the Romans and turn to Antiochus until 193, nor is it likely that the Roman Senate was blessed so early with the foresight to know they would.

What the envoys (in practice Caepio) did claim was probably closer to the allegations earlier raised by Hannibal's enemies: he had been in touch with the Seleucid king and was urging him to make war on the Romans, no doubt promising to bring in the Carthaginians on his side; the republic would never enjoy peace while its hate-filled former leader lived in its midst, free to take part in affairs and seek power afresh. It would have been a small step from this to demanding his handover, but in his absence the best they could add was what Livy reports, that 'such conduct should not go unpunished if the Carthaginians wished to convince the Roman people that none of [his misbehavings] had been done with their approval or with public sanction'.[17]

Faced with this unsubtle deposition the Punic senate—even had it been composed entirely of Barcid backers, even if both current sufetes were—could not counterargue. The Romans were militarily busy only with provincial wars in Cisalpina and Spain, and had a powerful navy plus plenty of veterans from the recent war with Macedon. Caepio and company had turned up officially out of the blue (they certainly had not been invited, nor had sent word ahead that they were coming), and everybody knew of at least one previous abrupt Roman démarche, the rape of Sardinia: some elderly senators had probably lived through it.

Even so—and even though the demand that Hannibal 'should not go unpunished' clearly implied that punishment should be at least decreed—the senate's reply took the limited form noted earlier: the Carthaginians would do whatever the Romans wished. This move quite possibly forced the envoys to declare what they did wish. Only after that were the penalties voted that

Nepos credibly reports (Livy mentions no penalties under any date but, as just noted, he plainly implies them here). The senate not only ordered ships to chase after the runaway ex-general but declared him an exile, seized his property and even demolished his house.[18]

But no one else was attainted and the Barcid faction remained to fight another day. As the crowds' reaction to his disappearance and then the Aristo episode in 193 both show, Hannibal left behind a strong network of friendships and popular support. His opponents do not seem to have succeeded in reimposing the old oligarchic control of affairs through the One Hundred and Four, for when some light is next thrown on Punic domestic affairs we read of three factions or groups competing politically: pro-Roman, pro-Masinissa (the old king was still very much alive) and 'those who favoured popular rule'.

Typically Appian, the reporter, fails to clarify when this was, and seems in fact to be generalizing about the whole postwar era—he names Hanno the Great, surely in his eighties by 195 if not dead, as the pro-Roman leader and Hamilcar the Samnite, who was active in the later 150s, as one of the two democrat chiefs. But it is clearly implied that politics remained a matter of competing leaders and groups, even if the leaders were the rich and well-born as usual. The citizen assembly continued to play an important part: to drive the pro-Masinissa faction-chiefs into exile in 152 Hamilcar the Samnite and his confrère Carthalo had to carry a popular vote, which they sought to shore up by persuading the citizens into an oath never to contemplate repeal. In turn the 'democratic' faction's ascendancy in the following years, leading to confrontation first with Masinissa and then with the Romans, was seconded by the Mighty Ones, who continued to direct foreign affairs.

Such consensus probably had not reigned at all times during the preceding 40 years, of course, but overall it points to a more open and flexible political life after 196 compared with before. Moreover it was the 'democrats' who in the 150s and after spearheaded resistance first to Masinissa and then, disastrously, the Romans. So, whether or not directly descended in political terms from Hannibal's supporters, they look like continuators and adapters of his methods and attitudes—and, in dramatic irony, the devisers of a national disaster that outdid his.[19]

VI

Hannibal's services to his city as sufete were certainly notable. True, he was not the architect of the renewed prosperity: that was due to the energy and resourcefulness of all his fellow-citizens, even if he had helped to set an example with his olive-plantations. But as suggested earlier, his financial reforms seem to have survived and made an impact, he eased the political strains that had been building up and he let greater flexibility, openness and indeed responsibility into public life. Arguably his achievements in one year of civil office far outdid those of his twenty years of military command—in constructive practical effects if not world renown.

The Romans' reaction to his reappearance in public affairs in 196 sharply contrasts with their indifference five years earlier, even though then he had still headed an army whereas now his leadership was civilian. Scipio, uninterested in hounding Hannibal in 201, was firmly opposed to it in 196 too, but his influence—despite his renown and his position as honorary first senator—had plainly declined. The Romans' intervention vividly illustrates, and unflatteringly, their worries at the prospect of conflict with the Great King of the East. But it revealed too the growth of a deeply ingrained ill-feeling towards the Carthaginians. This could not yet be called hostility (except towards Hannibal) but, over the decades and in spite of all their guest-friendships and contacts, it would strengthen into implacability.

This did not have to happen. The Romans' officious response in 195 to the allegations by Hannibal's enemies—whose self-interest was surely obvious to others besides Scipio—recalls their ruthless reaction to Hamilcar's military and political success in 237 which involved no menace to Italy: better to act high-handedly at once to snuff out a possible danger than sit quiet and see what might come. There is no sign that the Carthaginians harboured anti-Roman feelings, let alone schemes, nor that Hannibal had any such designs. True, after years of Masinissa's bullying and Roman lukewarmness, they broke the treaty of 201 by waging war against the Numidian without the Romans' (unobtainable) consent. But the king's provocation was obvious, nor had they any wish for a Roman war even then.

So it could be argued that if the Romans had followed Scipio's advice and left the Carthaginians to solve their own problems, relations between the two republics would have found a better footing. The reformed and peaceable Punic state would have posed no threat, would have promoted prosperity around the Mediterranean, might even have become a loyal ally—and there would have been no tragedy of 146. If so the Romans' vindictiveness in 195 was unusually shortsighted.[20]

This is probably too optimistic, all the same. The Carthaginians and Hannibal too were submissive because they were militarily powerless. It is a different question what might have happened over time, if Hannibal and his friends had remained dominant in political life while prosperity developed and the Romans entangled themselves in one foreign war after another.

Masinissa and his ambitions would have been a permanent thorn in Punic Africa's side, and action against him—as actual events were to show—could not be ventured without involving, in fact defying, the Romans. Hannibal would have made sure that, if it came to defiance, the republic was well equipped (its accumulating wealth has already been mentioned). It is not unthinkable, either, that a vigorously restored and Barcid-dominated state might eventually have looked for ways to reassert itself in foreign affairs overall, including allying with other states oppressed by growing Roman supremacy and high-handedness. Indeed in 174 Masinissa was to claim that the Carthaginians and Perseus of Macedon had exchanged envoys, though what their motives were is unknown (and the Romans for once seem not to have taken offence). The decision to interfere at Carthage in 195 probably owed something to fear of a Barcid-led return to independence; and however ill-grounded the fear was at the time, over the long term it was probably the right decision from the viewpoint of the Romans' own interests.[21]

XVII

THE END OF THE BARCIDS

I

Hannibal never came home. Received by Antiochus III as a friend and counsellor, he none the less failed to play a notable rôle in the events up to and during the Great King's war with the Romans. Originally he was neglected because the king still sought to settle his differences with the Romans by diplomacy; then he continued to be overlooked (we are told) owing to his ill-timed hobnobbing with Roman envoys at Ephesus in 193. They sought him out supposedly with specious hints that he might be able to return to Carthage, but in reality to stir suspicions in Antiochus' mind: a fairly predictable ploy that any experienced ex-general should recognize. He may have responded so as to sound out what the chances of return were—or to remind his host indirectly that he was not to be taken for granted. In either case it lacked tact. Even if he regained Antiochus' confidence by telling him of his boyhood oath 'never to bear goodwill to the Romans', the Seleucid monarch still failed to use him seriously when war did break out.[1]

There were other reasons for this. The exile's frankness would have done him no good if the stories told of it are true—like the cutting comment when Antiochus, showing off his sumptuously caparisoned military multitudes, asked complacently if they would be enough for the Romans: 'enough and quite enough for the Romans, however greedy they are'. This is probably *ben trovato* rather than true (a writer's idea later on of showing how the hero forecast débâcle and refused to flatter), unless it was a comment that Hannibal in fact growled to someone else after the display. More likely to be true is his barb at the expense of Phormio, a Peripatetic philosopher at Ephesus, whose lifetime lack of military experience did not deter him from lecturing for hours on generalship to Hannibal and an otherwise enraptured audience—'I have often seen many old drivellers, but one who drivelled more than Phormio I have not seen.' But Phormio's admirers probably included, even if not Antiochus, some of the royal court since it was Hannibal's new hosts who had invited him along.[2]

He was outspoken, and not entirely to others' taste again, when occasion-ally admitted to the royal council's strategic planning discussions. In 194 and 193, when everyone including the king was still wondering whether it might come to war with the Romans, he urged pre-emptive action: a small com-bined expedition—100 warships, 10,000 foot and 1,000 horse, under his own command naturally—to be sent to Italy via Africa to try to bring the Carthaginians into alliance and, with their aid or without, raise war against the Romans in their homeland (Livy later shows he was thinking of Etruria, Liguria and Cisalpine Gaul). Meanwhile the main royal forces should move into Greece as a first step towards invading Italy in his support. This riskily optimistic grand scenario supposedly impressed Antiochus, but that was partly because war was far from certain and therefore bold schemes could be comfortably touted. In any case, the upshot was that Hannibal sent ahead his Tyrian friend Aristo to sound out the Carthaginians: and when that mission collapsed so did royal interest, if it had not already faded thanks to Hannibal's meetings with the envoys from Rome.[3]

Despite the reported reconciliation between exile and king that followed, Hannibal was still not invited to council meetings for several months, so the reconciliation was at best on a personal level. Militarily the royal ear preferred to listen to Greek advisers, Alexander the Acarnanian and Thoas of Aetolia, who suggested only sideshow-jobs for the Carthaginian because plainly they resented him in any serious rôle. Nor was Antiochus himself too enthusiastic about entrusting a serious rôle to a lieutenant who might eclipse him in mili-tary prowess.

If Nepos is right that in 193 Hannibal sailed with five ships to encourage his fellow-countrymen to join Antiochus' war—only to give up when he reached the coast of Cyrene, more than 600 miles (1,000 kilometres) from Carthage—then this was his first employment by the Seleucid king since he had joined the court, but the story is unconvincing. Nepos has Mago the Barcid join his brother only to die, and Hannibal gives up because the Carthaginians have decreed banishment for Mago in turn; on Aristo's mis-sion in this same year Nepos is silent. Livy more believably reports that the idea of sending Hannibal had been discussed but, thanks to Thoas, nothing came of it. If the ex-general did ever visit Cyrene, with five ships or just one, it would have been *en route* from Carthage to Tyre in 195, for the coastal trip could hardly have avoided Cyrenaica. If he learned of a Punic decree of exile then, it was not about his long-dead brother Mago but himself.[4]

He was not given another council hearing until midwinter 192–191 when the king and his court were at Demetrias in Greece, with hostilities already under way. Now he urged a rather different strategy but still with the focus on Italy: Philip V of Macedon to be won over or neutralized, half the royal fleet to raid the Tyrrhenian coasts and half to bar the Ionian Sea to an enemy crossing and make it possible for Antiochus to invade Italy himself at an opportune moment. This time he did not (it seems) envisage landing in Italy to stir up preliminary revolts: instead Antiochus was to station all his troops in Epirus for an invasion in force. The council applauded his proposals, then acted on none of them.[5]

II

Antiochus may have been jealous of his guest's fame and suspicious of his devotion, but there was more to it. Hannibal's stress that war against the Romans needed to be fought primarily in Italy was strategically sound (like his stress on how needful support from Macedon was), but for him to urge this after his own failure there, and in so limited a form—even though it was just to be the opening stage—was counterproductive. The notion that he could land in Italy or Cisalpina with 11,000 troops and tie the Romans in knots was frankly nonsense. When he had arrived there in 218 with more than twice as many, recruiting locally thousands more, he still had not managed either to crush them in their homeland or prevent them occupying all of Punic Spain and Africa save Carthage itself. Besides, by the mid-190s no part of Italy was in any condition or mood to rise up one more time against the Romans: yet for an expedition to make any real impact he would have needed much more than Cisalpine allies. As for the 100 ships that he had also demanded, Antiochus' whole navy was not much bigger—when war started in 192 he could take only that many with him to Greece.[6]

With Hannibal also proposing to stop *en route* at Carthage, the king might be forgiven for wondering just where the exile's priorities lay. Obviously, to have the Punic republic on side would be a great advantage: but was it guaranteed that if Hannibal and his friends recovered power, even thanks to Seleucid forces, they would back the king after all, rather than keep Carthage neutral and prosperous? If a Hannibalic coup sparked dissension in the state—as was quite likely—would the general still go on to Italy as promised rather than stay in Africa to support his faction? If he stayed home, Antiochus would have wasted troops, ships and money. When Hannibal in turn began having conversations with the Roman envoys during 193, any such doubts might well seem justified. He was able to pacify the royal mistrust: but his later proposals in winter 192 left out any mention of Carthage.

In the war, the best the Great King could find for the greatest general of the age to do was bizarre: a rôle as naval commodore in the eastern Mediterranean which in summer 190 earned him and a small Seleucid fleet a trouncing by the Rhodians off Side in Pamphylia. With the peace-terms in 189 calling for him to be surrendered to the Romans, he had to find a new refuge.

Six more years of rootlessness followed. First a stay at Gortyn in Crete where (the story goes) he deflected local greed for his portable wealth by lodging jars brimming with gold and silver in the temple of Artemis, only for the locals to find after his departure that the jars were lead-filled with just a topping of valuables—a properly Hannibalic ruse if true. Next to the court of Artaxias king of Armenia, for whom reportedly he founded the city of Artaxata; then in service with Prusias king of Bithynia, who like the now-dead Antiochus III made use of him in war merely as a naval commander. At least Hannibal won his sea-battle this time, in Prusias' brief war with Eumenes of Pergamum, again using a characteristic surprise touch—poisonous snakes in clay pots hurled onto the enemy's decks to sow panic. And according to the Elder Pliny at least, he founded a city, Prusa, for his host.

But Prusias was an unreliable protector. When Roman envoys arrived in Bithynia late in 183 or at the start of 182 to insist on peace between the two kings, they added Hannibal's handover to the agenda once more, though it may not have been part of their original instructions, and with Prusias' acquiescence took steps to prevent another flight as they closed in on his country house. To escape the indignity of capture—he no doubt recalled Syphax the Numidian's confinement and early death—the elderly exile, now 64, took poison. His remains were entombed nearby, the memorial one day to be splendidly redone in white marble by another and more successful African leader, the emperor Septimius Severus from Lepcis Magna.[7]

III

The rise and fall of the Barcids' ascendancy at Carthage played itself out almost exactly across Hannibal's own lifetime. More narrowly, he and his kinsmen had dominated the affairs of the Carthaginian republic from the later stages of the Mercenaries' War to the last years of the Second Punic and then again, as argued earlier, during the middle 190s. It was a dominance shorter than that of the Magonids in the sixth and fifth centuries, but much more spectacular.

Punic politics, as argued earlier too, remained relatively competitive after 195 if still largely aristocratic, and the one-time Barcid group—or a similar one—continued to play a part. But no Barcids were associated with it, and no appeal was made to Barcid or Hannibalic memories even in Carthage's death-struggle with the old enemy 40 years later. If Hannibal and Imilce did have a son he did not live, or else he lived a thoroughly obscure life. Ironically, lasting fame and even respect sprang from those same enemies and their Greek friends: starting with Scipio's admiration for Hannibal, Cato's commendation of Hamilcar and Polybius' broad treatment of all three Barcid leaders.

The Barcid ascendancy had rescued the city and the republic in their blackest hour, created a land empire to rival or outdo the Romans', and raised Carthaginian fortunes to their zenith by bringing much of Italy under Barcid dominance and recovering most of Barcid Spain from its invaders. Then Roman resilience and Barcid mistakes brought the overstretched structure down. The day after peace was sworn in 201 found the republic in much the same condition as the day after Hippou Acra and Utica had surrendered in

237: all overseas territories lost, the homeland a smoking ruin, trade shattered and the treasury drained. That brought one more Barcid service, Hannibal's sufeteship, which revitalized public life and restored public resources—and with them public confidence—enough for the effects to endure practically to the end of the city's existence.

These feats were not due simply to three men's genius. On all the evidence, Carthaginian society had a vigour and resourcefulness matched by no contemporary republic save Rome, and by few if any of the monarchies. The Carthaginians' dogged resistance in the Mercenaries' War, their ability to supply settlers and other personnel for the conquests in Spain, the forces—glorious and inglorious—they put into the field and sent to sea during the Second Punic War, and their economic recovery after 201 and especially 196, all testify to the mettle of the people the Barcids led.

A great deal was surely owed to the unrecorded and unsung kinsmen and friends of Hamilcar, Hasdrubal and Hannibal who in practice operated the Barcid ascendancy at Carthage. The Barcid generalissimos were largely absentee leaders—present in Africa only between 241 and 237, around 228 and after 203 respectively. It was their men at Carthage who kept senate and people supportive, effectively handled the not always predictable tribunal of One Hundred and Four, no doubt filled public offices from year to year, and won over or neutralized potentially powerful rival interests like the group around Hasdrubal son of Gisco and the seemingly indestructible (if at times minute) faction of Hanno the Great. Without them the generals could not have maintained the dominance of affairs and policies that even Hannibal enjoyed until the last two or three years of his war, and it must have been with them—those who survived and had stayed loyal—that he staged his comeback in 196.

The Barcid ascendancy was an unusual phenomenon for a Hellenistic-era republic. The Romans did have a largely aristocratic system of politics but one more open and chequered, with no Roman family or coterie of friends able to dominate it for decades and largely exclude opponents from policymaking. Similar politics prevailed (so far as we know) in republics like Rhodes, Tarentum and Athens. In some others an open and fractious public life suffered transformation into monarchy virtual or real—notably Syracuse in the fourth and third centuries, where long periods of autocracy were merely punctuated by spasms of democracy.

At Carthage, a virtual power-monopoly was maintained through popular support and popular politics. It was not a virtual autocracy for, with every Barcid leader overseas, his supremacy at home rested on collaborators, whose support he could not automatically compel and whose own initiatives he (sometimes at least) had to follow. Moreover opposition to the ascendancy endured and found voices; nor is there any trace of prosecutions, show trials or violence against anti-Barcid Carthaginians. When popular support and popular political methods faded, the Barcid ascendancy was replaced by a power-oligopoly, but returned briefly in 196–195 and then left behind as a legacy (even if one not wholly intended by Hannibal) an energetic political life something like the Roman, which lasted till the city's final crisis. It was an extra irony that in time Roman politics would evolve in the opposite direction—from more and more fractious competitiveness into dictatorship and then an all-encompassing monarchy. Julius Caesar's career path would reverse Hannibal's.

IV

At times the Barcids, and Hannibal in particular, have been seen as standard-bearers of Hellenistic civilization (or a form of it) pitted against the alien advance of Rome; or, a little less epically, as protagonists of a multicultural Mediterranean confronting the levelling impetus of Roman imperialism. That any of them took such a view of themselves or found it taken by contemporaries is unlikely. Third-century Carthage had certainly adopted elements of Hellenistic civilization—notably urbanistic, architectural and military—but these no more transformed the Carthaginians into a Hellenized community than much bigger borrowings transformed the Romans 100 years later. Again, the Barcids were all notable city-founders, from Acra Leuce to Prusa, but no citizen of an ancient Phoenician colony would view city-founding as a Greek-inspired activity. And while Hannibal knew Greek thanks to Sosylus and wrote some books in the language, he hardly needed lectures from his friend on Cleomenes III of Sparta's recent and divisive reforms to prompt his own (far more limited) measures in 196.[8]

The overwhelming likelihood is that the Barcids saw themselves as the defenders and promoters of their own state's safety and power, and subordinated everything else to this. Certainly too they saw themselves as the Carthaginians best-qualified for defending the city's safety and promoting its power and prosperity—they would hardly have been useful leaders otherwise.

This is not to claim that their policies were all well judged, still less always the best. Was expansion into Spain a better long-term move than expanding within North Africa? Numidia had potential, as Masinissa afterwards was to show. Was focussing on a military establishment by land the most rational use of resources? Carthage's history, economy and location—including the strategic vulnerability of Punic Africa—arguably made strong naval forces just as vital (and the Barcids had the lessons of the previous Punic war to remind them). Was confronting the Romans over Saguntum a sound reaction to their embassy of 220, when restraint might have avoided war or, at least, might have forced the other side into more overtly aggressive moves that could have given the Carthaginians the moral high ground—and conceivably some military and diplomatic advantage as well?

Not all of Hannibal's military decisions look the best either. Could he have executed the march to Italy more efficiently so as to reach Cisalpine Gaul less late in the year and with something like the 50,000-plus troops who had followed him across the Pyrenees, or at any rate the 46,000 he had led over the Rhône? It would have made an incalculable impact on the war. Was it an effective long-term strategy not to follow Cannae with a march on Rome? And indeed was it defensible to invade Italy at all with no alternative offensive strategy to fall back on if the Romans failed to be cowed by two or three defeats—any more than they had been cowed by both defeats and natural disasters in the earlier war?

The lack of some alternative offensive strategy condemned his expedition to operating stagnantly in southern Italy while hoping for some new event or arrival to revitalise its efforts. Co-operation with Macedon and then Syracuse flopped: instead of achieving a concentration of fresh forces against the enemy, Hannibal managed to disperse not only Roman military efforts (a strategic plus) but likewise Carthaginian. When a new opportunity did occur—after the destruction of the brothers Scipio in Spain in 211, then in 207 on Hasdrubal's advance across the Alps with a fresh army—the Punic strategic response was pathetic.

Conceivably too Hannibal could have done more to shore up Barcid fortunes at Carthage, at any rate in the second half of the war when they began to fail. While the war went well the Barcid ascendancy was self-sustaining, but it was unwise to expect that to continue once a practical stalemate descended on operations, and plain folly to expect it after Punic and Barcid fortunes started to slide. From 218 if not earlier (we do not know when Hannibal's brothers went to Spain) until 201 the only Barcid brother to set foot in Carthage was Mago in autumn and winter 216–215, and his purpose was military. No doubt relatives as well as close family friends worked hard politically, as mentioned earlier, but with the tide turning it would have been politic for brother Hasdrubal, for instance, to pay a visit home to shore up allegiances, inspect the workings of administration and organize fresh forces. In the slow years after 211, in an off-campaign season, Hannibal himself might have risked it. In either case it might have revitalized both the Barcid group at home and the war-effort.[9]

Hannibal's taking the home front for granted was to be expected, for in contrast to his father and brother-in-law he had virtually no experience of Carthaginian political life before 201. Maintaining the Barcid ascendancy at home was, in effect, done for him. His political business managers at Carthage, unsung and unremembered, must have been both skilled and devoted—and probably he took all that for granted. What they might have achieved for Barcid interests, had the Barcid warriors during the war kept closer personal contact with their home city, can only be guessed.

This enduring detachment from home politics was one more mistake—and a serious one—of Hannibal's leadership. Of course he might argue that every general, even the greatest, makes mistakes. But few great generals have been at the same time the political leaders of their states: and of those few, none detached himself so completely from the ongoing business of politics and government at home. Since war and victories were his trademark, military defeat meant the end of his and his family's political mastery. Yet the continuing vigour of Barcid political interests after 201 surely testifies not just to the self-centred ineptitude of those who supplanted him, but also to the strength of the relationships built up over 30 years of success and—not least—to the charismatic appeal of Hannibal's own personality.

V

The Romans found it hard to decide about him. He was both a fearsome enemy, more fearsome than Pyrrhus or later on Mithridates of Pontus, and at the same time a figure with qualities worth admiring—in his energy, resourcefulness, leadership and devotion to his country practically a Roman manqué. Scipio Africanus opposed intervening against him in 195 and their supposed friendly meeting at Ephesus a couple of years later, even if invented, shows that the Roman hero was not remembered as a Hannibal-hater. Cato, who respected Hannibal's father and disliked Scipio, possibly saw some good points in Scipio's opponent too even if he judged the attack on Saguntum a breach of treaty.[10]

The non-Roman Polybius not only sought to be objective about the Barcids (and saw virtues in all of them) but even registers the opinion that Hannibal was justified to fight in 218. Of course he states this obliquely—his work was aimed at Roman as well as Greek readers—and he later qualifies it with the verdict that the general all the same acted too soon. Livy by contrast exemplifies Roman ambivalence: he offers the famous character-portrait at the start, with virtues vividly specified and then a list of generalized vices, follows it with a narrative noticeably respectful towards the foe, and accords him a stoically pathetic speech before his suicide. Cassius Dio's character-portrait, a lengthy collection of generalizations for an energetic and awe-inspiring commander, is almost entirely friendly. Poets too, like Horace and Silius, reflect the Romans' hate-and-love complex.[11]

What fascinated them, like Romans and Greeks generally and moderns too, was Hannibal the general, the breaker of armies and, most vividly of all, crosser of mountains—not the Hannibal who, it can be held, restored his country's prosperity later on and with it at least a modicum of democracy. Those achievements endured for nearly half a century but they lacked the éclat of war. Historical irony all the same ensured that the unforgettable military exploits, after a decade and a half of excitement and success, left his state toppled as a great power and its enemies poised to rule the Mediterranean. Once the Barcid era had ended, many Carthaginians might ruefully feel that their city could have fared better without it and its short-lived grandeur, had Carthage been left quietly to cultivate its garden in Africa instead.

Yet this would probably have been impossible, no matter who directed Punic policy after 241. To have Hanno the Great and his circle in charge, for instance, and favouring expansion within North Africa—not that we know of them favouring this—would not have guaranteed an untroubled existence. There was plenty of trade between North Africa and Italy and the Romans at times showed themselves aggressive in protecting their traders' interests (or using protection as a pretext), as in 240 towards the Carthaginians themselves and ten years later towards the Illyrians. A much-expanded Punic empire in North Africa and accompanying prosperity could have fuelled revanchist Punic designs on Sicily; even if not, the Romans' behaviour in 237 and 225, over Sardinia and when facing the Gallic invasion, suggests they would soon have begun suspecting just such designs.

Again, it is scarcely believable that Hanno in charge of affairs could have averted the mercenary and Libyan revolt; and it was this catastrophe that prompted Punic expansion into Spain, where richer resources beckoned than in Africa at the time. In turn the expanding Spanish empire would still have regularly risked Roman inquisitiveness, with unforeseeable results.[12]

The Carthaginians had thus been locked into a very narrow range of choices from 241 on: and that being so, the Barcid ascendancy, which brought them new wealth and power and, for a while, the chance of western Mediterranean supremacy, was probably their best course. An ultimate Barcid defeat was not inevitable either for, as we have seen, some crucial decisions (especially some of Hannibal's) could have been made differently to bring the opposite result.

As it turned out, though, the most permanent achievement of the Barcid era was fame and a glorious memory. Carthage went down to fiery destruction in 146—just over a century after Hamilcar first stepped into the light of history—but even if there were no Carthaginians left to remember it, the time of the Barcids was stamped on the memories and traditions of their enemies, partly in hostility (but this cooled over the centuries) and partly in admiration. As a result, imperfectly in places and extensively in others, we can in our own time appreciate the impressiveness of their achievement and the drama of their fall.

XVIII

SOURCES

I

What we know of the Barcid era is uneven. Much, though not enough, about Hamilcar's campaigns in Sicily and then North Africa, but barely anything of his years in Spain; again only an outline of Hasdrubal's time as general there; while by contrast the wars of Hannibal and his lieutenants are copiously—which does not always mean reliably—recorded. The most glaring deficiency of all is in the record of domestic Carthaginian affairs, for all we have are occasional glimpses (during the negotiations with Scipio in 203, for instance) and passing comments. The surviving sources are all literary, in other words are works composed by educated writers for similar readers. These all lived later than the events they record, some much later; were all Greeks or Romans; and all had interests of their own to illustrate, centred on the Hellenistic Greek world and the Romans' achievement of Mediterranean dominance. Works on the Carthaginian aspect of the same events once existed too, but disappeared probably before the Roman empire did.

The first important source, all the same, predates them and survives. In his analysis of city-state political systems Aristotle includes the Carthaginian, his sole non-Greek example. He judges it a well-balanced structure though not free from stresses, largely oligarchic but with an important though limited rôle for the ordinary citizen; mentions the tribunal of One Hundred and Four and notes both its power and that of the (undefined) pentarchies; and emphasizes as well as criticizes the weightiness of wealth in public life. His comments may amount to little more than a sketch and raise plenty of further questions, and he is describing the Punic polity of a century or more before the Barcids: but it is all we have apart from passing and sometimes ignorant remarks in other writers.[1]

The very first writers to treat of the Barcids were the Sicilian Philinus of Agrigentum, and the Roman Q. Fabius Pictor. Philinus wrote a history of the First Punic War, a fairly substantial one since he began the war itself only in his second book. There is no convincing sign that he went past 241 and he seems to have composed his work in the years following. By then Sicily was

212

under Roman rule, which did not improve his attitude towards the people who had sacked and ravaged his home city. By contrast Fabius, the first Roman historian—who also wrote in Greek—dealt with the whole of Roman history, paying special attention to its legendary opening centuries and to his own time. He had held a praetorship and, after the disaster of Cannae, led an embassy to consult the oracle at Delphi. His narrative reached 217 at least (Livy cites his Roman casualty figures for the battle of Lake Trasimene), and probably the end of the war. The papyrus fragment of Polybius' time, on some events in North Africa in 203, is possibly from an epitome of it.

Both writers took partisan stands on Roman–Punic relations. Philinus gave a questionable account of the start of the first war and very probably bathed Hamilcar's Sicilian campaigns in the eulogistic light that Polybius' own verdict reflects—Fabius can hardly have done so, and these two are the only primary sources known. Fabius in turn accused Hasdrubal, Hamilcar's successor, of greed and power-lust, claimed that Hannibal copied the same vices, and denied the latter the support of any leading person in his attack on Saguntum and the ensuing war against the Romans. All the same they both recorded events in detail and, a useful feature, from opposing points of view; both also convinced Polybius of their honest intent even if this had flaws in practice.[2]

Hannibal himself was a source. In 205 he had an account of his campaigns inscribed in Punic and Greek in the temple of Hera at Cape Lacinium; so at any rate Livy describes the contents, though Polybius cites them for nothing more than the Punic army statistics of 218. The Greek text of his treaty with Philip V of Macedon does survive in Polybius' verbatim quotation—the nearest we can come to anything composed by Hannibal himself.[3]

Just a little is known of other contemporaries. Hannibal's Greek friends and admirers, Silenus from Cale Acte in Sicily and Sosylus of Sparta, both wrote accounts of his doings as war-leader and may (either or both) have continued down to 195. But a papyrus fragment on a naval battle in Spanish waters, maybe the battle at the Ebro's mouth in 217, is all that remains of Sosylus' *Hannibalica*, and the famous story of the general's dream *en route* to Italy is Silenus' only substantial item still surviving.

Polybius is not enthusiastic about them. He sees Sosylus as capable of relaying gossip worthy of a barbershop (a sharp verdict, but not disproved by the plausible battle-narrative); and is contemptuous of writers who supplied Hannibal with gods and heroes to guide his way across the Alps, which hits very near to Silenus. On the other hand they recorded events from Hannibal's side in detail, and not his operations alone: Sosylus' Spanish sea-battle, and Silenus' figures (cited by Livy) for military booty captured at New Carthage in 209, show that both narrated the war as a whole and—on military matters anyway—soberly enough. No doubt they portrayed their friend and patron in the best light at all times. How much they reported, or even understood, of his enemies' military and political systems, or the constantly changing details of Roman commanders and magistrates, can only be guessed.[4]

Various other early writers are mentioned in our surviving sources, most of them just names: like the Chaereas whom Polybius brackets with Sosylus as a purveyor of barbershop tales, one Eumachus of Naples, and a Xenophon. Less misty is the Roman L. Cincius Alimentus, praetor in 210 and later on a prisoner of Hannibal's: he too eventually wrote a history of Rome which included his own times, in Greek like Fabius Pictor. As a high-ranking captive he was treated to conversations with the general at least on military matters, though his one recorded slice of information—figures for Hannibal's losses *en route* to Italy and army strength on arriving—is at best the product of misunderstanding or a confused memory. The innovative and pugnacious Cato the Elder, a veteran of the war, consul in 195 and the first to write history in Latin, likewise dealt with the era in later sections of his seven-book *Origines*, but only a few extracts survive thanks to quotation by later writers. One of them is the earliest known version of Maharbal's famous remark to Hannibal, uttered supposedly after Cannae but arguably in fact the day after Trasimene.[5]

With history-writing an established genre at Rome, a long succession of Latin as well as Greek authors covered the Punic Wars as part of their general narratives, but what they contributed to the surviving accounts cannot be identified. In the late second century, on the other hand, L. Coelius Antipater invented the Latin historical monograph with seven books on Hannibal's war. Although it too failed to survive it was much consulted by Livy and others, and Cicero rather grudgingly praises Coelius' efforts at literary stylishness. Coelius made use of Silenus, and maybe other pro-Barcid writers, as well as Roman sources; consulted not only historical works but items like preserved funeral orations; and drew his conclusions on debatable issues from careful consultation of the evidence available, for instance on how the consul Marcellus met his end in 208. An interest in literary style and dramatic scenes led him to cite Silenus' account of Hannibal's famous dream, and sometimes prompted more dubious touches—like running Scipio and his army through a near-disastrous storm on their voyage to Africa, whereas all Livy's other sources recorded a calm sea and prosperous voyage.[6]

Two first-century historians of Rome also loom large among Livy's fitful references to predecessors whom he consulted on the Punic-wars period and after. Claudius Quadrigarius and Valerius Antias, conventionally dated to the time of Sulla the dictator, gave much space in their lengthy works to the Punic wars. For such general histories, standard practice was to recount events year by year (as Livy and others do): hence the term annalists applied to the writers. Livy found these two particularly appealing, and not only on the Punic wars, for the quantity of detail they offered and their claim to have digested a broad range of earlier sources. Not so appealing as to blind him to some of their shortcomings, notably Valerius' feckless exaggeration of enemies slain and booty taken; yet he cites them a good deal more often than any other predecessors.[7]

II

Polybius is the oldest extant source. His lengthy history of recent times is incomplete: only Books 1–5 in full, plus excerpts—fortunately, many are lengthy—of most of the other 35. For Polybius recent times began in 220, when in his view all the affairs of the Mediterranean world began an interaction (*symplokē*) that was to culminate in Roman domination from east to west. But to clarify how the interaction originated he provides a sketch, in Books 1 and 2, of the main events preceding it: the First Punic War and the Mercenaries' War, followed by events in Greece, Roman expansion into northern Italy in the 230s and 220s and interwar Roman–Punic relations. His work as a result spans the era 264 to 146.[8]

Polybius is not only the earliest source but an acute, analytical and argumentative one. Thanks to 17 years at Rome from 167 (as a comfortably housed state hostage), he became an admirer of the Romans—their civic qualities, political system, military structure, imperial success—and a friend of the much younger P. Scipio Aemilianus, grandson of Hannibal's opponent. When Aemilianus outdid his grandfather by sacking, burning and depopulating Carthage in 146, Polybius was at his side. Long before this he had decided to write an account of 'how, and through what type of political system, almost the entire world was subdued in not quite fifty-three years and fell under the sole rule of the Romans'. The 53 years were from 220 to the overthrow and partition of Macedon, a state which itself had once conquered much of the world, in 167. It was a later decision to extend the narrative down to 146 to show, in not always favourable detail, how the Romans used their hegemony.

The history is not a plain narrative but also supplies regular comments, discussions, digressions and even extensive thematic essays: the most famous being his treatment of the Roman political and military systems in Book 6. To explain events required impartiality, perceptiveness and clarity, all of which he was confident he possessed. Likewise experience of warfare and politics, which again were no problem. And he had available a wide range of sources, all of them contemporary or near-contemporary with their times, from written accounts of the First and Second Punic Wars to participants and eyewitnesses of recent events.[9]

Book 3 ends with the Roman catastrophe at Cannae, and when the Punic war narrative resumes after Book 6 we have only the excerpts, most of them from the tenth-century Byzantine compilation authorized by the emperor Constantine VII. While some later sources, Livy above all, do follow Polybius as their own source when reporting the decades after 216, it is hard to be sure what is Polybian in their versions and what they take from other writers. The blending that took place can be seen plainly enough in Livy's telling of the first three years of Hannibal's war, where his Books 21 and 22 run parallel to Polybius' Book 3; not to mention in passages later in his work where he can be matched with a Polybian excerpt, for instance the accounts of Zama and its aftermath.[10]

Polybius' Roman and Greek focus widens to include Carthaginian matters only where these are relevant—or to him seem relevant—to his grand theme. The Punic Wars obviously do; so too the Mercenaries' War in Punic Africa, in his view an awful demonstration of the dangers such employees could pose to a state when they broke from control, and also a vital factor in the causes of Hannibal's war. He much admires Hamilcar and Hannibal: the father to the extreme of judging him the finest general of the First Punic War, and the son for his leadership and military genius, despite conceding he was not free of faults—and despite laying responsibility for the Second Punic War on both of them. But he is not interested enough in the Punic state or community to offer even an outline of Carthage's political system (a contrast to Book 6 on Rome's) or name any notable Carthaginian except military commanders: that Gisco was the name of the senator whom Hannibal summarily shut up in 203 we learn from Livy, while the sufete who spoke for Carthage in 218, in the fateful confrontation with the Romans' war-embassy, remains anonymous. Again, his comment that by 218 the Punic political system was tilted towards democracy is better than no comment at all, but still leaves us to make what we can out of Aristotle's sketch in the *Politics* plus occasional items like Hasdrubal's and Hannibal's election as generals, and Livy's brief mention of the postwar 'order of judges'.[11]

All that being said, Polybius has unique strengths. He consulted pro-Punic accounts like Hannibal's and Sosylus' as well as Roman ones, and was not over-trusting of either side (though at times hypercritical). In spite of his Roman connexions he is not prepared to give the Romans the benefit of the doubt every time: certainly not, for instance, over the rape of Sardinia in 237, while—cautiously but unmistakably—he sets out his opinion that the Carthaginians were justified in going to war in 218. In a different vein, his description of the special horrors of a Roman city-sacking is the more chilling for being matter of fact.

The Hellenistic equivalent of a Renaissance man, Polybius not only was a leader, diplomat and organizer in his own career but also contributed to military science (improved fire-signalling methods, for example), travelled widely, inspected sites and terrain, looked up documentary sources like Hannibal's inscribed memoir and the treaties between Rome and Carthage, and interviewed eyewitnesses (King Masinissa for instance). All these aspects show up in his history. On military, geographic and chronological matters he is a great deal more knowledgeable than our other sources, and he takes time out to describe and discuss them. Not that this does guarantees clarity every time— most famously over Hannibal's route from the Rhône to Cisalpine Gaul, but also for instance over the chronology and topography of the Mercenaries' War—but it is important that he realizes the need. In the same way his interest in explaining psychology and motivation is valuable even though not every explanation may convince: thus, famously, his theory of Barcid hostility and war-planning against Rome.[12]

III

Well after Polybius came the next two surviving writers, Diodorus and Livy, both of the later first century BC. Diodorus' *Historical Library*, a 40-book world history, offers only excerpts from its second half, mostly selected by medieval Byzantine copyists. A Sicilian himself, he devoted substantial space to the island's history and for the First Punic War drew on his fellow-Sicilian Philinus as well as on Roman sources. In turn, his few excerpts on the Mercenaries' War match Polybius' account so closely that efforts from time to time to thrust some intermediary fount between them remain unconvincing. By contrast, his invaluable few paragraphs on Hamilcar's and Hasdrubal's doings in Spain draw on some other writer, well informed, detailed and Barcid-friendly: it is tempting to think of either Silenus or Sosylus.

Diodorus' *modus operandi*, much of the time anyway, was to rewrite or abbreviate his source of the moment with few substantial changes; in other places (like his account of the fateful year 264) he uses more than one source but seems to be faithful to each in turn. This not very original way of writing history makes the lack of his full text the more deplorable, for that might have given a better view of what some of the pro-Punic sources were like.[13]

T. Livius, his younger contemporary, started his history of Rome around 30 BC and outdid all his predecessors in length (142 books—90 per cent of them on the centuries from 272 on) and in artistry. Of the 35 books surviving, Books 21 to 30 record the Second Punic War; then Books 31 to 39 provide most of the details we have of Hannibal's postwar fortunes, including his year as sufete. Like Diodorus, Livy is heavily dependent on his sources, but with much more reshaping and recasting of his finished narrative. As mentioned earlier he often draws on at least two accounts to create his own blend, something readily seen when one account is Polybius'. For the later third century and the first half of the second, besides Polybius he draws chiefly on Roman predecessors, with the already-noted partiality for Claudius and Valerius; but—at least by his own claim—makes use from time to time of a wider selection, including Fabius and Cincius. Whether he directly consulted all such works or merely reproduced citations made by a narrower group (Coelius and the late annalists have been urged) we do not know.

Livy follows Polybius in his praises of Hannibal's leadership and continues to be interested in—and sympathetic to—the general after 201. Nevertheless he makes it clear that the Romans were provoked into the war and had the moral fibre to win it. Literary grandeur apart, his value lies not just in basing his narrative partly on Polybius but in supplying detailed accounts of Roman affairs of every kind, materials that his industrious predecessors amassed from older records like the annals of the *pontifices*. Industrious himself (the

217

history took him about four and a half decades), he lacked direct experience of politics or warfare or the world outside Italy—rather like Polybius' favourite *bête noire* Timaeus—and could apply no great independence of judgement to issues. Therefore he reworks what his sources tell him: and so preserves a wealth of unique information, along with rather numerous mistakes and confusions. Now and then, he pauses to summarize the differing opinions among his sources that are causing him trouble (Hannibal's Alpine route and army losses, Fabius the Delayer's exact legal position *vis-à-vis* his deputy Minucius late in 217, Hannibal's route to Rome in 211, Scipio's booty from New Carthage). Patriotism plays its part too, for instance to distort the Ebro accord with Hasdrubal and import romantic tales about Scipio Africanus in Spain and Africa.

One result of Livy's methods and limitations is extensive scholarly scepticism about many items that lack Polybian corroboration and smell instead of annalistic inventiveness, or seem to. Minucius' self-abasement after being rescued by Fabius the Delayer from annihilation is one uncontroversial example, and so too is (or should be) the Senate's rejection of the peace negotiated in 203 by Scipio in Africa. The non-Polybian details reported for the elder Scipios' operations in Spain down to 211 are, some or all, dismissed as annalistic fictions too, which (on the other hand) may be oversceptical; likewise, on a smaller scale, the episode of Centenius Paenula in 212. Such controversies make it necessary to read Livy, even more than Polybius, with care.[14]

IV

Sizeable narratives of operations in both Punic Wars are provided by the late second-century AD Appian of Alexandria, in his history of Roman wars laid out by geographical regions: in particular the books *Hannibalica*, *Iberica* and *Libyca*. They are very uneven work. On second- and first-century wars Appian is generally sound: his telling of the Third Punic War in *Libyca*, for instance, is at least partly based on Polybius and puts no strain on a reader's credulity, nor does the lengthy account of the wars against Mithridates of Pontus. In glaring contrast, his accounts of the various theatres in the Second Punic War (those for Italy, Spain and Africa survive) call for constant caution.

It is not only that Appian fails to tell apart the Ebro and Tagus rivers, sites Saguntum north of the former, and still manages to identify it with New Carthage. His narratives teem with items missing from any other source and often incompatible with those in Polybius or Livy. Events in Africa between 204 and 202 are thus enlivened, not to mention a good many of Hannibal's in Italy. The Appianic battle of Cannae, for instance, is nothing like the standard version (among other things, he transfers to it Hannibal's stratagem at the Trebia—troops hidden in a ravine to ambush the enemy's rear). Hasdrubal's Ebro accord in Appian has provisos more plentiful and less believable than in any other source. Again, the elder Scipios' disastrous last campaign as Appian tells it is at odds with Livy's more thorough account.

Sometimes Appian does it the other way round, for example telling us nothing of the important operations (including at least one big victory over Hasdrubal brother of Hannibal) that Cn. Scipio carried out in 218 and 217 before his brother joined him. The younger Scipio's operations in southern Spain from 208 to 206 are run together and one battle fills in for both Baecula and Ilipa. Highly rhetorical speeches and occasional grotesque dramatizations (notably the hand-to-hand combat between Hannibal and Scipio at Zama) add extra colour and disbelief.[15]

All the same Appian cannot be ignored, even if he has to be used with care and some scepticism. Not all the details that he alone offers are incredible. Once the Tagus is substituted for the Ebro, for instance, his description of Hasdrubal's sway in Spain becomes plausible. Like other later writers he makes a Roman propaganda mess of the Italian traders episode during the Mercenaries' War and then the seizure of Sardinia; but he may well be right that the Romans allowed the Carthaginians to recruit soldiers in Italy during that war. A good deal of his narrative does, moreover, coincide with other sources' versions. Hannibal's oath is in the standard Roman version, as against Polybius' (and Nepos'); his army-strength on leaving New Carthage matches Polybius' figures; and the Appianic battle of Trasimene is largely the same as in Livy. Later on, like Livy and Diodorus, Appian too makes Hannibal massacre his reluctant Italian soldiery before embarking for Africa, not that this adds any probability to the tale.[16]

His treatment of the general, the only Barcid dealt with at length, is censorious in places. Political calculation and glory-hunting prompt Hannibal to start the war, he slaughters prisoners at times (plus the recalcitrant Italians), victimizes the family of a treacherous Italian ally, and as his fortunes start their decline he takes a winter holiday in Lucania with a mistress. Yet Appian gives him his due as well—mild treatment of Italian captives after Trasimene, Cannae lauded as a splendid victory, honours for the fallen commanders Gracchus and Marcellus, later on in Africa a (quite improbable) effort to make a treaty with Scipio which his fellow-citizens abort, and after Zama more wise counsel to the ungrateful Carthaginians about accepting Scipio's terms. This varied depiction again mirrors the ambiguities of the standard Roman tradition towards their most admired enemy.[17]

That Coelius was his basic source, at least for the Second Punic War, has been suggested. But Appian's way of so often combining factual material with fanciful, and reporting items that Livy—who did use Coelius—contradicts or ignores, points to a far more eclectic and uncritical blending of borrowings, not to mention a strong dash of carelessness. This means that Appianic items on their own cannot be automatically treated as sound evidence merely omitted by other writers: scrutinized carefully, some may pass muster while others have to be left in doubt or be rejected. Overall his treatment of the period suggests that he preferred annalistic sources (a great contrast to his account of the final Punic war) and put them together fairly uncritically—not to mention ignorantly at times.[18]

V

Other sources are less extensive. In the later first century BC Cornelius Nepos included a three-paragraph biographical sketch of Hamilcar and a lengthier one (13 chapters) on Hannibal among his collection of lives of distinguished foreign generals. As far as they go these are useful at least for various details—we owe him our knowledge of Silenus and Sosylus being in Hannibal's entourage—and, interestingly, he gives as much space to Hannibal's life after the war as to all his earlier career. Except for the general's suicide, these later details are not matched in Livy or other major sources, but one or more turn up in other lesser writers like Justin. At the same time, compression (like covering the years from 216 to 203 in one paragraph) and various errors or confusions (he places the events of late 217 after Cannae, and misunderstands Hannibal's postwar position) limit what he has to offer.[19]

The philosopher and biographer Plutarch, of the late first and early second centuries AD, wrote no biography of a Carthaginian and his life of Scipio does not survive. Those of Fabius the Delayer and the pugnacious Marcellus treat largely of their subjects' doings in the Second Punic War. They contribute to the record of events, usually from Roman sources (Livy included), but the occasional sayings and anecdotes of Hannibal that Plutarch includes—like the jest to Gisco before Cannae—must derive directly or indirectly from a Punic source, perhaps Silenus or Sosylus again.

The third-century AD consular historian L. Cassius Dio treated the Punic Wars period at some length in his 80-book general history of Rome. But all that remains of Dio before his Book 36 (the late Republic) is a collection of excerpts, mostly short, and the sizeable epitome of his work that the retired Byzantine administrator John Zonaras made in the eleventh century. Dio's history rests almost entirely on Roman and pro-Roman sources (though he claims he read every work relevant to his theme, which for this period ought to include Sosylus and Silenus at least). He relays, for example, the story that Roman envoys went to Hannibal during the siege of Saguntum; has Hannibal after Trasimene advance down the Tiber valley towards Rome; reports Maharbal's advice to him after Cannae as Livy does and narrates the Metaurus campaign much again as in Livy. Likewise he makes the Romans refuse to ratify Scipio's peace-terms in 203 until Hannibal has departed Italy.[20]

There is also Silius Italicus. An eminent ex-consul in the later first century AD, he composed a lengthy epic poem, *Punica*, on Hannibal's war—the longest epic poem in Latin and the least inspired. A collection of episodes told in standard epic form and heavily imitative of Vergil, it offers plenty of sonorous names and similes, Homeric-style combats (including between gods, not to mention Scipio versus Hannibal again), and Scipio—who we learn is really the son of Jove—at one stage summoning up the ghosts of past Roman heroes and heroines for consultations. The poem uses Roman historical sources, notably Livy, and adds no special information of its own apart from naming Hannibal's wife and giving them a son, both of which items may or may not be accurate. An effort has certainly been made to see a pre-Livian source behind Silius' telling of the war's preliminaries, so as to use him as a foil to the supposed bias and distortions in Polybius and Livy, but it is hard to find this plausible.[21]

Late Roman historical writers add only incidentally to the register. Eutropius, a retired senior administrator in the later fourth century who composed the most concise of Roman histories for the presumably easily distracted emperor Valens, summarizes the entire period from 264 to 201 in ten pages. His most useful contribution (not always believed) is the date of the battle of the Aegates islands in 241. The much more useful Justin, probably again fourth century in date, epitomized a lengthy history of the non-Roman world by the Augustan-age writer Pompeius Trogus, with valuable if concise information about Carthage's earlier times and equally abbreviated references to Barcid doings—mostly on their Spanish conquests, Hannibal's exile and his dealings with Antiochus III. That we lack Trogus' full work is a pity since, on Justin's showing, he was sensible and well informed.[22]

Orosius, a Spanish church presbyter oppressed by the disasters befalling the now Christianized empire early in the fifth century, put together a seven-book world history to show carping pagans that these were nothing compared to the calamities of past times. He deals with the period of the first two Punic wars in 20 pages, much of them devoted to pious lesson-drawing. His account follows standard Roman tradition, for instance on Hannibal's oath, and goes back, probably indirectly, to Livy.

Briefer sources need mention too. Anecdotal compilations include Valerius Maximus' nine books (from the reign of Tiberius) of famous deeds and sayings by Roman and foreign leaders, in which Hamilcar, his sons and even Hasdrubal son of Gisco contribute mostly well-known items. Julius Frontinus, ex-governor of Britain and City water-services commissioner, late in the first century AD put together four books of anecdotes on military stratagems, which for Roman history seem to draw much from Livy and naturally offer some items from the Barcid era. A generation or so later a skilful rhetorical writer, one Florus, boiled down Livy's and others' accounts of Roman wars to Augustan times into a fluent two-book compendium, occasionally useful if also prone to error and exclamations. In the 160s AD a Greek rhetorician, Polyaenus, tried his hand too at stratagems-collection, of minimal use to Barcid history.

At some period, probably the late empire, an anonymous person compiled a series of one-paragraph biographies of notable men in Roman history (and three women including Cleopatra) down to the end of the Roman Republic.

Hannibal and some of his Roman contemporaries figure among them, but the entries are merely skeleton résumés—which does not save them from various careless mistakes. Unlike Aurelius Victor's similarly compacted lives of the Roman emperors, very little of independent value can be found in *De Viris Illustribus*. It stands as a sobering illustration of how not to compress.[23]

A few other writers supply miscellaneous information. The Augustan-age writer Strabo in his world geography describes not only the topography but also the ethnography of Spain, Italy and Africa as well as other lands; Pliny the Elder's encyclopaedia contributes a great variety of individual items (it mentions the rich silver mine at Baebelo, for instance); a hundred years later the Greek Pausanias wrote a travel account of Greece with one or two bits of relevant information, and useful too is Ptolemy's *Geography*, a catalogue of countries, peoples and cities. And late Roman itineraries— catalogues of major routes with their towns and distances—have their uses, as does the epitome of Stephanus of Byzantium's sixth-century geographical encyclopaedia.

APPENDIX
Special notes

1 Hamilcar's daughters, and other family questions (chapter II, note 2)

Appian, *Hann.* 20.90, mentions a military commander Hanno as Hannibal's nephew (kinship doubted by Lenschau, *RE* 7.2357); he was son of Bomilcar 'the king' (Pol. 3.42.6), so if Appian is right about the kinship it would mean that his mother was a sister of the general. A daughter promised by Hamilcar to Naravas in about 240 (the original of Flaubert's Salammbô): Pol. 1.78.8. Livy 29.29.12 mentions 'a Carthaginian noblewoman, daughter of Hannibal's sister', who by 206 was widow of another Numidian prince, Oezalces: she may have been a sister to Hanno son of Bomilcar (cf. chapter XIII).

Seibert suggests that Hannibal may not only have been reared, but even have been born, in his father's Sicilian camp (*Hann.* 9 note 12). But this was hardly the place for a baby and its mother—still less so after the move to Eryx in 244, when a second son probably arrived too. Hasdrubal's birth-date: Diod. 25.19, lines 9–10 (actually from the Byzantine versifier John Tzetzes (chapter V note 15)) describes him as 12 and Hannibal as 15 in late 229, which is wrong arithmetically but may be right on the difference between their ages.

Seibert, *Hann.* 20, notes too that, according to Val. Max. 9.3 ext. 2 and Cassiodorus, *Chronica, Anno Urbis Conditae* 524, Hamilcar had four sons and—as a fourth never appears in history—infers that the newborn fourth formed part of a major infant-sacrifice which, he further infers, took place during the Mercenaries' War. But Valerius describes all four as Hamilcar's lion-cubs being *raised* to destroy Rome. It is likelier that the numeral is due to a fuzzy awareness that Barca had more children than just three sons. Or the numeral in these texts may be mistaken: in Valerius' text the preceding word is 'odium', which could have corrupted a 'iii' to a 'iiii' or 'iv'—and Cassiodorus' item seems to come from Valerius.

2 The artificial ports at Carthage (chapter II, note 5)

Nearly all the datable remains are from the second century BC, hence the excavators' view that the ports were built in Carthage's final years. But those years may mark refurbishments and repairs (H. Hurst, *Antiquaries' Journal* (1979) 27; and in *Atti del I Congresso Internazionale di Studi Fenici e Punici . . . 1979* (Rome 1983) 2.609). To start so colossal a project in an era when the Carthaginians were forbidden by treaty to have a navy, and were terrified at any prospect of clashing with the Romans (then the only major power with one), was pointless expense. True, Livy reported Roman complaints about Punic warship-building then (*Epit.* 47, 48, 49), but ships alone do not a port make, and even the ships may have been anti-Punic propaganda.

True again, there is an almost complete lack of late fourth- and third-century material—only a third-century coin of Tarentum and one struck at Carthage in the period 241–221 or just after (Hurst, *Antiq. J.* (1979) 27)—but a late third-century date is possible enough, most probably the first decade of the Second Punic War (cf. chapter VIII §IV). It does make more sense for the ports to date to an era of Punic naval power (so too Seibert, *FzH* 111–13). Seibert suggests the interwar years of 241 to 218; but when the Second Punic War began Punic naval strength was woefully low (chapter VIII §II). By contrast, Romans raiding the Punic coast in 210 learned from prisoners that the Carthaginians were readying a massive fleet (Livy 27.5.13). True, Punic naval forces after 210 never exceeded 70 to 100 ships (cf. Lazenby (1978) 197), but if the naval port was being or had recently been constructed the Carthaginians may yet have had hopes. Refurbishments one or two generations later could point to both ports then being used for Carthage's prosperous marine commerce.

3 Carthaginian revenues (chapter II, notes 10–11)

(i) Tribute of 'Lepcis' in 193 (Livy 34.62.3): Lepcis, later Lepcis Magna, was a big and flourishing Phoenician colony, but 360-plus talents a year would be a colossal sum to pay in tribute. Yet Lepcis certainly lay in an area called Emporia as Livy states (rightly, despite W. V. Harris, *CAH*² 8.145, and map, *ibid.* 144; see chapter II note 10) and had prosperous neighbours, Oea and Sabratha.

Leptis Minor in its turn was not by the Lesser Syrtes but at the southern end of the gulf of Hammamet further north; nor was it as important as Lepcis, so a daily talent of tribute is unthinkable from it alone. But though Livy clearly singles out 'Lepcis' (*or* 'Leptis') itself as paying the talent—'una civitas eius [sc. regionis] Lepcis; ea singula in dies talenta vectigal Carthaginiensibus dedit' (34.62.3, where *ea* can hardly refer back to the understood *regionis*)—this may be a misreading of his source: cf. Briscoe (1981) 143–4; Mattingly (1994) 50. Leptis Minor did stand close to the fertile Emporia region south-east of Carthage, the later Byzacium (Pliny, *NH* 5.24). Moreover Masinissa in 193 coveted Emporia—this is in fact why Livy mentions the region and 'Lepcis'—a lust that fits the area adjoining his kingdom better than territory far away to the east, even if that region counted as part of Emporia.

Briscoe (1981) 143–4 is probably right then to suggest that Leptis Minor served as the administrative centre for Emporia (Hadrumetum and Thapsus were more important cities, but were independent allies of Carthage). Cautiously then the daily talent can be taken as paid by Emporia as a whole—even perhaps including Lepcis Magna and its neighbours far to the east.

(ii) Carthage's Spanish revenues: We have only one indicator, the output of a silver mine at Baebelo—site unknown—which yielded Hannibal 300 pounds daily according to the Elder Pliny (33.97). In Roman *denarii* this would be about 25,000 a day, or just over 4 talents (cf. Frank (1933) 47). But that would make Baebelo by itself produce nearly 1500 talents a year; more likely Pliny's figure is exaggerated, optimistic or flawed. Perhaps the whole of the Spanish empire by 218 paid 1,500 a year—much of it no doubt spent in the province. Incidentally the silver mines near New Carthage in the second century BC likewise yielded 25,000 drachmas/*denarii* a day 'to the Roman people', according to Polybius (cited by Strabo 3.2.11, 148C).

Whatever the wealth of Spain, Kahrstedt's estimate ((1913) 135–7) of Carthaginian income in 218 of up to 6,000 talents seems wildly optimistic, and not much less so the 2,800 a year he supposes for 200–191.

4 Carthaginian population in the third century (chapter II, note 12)

Strabo 17.3.15, 833C, reports 'seventy myriads of men [i.e. persons] in the city' in 149. K. J. Beloch estimated 200,000–300,000 in the city (*Die Bevölkerung der griechisch-roemischen Welt* (Leipzig (1889) 467); Kahrstedt 125,000–130,000 in 218, including 20,000 non-Carthaginians ((1913) 23–4, 133). Warmington (1964) 150 reckons some 400,000, including slaves and foreign residents; Picard (1961) 61 about 100,000 for the city proper and 100,000 for Megara. Tlatli reckons 243,000 all told in the city and Megara, plus some 400,000 in a territory of 18,000 square kilometres ((1978) 107–9, 117–18, 124), perhaps rightly, but that area is too large—it includes cities like Utica, Hippo and Mactar which did not belong to Carthage's own city-territory. Huss (1985) 51 accepts Strabo's figure, whereas Ameling (1993) 205–6 holds to a broad range of 90,000–225,000.

Two hundred thousand citizens, with their families, for city and territory together can only be a rough estimate, but the total of men, women and children would then range between 571,000 and 714,000, depending on what percentage was male in the total population (probably between 28 and 35 per cent: cf. Brunt (1971) 59, 116–17). Additional to these would be any Libyans dwelling in Carthage's own territory, plus resident aliens, and slaves—surely another 100,000 at least.

The Libyans outside the city's territory, the North African allies like Utica and Hippou Acra, and their slaves, are a separate matter. For the city and empire in 218 Kahrstedt's detailed estimates come to about 2.1 million apart from the recently won Spanish territories ((1913) 133), but include implausibly low estimates or guesstimates for the city of Carthage (above) and for the Libyan subjects (650,000); Ameling (1993) 225 likewise estimates the Libyans at under a million. If instead there were 700,000–800,000 people in Carthage and its own territory, plus 1.5–2 million Punic allies, subject Libyans and their slaves, and 1.5 million in Hasdrubal's Spain—quite possibly too low a guess, Kahrstedt thinks 2 million—then the total population under Barcid leadership around 221 would be 3.7 to 4.3 million. For comparison, Rome and Italy together Brunt estimates at 3.5 million in 225 ((1971) 59–60).

5 Naravas' family (chapter III, note 7)

Naravas seems to be the *Nrwt* mentioned on a Libyan inscription set up in 129 or 128 BC near Mactar by Nrwt's grandson *Wlbh* (Picard (1966) 1257–65; Huss (1985) 60 note 65). It names Nrwt's father as Zililsan, known from an inscription of 140 or 139 at Thugga as father of Gaia (G. Camps, *Masinissa ou les débuts de l'histoire* [= *Libyca* 8 (1960)] 283). This is the royal family of the Massyli in eastern Numidia. If the identification is correct, Naravas was brother of Gaia, whose famous and long-lived son Masinissa was born around 240. Another brother, Oezalces, late in the Second Punic War married a daughter of one of Hannibal's sisters (Livy 29.29.12): see chapter XIII.

6 Massiliot colonies in south-eastern Spain (chapter V, note 12)

Strabo (3.4.6, 159C) mentions the three Massiliot 'little towns' (πολίχνια) in the present tense (ἐστίν), which itself rules out Acra Leuce, a 'very large city' and a Punic one from Hamilcar's day, being one of them. He sites them 'not far from' the Sucro river (modern Júcar) and names one: Hemeroscopeion, the Roman Dianium, which apparently was at modern Denia by Cape de la Nao, 36 miles/60 kilometres south of the Sucro (Rouillard (1982) 427). Stephanus lists an Alonis (s.v.) as a 'Massiliot city', and other evidence places this near Alicante (Mela 2.93; *Itin. Rav.* 304), but it does not count very obviously as one of Strabo's three. If all three were near to or south of Cape de la Nao, Strabo's phrase loses all meaning; why not describe them instead as 'not far from' the cape?

7 The Saguntines' fractious neighbours (chapter VII, note 9)

Livy calls them Turdetani and Turduli, Appian Torboletae or Torboletes, but none of these suits the region. By contrast the town of Tyris or Turis, at the mouth of the nearby river still called the Turia, existed until the first century BC and is altogether apt (Hoyos [1998] 188–9). In Latin its people would be called Turitani; in Greek 'Tyrieis','Turietae/-tes', 'Tyristae' or the like. The 'Thersitae' who, along with the Olcades and others, supplied troops to North Africa early in 218 (Pol. 3.33.9) may again be these people in yet another Grecized form; the Thersitae are otherwise unknown and efforts (Walbank 1.362; Huss (1985) 297) to identify them as Tartessii or Turdetani are less plausible.

8 The grand army at the start of 218 (chapter VIII, note 15)

On the expeditionary army, recent discussions include Walbank 1.366; Lazenby (1978) 33–4; Scullard, *CAH²* 8.40; and Lancel, *Hann.* 103–4, who all doubt Polybius' starting total; so does Seibert, *FzH* 179–83, suggesting 70,000 infantry and 10,000 cavalry. By contrast Barreca (1983–4) 44–5 defends Polybius' total, and Goldsworthy (2000) 154, 158–9 accepts it without discussion. No one suggests that Polybius' figure may include the 15,000 men Hannibal assigned to his brother Hasdrubal.

Livy's details about the disillusioned Spanish troops (21.23.4–6) are fuller than Polybius' and look well based, perhaps from a Hannibalic source like Silenus—directly or via Coelius. If we suppose a fighting loss of 7,000 in north-eastern Spain, which seems plausible if losses were serious (8 per cent of an expeditionary total of 87,000), this plus the dismissed troops and Hanno's corps would add up to 28,000. Hannibal would then indeed have had 59,000 to lead over the Pyrenees.

Interestingly the Roman prisoner of Hannibal's, L. Cincius Alimentus (cf. Hoyos (2001a) 78), who conversed with the general around 206, later wrote a history of Rome and estimated the Punic army at 80,000 foot and 10,000 horse on its *arrival* in Italy (Livy 21.38.3–4). Perhaps he misremembered a rounded-up estimate of Hannibal's of the original numbers departing for Italy. The figure certainly does not refer to Hannibal's strength after the Boii and others joined his army in north Italy, for he still had only some 40,000 men at the Trebia: see §9 below.

9 Hannibal's route to Italy and numbers on arrival: some views (chapter VIII, notes 23–4)

(i) On the general's constantly discussed route recent studies include Proctor (1971); Lazenby (1978) chapter II; Connolly (1981) 153–66; Huss (1985) 298–306 with 298 note 35; Seibert (1989), also *FzH* 191–200 (with a thorough bibliography of Hannibal's pass from 1820 to 1993) and *Hann.* 96–113. Seibert holds that identification of the pass is impossible and he is probably right. Less plausible is his theory that the Punic army went in two corps via two passes, thus explaining—he thinks—why some of Polybius' and Livy's details diverge ((1989) 72–3; *FzH* 198; *Hann.* 106). Now neither writer, nor any later one, shows any awareness of this division, and in fact Livy's account of the whole march largely draws on Polybius. Discrepancies could have arisen if one or more previous writers had tried to clarify the route from their own, sometimes faulty, geographical knowledge or guesswork, and if Livy reflected the guesses (he was interested in the topic himself).

(ii) While Hannibal claimed that he had only 20,000 foot and 6,000 horse on reaching Italy, some scholars hold that he left another 8,000 out—light-armed pikemen and Balearic slingers, both mentioned at the Trebia by Polybius (3.72.7)—to make his victories against huge odds seem still more glorious: thus Delbrück (1920/1975) 1.361–2; Ridley (1987) 162; Seibert, *FzH* 181, 212; *Hann.* 112. Delbrück, 361, holds that the heavy infantry alone must have totalled 20,000 on arrival, because otherwise they would have been too few, after Trebia and Trasimene, to carry out the tasks they did at Cannae. If so Hannibal really brought 34,000 troops into Italy.

But at the Trebia in December 218 he had about 40,000 men in all, including by then 10,000 horse (Pol. 3.72.8–9; Walbank 1.404–5; Lazenby (1978) 56)—and this after 'all the neighbouring Gauls' had rallied to him and supplied troops (3.66.7). If he had reached Italy with 34,000 men, then these new allies can have numbered only about 6,000 and have been mostly cavalry since his cavalry total had risen by 4,000 (so Delbrück, 361). This is implausible, and it also contradicts Polybius' evidence for substantial Gallic infantry at the Trebia (3.72.8, 74.4 and 11): for one thing Hannibal's 20,000 infantry in that battle consisted of Spaniards, Africans *and* Gauls (72.8). Much more likely then the general had gained 4,000 horse and 10,000 or so foot, including some light-armed, from his new allies.

Even if he left the several hundred-odd Baleares out of his Lacinian record, he must have counted his own pikemen—themselves Africans and Spaniards—among the African and Spanish foot (so too Walbank 1.366; cf. Connolly (1981) 187). Nor did these pikemen likely total 8,000, for of that total at the Trebia some would be Gauls (cf. Lazenby, 81). In other words his African and Spanish regular infantry probably numbered more than 12,000. Moreover, as most of the casualties at Trebia and Trasimene were to fall on his Gauls, the Africans and Spaniards would not have been too many fewer at Cannae in 216 (cf. Goldsworthy (2000) 180, 189, 207) though admittedly some men had died of cold in winter 218–217.

He of course had pikemen at Cannae too (Pol. 3.113.6) but likely enough many were Gallic again (*contra* Goldsworthy, 207; see Lazenby, 81; Connolly, 115, 117–18; Wise (1982) 17 suggests 6,000 were). In rearming his African troops after Trasimene with his plentiful haul of captured Roman weapons (3.87.3) he may well have armed the highly trained African pikemen at least, thus adding them to the regular infantry (on these pikemen's military quality, cf. Lazenby, 14–15). Even if not, it is unconvincing to suppose his regular infantry was only 9,000–10,000 strong at Cannae.

10 'De dignitate atque imperio certare'
(chapter X, note 9)

The original source or sources for Hannibal's statement to his Roman captives—Silenus, Sosylus, Fabius or the like—no doubt used Greek terms like
τιμή and ἀρχή; for a Latin version of ἀρχή Hannibal or his interpreter could
have said *potestas* or maybe *dicio*. *Imperium* looks like Livy's rewording or maybe
a recent annalist's, for by their time it could mean 'empire' as well as 'power'
or 'command'—not in Hannibal's day, though (cf. Hoyos [1998] 130). Livy
himself probably had all these senses in mind.

11 Independent Roman corps operating in Italy
(chapter XI, note 3)

Hanno's and Hannibal's victories over such forces in 213 and 212 are one or
both rejected by Kahrstedt (1913) 265–6, and Briscoe (1989) 54 note 52.
Seibert, *Hann.* 288, accepts the earlier but (294 note 33) rejects the later; both
are accepted by de Sanctis, 3.2. 264, 383, by Huss (1985) 359 note 184, 365,
by Lazenby (1978) 102, 113, and by Kukofka (1990) 76–7 with modifications.
Appian, *Hann.* 9.37, 11.45–7, confuses the defeat of C. Centenius' 'army'
after Trasimene in 217—in reality Centenius led the consul Servilius' cavalry—with the disaster of M. Centenius Paenula the ex-centurion (perhaps
appointed a *praefectus*) in Lucania in 212; but this is hardly a warrant for disbelieving the Paenula incident which Livy reports.

Irregulars in 209 forced to surrender: Livy 27.16.9. Some had been
brought over from Sicily by Valerius Laevinus and combined with Bruttian
deserters for operations in Bruttium. Livy 27.12.4–6 avoids naming any commander; cf. chapter X note 13. Note too another independently operating
force in 208, a column of Roman troops marching on their own from Tarentum towards Locri when ambushed at Petelia by Hannibal (27.26.4–6).

12 Debated aspects of the Italian campaign of 207
(chapter XII, notes 12–13)

Though Livy seemingly makes Hannibal move from the territory of Larinum
in east-central Italy to the Sallentine peninsula, 'agri Larinatis' in his text may
be a copyist's mistake for 'agri Tarentini' (27.40.10, where most MSS actually
offer 'laritanis', 'laritani' or 'lartiani'): thus Huss (1985) 392. Certainly the general is soon after reported departing 'ex agro Tarentino' (40.12). But Livy fails
to explain why Hannibal should be marching into the heel of Italy at all—for
forage? Or is 'in Sallentinos' an error for some other and more northerly destination (e.g. 'Salapitanos')?

Whether the rest of the reported marching and fighting could have fitted
between mid-March, when the consuls entered office and joined their armies,

and mid-June when Nero left Apulia for the north, is hard to decide but looks a little dubious (the battle of the Metaurus was fought on 22 June by the Roman calendar, according to Ovid, *Fasti* 6.769–70. Cf. Walbank 2.270–1, answering de Sanctis' scepticism (3.2.560–1); cf. Derow (1976) 280–1; Seibert, *FzH* 244–5).

Seibert (*Hann.* 382–4) sees Canusium as Hannibal's intended junction-point and the brothers as having conflicting views ('Meinungsverschiedenheiten'), while also supposing (385) that Hasdrubal had got in touch with Hannibal as soon as he reached Italy. He rightly notes (383–4) that a junction in Umbria implied moving against Rome. But it need not follow that this meant giving up the Punic-held south, for Hannibal had garrisons in key cities.

At the battle of the Metaurus, Seibert (*Hann.* 389, 391) judges Nero's decisive tactical manoeuvre as fiction from a Nero-friendly tradition—a very early one if so, since Polybius reports it—which copied Hannibal's decisive cavalry manoeuvre at Cannae. Instead he credits the other consul Livius with working around Hasdrubal's flank to strike the decisive blow. But not only is this an arbitrary treatment of Polybius' evidence as well as Livy's; it virtually implies that Nero's presence was unnecessary, for until he made his manoeuvre his troops played no part in the battle. (Nor, it may be added, is Nero's infantry manoeuvre very similar to Hannibal's cavalry coup at Cannae.) Why not infer then that his famous march and reinforcement of Livius were invented too? Seibert also denies Nero's decisive rôle in urging a battle and assigns the decision to Livius (386–7, 391)—even though before Nero's arrival the latter was avoiding combat and gave his unexpectedly arriving colleague a decidedly 'frostige Begrüßung' (386).

Livy claims that Nero's return to Apulia was swifter ('citatiore agmine') than the outward one—it began the night after the battle and took six days (27.50.1), while the battle itself was fought the day after he joined Livius (27.46.5 and 11). If the Metaurus was fought on 22 June, this would date Nero's expedition—500 miles (800 kilometres) of marching plus a major battle—from about 12/13 June to 28/29 June, a clear impossibility. De Sanctis (3.2.556) suggests Nero and his cavalry took six days to return while the infantry took longer, for he holds (553) that Hannibal moved towards Larinum now, not at the start of the year—giving Nero only some 190 miles (300 kilometres) thither from Livius' army—but on this see Lazenby (1978) 185. Three to four weeks' absence is a safer estimate.

Seibert's efforts (*Hann.* 385 note 36) to shield Hannibal from blame for not noticing Nero's absence ('angesichts der kriegerischen Praxis völlig normal') or, if he did notice it, for not taking advantage of it, are hardly persuasive. And if Nero knew that his absence would be 'völlig ungefährlich' for the Romans because Hannibal would not stir, this puts the latter's military sagacity by 207 in just as poor a light.

13 The peace talks in 203 and *P. Ryl.* 3. 491
(chapter XIV, note 12)

P. Ryl. 491, published in 1938 (Roberts (1938)) and generally seen as pro-Carthaginian in tone, does not mention an attack on Scipio's envoys, but it is too fragmentary for disproof and its supposed bias is quite unprovable (Hoyos (2001a)). Just as likely if not more so, it could be a précis of a pro-Roman account, maybe even Fabius Pictor's. Whatever its background, it does not impugn Polybius' account.

Plutarch meanwhile has a story of Scipio telling the Carthaginians that, because they had recalled Hannibal, he would not continue the armistice 'even if they wished it' unless they paid a further 5,000 talents (*Moralia* 196C–D); but this tale is not plausible. Having brought Hannibal home the Carthaginians would scarcely be interested in paying to continue the armistice; and Eutropius (3.22) has Scipio prescribe a similar penalty when Hannibal himself supposedly asks for peace before Zama. So at best Plutarch's story is a glimmer of a more pro-Punic and anti-Scipio tradition: thus de Sanctis, 3.2.533 note 161, and Huss (1985) 414 note 90; while Mantel (1991) 121–2 sees it as a distorted annalistic item.

14 The 'quaestor' at Carthage in 195
(chapter XVI, note 3)

That 'quaestor' means *rb* (*rab*) and head of finance is argued most fully by Huss (1979), but the case is not completely certain. Finance officials are attested—*mhsbm*, 'the accountables'—but, it seems, no *rab* of the *mhsbm* (Sznycer (1978) 585; cf. Huss (1985) 465) even though *rab* means simply 'chief' and is also used with other offices, e.g. *rab kohanim*, 'chief of priests' (Huss, 543). Livy's Latin, of course, may mean not '*the* quaestor' (the usual supposition) but, just as likely, '*a* quaestor' and so may refer to one uncooperative member of 'the accountables'. True, Gades in 205 had two sufetes and one 'quaestor', all of whom Mago murdered for disloyalty (Livy 28.37.2); but Gades, a town much smaller than Carthage, may well have had only one *mhsb*. In any case Latin writers are not consistent in naming Punic magistracies, so a 'quaestor' recorded at one city does not inevitably prove one at another; for inconsistencies compare Livy calling Hannibal in 196 'praetor' (33.46.2) but writing of 'sufetes' in 193 (34.61.15), while Justin terms him 'consul' at the time of his flight (31.2.6); and on Nepos' confusions see chapter XV note 7.

15 Hannibal, Cyrene and Siwa (chapter XVII, note 4)

Along with holding that Hannibal visited Cyrene in 193, Seibert (*Hann.* 514 and on his Map 10) supposes that he travelled inland to the oracle of Zeus

Amon at the oasis of Siwa, for later he believed in a prophecy of Amon about his place of burial (Pausanias 8.11.1; Appian, *Syr.* 11.44; Tzetzes, *Chiliades* 1.801–22). Of course he would not have had leisure to go to Siwa during his flight in 195. But Appian and Tzetzes pretty clearly imply that Hannibal had been sent the prophecy, perhaps after submitting a written query. No actual visit to the oasis should be supposed.

TIME-LINE

233

228 or 227	Hasdrubal visits Carthage
227/226	Foundation of New Carthage; Roman interest aroused
225 (spring)	Ebro-accord between Hasdrubal and the Romans; probable date of first Saguntine–Roman diplomatic links
225–222	Romans defeat Gallic invasion of Italy, and subdue Cisalpine Gaul
221	Hasdrubal assassinated; Hannibal elected general; subdues Olcades
220	Campaign in central and northern Spain; Vaccaei and Carpetani defeated
(autumn)	Roman envoys see Hannibal at New Carthage
219 (prob. Apr./May– Dec.)	Hannibal besieges Saguntum
218	Romans declare war at Carthage
(June–Nov.?)	Hannibal's expedition to Italy
	Cn. Scipio operates in north-eastern Spain
(Nov.–Dec.)	Battles of the Ticinus and the Trebia
217	Hannibal enters Etruria; crossing of the Arno marshes
(June)	Battle of Lake Trasimene; Hannibal marches to Apulia; Fabius Maximus dictator at Rome; operations in Campania
	Victories of the Scipio brothers in Spain
216 (Aug.)	Battle of Cannae
215	Defections to Hannibal begin in Campania and southern Italy; further operations in Campania; treaty with Philip V of Macedon
	Hasdrubal in Spain defeated at Hibera
	Hiero of Syracuse succeeded by his grandson Hieronymus
214	Hannibal's operations in Campania and Apulia; Hanno defeated at river Calor
	Hieronymus assassinated; Hippocrates and Epicydes ally Syracuse with Carthaginians
213	Arpi in Apulia defects to the Romans; Marcellus besieges Syracuse
212	Tarentum defects to Hannibal; likewise Metapontum, Thurii and Locri; first battle of Herdonea
	Romans besiege Capua; Marcellus takes Syracuse
	Successes of Scipio brothers in southern Spain; Saguntum restored to its citizens
211	Hannibal's march on Rome; Capua surrenders to the Romans

211	Destruction of the Scipios in Spain
210	Second battle of Herdonea; battle of Numistro
209	Fabius captures Tarentum; P. Scipio the younger captures New Carthage
208	Consul Marcellus killed; Scipio defeats Hasdrubal, brother of Hannibal, at Baecula; Hasdrubal sets out for Italy
207	Hasdrubal's arrival in Italy and destruction at the river Metaurus
206	Hannibal stagnant in Bruttium; Scipio defeats Hasdrubal son of Gisco at Ilipa
	Hasdrubal son of Gisco wins over Syphax of Numidia as Punic ally
205	Scipio as consul operates in south Italy; Mago brother of Hannibal, in Liguria
	Philip V makes peace with Romans
204	Scipio as proconsul invades Punic Africa
204/203 (winter)	Scipio destroys Punic and Numidian armies near Utica in night attack
203	Hasdrubal son of Gisco and Syphax again defeated at the Great Plains; Masinissa made king of all Numidia
	Carthaginians make peace with Scipio; Hannibal recalled from Italy
202	War resumes; battle of Zama (October)
201	Peace treaty ends Second Punic War
200	Indemnity-money scandal
200–197	Second Macedonian War and defeat of Philip V
199(?)	End of Hannibal's generalship
196	Hannibal becomes sufete and enacts reforms
195	Roman embassy prompts Hannibal into self-exile; joins Antiochus III at Ephesus
193	Aristo of Tyre visits Carthage
191	Hannibal as naval commodore for Antiochus in eastern Aegean
190	Battle of Magnesia
189	Antiochus makes peace with Romans; Hannibal forced to leave his kingdom
189–186(?)	Hannibal's wanderings
186(?)–183	Hannibal in Bithynia including service as King Prusias' admiral
183	Roman embassy to Prusias; suicide of Hannibal
149–146	Third Punic War and destruction of Carthage by P. Scipio Aemilianus

NOTES TO THE TEXT

I THE HEIGHTS OF HEIRCTE AND ERYX

1 Hamilcar at Heircte (or 'Hercte'): Pol. 1.56–7. Properly speaking it was the fort in the pass that had this name (Thiel (1954) 254 note 618) but the mountain's ancient name is not known. Earlier Roman attack on fort 'Hercte', supposedly with 40,000 foot and 1,000 horse: Diod. 23.20 (in 252/251?). The First Punic War's eighteenth year began in midsummer 247: Walbank, 1.119–20.

2 For the theory that the Romans originally meant to fight not Carthage but Syracuse see A. Heuss, *Der erste punische Krieg und das Problem des römischen Imperialismus*, 3rd edn (Darmstadt 1970); J. Molthagen, 'Der Weg in den ersten punischen Krieg', *Chiron* 5 (1975) 89–127; more fully Hoyos (1998) 47–99.

3 Naval losses from 255 to 249: Pol. 1.37.1–2, 39.6, 51.11–12, 54.8; Diod. 24.1.7–9; Thiel (1954) 236, 251, 279–89. Readable short accounts of the war are Caven (1980) 18–66; Scullard (1989a) 537–69; a full history in Lazenby (1996); while the naval side is thoroughly and interestingly studied by Thiel, 61–338. Census figures: Livy, *Epit.* 16 and 19 (292,200 and 241,700); Brunt (1971) chapter III.

4 Negotiations with Regulus: Lazenby (1996) 101–2; Hoyos (1998) 116–18.

5 Carthalo's raid: Zon. 8.16 (Carthalo scared off by the *praetor urbanus*, who was based in the City; note too the new citizen-colonies of Alsium and Fregenae founded on the south Etruscan coast in 247). Economic strains: cf. Picard (1967) 57–9; Hoyos (1994) 265–6. Ptolemy declined to lend: Appian, *Sic.* 1.1–2. Fleet neglected after 249, and overloaded, undermanned and poorly trained in 241: Pol. 1.61.4–5; Zon. 8.17; Thiel (1954) 306–11; Lazenby (1996) 144–5, 150–5. Privateering Roman raids: Zon. 8.16; cf. Thiel, 299 note 768; Lazenby, 146–7.

6 Hecatompylus–Theveste–Tebessa: Pol. 1.73.1; Diod. 24.10.1–2, cf. 4.18.1; de Sanctis, 3.1.176 note 79. On motives for expansion in the 240s cf. Hoffmann (1962) 14–15. On the fertile Tebessa uplands see Fentress (1979) 32–3, unnecessarily doubting that Hecatompylus was Theveste. 'Thinking that they had rational grounds', Pol. 1.72.1; Hanno involved, *ibid.* 3.

7 Zon. 8.16 (mutiny repressed, episode at Drepana); Pol. 1.56.2–3 (raid and move to heights). Frontinus' tale of a supposed ruse by 'Barca' to enter Lilybaeum despite Roman warships (*Strat.* 3.10.9) is not about him at all (despite de Sanctis, 3.1.238; L. Pareti, *Storia di Roma* 2 (Turin 1952) 166–7) but was performed by another general, Hannibal son of Hamilcar, in 250 (Pol. 1.44; Thiel (1954) 266–9) and Frontinus or his source got confused.

8 See Hoyos (2001c).

9 Kromayer estimated Hamilcar's army at 15,000–20,000 (in Kromayer and Veith, *AS* 3.1.10), as do Walbank (1.121) and Scullard ((1989a) 564), but Thiel (1954) 299 note 766 rightly disbelieves this. Perhaps 30,000 at battle of Panormus in 250: Lazenby (1996) 121. Twenty thousand mercenaries from Sicily in 241: Pol.

1.67.13. Lilybaeum was garrisoned by 7,700 in 250, soon reinforced to over 20,000 (Diod. 24.1.1–2; Pol. 1.44.2, 45.8; Thiel, 263–4). Hamilcar's cavalry: 200 are mentioned at Eryx in 243 (below) but the Heircte heights had much more room and resources. Roman force was 'evenly matched' with his: Pol. 1.57.6; de Sanctis improbably supposes an entire consular army (3.1.179), meaning some 20,000 men. Kromayer, 23, places the Roman camp south of M. Castellaccio on Cuzzo Gibelliforni, as good a guess as any (Hoyos (2001c) 494).

10 Operations from the Heircte heights: Pol. 1.56.9–57.8, cf. 1.74.9. Lancel (1992) 388 thinks raids on Italy continued from 247 through to 241. Italium: Diod. 24.6. Like de Sanctis (3.1.178 note 83), Manni takes Longon to be an unknown river near Catana ((1981) 114, 193). Lazenby (1996) 148 sees it as a raid into Catana's territory perhaps to put pressure on Hiero of Syracuse nearby. But Longane near Mylae, attested on coins and an inscription (Manni, 197), is called 'Longone' by Stephanus of Byzantium (s.v., citing the fourth-century Syracusan historian Philistus), so 'Longon' is not an impossible variant; Κατάνης φρούριον could be a copyist's error for Μεσήνης φ. (compare the probable error of Αἴγεστα replacing Ἐχέτλαν at Diod. 23.3, and the definite one Λιγάτινος, meaning Λυτάτιος, at 24.11.1). Panormus–Agrigentum road: attested by a milestone probably of 252 or 248 set up by the consul C. Aurelius Cotta (*ILLRP* 1,227; Verbrugghe (1976) 19–22).

11 Hamilcar's family: chapter II. Seibert supposes winter visits to Carthage (*Hann.* 9 note 14) but winter sailing was very dangerous. On *brq/baraq* see Gsell, *HAAN* 2.252 note 7 (noting that it might instead mean '[Ba'al] has blessed', from the verb *brk*—though he might have added that this seems less suitable for the military Hamilcar); Picard (1967) 19; Sznycer (1978) 552–3. The claim that Hamilcar's family had come from Barce, a Greek city near Cyrene (R. G. Austin, *P. Vergili Maronis Aeneidos Liber IV* (Oxford 1955) 43), is an unfounded guess. Numidian prince's admiration: Pol. 1.78.1–8 (Naravas).

12 Move to Eryx: Pol. 1.58.2; Diod. 24.8. Kromayer, in Kromayer and Veith, *AS* 3.1.32–5, with his Map 2; Thiel (1954) 301. Temple of Venus Erycina: de Sanctis, 3.1.173 note 73; Walbank, 1.118–19. Eryx townsfolk transferred to Drepana in 259: Diod. 23.9.4; Zon. 8.11. A surviving line from Naevius' late third-century epic poem on the war, 'superbiter contemtim conterit legiones' ('haughtily, scornfully he wears down the legions') may refer to Hamilcar, on Eryx or earlier at Heircte: cf. Warmington (1936) 64, frg. 38. Hamilcar, 'Vodostor' and Fundanius: Diod. 24.9. *Circa* 1 May for consuls entering office: Morgan (1977) 90–1. The Gallic deserters: Pol. 1.77.4, 2.7.7–10.

13 New Roman fleet and battle of the Aegates islands: Pol. 1.59–61; Diod. 24.11; Zon. 8.17 (with Hanno's fate); Florus 1.18 [2.2] 33–6; Eutrop. 2.27.3, with the date convincingly defended by Morgan (1977) 109–12; other sources at Broughton, *MRR* 1.218; Thiel (1954) 302–16; Walbank, 1.124–6; Lazenby (1996) 150–7. Attack on Eryx, 2,000 Punic troops slain: Oros. 4.10.8. Peace-talks and terms: Pol. 1.62.1–63.3; 3.27.1–6; Diod. 24.13 (mentions Gisco); Nepos, *Hamil.* 1.5; Appian, *Sic.* 2.1–4 (a confused blend of first and final drafts); Zon. 8.17; de Sanctis, 3.1.184–9; Walbank, 1.126–7, 355; Schmitt, *SVA* 3.173–81; Huss (1985) 249–51; Scardigli (1991) 205–43; Hoyos (1998) 118–23, 130–1. The 1,000 talent down-payment possibly represented about one year's Punic state revenues: chapter II §III. Hamilcar's promises to the troops: Pol. 1.67.12; Appian, *Iber.* 4.15.

14 Hamilcar's final actions in Sicily: Pol. 1.66.1, 68.12; Zon. 8.17. Punic generalship indefinite in duration: Gsell, *HAAN* 2.420–1; Huss (1985) 478. Official scrutiny: Gsell, 2.188, 205–7; Picard and Picard, *LDC* 128, 142–6; Huss, 464, 478.

15 Politics at Carthage in mid-century: chapter II. Hanno undermined war-effort in Sicily: Thiel (1954) 294–7, 306; Picard (1967) 60–1; Picard and Picard, *LDC* 198; Huss (1985) 246 note 232; Scullard (1989a) 563. Seibert severely criticizes Hamilcar's leadership at both Heircte and Eryx for stubbornness and failure to exploit advantages like Punic naval superiority before 242 (*FzH* 89–94; *Hann.* 8–11).

II CARTHAGE

1 Descent from Belus and Barca, Silius 1.71–6, 15.745–8. Ba'lu king of Tyre in early seventh century: Nina Jidejian, *Tyre through the Ages* (Beirut (1969)) 46–9, 246; W. Röllig, *Kl P* 4.1028 s.v. 'Tyros'. Tyre did have other kings with similar names, for instance Ithobaal in the first half of the ninth century (Jidejian, 39–41, 246), Baal in the sixth (*ibid.* 56, 246–7). Punic names: Sznycer (1978) 550–1—over 500 known from inscriptions. The two Hamilcars: see next note.

2 Hamilcar 'admodum adulescentulus', Nepos, *Hamil.* 1.1. *Adulescentulus* and *adulescens* can be very elastic—for instance Cicero retrospectively terms himself 'adulescens' as consul aged 43 (*Philippics* 2.46.118) and to Sallust a 37-year-old Caesar is 'adulescentulus' (*Catilina* 49.2; cf. Lewis and Short's *Latin Dictionary*, s.v. 'adulescens'). Hamilcar about 30 in 247: similarly Picard (1967) 64, puts his birth around 280–75. T. Lenschau, *RE* 7.2302–3, wants him born by 285 so as to identify him as the Hamilcar prominent in the war from 260, but Nepos is emphatic: Barca's first command was in the 'temporibus extremis' of the war. See also Walbank, 1.80; Huss (1985) 228 note 74. Hanno son of Bomilcar, Pol. 3.42.6; Bomilcar called 'the king' (i.e. sufete?), Appian, *Hann.* 20.90; Huss (1983) 25–32, (1991) 118–23.

Hannibal's birth-year: in early 237 he was nine (Pol. 2.1.6 and 3.11.5; Livy 21.1.4), at the end of 202 'more than 45' (Pol. 15.19.3; cf. Livy 30.37.9); see Lenschau, *RE* 7.2323 s.v. 'Hamilkar (7)'; Seibert, *Hann.* 7 note 2, 9 note 12. Mago in 218, Pol. 3.71.8 ('young'), etc.; born in 242, surmises Picard (1967) 65. On Hamilcar's daughters and other family questions, see Appendix §1.

3 Byzacium estates: Livy 33.48.1; the inference of wealth is Picard's (1967) 20–1. Birth and wealth required: Aristotle, *Pol.* 2.11.8–9, 1,273a, 'they believe that magistrates should be chosen on the basis not only of birth but also of wealth; for it is impossible for a poor man to govern well and to have the time'. Bribery, 2.11.10–12; still prevalent and public in later times, Pol. 6.56.1–4. Ameling (1993) 171–5 seeks to temper these verdicts.

4 Hanno's sobriquet: Appian, *Iber.* 4.16, *Lib.* 34.145, 49.213; Zon. 8.22; Huss (1979) 230 note 40, and (1985) 464, sees it as rendering Punic *rb* (*rab*), 'great one' or 'chief', and meaning not age or eminence but the head of the state finances (cf. chapter XV §III). But that this office could be held by Hanno for decades during the Barcid supremacy—and that only he, and a couple of other Hannos in other eras, were remembered for it by having it as their sobriquet—is not convincing. His alleged enmity towards Hamilcar during the 240s: cf. chapter I with note 15. Not hereditary (*contra* for instance Gsell, *HAAN* 2.253; Hoyos (1994) 270 tentatively)—Livy limits it to Hamilcar and his sons (21.3.2, 10.11 'paternas inimicitias', 23.13.6 'simultas cum familia Barcina') and Silius, writing about Hanno's 'odiis gentilibus' towards Hamilcar's son (*Pun.* 2.277), may have no more than that in mind; in any case this is a poet who affirms that Regulus had been crucified in public (2.343–4). Loreto similarly sees the decisive break between Hanno and Hamilcar coming as late as 237 ((1995) 205, 207–8, cf. 138, 161).

5 The ports, especially the circular one, have been extensively studied as part of the 'Save Carthage' project: see for instance Picard (1983) 34–7; Huss (1985) 47–8;

L. E. Stager and H. Hurst in Ennabli (1992) 75–8 and 79–94; Lancel (1992) 192–211 = English tr. 172–92). See Appendix §2.

6 On Carthaginian history and culture see, e.g., Lancel (1992); Huss (1985); Picard (1968); Picard and Picard (1983); Warmington (1964). On the archaeological remains, Ennabli (1992); Niemeyer *et al.* (1996). Timaeus on the foundation-date: *FrGH* 566 F60. Extent of city: Strabo 17.3.15, C833; Appian, *Lib.* 95.448–96.455, 117.555, 128.610–13; Gsell, *HAAN* 2, chapter I; Tlatli (1978) chapters III–IV; Huss (1985) chapter IV; Scullard (1989a) 499–503; Lancel (1992) chapter V. The Numidians: Gsell, 2.99–100, 306–8. On the Carthaginian empire, Whittaker (1978). The Pyrgi tablets: e.g. J. Ferron, in *Aufstieg und Niedergang der Römischen Welt*, 1.1, ed. H. Temporini (Berlin and New York 1972) 189–216; Tusa (1974) 88–9; Lancel (1992) 101–2. Treaties with Rome: Pol. 3.22–4; cf. Walbank, 1.339–49; Scardigli (1991) 47–127; Cornell (1996) 210–14, 388.

7 King Hamilcar's mother: Herodotus 7.165. Hamilcar Barca and Naravas: Pol. 1.78. Later granddaughter's royal marriages, and Sophoniba's: chapter XIII note 2. Background of Punic agents Hippocrates and Epicydes: Livy 24.6.2. On intermarriage cf. Picard (1961) 82–3.

8 Carthaginians jealously guarding their western trade monopoly: Strabo 3.5.11, 175C, 17.1.19, 802C; but see Whittaker (1978) 61, 80–1. On Carthaginian Sicily see especially Hans (1983). For the one, dubious clash between Carthaginians and Massiliots, a supposed 'battle of Artemisium', see Sosylus, *FrGH* 176, F1, with Jacoby's commentary (*Kommentar* vol. BD, 605); Huss (1985) 67. Punic adoption of Greek usages: e.g. Picard (1964) 96–118, 194–5; Picard and Picard (1983) 55–9; Hahn (1974); Lancel (1992) 360–7. Coinage: Jenkins and Lewis (1963); Huss (1983) 489–93.

9 Punic religion is well discussed by Huss (1985) chapter XXXVI; Lancel (1992) chapter VI. On child sacrifice: L. E. Stager in Pedley (1980) 1–11; Lancel, 268–76; Fantar (1995) 74–7 is sceptical. The *molk* of 310: Diod. 20.14.4–7 (emphasizing that it was exceptional). Silius Italicus has a story about Hannibal being ordered by the priests to hand over his son for sacrifice, and refusing (4.763–829), but this is obviously a fancy (though Seibert, *Hann.* 20 note 60, thinks there may be something to it and also (19–20) that a *molk* may have taken place during the African revolt of 241–237, despite the lack of evidence. Neither idea persuades, cf. Appendix §1).

10 'Lepcis' on the 'ora minoris Syrtis': Livy 34.62.3 (*Leptis* in some MSS). The Emporia region stretched from the Lesser to the Greater Syrtes (gulf of Gabès to gulf of Sirte): Gsell, *HAAN* 2.127–8; Lancel (1992) 111, 278, 430; cf. Mattingly (1994) xiii, 1, 50–2, 218. The daily talent is disbelieved by Kahrstedt (1913) 134–5, and Walbank, 3.491; but Gsell, 2.319, and de Sanctis, 3.1.32 note 88, judge it as revenue from Lepcis plus its surroundings. See Appendix §3.

11 Roman republic's estimated income from 200 to 157: T. Frank, *An Economic History of Rome*, vol. 1: *The Republic* (Baltimore 1933) 126–41; Nicolet (1978) 1.255–7. Rhodian customs-duties: Pol. 30.31.7–12; Walbank, 3.458–60. Rhodian customs-duties before 167: Pol. 30.31.7–12; Walbank, 3.458–60. Punic war-indemnities in 241, 237 and 201: chapter I §v, chapter IV §1, chapter XV §1 (that of 241 was perhaps suspended during the Mercenaries' War, Hoyos (1998) 125). Revenues of Athens at the start of the Peloponnesian War, reportedly 1,000 talents: Xenophon, *Anabasis* 7.1.27, cf. Thucydides 1.99.3; R. Meiggs, *The Athenian Empire* (Oxford 1972, repr. 1987) 258–9. Syracusan indemnity: Pol. 1.16.9–10, 17.3; Diod. 23.4.1; Zon. 8.9.11 (Eutropius, 2.19.1, improbably claims 200 talents); Hoyos (1998) 106–7.

12 Population of Carthage: Appendix §4. Resident non-citizens: cf. Huss (1985) 501–2. Adult men: this follows P. A. Brunt's calculation of them as 28–31 per cent of total population, at any rate in third-century BC Italy ((1971) 59, 116). Punic citizens sent out as colonists: Aristotle, *Pol.* 2.11.15, 1273b; 6.5.9, 1320b. Roman citizens in 247: Livy, *Epit.* 19. In 225, with Roman and Italian allied manpower together reported as 770,000 (probably too high): Pol. 2.24–5; cf. Brunt, chapter IV. Population of the empire: Appendix §4. Slaves: Huss, 499–500.

13 Aristotle on the political system: *Pol.* 2.11.1–9, 1272b–1273b; 4.7.11, 1293b ('threefold aim' (Penguin tr.)); Picard and Picard, *LDC* 141–6; Huss (1985) chapter XXX. Cf. Pol. 6.43.1, Walbank, 1.724, and Huss, 458 note 1, for other admirers. The kingship: Ameling (1993) chapter II. The sufetes: Gsell, *HAAN* 2.193–200; Picard (1963); Sznycer (1978) 567–76; Bacigalupo Pareo (1977); Huss (1983) and (1991) 118–23; Scullard (1989a) 490–1. Occasionally there might be four rather than two sufetes in a year (W. Huss, *Muséon* 90 (1977) 427–33). Generals: Bengtson (1952); Picard (1968) 115–23; Ameling (1993) 83–117; Hoyos (1994) 249–56. Plurality of offices: Aristotle 2.11.13, 1,273b.

14 *H'drm*, Huss (1985) 462, (1991) 124–7. Senate's powers: Gsell, *HAAN* 2.202–4, 215–26. Decided peace and war: cf. Hoyos (1994) 262–4; below, chapter XVI note 21. On the term *rab*, see Huss (1979), (1985) 465 and (1991) 129, who suggests that on its own this was the title of Carthage's presumed magistrate for finances; but see Appendix §14. Public scribes (*sprm*): cf. Pol. 3.22.8 (first treaty with the Romans); Sznycer (1978) 585 (also for market inspectors). Boards of Five (pentarchies): Aristotle, *Pol.* 2.11.4, 1273a13–20; cf. 3.1.7, 1275b12–13. Ban on Greek: Justin 20.5.12–13 (a date around 370). Inner council of senate: Pol. 10.18.1, 36.4.6; Livy 30.16.3 'sanctius consilium'; Walbank, 1.76, 2.218; Huss (1985) 462–3 and (1991) 125.

15 Tribunal of One Hundred and Four: Aristotle, *Pol.* 2.11.2, 1272b ('104'); 2.11.4, 1273a ('100'); Justin 19.2.5 (100 judges created from among the senators). *Ordo iudicum:* Livy 33.46.1–7. See, e.g., Susemihl and Hicks (1894) 341–3, 348–9; Gsell, *HAAN* 2.205–8; Sznycer (1978) 579–81; Huss (1985) 464; Ameling (1993) 83–5; and cf. below, chapter VI §III; XV §II.

16 Citizen assembly: Aristotle, *Pol.* 2.11.5–6, 1273a; Pol. 3.13.3–4 (election of Hannibal as general), 6.51.2–7; Livy 33.46.6–7; Gsell, *HAAN* 2.225–31; Sznycer (1978) 581–4; Huss (1985) 463–4; Hoyos (1994) 262–4. Poorer Carthaginians excluded: so for instance Gsell, 2.228, and Sznycer, 583, because Polybius distinguishes between 'citizens' and 'artisans' at New Carthage in 210 (10.16.1, 10.17.6–9); but see Walbank, 2.216; Scullard (1989a) 491–2. Evidence for formal clientships, perhaps including freed slaves: Huss (1985) 497–9.

17 Magonids: Justin 18.7.2–19.3.12; Herodotus 7.165; Diod. 13.43.5, 14.54.5. Fourth-century Hanno the Great: Aristotle, *Pol.* 5.6.2, 1307a; Justin 21.4. Bomilcar's attempted coup: Diod. 20.43.1–44.6. See, e.g., Gsell, *HAAN* 2.186–91, 245–52; Picard and Picard, *LDC* chapters II–III; L. J. Sanders, *Historia* 37 (1988) 72–89; Lancel (1992) 127–32 (= English tr. 110–15); Ameling (1993) chapter II.

III THE REVOLT OF AFRICA

1 Outbreak of the Truceless or Mercenaries' War: Pol. 1.66–70; Diod. 25.2; Gsell, *HAAN* 2.101–5; Huss (1985) 252–5; Loreto (1995) 45–113; Hoyos (1999). Rebel coinage (cf. Pol. 1.72.6): for instance Jenkins and Lewis (1963) 43, 51; W. Huss, *Schweizer Münzblätter* 150 (1988) 30–3; E. Acquaro, in Devijver and Lipinski (1989) 137–44; Howgego (1995) 113–14.

2 Troops' irritation with 'the generals who had made the promises': Pol. 1.67.12; cf. Appian, *Sic.* 2.7. Gisco's fate: 1.80.10–13. Prosecution of Hamilcar: Appian, *Iber.* 4.16, *Hann.* 2.3; dating accepted for instance by Lenschau, *RE* 7.2356; Gsell, *HAAN* 2.255; Picard (1967) 74 and (1968) 120; Loreto (1995) 205–6, who implausibly argues for different charges arising out of the war in Africa. *Contra*: de Sanctis, 3.1.377 note 16; Walbank, 1.140, 151; Hoyos (1994) 261–2.

3 'The leading men' or 'the men in power', τοὺς πολιτευομένους (Appian, *Iber.* 4.16; the Loeb translation is less satisfactory, 'the chief men in the state'). The verb basically means 'to be in public life', but can also mean 'to be in government' or 'to administer affairs'. Since Hamilcar's enemies must have been in public life too, the stronger sense seems to be what Appian intends (similarly Loreto (1995) 208–9). Hasdrubal 'the most popular', Appian, *ibid.*; his youth and the alleged sexual relationship, Nepos, *Hamil.* 3.2; Livy 21.2.3 ('uti ferunt'). Diodorus on Hamilcar in 237: 25.8. The widespread idea that Hamilcar at this time was at odds with the dominant faction, or with the oligarchy as a whole (de Sanctis, 3.1.376–7; Gsell, *HAAN* 2.253–4; Picard (1967) 60, 68; Scullard (1980) 184), hardly squares with such evidence as we have (Hoyos (1994) 258–61, 267; Loreto, 208–9).

Appian shifts the prosecution to 237, perhaps through linking it with a supposed joint appointment of Hamilcar and Hanno to subdue the Numidians, following the Mercenaries' War; Hamilcar uses the appointment as a clever way to escape trial (cf. also *Hann.* 2.3). In reality, if any operations against the Numidians occurred, they were part of the mopping-up near the end of that war when the two generals were again co-operating. Hamilcar's appointment immediately following the war was to Spain.

4 Seibert defends Hanno against Polybius' biased presentation (*FzH* 96 note 52; cf. Walbank, 1.140, and Huss (1985) 258). But it remains true that he did not shine in his operations. Loreto (1995) 135–7 maintains that Hanno then led his surviving troops back to Carthage, where some formed Hamilcar's army in turn. But it is hard to believe that Polybius—especially in his anti-Hanno mood—would have left that out, and in fact he indicates that the army was formed partly of later-enrolled mercenaries (75.2). Hamilcar's army may have included some of the 2,743 Punic prisoners of war sent home, ransom-free, by the Romans (Pol. 1.83.8; Val. Max. 5.1.1 and Eutrop. 2.27 give the number) if the restoration occurred about this time: cf. Hoyos (1998) 124.

Multiple generalships: Gsell, *HAAN* 2.422–3. Adherbal in overall command in 250–249: Pol. 1.44.1, 53.2–3; Gsell, 422 note 6; Thiel (1954) 281; Walbank, 1.109, 116; Lazenby (1996) 126. Hamilcar appointed, Pol. 1.75.1; but as commander-in-chief, Picard and Picard, *LDC*, 206; Huss, 258; Scullard (1989a) 567; Lancel (1992) 392; Hoyos (1994) 250–1. Carthaginians urged both generals to avenge Gisco: Pol. 1.81.1. Hamilcar 'called Hanno to him': 1.82.1. Carthaginians surprised by their quarrel: Seibert, *FzH* 101 note 71.

5 Punic naval strength in 241–240: Pol. 1.73.2 (triremes and the smaller 50-oar ships). Rebel numbers: Pol. 1.67.13, 73.3; Nepos, *Hamil.* 2.2. De Sanctis, 3.1.375 note 11, and Walbank, 1.139, are probably right to judge the Libyan figure (70,000) exaggerated, despite Loreto (1995) 87–9, 119–21. Battle of the Bagradas: W. E. Thompson, *Hermes* 114 (1986) 111–17; Loreto, 137–48. Siege of Utica raised: Pol. 1.75.3, explicitly; cf. Huss (1985) 259 note 59; sceptics include Walbank, 1.143; Seibert, *FzH* 99 note 63; Loreto, 139, 151. Though Polybius later writes of the defeated rebels fleeing back to their camp outside Utica (1.76.9), he reports Hamilcar pursuing them part of the way at least (76.10) and their leader Spendius is next found following him into the Libyan countryside

(77.1 and 4). Hamilcar possibly had Hanno's help in raising the siege of Utica—Hanno and his forces were somewhere in the background (cf. previous note).

6 Relations with Hiero and the Romans: Pol. 1.83.2–11; Nepos, *Hamil.* 2.3; Appian, *Sic.* 2.10; Zon. 8.17; Hoyos (1998) 123–6, suggesting (125) that the indemnity was waived until war's end. But the story that Roman envoys tried to mediate in the struggle (Appian, *Sic.* 2.11, *Lib.* 5.19; Zon. *ibid.*; accepted by Huss (1985) 257, and Loreto (1995) 198) is not to be believed; at best it misunderstands or embroiders the rôle of their protest embassy. Spendius' 'Fabian' tactics, Pol. 1.77.2.

7 Naravas' family: Appendix §5. Naravas and Hamilcar's victory, Pol. 1.78.1–12; policy of mercy to prisoners, 78.13–15, 79.8. Veith identifies the victory-site, a plain circled by mountains, as near the hill-town of Nepheris 18 miles/30 kilometres south-east of Tunis (in Kromayer and Veith, *AS* 3.2.539–41); de Sanctis prefers a site north of the Bagradas (3.1.378 note 19; cf. Seibert, *FzH* 99 note 64); Loreto ((1995) 153) suggests the mountains 6–10 miles (10–15 kilometres) west of Tunis but remarks that the lack of help from Tunes for the rebels would indicate a relatively distant site, which seems contradictory. If Veith is right, Hamilcar could have been trying to command a supply-route from the Cape Bon region. But possibly enough the encounter was much further inland.

8 Hanno's activities: in Kromayer and Veith, *AS* 532 inferred confrontation with Mathos besieging Hippou. Loreto, supposing instead that Hanno had marched back to Carthage even before Hamilcar left there (note 4 above), then has him remain at or near the city until he went to join Hamilcar ((1995) 137, 160).

9 Revolt in Sardinia, Pol. 1.79.1–7; massacre of Gisco and other prisoners, 79.8–80.13; Hamilcar's no-quarter policy, 82.2 (with Polybius' implied approval; cf. 81.7–11). Trampling by elephants: inflicted by the regent Perdiccas on selected opponents in 323 after Alexander's death (Curtius, *Historia Alexandri* 10.9.18; Scullard (1974) 78). Much or most of Libya submitting only after Spendius' and Autaritus' débâcle, 86.2.

10 Union of armies and quarrel with Hanno, Pol. 1.82.1–5; Hamilcar became supreme general, 82.5 and 12. Seibert and Loreto similarly infer differences over how to wage the war, rather than an unattested ancient feud (Seibert, *FzH* 101 note 71; Loreto (1995) 161). Soldiers' decision: cf. Eucken (1968) 73; Huss (1985) 477; Hoyos (1994) 250; Loreto, 165–6.

11 The reconstruction in Picard (1968) 117–19, and Picard and Picard, *LDC* 207–8, of the politics behind Hamilcar's election to supreme command is imaginative, circumstantial—for instance giving a substantial rôle to Hamilcar's putative son-in-law Bomilcar—and largely based on assumptions. They also see Hamilcar's election as chief general as establishing his mastery of the Punic state.

12 Fleet lost, Pol. 1.82.6. Mathos' siege of Hippou Acra, 70.9, 73.2, 77.1, cf. 79.14; on Utica, note 5 above. Their 'senseless' defection, 82.8–9 (ἀλόγου); cf. Loreto (1995) 160, 163–4. Pro-Carthage factions deposed: since both cities were (it seems) treated fairly mildly after the war, this is best accounted for if loyalists recovered control then. Hippou and Utica, to show their keenness for their new cause, treated the Carthaginians within their walls with the usual pitilessness: 82.9–10. Carthage besieged: 82.11.

13 Hardships of the besiegers: Pol. 1.82.13, 84.1–2; Diod. 25.4.1. Recruits after breakout, Pol. 84.3. Walbank, 1.146, suggests the rebel army totalled no more than 20,000; Loreto ((1995) 169, 172) accepts Polybius' figure. 'The Saw', Pol. 85.7 (in *Salammbô*, chapter 14, Flaubert more evocatively if misleadingly calls it 'the defile of the Axe'); Veith locates it close to modern Hammamet and the sea about 30 miles/50 kilometres south of Carthage (in Kromayer and Veith 3.2.546–54), but Polybius' description is too brief and general for any precision.

Hamilcar's conduct: cf. de Sanctis' remarks, 3.1.382 ('certo non senza perfidia'); Walbank, 1.147; Loreto, 176, defends it.

14 Fates of Spendius and Hannibal, Pol. 1.86. Hamilcar's move north prevented Mathos joining up with Hippou and Utica rebels: thus Meltzer (1896) 385; Loreto (1995) 185. Seibert, *FzH* 105 note 92, scathingly but unpersuasively judges the move 'kopflos'. Walbank, 1.148, and Huss (1985) 265 note 100, see it only as a move to maintain his communications; Veith, in Kromayer and Veith, *AS* 3.2.556, supposes that Hannibal's force was virtually annihilated, but that is not Polybius' implication (86.5, many killed, all driven from camp).

15 Reconciliation between Hamilcar and Hanno, 1.87.1–6 (Polybius, 86.5, writes as though both generals needed persuasion, which looks like an effort to play down Hamilcar's reluctance); Seibert, *Hann.* 21–2, also sees it as a compromise; cf. Loreto (1995) 186. Hanno already general, 86.3. A political comeback by him: Walbank, 1.148; Picard and Picard, *LDC* 208–9; Scullard (1989a) 568. Troops from Carthage reinforcing Hamilcar, 87.3 ('arming the remaining men of military age, as though now running the last lap [i.e. in a supreme effort], they sent them off to Barca'). Tunes: Veith, in Kromayer and Veith, *AS* 3.2.557, thinks some troops remained there until Mathos summoned them to his last stand, but this seems very unlikely. Operations around 'Leptis' and final battle, Pol. 87.7–10; no doubt Leptis Minor on the Byzacium coast, near Hadrumetum which would be one of the 'other cities' mentioned (Gsell, *HAAN* 2.122 note 4; Walbank, 1.148); not the bigger and more famous Lepcis (*sic*) Magna hundreds of miles to the east, despite Loreto being tempted by this ((1995) 187). Death of Mathos at Carthage, 88.6. Utica and Hippou fearful: 88.3–4, echoed by Diod. 25.5.3. Terms given them: 88.4; Gsell, 123; Walbank, 1.149. Punic rule extended around this time: Diod. 25.10.1, 26.23 ('Micatani'—maybe the Muxsitani of a district (*pagus Muxsi*) west of Utica and Hippou Acra; cf. Lancel (1992) 280); Nepos, *Hamil.* 2.5; see also chapter IV. Chronology: Pol. 88.7; Diodorus' 4 years 4 months (25.6) is impossible to match with other chronological indicators; cf. Walbank, 1.149–50; Loreto, 211; Hoyos (2000a). Mercenaries driven from Sardinia to Italy: Pol. 79.5, 88.8.

16 Debased coinages: Robinson (1956/1978) 9; Jenkins and Lewis (1963) 43; Howgego (1995) 113–14, noting Punic silver 15–33 per cent pure, rebel 25–43 per cent. The rebels overstruck many older Punic coins with their own dies.

17 'Mastia Tarseiou [or Tarseion?]': Pol. 3.24.2 and 4; Walbank, 1.347; Huss (1985) 150–1; Barceló (1988) 134–5, doubting that its site was Cartagena; Scardigli (1991) 107. Punic help to Gades: Justin 44.5.1–4, claiming a Punic conquest of Iberia. Barceló, chapter IV, shows that such claims have no basis; so too González Wagner (1989), but he assumes (156) without warrant that after 241 Carthaginians were barred from direct access to Spanish trade.

IV BARCA SUPREME

1 Chronology: chapters III note 15, V note 16. Punic field forces: Veith, in Kromayer and Veith, *AS* 567–71, estimated 40,000 (versus 30,000 rebels) in Mathos' last battle. 'Formed a political group', etc.: Diod. 25.8, tr. Walton; on the textual questions, Walton (Loeb edn, 11.152); Loreto (1995) 206 note 31; Hoyos (1998) 151 note 2.

2 Hamilcar's appointment to Spain: Hoyos (1994) 258–9. Loreto (1995) 205–10 tries to show that it gave Hamilcar domestic political dominance, but it is much likelier that his already-won dominance brought him the appointment. On Picard's view that Hamilcar now carried through a 'révolution démocratique'

(Picard (1967) 75–7, 216–17, (1968) passim) cf. Hoyos, 262–70. The idea that Hanno was initially re-elected general, only to be dismissed later at Hamilcar's instigation (Loreto, 201, 205–8), reads too much into Appian, *Iber.* 5.17, and also depends on dating the operations in Numidia after the Sardinia crisis (against which, chapter III note 15). The command effectively open-ended: Diodorus terms it explicitly so (εἰς χρόνον ἀόριστον) but this may be a rationalization, since in practice a war in so distant a theatre, against an indefinite range of enemies, would be over only when the commander declared it over. On the Sardinia crisis, Loreto, 198–9; Hoyos (1998) chapter IX, both with detailed citations of earlier scholarship; also Carey (1996), who holds to the view that the Romans treated the island as *terra nullius.*

3 Carthaginians 'at first sought to come to an agreement': Pol. 3.10.1. Embassy of ten: Oros. 4.12.3; Hoyos (1998) 137. Allegations about traders: 3.28.3–4; Appian, *Iber.* 4.15, *Lib.* 5.19; Zon. 8.18 (Appian and Zonaras take them seriously). Ancient and modern explanations for the crisis: Hoyos, 140–3; Goldsworthy (2000) 136 is undecided but, implausibly, thinks the change of consuls influenced the policy switch. The 1,200 talents payable as a lump sum: Pol. 3.27.8 (the terms do not mention instalments); Hoyos, 141. Finances confiscated: Picard (1967) 76, seeing the aim as to undermine Carthage's economy; Loreto (1995) 199 (to prevent a war of revanche); Hoyos, 141–2. The 1,200 talents, incidentally, may represent what the Romans judged to be a year's total revenue of the Punic state: chapter II §III.

4 A third embassy, accepting the terms, may have been sent: Orosius seems to have five—two pairs (doublets?) and a final one; Hoyos (1998) 137–8. The Romans may not have sent their own forces to Sardinia until 235: Hoyos, 139–40.

5 Hasdrubal as trierarch, Pol. 2.1.9; on the position cf. Walbank 1.109, 153; below, chapter X note 6. Hannibal's relative Mago in 215, Livy 23.41.1–2: perhaps a son of brother-in-law Hasdrubal, suggests L.-M. Günther (in *Die Neue Pauly* 5 (1998) 171 and 7 (1999) 701, citing K. Geus, *Prosopographie der literarisch bezeugten Karthager* (Leiden 1994: Studia Phoenicia 13)). But Livy's 'ex gente Barcina' hardly points to so close a link—contrast 29.29.12 for a niece—and a militarily active nephew was more likely to serve with his uncle, as Hanno son of Bomilcar did. This Mago could be a cousin, for Hamilcar need not have been an only child. Mago the Samnite, Pol. 9.25.1–6. Bomilcar the 'king': chapter II note 2 and, on the ancient kingship, *ibid.* note 12; Loreto (1995) 208 sees him as a Punicised Numidian king, but though Punic–Numidian marriages were common enough (note 2 above), no other known Numidian lord of this era had a Punic name. Picard sees Bomilcar as crucial to Barcid political fortunes in and after the Mercenaries' War: (1967) 68–75, 149, (1968) 118; Picard and Picard, *LDC* 207–8; cf. Lancel, *Hann.* 25, who thinks he was also the admiral in the Hannibalic War (24). On Hasdrubal going to Spain cf. Hoyos (1994) 260–1. Himilco in 216, Livy 23.12.6; cf. Maharbal's father's name, 21.12.1. Incidentally Plutarch, *Fabius* 17, names as 'Barca' the officer—Maharbal in Livy (22.51.1–4)—who advised Hannibal after Cannae to march on Rome, which just possibly might go back to some source misunderstanding a Barcid kinship of Maharbal's. Gestar (an invented name?) in 218, Silius 2.390. Hanno versus Hasdrubal in 218, Zon. 8.22; Huss (1985) 294 note 4 guesses Hasdrubal son of Gisco, cf. Seibert, *Hann.* 59 note 48. Loreto, 208–10, speculates about Hamilcar's various sources of political support around 237. Muttines of Hippou Acra: Livy 25.40.5. Punic senators as Barcid councillors: Pol. 3.20.8 (Romans in 218 demanded handover of Hannibal 'and the senators [?—συνέδρους] with him'), 7.9.1 (γερουσιασταί, mentioned in treaty with Philip V of Macedon in 215), 10.18.1 (members of the senate and its inner council

captured at New Carthage in 209); Chroust (1954) 67 note 34, 77–8; Walbank, 1.334–5, 2.44–5; Seibert, *Hann.* 242 note 86.

6 Hamilcar's Spanish expedition unauthorized by élite: Appian, *Hann.* 2.4; Zon. 8.17; cf. Oros. 4.13.1. Against this claim, Hoyos (1994) 258–9 with earlier references; Lancel, *Hann.* 47 thinks it originated with Fabius Pictor. Pictor's criticisms of Hasdrubal and Hannibal: Pol. 3.8.1–8. Barcid Spain virtually independent: notably Schwarte (1983); Blázquez and García (1991) 38–40; more hesitantly Goldsworthy (2000) 137–8, 152; against, Hoyos (1994) citing earlier discussions. 'Enriched Africa': Nepos, *Hamil.* 4.2. Largesse: Appian, *Iber.* 5.18, 6.22, and *Hann.* 2.4. On Barcid political dominance after 237 cf. Hoyos, 270–4. On the later Barcid connexions with Numidian royalty: chapter XII §I.

7 Hannibal's oath: Pol. 3.11.5–9 (μηδέποτε Ῥωμαίοις εὐνοήσειν, often rendered 'never to be a friend to the Romans', as Nepos and Livy do); Livy 21.1.4 (later Roman version), 35.19.3–6 (Polybius' version); Nepos, *Hann.* 2.4 (like Polybius'); Silius 1.70–119; Appian, *Hann.* 3.10; still other versions, following the Roman tradition as do Silius and Appian, are listed by Walbank, 1.314. Ba'al Hammon or B. Shamim: Polybius writes 'Zeus', Nepos 'Jupiter best and greatest'; of course no source supplies the Punic name. B. Hammon was the chief deity in the Punic pantheon in this era (chapter II with note 9); B. Shamim it seems was the god whom Greeks usually identified as Zeus. Picard (1967) 27–9 prefers Shamim; Barré (1983) 12–13, 40–57, stresses that fixed identifications are unlikely and sees 'Zeus' in Hannibal's treaty of 215 with Philip V of Macedon as Hammon.

8 Oath-story reminiscent of 'einer hellenistichen Geschichtsnovelle', Groag (1929) 20 note 1. Invented by Hannibal or others: Hoffmann (1962) 37–8; Errington (1970) 29. Hamilcar not leaving Hannibal behind: Seibert, *Hann.* 27–8. Very probably the story was not publicly known before 193 (cf. Sumner (1972) 472), so it is no surprise if Fabius Pictor—writing around 200—did not have it (Badian (1966) 3–4; Errington, 25–30; Seibert, 28 note 13). Hannibal's loyalty to Hamilcar's guidance: e.g. Pol. 3.12.3–4, 14.10; Livy 21.4.2, 43.15; Zon. 8.21.

V HAMILCAR IN SPAIN

1 Justin (44.5.4) calls Hamilcar's army a 'large force' ('cum magna manu'), which is not of much use. Hannibal's forces in North Africa in 218, Pol. 3.33.9–12; Punic field army by late 238, chapter IV note 1; forces in Spain in 228, Diod. 25.12 (elephants, 25.10.3). Görlitz (1970) 31 arbitrarily guesses a 30,000-strong army in 237. Hamilcar sailed to Spain: Diod. 25.10.1; Nepos, *Hamil.* 4.1; accepted by de Sanctis, 3.1.394, and Scullard (1989b) 23. Other sources merely mention him crossing the straits of Gibraltar (Pol. 2.1.6; Silius 1.141; Appian, *Iber.* 5.17, Hann. 2.4) which does not amount to having him march there—although Gsell, *HAAN* 3.124–5 (admitting it would be 'une marche longue et pénible') thinks it does; so too Huss (1985) 270 note 9; Seibert, *Hann.* 28; Lancel, *Hann.* 55; and Barceló (1998) 20. Walbank, 1.151–2, is undecided.

2 Spain before 237: Harrison (1988); S. J. Keay, *Roman Spain* (London 1988) 8–24; Fernández Castro (1995); Richardson (1996) 9–16. Tartessus: K. Abel in *KI P* 5. 531; Harrison, 51–9, 69–73; T. Júdice Gamito, *Social Complexity in Southwest Iberia 800–300 BC: The Case of Tartessos* (Oxford 1988: BAR International Series 439); Fernández Castro, chapters 12 and 14. The early Magonid expedition to rescue Gades (chapter II note 16) may have helped in Tartessus' collapse (cf. Picard and Picard, *LDC* 66; Huss (1985) 68). On third-century Spanish soldiery and

soldiering, Connolly (1981) 150–2. Aspects of the Barcids' rule in Spain are discussed by Barceló (1989), Hoyos (1994), Lancel, *Hann.* chapter II.

3 Hamilcar's first campaign: Diod. 25.9 (boastful Celts), 25.10.1 (where the Loeb version, 'the Iberians and Tartessians, together with the Celts, led by Istolatius and his brother', does not translate what Diodorus writes). Diodorus' accuracy about 'Tartessians' is urged too by Eucken (1968) 81–3. On Turdetani and Turduli see A. Schulten in *RE* 7A.1378–80; Knapp (1980); Fernández Castro (1995) chapter 17. Ancient geographers, not to mention non-geographical writers, are loose and contradictory about the extent and content of Turdetania; Strabo even includes the Phoenician settlements (3.2.13). Celtici in south-west Spain: Pol. 34.9.3 (= Strabo 3.2.15, C151); Strabo 3.1.6, 3.3.5 (C139, C153); Pliny, *NH* 3.1.13, 4.22.116. Hamilcar campaigned eastwards: Gsell, *HAAN* 3.130; Walbank, 1.152 (inferring Turdetanians and 'east coast Iberians'); Vollmer (1990) 119–20; Lancel, *Hann.* 64. Picard and Picard reinterpret Diodorus—the 'Turdetani' subjugated first, then a Celtiberian incursion under Istolatius and Indortes in 235: *LDC* 216–17. Iberian and Celtiberian mercenaries in Punic armies (outside Spain at that): e.g. Pol. 1.17.4, 1.67.7, 3.56.4, 14.7.5; Livy 30.7.10. Celtiberians in Turdetanian service in 195: Livy 34.19.1. Gades' new coinage: Robinson (1956/1978) 10–11; Lancel, *Hann.* 65.

4 On the Baetis valley and surrounding lands: Fernández Castro (1995) chapter 17; Ruiz Rodríguez (1997). The land, topography and cultural heritage of Andalusia are evocatively treated by Jacobs (1990); geographical analysis in Lautensach (1964) 443–51, 572–609. Indortes 'routed' (τραπείς), Diod. 25.10.2. Treatment of Gisco and other captives: Pol. 1.80.13. To Huss ((1985) 272) the savage treatment of Indortes suggests he had made an agreement after his initial defeat and then broken it, so was seen as a renegade—but there had been no defeat and the inference from Diodorus' wording is implausible.

5 Chronology from coins difficult: Robinson (1956/1978) 10 estimates that Gades' first Barcid series lasted a few years before the finer new issues began around 235, but no certainty is possible. 'Many cities throughout Iberia': Diod. 25.10.3. Wealth accrued: Nepos, *Hamil.* 4.1; Strabo 3.2.14, C151. On the Sierra Nevada and Las Alpujarras: Jacobs (1990) 37–40. On the south-eastern ranges (Sierras de Cazorla, Segura, etc.) and the wilderness lands they embrace: Lautensach (1964) 593–4, 609–15, 625; Jacobs, 25–6, 40–2.

6 Naravas' family: Appendix §5. 'Mostly loyal': Livy 40.17.2 mentions that Masinissa's father Gaia, who died around 210, had once taken territory from the Carthaginians who later received it back from Syphax. This would suggest a Punic–Massylian clash (cf. Walsh (1965) 150) but no details are given and it may not be correctly reported. Surviving Numidians 'were made slaves and liable to tribute', Diod. 25.10.3: with ἐδουλώθησαν φόρους τελέσοντες (Dindorf's Teubner edn) an emendation preferable to ἐ. φ. τελέσαντες (Walton's Loeb), 'were made slaves having paid tribute', for no earlier tribute is known; the manuscript's τελέσαντες has to be emended one way or the other. Massyli and Masaesyli: Gsell, *HAAN* 3.174–8 (who sees no Punic rôle in the formation of the two kingdoms); J. Desanges, in Nicolet (1978) 2.645–9; Fentress (1979) 43–4. Their auxiliaries in 218: Pol. 3.33.15. Syphax attacked by Massyli and Carthaginians, around 212: Livy 24.48–9.

7 By locating Acra Leuce in the upper Baetis valley Sumner (1967) 211 rejects that Hamilcar reached the east coast; but see below. Foundation date: Lancel, *Hann.* 66 surmises around 235, which is surely too early. On the imaginary Punic–Roman confrontations in the 230s: Hoyos, *AHB* (1990) 31–6, and (1998) chapter X. Alleged embassy to Hamilcar: Dio, frg. 48; Hoyos (1998) 147–9 (listing earlier

discussions; sceptical); Lancel, *Hann.* 65 ('probablement apocryphe'), 73 (accepting it, as does Barceló (1998) 23); Richardson (1996) 19 is dubious.

8 Cato placed Hamilcar on a par with Pericles, Curius Dentatus and other classic heroes, above any king: Plutarch, *Cato Maior* 8.14; cf. Hans (1991). Alleged anger and war-plan: Pol. 2.36.4; 3.9.6–8, 10.4–5, 12.7–13.2, 14.10, 15.9–11 (etc.); Nepos, *Hamil.* 1.4, 3.1, 4.3; Livy 21.1.5–2.2; Val. Max. 9.3 ext. 2–3; Silius 1.60–3, 77–80, 106–19, 140–3; 2.296–8; 13.732–51; Florus 1.22 [2.6] 2; [Victor], *De Vir. Ill.* 42.1; Oros. 4.13.1, 14.3; Zon. 8.17, 21; cf. Appian, *Iber.* 9.34, *Hann.* 3.10 (oath-story, but he offers a different tradition as well—see below). No such report in Diodorus, despite many character descriptions of Hamilcar, Hannibal and his brother Hasdrubal (23.22, 24.5, 25.8, 26.2, 26.24, 29.19). For modern views pro and con see Hoyos (1998) 152 notes 6–7; add Loreto (1995) 83–4, 200–2 (belief that war-plan existed from 241); Lancel, *Hann.* 55–7, 64–6 (disbelief in war-plan); Cornell (1996) 14–18, and Goldsworthy (2000) 146–50 (conditional acceptance).

9 Fabius Pictor: Pol. 3.8.1–8. Appian blames the Second Punic War on Hannibal alone: *Iber.* 9.35, *Hann.* 3.9–10. This view hardly sits comfortably beside the one that Hamilcar made him swear eternal enmity against the Romans, but Appian carefully separates the two. This might suggest that the Hannibal-alone view was the older, and therefore existed before the 190s. Just as likely, though, a later independent-minded historian (which incidentally rules out Appian in the *Hannibalica* and *Iberica*) might have come up with it. Cato the Censor, in the history written in his old age, blamed the Carthaginians for six treaty-breaches down to 219, and these probably included several alleged ones in Barcid times (*Origines*, frg. 84P). This *might* reflect criticisms uttered then (cf. B. D. Hoyos, *AHB* 1 (1987) 112–21, and 4 (1990) 31–6; (1998) 146–7), but equally could be Cato's hindsight three-quarters of a century later.

10 Punic quinqueremes in 218: Pol. 3.33.14 (50 in Spain, but 18 of them unequipped); Livy 21.49.2–4 (55 sent against Sicily and Italy); Thiel (1946) 35–8. Roman fleet in 229: Pol. 2.11.1. Fleet and army in 219 (no figures): 3.16.7, 18.3–19.13; cf. Walbank, 1.327. Once the Second Punic War began, the Carthaginians did again build substantial naval forces: 70 quinqueremes could be sent against Italy and Sardinia as early as 217 (Pol. 3.96.8), for instance. Son-in-law Hasdrubal was Hamilcar's *trierarchos*: chapter IV note 5.

11 Improvements to upper Baetis towns: Fernández Castro (1995) 272–3.

12 Acra Leuce (Diod. 25.10.3) = Lucentum/Alicante: de Sanctis, 3.1.396; Gsell, *HAAN* 3.131; Schulten (1935) 11, 84; Bosch Gimpera (1955) 30; Richardson (1996) 17. Massiliot colonies: Strabo 3.4.6, C159; cf. Appendix §6. Already a Greek colony: Rhys Carpenter, *The Greeks in Spain* (Bryn Mawr 1925, repr. 1971) 56; A. García y Bellido, *Hispania Graeca* (1948) 2.59–60, cited by Barceló (1989) 170 note 9; Schulten (1952) 231; Richardson, 17; Fernández Castro (1995) 234. Site of Alicante: Lautensach (1964) 617. On Hippo 'Zarytos': Huss (1985) 36 note 145.

13 Problems with Acra Leuce being at Alicante: Beltrán (1964) 89–90; Sumner (1967) 208–10, 211 note 22, who places it near Castulo, noting (210 note 20) Urgao which in Roman times bore the epithet 'Alba'; Blázquez and García (1991) 45–56, and Barceló (1996) 47, (1998) 23 echo this. Picard and Picard, *LDC* 218 places it on the coast at La Albufereta, and Rouillard (1982) 427 there or at Tossal de Manises (both lie just north of Alicante). Barceló once preferred Villaricos or Baria well to the south-west ((1988) 119–21, cf. (1989) 170–1); Vollmer (1990) 119–22 has it in the mountain lands south of the river Segura. Undecided: Scullard (1989a) 23–4, and Lancel, *Hann.* 66. For the argument that, if Acra Leuce

was at Alicante, Hasdrubal's New Carthage would have required abandoning it: Barceló (1988) 120–1, (1989) 171. Mastia and Mastiani: Pol. 3.24.4, 33.9; Avienus, *Ora Maritima* 449–52 ('urbs Massiena' in a sheltered gulf); St. Byz. s.v. Μαστιανοί; Walbank, 1.347; Huss (1985) 152; Barceló (1988) 134–5 (but sceptical of Mastia being Cartagena); Richardson (1996) 18–19.

14 Climate of Elche: Beltrán (1964) 90. Hamilcar's death: Diod. 25.10.3–4. Castrum Altum: Livy 24.41.3 ('locus est insignis caede magni Hamilcaris'). The great Livian editor Arnold Drakenborch (1746) proposed 'Album' with explicit reference to Diod. 25.10.3, but without printing it in his text; two later editors, Kreyssig and Bekker, did print 'Album' and the change has been accepted virtually without discussion since, often and paradoxically with a reference to Drakenborch (cf. Hoyos (2001b) 80–1).

15 Young Hasdrubal three years Hannibal's junior: John Tzetzes, *Chiliades* (Byzantine versification of Diodorus, Dio and Dionysius of Halicarnassus) in Diod. 25.19, lines 9–10 (but he terms them 12 and 15 years old in 229/228, so his accuracy is not certain). Mago a young man in 218, 'trained from boyhood [etc.]': Pol. 3.71.6. Hamilcar 'rearing lion-cubs': Val. Max. 9.3 ext. 2; Zon. 8.21; Cassiod., *Chronica, Anno Urbis* 524.

16 Sosylus and Silenus: Nepos, *Hann.* 13.3 singles them out as the prime historians of the war. Sosylus' fragment, on a sea-battle in Spanish waters, is at *FrGH* 176 F1. Polybius on Sosylus' 'barbershop gossip', 3.20.5. The romantic notion that Sosylus was not just Hannibal's Greek tutor (and only from 221) but his adviser on warfare (Zecchini (1997)) is quite implausible. Greek mercenary officers in this era: the famous Philopoemen of Achaea served twice thus in Crete (Pausanias 8.49.7; Plutarch, *Philop.* 13). Greek mercenary troops in Hannibal's service, Pol. 11.19.4.

17 Hamilcar spent 'nearly nine years' in Spain and died ten years before the Second Punic War began: Pol. 2.1.7, 3.10.7; cf. Nepos, *Hamil.* 4.3 'nono anno'; Livy 21.2.1 'novem annis'. Cf. Lenschau, *RE* 7.2307–8; de Sanctis, 3.1.393 note 40, 397 note 52; Sumner (1967) 213 note 27; Hoyos (1998) 139; Loreto's argument ((1995) 213 note 17) that he reached Spain only at the end of 237 is unclear and implausible. Hasdrubal's eight years: Pol. 2.36.1; Livy 21.2.1 ('octo ferme annis'); Diod. 25.12 gives nine, as also for Antigonus Doson of Macedon (25.18), who likewise ruled from 229 to 221. Hamilcar's end: Pol. 2.1.7–8; Diod. 25.10.3–4, 25.12; 25.19, lines 4–21, for Tzetzes' versified and not entirely faithful retelling. Other versions: Nepos, *Hamil.* 4.2; Frontinus, *Strat.* 2.4.17; Appian, *Iber.* 5.19–21; Justin 44.5.4; Zon. 8.19. The Orissi/Oretani: Pol 3.33.10 Ὀρῆτες; Strabo 3.1.6, C139; 3.3.2, C152; 3.4.1, C156; St. Byz. Ὠριτανοί, citing the second-century BC geographer Artemidorus; *ILS* 5901 (attesting an Oretanian bridge over the river Jabalón about 15 miles/25 kilometres south-east of Ciudad Real); A. Schulten, *RE* 18.1018–19 s.v. 'Oretani', 'Oretum', and (1952) 200–1; Walbank, 1.362; Alföldy (1987) 37–9, 46–52; Ruiz Rodríguez (1997) 186–8. Castulo and 'Orisia' are named as their chief centres by Artemidorus and Strabo; as Castulo—south of the Sierra Morena and in prime silver-mining country—was surely under Punic hegemony by 229, the Orissi/Oretani who attacked Hamilcar very probably came from the Anas river-lands north of the mountains.

18 Ilucia (Livy 35.7.7) is Sumner's candidate ((1967) 210 note 20), partly because he locates Acra Leuce in the upper Baetis valley; Ilucia was probably the same as Ilugo, in the Sierra Morena (Schulten, *RE* 9.1091, and (1935) 196; Hoyos (2001b) 79). 'Helice' as Belchite, south of Saragossa: Beltrán (1964) 91–3. Near Albacete on the La Mancha plains: Picard (1967) 84. Alce: Livy 40.48.1; *Itin. Ant.* 445.5 ('Alces' between Laminium and Titulcia); E. Hübner, *RE* 1.1338; it stood some

30 miles (50 kilometres) south-west of Toletum, at or near modern Villacañas. Jacob (1985) 260 assumes Helice to be Ilici near Lucentum, with no discussion.

19 Elche de la Sierra: A. García de Bellido in R. Menéndez Pidal (ed.), *Historia de España* 1.2 (Madrid 1960) 369; Barceló (1989) 172–3, (1998) 27; criticized by Beltrán (1964) 91, because of the terrain's difficulties. Ilunum, Turbula and Segisa: Ptolemy, *Geogr.* 2.6.60, with detailed notes by C. Müller (Paris 1883); Miller (1916/1964) 181 less plausibly identifies Ilunum with Ilugo, near Castulo. Arcilacis: Ptolemy 2.4.9 and 2.6.60; E. Hübner, *RE* 2.602; A. Tovar, *Iberische Landeskunde* 1: *Baetica* (Baden-Baden 1974) 181. The final -*s* is for Greek convenience, like 'Saltigis' and 'Iliturgis'. Ptolemy also repeats, for instance, the later town Salaria (2.6.58 and 60). Aurinx (Livy 24.42.5)/Orongis (28.3.2, 4.2)/Aurgi: Schulten, *RE* 18.1160; Scullard (1970) 262 note 60 sees Livy's two towns as one but places it nearer the Baetis.

20 Castrum Altum etc.: Livy 24.41.3–11; Hoyos (2001b) 76–83. The two Bigerras: Müller (1883) 183 on Ptolemy 2.6.60; Schulten (1935) 84. Bogorra on the river Madera (Müller calls it 'Bigorra') lies in the Sierra de Alcaraz, not far north-west of Elche de la Sierra but across very rugged mountains (*Nuevo Atlas de España* (Madrid 1961) 307). Müller (183, cf. 180) places the other Bigorra at 'Becerra' near the upper Baetis/Guadalquivir, in fact Peal de Becerro 15 miles (24 kilometres) east of Úbeda (Hoyos (2001b) 82). Campaign debatable: Lazenby (1978) 129; Seibert, *Hann.* 251–2 (under date 215); cf. below, chapter XI §III.

21 That the king of the Orissi offered to mediate between Hamilcar and the defenders of 'Helice' and that Hamilcar then agreed to retreat, only to be attacked *en route* (Picard (1967) 84; Lancel, *Hann.* 67), is a very odd misreading of Diodorus. The oxen and burning wagons (in Frontinus, Appian and Zonaras) are accepted by Tarn (1930) 92; Sumner (1967) 209 note 11. 'Vettones': Nepos, *Hamil.* 4.2. Hamilcar's age: cf. chapter II note 2.

22 'Totam locupletavit Africam', Nepos, *Hamil.* 4.1. Polybius on Hamilcar: e.g. 1.62.3, 64.6; 2.1.7; 3.9.6–12.4. Diod. 24.5, 9.3, 13; 25.3.1, 8, 10. Cato on Hamilcar, note 11 above; Livy 21.1.3–2.2; Silius 1.70–119, 13.732–51.

23 Fabius Pictor's strictures on Hasdrubal: Pol. 3.8.1–5. Rule by first citizen, cf. Thucydides 2.65.9. Barcid coins: e.g. Robinson (1956/1978); J. Navascués in *Homenaje al Profesor C. de Mergelina* (Murcia 1961–2) 665–86; Villaronga (1973) 45–63; Acquaro (1974), (1983–4); Sznycer (1978) 566–7; Picard (1983–4) 76–9; Scullard (1989b) 25, 39–40; Blázquez and García (1991) 47–50; Seibert, *FzH* 42 note 179; Lancel, *Hann.* (1995) 71.

24 Pol. 3.14.10.

VI HASDRUBAL'S CONSOLIDATION

1 Diod. 25.12 ('broke camp', ἀναζεύσας, military term); Pol. 2.1.9; Appian, *Iber.* 6.22. Hasdrubal, younger than Hamilcar on all the evidence, yet enjoying major political influence as early as 241, was surely born no later than 270. Huss infers from the 100 elephants, plus Appian's report of the Carthaginians then sending 'another army' to Spain, that when Hamilcar perished he was in Africa ((1985) 274); but Appian writes that he was in Spain. In any case it was wintertime—were Hasdrubal in Africa he would have had to stay there for months. For Lascuta, Scullard (1974) 156.

2 'By both the army and the Carthaginians', ὑπό τε τοῦ λαοῦ καὶ Καρχηδονίων: λαός can also mean the 'people' (as at Diod. 22.2.2) but both context here and comparison with Hannibal's later election point to the other meaning (as at 22.8.2); cf. Huss, 274. When an earlier general Mago was killed in Sicily in 383, 'the

Carthaginians'—his citizen troops?—gave him a splendid funeral there and installed his son as general (Diod. 15.15–16). Hasdrubal chosen by the citizen soldiery: cf. Warmington (1964) 207. Citizen troops and officers in Barcid times: Pol. 1.73.1, 75.2, 79.2, 87.3; 7.9.1 and 4 (Hannibal's treaty with Macedon); 15.11.2–3; Livy 21.5.5, 30.33.5; Appian, *Lib.* 9.35, 40.170. Except in North African wars, most military Carthaginians in this era were probably officers, for no citizen fighting-units are attested. On Punic citizen soldiers generally: Ameling (1993) chapter VII.

3 Hasdrubal and Orissi: Diod. 25.12. Fourteen towns: Ptolemy 2.6.58. Eucken (1968) 84 disbelieves the total for elephants and thinks Diodorus' troop numbers represent Punic Spain's total potential manpower, but it would be better to suppose that these were Hasdrubal's total forces in arms and that he used only part of them against the Orissi. Other units would keep watch over other regions of the province.

4 Diod., 25.12. Congress: Picard (1967) 86, 141; cf. Huss (1985) 275, 'die stimmberechtigten Angehörigen der iberischen Stämme'. Dionysius of Syracuse *et al.* elected *strat. aut.*: N. G. L. Hammond, *A History of Greece to 322 BC* (Oxford 1959) 472 (Dionysius), 518 (Dion and his brother); Eucken (1968) 85; K. Meister, *OCD*³ 37, s.v. Agathocles; B. M. Caven, *ibid.* 476, s.v. Dion; B. D. Hoyos, *Antichthon* 19 (1985) 39–40. Silenus, etc.: Hoyos (1998) 280–1.

5 Alexander as *hegemon*: A. B. Bosworth, *Conquest and Empire: The Reign of Alexander the Great* (Cambridge 1988) 189–91. Pyrrhus: P. R. Franke, *CAH*² 7.2 (1989) 479. Antigonus and Aratus: Pol. 2.54.4; Plutarch, *Aratus* 41.1; Walbank, 1.252–6. Senators from Carthage: cf. Pol. 7.9.1 and 4 (σύνεδροι, γερουσιασταί); Walbank, 1.334–5, 2.44–5; Hoyos (1994) 257. Officers in the advisory council: Pol. 3.71.5, 9.24.5; Livy 22.51.4; Walbank, 2.153.

6 Fabius Pictor in Pol. 3.8.2–4 (my translation). Diodorus' excerpts do not mention the episode though Diodorus' original may have. 'Feeling suspicious', ὑπιδόμενον (8.4; unnecessarily amplified by Paton's Loeb translation into 'suspicious of their intentions'; similarly Scott-Kilvert's Penguin). Episode disbelieved by, e.g., de Sanctis, 3.1.398; Huss (1985) 275 note 56; Seibert, *Hann.* 41–2.

7 Flaminius' bill in 232: Broughton, *MRR* 1.225; Barcid generals' position *vis-à-vis* Carthage: Ameling (1993) 101–7; Hoyos (1994) 246–59, cf. (1998) 150–1. 'Among the Carthaginians [etc.]': Pol. 6.51.6. On the supposed democratic revolution of 237: Hoyos (1994) 262–70, as against for example Picard (1968). Citizenship to foreigners: Ennius, *Annales* 234–5, ed. Skutsch, as emended by Skutsch, 414–16 (= 276–7 Warmington, with slight textual differences); Livy 21.45.6. Tribunal of One Hundred and Four: chapter II §III.

8 Fate of son of Gisco: chapter XIII note 16. In Aristotle's time lawsuits were judged by one or more of the Boards of Five (Pol. 2.11.7, 1273a); possibly these boards were given other jobs to do by Hasdrubal—or were abolished. By 193 the sufetes themselves heard cases (Livy 34.61.15; cf. chapter XV §v) and it is not known when this started. Groag thinks Hasdrubal sought to reform the tribunal of One Hundred and Four but failed ((1929) 27 note 3, 119), while Picard ((1968), cf. (1967) 75–7, 216–17) credits Hamilcar with it: above, chapter IV note 2.

9 Power and arrogance of the 'ordo iudicum' by 196: Livy 33.46.1. Fabius Pictor blamed Hannibal alone, as Hasdrubal's heir in wilfulness, for the Second Punic War: Pol. 3.8.5–8. Punic envoys to Scipio Africanus in 203 were already blaming him: Livy 30.16.5; cf. Hoyos (1998) 151. For contacts between third-century Fabii and at least one aristocratic Carthaginian house: Livy 27.16.5; Hoyos, 151. Hanno still survived in 203 according to Appian, actively anti-Barcid as ever (*Lib.* 34.145).

10 Diod. 25.12; Pol. 2.13.1 (cf. Walbank, 1.167). Καινὴ πόλις at e.g. 3.13.7, 15.3, 33.5, 56.3, 76.11; 10.7.5. Καρχηδών, sometimes defined as ἡ ἐν Ἰβηρίᾳ or the like, at e.g. 10.6.8, 8.6, 16.1; 11.31.1.

11 Thus Groag (1929) 29; much more colourfully Picard (1967) 86–7, 'l'audace [i.e. du nom] était presque sacrilège', 'Asdrubal . . . créait une troisième Tyr'; cf. Picard and Picard, *LDC* 219. More cautiously Schwarte (1983) 59; Lancel (1992) 398. Fabius' claim, note 6 above. Mastia: chapter IV note 13.

12 Hasdrubal's palace and alleged royal aspiration (φάσιν, 'they say'): Pol. 10.10.9. Neapolis (Nabeul): Gsell, *HAAN* 2.141; Huss (1985) 72, noting that the Punic name could have been Qart-hadasht. Neapolis-Macomades: Gsell, 2.126; Schwabe, *RE* 14 (1928) 161; Huss, 72 ('Mqmhds [i.e. *Maqom-hadashî*] = neuer Ort'). Another Macomades lay some 190 miles (300 kilometres) east of Lepcis Magna, with the alternative name of Pyrgos Euphranta (Gsell, 2.118–20; Schwabe, *ibid.*). Numidia had one between Cirta and Theveste, about 190 miles south-west of Carthage: Dessau, *RE* 16 (1935) 161, also registering a Macomadia Rusticiana of Roman date. Lepcis Magna another 'Neapolis': Pseudo-Scylax, *Periplus* (*ca.* 325 BC) 110 (cf. Müller (1855/1965) 1.87); Strabo 17.3.18, C835; Ptolemy, *Geogr.* 4.3.13; Gsell, 2.121; Windberg, *RE* 16 (1935) 2131. Ptolemy's 'Old Carthage' in north-east Spain (2.6.63) as probably Strabo's little-known Cartalia (3.4.6, C159): Müller (1883) 187; Schulten, *FHA* 6.233; Jacob (1985) 265 tentatively identifies Ptolemy's entry with Onusa/Oinoussa and as today's Peñíscola just south of the Ebro estuary. Citium in Cyprus originally a Qart-hadasht: *Kl P* 3.223–4. Aristotle on Carthaginian colonies: chapter II note 10. Carthage's 'Neapolis' district: Diod. 20.44.1 and 5; Lancel (1992) 160–1. Cf. too a suggested Phoenician origin for Neapolis in Sardinia: S. Moscati, *Fenici e Cartaginesi in Sardegna* (Milan 1968) 61–2 (against this, E. Lipinski in Devijver and Lipinski (1985) 69).

13 Link: Huss (1985) 276. Romans impressed: Pol. 2.13.3–4.

14 Polybius describes New Carthage at 10.9.8–11.4; cf. Walbank, 2.205–12; Scullard (1970) 48–55. Silver mines: Pol. 34.9.8. Appian somehow acquired the notion that Hannibal was the founder, and did so on the site of Saguntum (*Iber.* 12.47).

15 Diod. 25.12; St. Byz., s.v. Ἀκκαβικὸν τεῖχος (p. 60 Meineke); Jacob (1985) 253, 356, pointing to another city that Stephanus reports near the straits, with the interesting name of Τρίτη ('Third': St. Byz., 638), which Jacob thinks may really be another name for Accabicon and would mark it as a Punic foundation after Acra Leuce and New Carthage. Interestingly if enigmatically, Stephanus registers 'Caccabe', Κακκάβη, as one of various alternative names for Carthage in North Africa (s.v. Καρχηδών; Huss (1985) 38 note 5). Conceivably Accabicon Teichos, embodying Semitic *akaba* 'landing place' according to Jacob (253), might be a similarly alternative name, from some source, for New Carthage. Positioning it 'by the Pillars of Hercules' would then count as a very rough approximation.

16 Tiar: *Itin. Ant.* 401. The Teari or Tiari Iulienses of Pliny (*NH* 3.23) and Ptolemy's Tiar Iulia (2.6.63) must have been a different community further north (Schulten, *RE* 4A (1934) 99–100 s.v. 'Tear [2]'; 6A (1936) 761 s.v. 'Tiar [2]')—unless both writers have made a mistake about the site, which is possible: cf. B. D. Hoyos, *Historia* 28 (1979) 449–53, on Baetican mislocations by both. As for the name Tiar, besides the name-form Tharros in Punic Sardinia compare also the well-known Mactar in Punic North Africa. Schulten also (761) views the name Tiar as non-Iberian, though he links it to places in the Aegean.

17 Pol. 2.13.3–4; Walbank, 1.168. Polybius on the Barcid revenge-war plan (first at 2.36.4): chapter V notes 8–9. Date of the accord with Hasdrubal: Hoyos (1998) 156–8.

18 The Romans 'smoothing down and conciliating' Hasdrubal: Pol. 2.13.5–7. Roman dispositions in 225: 2.23.6, 24.1, 27.1; Walbank, 1.196–203; Seibert, *Hann*. 48–9; Bender (1997) 96–8; Hoyos (1998) 156–7. Romans saw their chances on a knife-edge: cf. Pol. 2.22.7–8 on how 'they were falling into constant terrors and alarms' and making furious preparations, well before the Gauls had even stirred from their own land; cf. 2.15.5, and Diod. 25.11.2 with Walton's note. Against the notion that the accord with Hasdrubal was influenced or even prompted by Massilia (still in Lancel, *Hann*. 74–5; Rich (1996) 20–1; Bender, 95–6) see Barceló (1996) 47–9; Hoyos, 170–1.

19 No Roman approach to authorities at Carthage: this emerges from Pol. 3.21.1–2; cf. Walbank, 1.169–70; Hoyos (1998) 154–5. 'Carthaginians not to cross': Polybius' wording (2.13.7 and elsewhere); Hoyos, 154. Bender (1997) 96–7, very oddly sees the accord, which was all about military movements by land, as intended to check a supposed (unattested) growth in Punic sea-power. Barceló (1996) 53–4, no less oddly, assumes it banned Roman trade south of the limit (which for him is the river Segura).

20 Hasdrubal's northern frontier: Appian, *Iber*. 6.24; Sumner (1967) 215–17; Hoyos (1998) 172. Silius Italicus too, for what he is worth, seems to view the Tagus valley as under Hasdrubal's sway (1.151–5). Hasdrubal the diplomat: Pol. 2.36.2; Diod. 25.11; Livy 21.2.5 and 7; Appian, *Iber*. 6.23. Silius unsurprisingly prefers him to rule 'furiis iniquis', be 'asper amore sanguinis' and enjoy being feared by all, a typical Hellenistic tyrant in fact (1.144–54). Armies wintering in Lusitania in 210–209: Pol. 10.7.5 with Walbank, 2.202; cf. Livy 22.20.12, 21.5 (army retiring to coastal Lusitania in 217). Gold in Lusitanian rivers: Strabo 3.3.4, C153; Mela, 3.8; Pliny, *NH* 4.115, 33.66; Silius 1.155; Schulten (1952) 203.

21 On the communities of the central plateau cf. Alföldy (1987). Mons Idubeda/Cordillera Ibérica (or Sistema Ibérico): Strabo 3.4.10, C161; Schulten (1952) 242–3. Carpetani: Pol. 3.14.2–3, 10.7.5; Livy 21.23.4–6. Spanish troops in 218: Pol. 3.33.9, cf. Walbank, 1.362–4; on the Ilergetes, Hoyos (1998) 183. Olcades: below, chapter VII note 4. Off-and-on Celtiberian support for the Romans, Lazenby (1978) 127, 130; hostility, 126, 130, 144, 152–4, 209–11. Celtiberian troops served professionally: Pol. 14.7.5; Livy 24.49.7, 30.7.10; Lazenby, 144. Emporitan coinage: Guadán (1969) 157–8. Indibilis and Mandonius: Lazenby, 126, 130, 139–54.

22 Saguntine messages: Pol. 3.15.1–2, implying messages over quite some time; Hoyos (1998) 182–5, 190–2. Before 220 Punic–Saguntine relations peaceful, Punic hegemony not at Ebro: 3.14.9–10. Saguntum's neighbours: Hoyos, 187–91; see Appendix §7. Seibert, *Hann*. 50, supposes that Hasdrubal did conquer the coastlands up to the Ebro (Saguntum apart) because Hannibal in 221–220 campaigned inland. But the inference does not follow and Polybius records the obedience of the territories up to the Ebro only from late 220 (3.13.9).

23 Territory: Punic North Africa (both the Carthaginians' own territory and that of their Libyan subjects) on Picard's estimate covered some 20,000–40,000 square miles, about 52,000–104,000 square kilometres: (1961) 60–1; cf. also chapter II note 10. Hannibal's mining works and Baebelo mine: Pliny, *NH* 33.96–7; below, Appendix §3. Where Baebelo lay is unknown: the Sierra Morena (Schulten, *FHA* 3. 45; Blázquez and García (1991) 34) and the New Carthage area (Scullard (1989b) 8.41) are guesses; so too Acci, modern Guadix east of Granada (based on a possible emendation—*Accitani* in place of *Aquitani* or *aquatini*—in Pliny's text), but the Guadix area is not known for silver.

24 Diod. 25.12; Livy 21.3.2–4.1 (Hanno's sexual and monarchic allegations), cf.

Nepos, *Hamil.* 3.2; Nepos, *Hann.* 3.1 (cavalry command). Barceló (1998) 26 still believes that Hannibal may have returned to Carthage during the mid-220s, but this contradicts Polybius (15.19.3)—and Livy (30.38.9). Livy, in stating that Hannibal when summoned to Spain served three years before succeeding Hasdrubal (21.4.10), allows the surmise that he was appointed cavalry commander in 224.

25 Livy 21.4.3–8 (Hannibal's prowess), adapted by Silius 1.239–67; Appian, *Lib.* 6.23 (Loeb tr.); Pol. 9.25.5 (Hannibal and friend Mago). Silius on Hasdrubal: note 20 above. Hasdrubal's murder: Pol. 2.36.1; Diod. 25.12; Livy 21.2.6; Val. Max. 3.3 ext. 7; Silius 1.165–8 (placing it in the palace); Appian, *Iber.* 8.28, *Hann.* 2.8; Justin 44.5.5. Polybius gives the murderer's motive simply as 'personal wrongs': compatible enough (despite Walbank, 1.214) with the more circumstantial details in Livy *et al.* General for eight years: Diodorus gives him nine but Polybius and Livy (21.2.3) eight, Livy with a qualification ('octo ferme annos', *nearly* eight) that suggests he follows here a source more precise than Polybius; cf. Sumner (1967) 213 note 27; Hoyos (1998) 139. Seibert, *Hann.* 51–2, sets the murder in summer, followed by Barceló (1998) 34. Hasdrubal's age: note 1 above.

VII HANNIBAL IN SPAIN

1 Hannibal's election: Pol. 3.13.3–4; Nepos, *Hann.* 3.1; Livy 21.3.1; Silius 1.182–89; Appian, *Iber.* 8.29, *Hann.* 3.8; Hoyos (1994) 249–50. Barceló's notion that Hasdrubal's death left a power-vacuum at Carthage ((1996) 54, (1998) 30, 33) contradicts all evidence. Appian and Dio also have Hannibal elected supreme general in 203 (*Lib.* 31.129; Zon. 9.13.10), probably a misunderstanding or invention like much else in their narratives. Character portrait: Livy 21.4.1–8 (virtues) and 4.9 (vices); Pol. 9.25 (greed). Livy had probably not read that part of Polybius' history when he composed his Book 21. Visit to Gades, Livy 21.21.9; made much of by Silius 3.4–61.

2 Imilce: Livy 24.41.7 (home town); Silius 1.62–7, 97–107 (claiming for her a noble ancestry, 'clarum genus'), 4.775, 806. Hanno the nephew: chapter II note 2. Mago the kinsman, captured by the enemy in Sardinia in 215 (Livy 23.41.1–2; chapter IV note 5), was not commander of the defeated Punic army though he was probably a senior officer in it. Maharbal's father: chapter IV note 5. Mago the Samnite: Pol. 9.25.1–6 and chapter IV note 5. Hannibal Monomachus: only known from 9.24.5–8 where Polybius stresses his cruelty to enemies (unless he is also the Hannibal at 7.2.3–6; cf. below, chapter X note 6). Gisco: Plutarch, *Fabius* 15 (ἰσοτίμου).

3 On the ports of Carthage see chapter II note 5, and Appendix §2. Seibert's dating to the interwar years (*FzH* 111–13) is unpersuasive given that Punic naval forces in 218 were so skimpy (chapter VIII §II). Orders to Hasdrubal in 215: Livy 23.27.9–10. Syracusan envoys: Pol. 7.2.1–4; Livy 24.6.7.

4 Olcades campaign: Pol. 3.13.5–7; Livy 21.5.3–4; Hoyos (2002). Sumner (1967) 216 suggests the area around Altea (Polybius names their stronghold Althia) and Alcoy: but Alcoy's name is Arabic, it lies inland across mountains (which would have divided the tribe even more vulnerably), and it is a far stronger site than seaside Altea. Olcades fugitives: Pol. 3.14.3. Alce: Livy 40.48.1, 49.2; *Itin. Ant.* 445 'Alces'; probably Villacañas in Ciudad Real province (Miller (1916/1964) 173). The Carpetani stretched northwards from Toletum: Alföldy (1987) 60.

5 Hannibal dominant up to Ebro by 220: Pol. 3.14.10. Ironworking in the Cordillera Ibérica: Fernández Castro (1995) 362–3.

6 The Vaccaei and their resources: Domínguez-Monedero (1986) 244–55.

7 Pol. 3.14.1; Livy 21.5.5–6 (booty, 5.8). Hannibal tricked: Plutarch, *De Mulierum Virtutibus* 10 (= *Moralia* 248e), and Polyaenus, *Strat.* 7.48, both plainly from the same source but with some variations; Walbank (1.317), Scullard ([1989a] 32), and Seibert (*Hann.* 53–4) treat the story more indulgently.

8 Pallantia (mod. Palencia) and Intercatia versus Romans: e.g. Appian, *Iber.* 53.222, 55.231–2, 82.354–7; *Historia de España* (1982) 91–2, 107–8, 302. Carpetani and 'neighbouring peoples' defeated, Pol. 3.14.3–8; Walbank, 1.318; H. M. Hine, *Latomus* 38 (1979) 891–901; Scullard (1989a) 32–3. Timoleon's victory (341): Diod. 16.79–80; Plutarch, *Timol.* 25–8; N. G. L. Hammond, *A History of Greece to 322 BC* (Oxford 1959) 578.

9 'None of the peoples', Pol. 3.14.9 (Loeb tr., modified). That Hannibal imposed effective rule over north-central Spain is sometimes supposed (e.g. Scullard (1989a) 33) but Polybius' careful phrasing does not amount to this. Saguntine neighbours: Pol. 3.15.8; Livy 21.6.1, 12.5; Appian, *Iber.* 10.36; Hoyos (1998) 187–91; Appendix §7. Romans kept informed: Pol. 3.15.1; Livy 21.6.2–3. Envoys: Pol. 3.15.2–5; cf. Livy 21.6.3–8, 9.3–11.2 (distorted version).

10 This siege-embassy is already in Cicero, *Philippics* 5.10.27; on the later embellishments and their implausibility, Hoyos (1998) 202–4.

11 Party strife and Roman arbitration at Saguntum: Hoyos (1998) 184–95. 'What most Saguntines wanted': that is, to judge by the extraordinary tenacity of the town throughout its lonely eight-month siege in 219. There is no basis to the fancy that it was Greek and Italian merchants living there who instigated Saguntum's links with Rome (Barceló (1996) 54).

12 Hannibal seemingly saw Saguntines as Roman allies: Pol. 3.15.8. Had avoided confronting them: 3.14.10. 'Solemnly called on' (3.15.5 διεμαρτύροντο): cf. on this meaning Walbank, 1.321; Sumner (1972) 477; Hoyos (1998) 204–5, who notes 'emphatically warned' as another translation. The Loeb translation, 'protested against [his attacking Saguntum]' is wrong, and still worse the Penguin rendition of 'trust' or 'good faith' (πίστις) as 'sphere of influence'.

13 On the Romans' attitude to defeated foes, cf. Hoyos (1998) 201–2.

14 Roman envoys' manners: a youthful Roman ambassador to the queen of the Illyrians in 230 had been so outspoken that he was assassinated (Pol. 2.8.9–12). Supposed Barcid war-plan, chapter V note 8; Romans knew it at least from 221, Pol. 2.36.4; interview confirmed it, 3.15.12, 16.1. Polybius judges revenge-war as justified: 3.10.4, 15.9–11, 28.1–3, 30.3–4; Hoyos (1998) 165–6. Hannibal's anger, Pol. 3.15.9 ('overall he was full of unreason (πλήρης ἀλογίας) and violent anger'), cf. Eckstein (1989); on his claim to Punic *fides* (15.7 'it was an ancestral principle of the Carthaginians (πάτριον γὰρ εἶναι Καρχηδονίοις)' etc.) see Hoyos, 206.

  The idea that Polybius, or some earlier writer, invented the anger (e.g. Walbank, 1.322–3; Mantel (1991) 73) is unconvincing: if this was invented, why not invent a more 'apposite' set of complaints at the same time? Instead, Polybius has to upbraid Hannibal for not making apposite ones and then supply them himself. The interview was no doubt reported by Hannibal's own author-companions Silenus and Sosylus, maybe too by Fabius Pictor who could have used the envoys' later report or their reminiscences.

15 Envoys go to Carthage, 'seeing clearly that there must be war': Pol. 3.15.12. Non-committal Punic answer: in Livy's version, which falsely makes them go on their mission in 219 while Saguntum is under siege, they do at least get such an answer (21.9.3–10.1, 11.2). Hannibal asked for instructions: Pol. 3.15.8; cf. Appian, *Iber.* 10.37, claiming numerous secret messages and padding out the story with envoys from the 'Torboletae'; although some accept Appian's extras (e.g. Walbank, 1.323;

Schwarte (1983) 64–5; Scardigli (1991) 277; Seibert, *Hann.* 58–60), these are implausible (Hoyos (1998) 210).

16 Hannibal given a free hand: Appian (*Iber.* 10.37) specifies this, but it was so obvious that Polybius could leave it out. If the Roman envoys were still at Carthage and thus could take home this news before year's end, it makes the Romans' inactivity over Saguntum in 219 still more marked. Against suggestions (e.g. by Groag (1929) 66; Caven (1980) 92–3) that the Punic authorities tried to limit him in one way or another, see Hoyos (1998) 220. Pretended arbitration, Appian 10.38.

VIII THE INVASION OF ITALY

1 Eight months' siege: Pol. 3.17.9; Livy 21.15.3; Zon. 8.21.10. The envoys to Carthage in 218 almost certainly included the consuls of the previous year, who laid down office on 15 March by the Roman calendar (Hoyos (1998) 234–5, citing earlier discussions). But how closely the Roman calendar in this era matched the solar year is much debated. On the problems with chronology: Walbank, 1.327–8; Sumner (1966); A. Astin, *Latomus* 26 (1967) 581–2; Rich (1976) 28–40; Eckstein (1983); Huss (1985) 282; F. Walbank, *Selected Papers: Studies in Greek and Roman History and Historiography* (Cambridge 1985) 299–304; Seibert, *FzH* 137–41; Rich (1996) 29; Hoyos, 221, 234–6.

2 Alexander's seven-month siege of Tyre in 332: A. B. Bosworth, *Conquest and Empire: The Reign of Alexander the Great* (Cambridge 1988) 65–7. Site of Saguntum: Schulten (1935) 31, 35–6; Walbank, 1.329–30; K. Abel, *Kl P* 4.1500–1. 'Hardships and anxiety': Pol. 3.17.9. Hannibal wounded: Livy 21.7.10; Zon. 8.21.10. Oretani, Carpetani, Maharbal: Livy 21.11.13–12.2 (on this officer cf. chapter IV note 5).

3 Second Illyrian War distracted the Senate, Pol. 3.16.4–5. His account of the war (3.16, 18–19) virtually ignores the rôle of one of the consuls, Livius. Cf. Walbank, 1.324, 327; Rich (1976) 41–3; Hoyos (1998) 222, 225–6. Debate in 219 over Saguntum: Livy 21.6.4–8, 7.1; Silius 1.609–94, with poetic flexibility stretching his into 218; Appian, *Iber.* 11.43, as usual adding various embellishments. Most scholars read this evidence as supporting Dio's claim (frgs 55.1–10, 57.12; Zon. 8.22.1–3) that there was debate only in 218 after Saguntum had fallen (and after Hannibal had begun his march). But see Groag (1929) 70–3; E. S. Staveley in *CAH²* 7.2.451, 453; Hoyos, 226–32. On the leaders in debate see Hoyos, 228–30.

4 Fabius Pictor in Pol. 3.8.1–8. Appian has the anti-interventionists resorting to absurdity—the Saguntines, though under siege, were still free as (supposedly) guaranteed in Hasdrubal's accord, therefore did not need help (*Iber.* 11.43). This looks like Appian's own notion of rhetorical effectiveness.

5 Booty from Saguntum: Pol. 3.17.10, cf. 17.7; Livy 21.15.1–2 (who contributes that the money was raised from selling plunder; this must be from another source). Its political use, Hoyos (1994) 271. Diodorus' denial of booty (25.15) is not to be trusted.

6 Appointment of Hasdrubal, troop transfers, ships: Pol. 3.33.5–18 (on the corps of 'Thersitae' see Appendix §7), followed by Livy 21.21.9–22.4. Polybius transmits the details given by Hannibal in an inscription at Cape Lacinium in southern Italy. Thirty-seven elephants: Pol. 3.42.11 and Appian, *Hann.* 4.13. Roman warships in 218: Pol. 3.41.2; Livy 21.17.3. If Hannibal appointed his brother trierarch, as Hamilcar had his son-in-law (chapter IV note 5), it is not mentioned, though Hasdrubal when commander in Spain did lead a fleet in 217, ingloriously. Huss (1985) 297–8 follows Groag (1929) 104 note 1, in simply guessing that the

Carthaginians had already elected Hasdrubal general for Libya, i.e. North Africa, but nothing supports this.

7 Hannibal's agents, and his knowledge of north Italy: Pol. 3.34.1–6, 48.10–12; cf. Hoyos (1998) 248 note 25. Hannibal changed plans: W. Hoffmann, *RhM* 94 (1951) 79–82; (1962) 44–6; Bender (1997) 104–5; against this view cf. Walbank, 1.365. Troops in winter quarters and after: Pol. 3.33.5, 34.6 and 9; so too Livy 21.21.2–8.

8 Informants about Italy: de Sanctis, 3.1.407, supposes—presumably by analogy with Greek political exiles—that 'Italian refugees' must have betaken themselves to Hannibal's camp; but no refugees are attested. Guest-friends: Q. Fabius the Delayer enjoyed *hospitium* with the family of one aristocrat, Carthalo, later commandant at Tarentum (Livy 27.16.5); other aristocrats' connexions are attested in 195 (33.45.6) and many must have been of long standing, for peace had returned only six years before; cf. Ameling (1993) 264. On Hannibal's likely calculations, cf. de Sanctis, 3.1.406–8, 3.2.9–12; Groag (1929) 79–96; Picard (1967) 128, 134–7; Picard and Picard, *LDC* (1968) 238–41; Hoffmann (1961/1974) 56–7; Lazenby (1978) 29–32; Nicolet (1978) 2.614–20; Caven (1980) 93–5, 98–9; Hampl (1983–4) 28–9; Huss (1985) 294, who unnecessarily supposes that the invasion-plan could not have occurred to anyone less than a genius; Briscoe (1989) 46; Seibert, *Hann.* 63–9, 541–3, cf. *FzH* 152–62. Hannibal expected reinforcements: thus Hasdrubal in 215 was told to go (Livy 23.27.9), though he was prevented, and a force from Africa did make it then (23.13.7, 41.10).

9 On Hannibal's march-chronology cf. below, note 23. Hanno the commandant in north-east Spain: Pol. 3.35.4; Livy 21.23.3. Zonaras calls him Banno which Huss (1985) 299 note 42 thinks correct (cf. Seibert, *Hann.* 96 note 119), but this is probably a copyist's slip: the name Hanno is repeated at Pol. 3.76.5 (Livy, 21.23.3 and 60.5, follows Polybius). Sound remarks on the strategic insignificance of Spain-beyond-Ebro by de Sanctis (3.2.9–10), though Lazenby argues for its supposed importance to Hannibal's communications ((1978) 33), and Huss implausibly sees its conquest as necessary to a successful crossing of the Pyrenees (298–9). Emporiae as Roman bridgehead: Pol. 3.76.1; Livy 21.60.2.

10 Spanish rivers, Hallward (1930) 36; Warmington (1964) 212; Lazenby (1978) 33; Scullard (1980) 204. Food availability, Lazenby, *ibid.* Regrouping the army before the Pyrenees: Proctor (1971) 45. Lulling the Romans: de Sanctis, 3.2.8–10; Scullard, *ibid.* Consular year began on 1 March (previously in May) probably from 222: de Sanctis, 3.1.107; Broughton, *MRR* 2.638–9; Rich (1976) 19. Sempronius set out before Scipio, probably in June/July: Hoyos (1998) 258–9, citing earlier studies.

11 Eight hundred *stadia* in ten days: Pol. 3.50.1; treated as Hannibal's more-or-less average marching rate by Lazenby (1978) 35, 275; as below average by Proctor (1971) 26–7, 29. Roman imperial armies averaged 23.7 kilometres (16 Roman miles) a day, Proctor, 31–2; though A. K. Goldsworthy, *The Roman Army at War* (Oxford 1996) 109–10, stresses such rates were under optimum conditions only.

12 Caven (1980) 98–101, suggests this less likely scenario; believed by Santosuosso (1997) 170. Punic spy: Livy 22.33.1; Dio in Zon. 9.1.1. Hoffmann (1957/1974) 55–6, (1962) 48, stresses the danger to Carthage if the Romans invaded North Africa.

13 Cavalry skirmish: Pol. 3.45.1–3; Livy 21.29.1–4. Hannibal's decision: Livy 21.29.5–6; disbelieved by Lazenby (1978) 37; in fact most or all scholars suppose he was anxious to avoid battle with Scipio entirely. His expectation of Scipio returning, cf. Pol. 3.61.1–4 (claiming his later surprise at the consul's swiftness). On arbitrary grounds Walbank, 1.395–6, disbelieves this report.

14 On dating the artificial ports see chapter II note 5 and VII §1.

15 Cape Lacinium numbers: note 6 above. 102,000 troops: Pol. 3.35.1; Livy 21.23.1; Appian, *Hann.* 4.13. Hannibal suffered 'great loss', gave Hanno 10,000 foot and 1,000 horse, and sent home 'the same number' (3.35.3–6; malcontent Carpetani and others, according to Livy 21.23.4–6). We should not assume these latter included many horsemen. For more details about the grand army see Appendix §8.

16 Syrian and Egyptian forces in 217 (68,000 versus perhaps 55,000 (Polybius claims 75,000)): Pol. 5.65.1–10, 79.2–13; Walbank, 1.589–92, 607; P. Green, *Alexander to Actium: The Historical Evolution of the Hellenistic Age* (Berkeley and London 1990) 289–90. Roman land forces in 218 totalled 27,000 citizens and some 44,000 allies, according to Brunt's careful calculations ((1971) 417–19, 678).

17 Consuls of 219 as envoys: Seibert, *Hann.* 83; Hoyos (1998) 234–5; cf. Goldsworthy (2000) 145 (sending them to Carthage in 219 *as* consuls!); disbelieved by Vollmer (1990) 137–8. It is not clear whether the Roman calendar was in accord with the true solar year (Seibert, *FzH* 346–52; Hoyos, 235), but any discrepancy looks likely to have placed it ahead—so *Idus Mart.* 218 might actually have been early March or late February. Envoys demand handover, Pol. 3.20.6–8 (see chapter V note 5); war let fall, 33.2–4. Visit to Melqart's temple: Livy 21.21.9; Huss (1985) 235, speculates about what Hannibal did there.

18 Monomachus: Pol. 9.24.5–8 (cf. Livy 23.5.12–13, Roman propaganda); cf. Walbank, 2. 153; Seibert, *Hann.* 111 note 180. The dream: Cicero, *De Divinatione* 1.49, citing Silenus via Coelius Antipater; Livy 21.22.5–9 (does not mention Hannibal being summoned before the gods); Dio, in Zon. 8.22.9; Val. Max. 1.7. ext. 1 and Silius 3.163–216 rephrase Livy. Cicero dates the dream simply 'after the sack of Saguntum', but (*contra* Seibert, *FzH* 184) this hardly contradicts Livy's dating it to the march. Dio both gives a version closer to Silenus' than Livy's—adding other fabulous details perhaps again from Silenus' propaganda (cf. Polybius' strictures, 3.47.8, 48.7–9)—and also implies the dream occurred during the march. Barceló (1998) 47 impossibly imagines that in Livy the dream foretells Hannibal's ruin and Carthage's defeat.

19 Aerenosii, etc.: Pol. 3.35.2; Livy 21.23.2. Indibilis 'always' pro-Punic: Pol. 3.76.6–7; Hoyos (1998) 183. His close links to the Lacetani and others: Livy 25.34.6; 28.24.4 and 26.7; Walbank, 1.410. Ilergetes of the interior: Strabo 3.4.10, C161; Walbank, 1.366. Note the Ilergetan cavalry squadron already in Hannibal's army: Pol. 3.33.15; Livy 21.22.3. Ausetani and Lacetani as Punic allies, 21.61.8—though this episode probably followed Cn. Scipio's victory at Cissis, 60.1–9. Coastal Ilergetes: Pliny, *NH* 3.21; Jacob (1985) 252, noting the 'Ilaraugatae' of Hecataeus, frg. 14; Hoyos (2001b) 69–70. Just possibly the Bargusii were around the later Barcino (Barcelona) for, with the pro-Punic Lacetani and Ausetani hemming them in, friendliness towards the Romans would be natural; though Schulten (*FHA* 3.47) prefers them well inland, on the northerly reaches of the Llobregat around the town of Berga. Troops sent home: note 15 above.

20 Hannibal won over the Gauls, Livy 21.24; earlier conciliation, 21.20.8; some forced to give passage, Pol. 3.41.7. According to Polybius he had been 'very fearful' of possible resistance to the army crossing the Pyrenees (40.1), which is odd as Polybius fails to mention any such fear when actually narrating the crossing (35.7).

21 Army size at Rhône, Pol. 3.60.5. Garrisons in southern Gaul: Picard (1967) 163–7; Seibert (1989), *FzH* 182–3, 193, 212, *Hann.* 98; contrast Goldsworthy (2000) 167. Seibert supposes that reinforcements later used this route from Spain to Hannibal until 207, though he concedes that the one force recorded (Bomilcar's in 215) went from North Africa.

22 Napoleon's losses in the first months of his Russian invasion: Chandler (1965/1993) 754–5, 781–2; C. Duffy, *Borodino* (London 1972) 51, 62, 161. The destruction of the army in the retreat from Moscow actually involved the loss of fewer troops.

23 A lucid chronology of the entire march in Lazenby (1978), Appendix iii; earlier analysis in de Sanctis, 3.2.77–81 (who dates the march from April to September rather than May/June to October/November). The one clear indicator of time is that the army reached the summit of the pass close to the astronomical setting of the Pleiades (Pol. 3.54.1; Livy 21.35.6), meaning early November. Though often treated as a loose or approximate datum (e.g. by de Sanctis and by Walbank, 1.365–6, 390) it is convincingly defended by Proctor (1971) 13–15, 40–5, 75–82; Lazenby (1978) 29, 32–3; and Seibert, *FzH* 176–8. In turn its final stages, from the Rhône on, can be worked out almost day by day from Polybius' account, as Lazenby shows. Losses inflicted by Allobroges *et al.*: Pol. 3.51.7, 53.1–3; cf. 51.3–5 (animals lost). Losses on the descent, 3.54.4, 56.2; army's spirits damaged, 3.54.1–2 and 7.60.3–4. Plains of Italy: 3.54.2–3; Livy 21.35.7–9. On Hannibal's impossible-to-identify route cf. Appendix §9.

24 Army strength after reaching Italy, Pol. 3.56.4 ('fewer than twenty thousand' (2.24.17) is a careless misstatement or maybe a copyist's mistake (δισμυρίων written for τρισμυρίων)). The mention of the Insubres' territory (56.3) is generally seen as just a loose Polybian reference (Walbank, 1.392; Huss (1985) 306 note 82), but this is not obvious. Nor, *contra* Seibert (*Hann.* 106 note 163; cf. previous note), need it reflect a source different from Livy's, who has Hannibal arrive among the Taurini (21.38.5). Dio does report desertions during the Alpine crossing (Zon. 8.23.6), though he may draw this either from a source or from personal inference. Balearic slingers: those involved in his troop-movements between Spain and Africa constituted about 1,400 in a total of 31,000 (Pol. 3.33.12–16); even if he himself took another 1,000 with him, their numbers too must have thinned. On some other reckonings see Appendix §9.

25 Pol. 3.60.8–13. Bender (1997) 98–105, disbelieving in any advance soundings by Hannibal, thinks that the Gauls had rebelled because the Romans founded the colonies Placentia and Cremona in their midst, and came over to him only once he showed his military strength by smashing the Taurini. But thus to dismiss Polybius' and Livy's reports of the earlier soundings is unconvincing. It was common sense for the Gauls to put off giving the invader any help until he reached their territories—which he did after the Ticinus skirmish (3.66.7, cf. 67.6), *before* his big victory at the Trebia.

26 On the near-disaster of the march, Hoyos ((1983) 171–3; Shean (1996) 175–80; Bender (1997) 98–9), improving on Hoffmann (cf. note 7 above), judges the whole expedition as 'the foolhardiest improvisation'. By contrast Barreca (1983–4) 45–6, thinks that Hannibal had allowed for heavy losses. Gallic migration into north Italy: Pol. 2.17; Livy 5.34–5; Salmon (1982) 34–7; T. J. Cornell, *OCD³* 625. Gaesati: Pol. 2.22.1–6, 23.1; Walbank, 1.194–5. Losses on the descent 'nearly as heavy' as in the Alpine fighting, Pol. 3.54.4; quality of army at Pyrenees, 39.8.

27 Seibert argues that P. Scipio sent on only about half his army with his brother (*Hann.* 104–5; earlier too Errington (1971) 65; *contra* Pol. 3.56.6 and Livy 21.32.3–5) because Cn. Scipio in 217 had only some 35 of the consul's original 60 warships; but for a different explanation see Lazenby (1978) 127; on Cn. Scipio's forces, Brunt (1971) 646–7. In any case warships, unless very numerous, did not convey whole armies themselves but escorted transports: cf. Walbank, 1.377, 431. Romans worried about Punic reinforcements from Spain, Pol. 3.97.3.

Importance of Africa: Hoyos (1983) 178; cf. Seibert, *Hann.* 488. P. Scipio's decision is almost universally judged as sound—even as pivotal to ultimate Roman
victory: e.g. Kahrstedt (1913) 384, 'darum hat es [Rom] den Krieg gewonnen'; de
Sanctis, 3.2.436; Hallward (1930) 57; Errington (1971) 80; Scullard (1970) 29;
Lazenby, 52; Hampl (1983–4) 26; Seibert, *Hann.* 490, 'die Karthager verloren den
Krieg nicht in Italien . . . sondern in Iberien'; Lancel, *Hann.* 119–20; Santosuosso
(1997) 182.

28 Naval raids on North Africa: below, chapter XII §I. Hasdrubal's planned march
to Italy in 215 and defeat at Ibera, Livy 23.27.9–29.17; chapter XI §III.

IX THREE GREAT VICTORIES

1 Battle of the Trebia: Pol. 3.71–4; Livy 21.54.1–56.8; Appian, *Hann.* 7.24–9; Zon.
8.24.4–5; Walbank, 1.404–8; Lazenby (1978) 56–8; Seibert, *FzH* 213–15, and
Hann. 126–9. Freedom propaganda, Pol. 3.77.3–7; doubted by Erskine (1993) on
the ground that it was a Greek concept and possibly a Polybian invention, but the
content of Hannibal's known treaties with Italian states (chapter X §I) shows
what was meant. Brundisine garrison-commander: Pol. 3.69.1–4; Livy
21.48.9–10, naming him Dasius. Groag's idea ((1929) 79) that Hannibal meant to
base himself in the Po region, while rousing revolt among Rome's Italian allies,
does not convince. Gauls and Hannibal in winter 218–217: Pol. 3.78.1–6; Livy
22.1.2–4; Zon. 8.24.8 (with even more fanciful disguise-details); Polybius' generalization (23.13.1) that Hannibal was never plotted against by his men cannot be
treated on its own as literal fact. Walbank, 1.410, and Seibert, *Hann.* 139–40,
think the disguise-tale worthless, unlike Rawlings (1996) 89. Hannibal's forces:
variously estimated by, e.g., Kahrstedt (1913) 406; de Sanctis, 3.2.114–15;
Lazenby, 65.
2 Livy reports a failed winter attempt to cross the Apennines (21.58), widely disbelieved as a mere embroidered doublet of the successful spring crossing (e.g. de
Sanctis, 3.2.97; Hallward (1930) 8.44 note 2; Lazenby (1978) 59–60; Briscoe
(1989) 49; Lancel, *Hann.* 149), but accepted by Seibert, *Hann.* 139. Other supposed operations during the same winter (21.57.5–59.9) do look very dubious: de
Sanctis, 3.2.96–9. The Arno marshes: Pol. 3.78.6–79.12; Livy 22.2.1–3.1; Zon.
8.25.3; Walbank, 1.413; Lazenby, 60–1. Hannibal blinded in one eye: Pol. 3.79.12;
Livy 22.2.11; Silius 4.751–5; Juvenal, *Satires* 10.158; Oros. 4.15.3. Eye badly damaged: Nepos, *Hann.* 4.3. Seibert, *Hann.* 148–50, is altogether sceptical about the
supposed rigours and suggests Punic propaganda magnified Hannibal's handicap
to link him with the one-eyed and glorious Philip II of Macedon; but the ailment
is never mentioned otherwise and its origin in the marshes is circumstantially
attested.
3 On the losses at Trasimene see Lazenby (1978) 65; Seibert, *Hann.* 153–4.
4 Punic fleet off Pisae: Pol. 3.96.8–10, cf. Livy 22.11.6–7; see Seibert, *Hann.* 156.
Less plausibly, Hoffmann (1961/1974) 339–40 supposes the fleet really meant to
harass Roman communications to Spain. Hannibal's first message by sea to
Carthage, Pol. 3.87.4–5; Africans rearmed, 87.3, 114.1; 'having become very confident', 86.8. Lancel, *Hann.* 158–9, and Shean (1996) 180–1, defend the decision
not to advance on Rome in 217; Walbank, 1.421, and Lazenby (1996) 41, hold
that he never meant to attack the city. Cf. note 8 below on Maharbal.
5 Punic army's battered state and ensuing recovery: Pol. 3.87.2–3, 88.1–2; Shean,
ibid. Plunder and slaughter, 3.86.8–11, 88.3–6. Huss (1985) 319 note 186 dis-
misses the killings (86.10–11) as merely anti-Punic propaganda; A. Toynbee,

Hannibal's Legacy, 2 vols. (Oxford 1965) 2.24 note 3 imagines that Hannibal perhaps suspended killing when he marched through allied territories (this would require accuracy about both boundaries and individuals' identities). Fabius' edict to farmers, Livy 22.11.4.

6 On the operations in the second half of 217 see (e.g.) Lazenby (1978) 66–73; Seibert, *Hann.* 164–77, 182–3. The three Campanian aristocrats, Livy 22.13.2–3. The famous episode of the cattle with blazing horns (Pol. 3.93.3–94.6; Livy 22.16–18; Plutarch, *Fabius* 6–7; Appian, *Hann.* 13.57–15.65; minor sources in Walbank, 1.429) is rejected by Seibert as a legend or distortion aimed against Fabius, and he infers a more straightforward ruse (*Hann.* 170–1). But this would have served the same supposed purpose, leaving unexplained why anyone should invent the more complicated one.

7 Hannibal's supply problems: Livy 22.32.3, 40.8–9, 43.2–4 (with rumours about the Spaniards). Cannae-depot taken, Pol. 3.107.1; in mid-year, Walbank 1.441. Erdkamp (1998) 163–5 argues that the army had gathered enough supplies during 217, but it is hard to see how they could have lasted until mid-216 or how the Gerunium district instead—with the Roman army at close range—could feed men and horses for months. Battle at the Ebro: Pol. 3.95–6; Livy 22.19–20; fought some time before Trasimene (despite Pol. 3.95.2 mentioning summer-time), cf. de Sanctis, 3.2.231–2, 664. Romans sought battle in 216: Pol. 3.107.7, 108.1–2 ('the decision of the Senate'). Joke to Gisco: Plutarch, *Fabius* 15. Cannae: Seibert, *FzH* 228–32 (lengthy bibliography on particular issues, 227–8), and *Hann.* 189–98 (detailed list of all ancient sources, 191). See also Kahrstedt (1913) 427–34; de Sanctis, 3.2.126–59; Walbank, 1.435–48; Brunt (1971) 419, 648, 671–2, estimating the Roman army at no more than 45,000, with 30,000 slain or otherwise lost; Lazenby (1978) 75–85; Connolly (1981) 183–8; Samuels (1990); Lancel, *Hann.* 169–77; Santosuosso (1997) 176–80; McKnight (1998); and cf. Sabin (1996).

8 Romans expected Hannibal to march on city: Pol. 3.118.6; Livy 22.55.1. Troops at Rome: Livy 22.57.7, 23.14.2; Fitton Brown (1959) 367 note 10; Brunt (1971) 648–9; Lazenby (1978) 90–1; Seibert, *FzH* 383–4, *Hann.* 207–8 with note 130; Lazenby (1996) 41. Maharbal's proposal: Cato, *Origines* frgs 86–7P; Coelius, frg. 25P (both from Gellius, 10.24.6–7); Livy 22.51.1–4 (Maharbal's epigram, not in Cato, was probably not in Coelius either); Val. Max. 9.5 ext. 3; minor sources in Hoyos (2000b). Livy makes Maharbal commander of the right wing, 46.7, whereas Hasdrubal and Hanno were the wing-commanders according to Polybius (3.114.7, 116.6–8): note, though, that Appian has Maharbal command a cavalry reserve (*Hann.* 20.91). The anecdote is disbelieved (e.g.) by Huss (1985) 332 note 281; Seibert, *Hann.* 198–9; Lazenby (1996) 39; but there are grounds for believing it in its basic form. Maharbal probably first gave his advice after Trasimene: Hoyos (2000b).

9 Hannibal expected Romans to offer terms, Livy 22.58.2–9. Lord Montgomery of Alamein, *A History of Warfare* (London 1968) 97, comments on his lack of siege equipment; Seibert, *Hann.* 201, on his aversion ('Abneigung') to sieges—but both nevertheless hold that he should have marched (Montgomery, *ibid.*; Seibert, 198–203, 224, 484; so too Huss (1985) 332–3 and Barceló (1998) 59–60). Goldsworthy is undecided, (2000) 215–16. That Hannibal was right not to march is strongly argued by, for instance, Mommsen, *HR* 2.141; de Sanctis, 3.2.202–3 (Maharbal offering 'consiglio, più che spavaldo, pazzo'); Hallward (1930) 55 (Hannibal's 'deep strategic insight'), cf. 61; Fitton Brown (1959); Hoffmann (1962) 73–4; Picard (1967) 180–1; Görlitz (1970) 99–100; Lazenby (1978) 85–8, (1996) *passim*; Caven (1980) 141; Lancel, *Hann.* 177–8, cf. 158–9; Shean (1996);

McKnight (1998) 13—not to mention by the general himself in G. Brizzi, *Annibale: Come un'Autobiografia* (Milan 1994) 173–4.

10 Masinissa's capture of Cirta in 203, Livy 30.12.5–10; on its site, *OCD*[3] 333. Destruction of L. Postumius Albinus' army in north Italy: Livy 23.24.6–13; Pol. 3.118.7; Frontinus, *Strat.* 1.6.4; Zon. 9.3.3; Broughton, *MRR* 1.253. On possible *legiones urbanae* in the city: Livy 23.14.2, accepted by Lazenby (1978) 85; not by Seibert, *Hann.* 186 note 16, 207 note 130.

11 Fictitious though Maharbal's comment about speed and surprise may be in Livy—'they will learn of my arrival before my approach' (22.51.2; not in Cato's or Coelius' quoted versions (note 8))—it makes the crucial point: cf. Hoyos (1983) 177. Fertility of Samnium in central Italy, Pol. 3.90.7; of Campania, 91.1–2; of the territory around Rome, 9.6.9–7.1. Marcellus and Pera: Lazenby (1978) 90–1, with references. Alarm at Rome in 211: Pol. 9.6.1–3 ('universal alarm and fear', though perhaps an exaggeration); similarly Livy 26.9.6; Appian, *Hann.* 39.165–6, 40.173. Possible speed of army to Rome: cf. chapter VIII note 11; also Lazenby, 85. Extent of Rome's walls reckoned at 11 kilometres (6.6 miles): Starr (1980) 16. Twenty-three slaves crucified in late 217 for plotting 'in the Campus Martius' (just outside the then walls), Livy 22.33.2. Betrayal of Tarentum in 213: Pol. 8.24–31; Livy 25.7.10–9.17; Lazenby, 110–12.

12 Mago at Carthage, Livy 22.11.7–12.5. Hannibal had to stay in the south or potential defectors would be discouraged: thus Caven (1980) 149; Lazenby (1996) 41–2. Booms etc. across the Tiber, Shean (1996) 167, who sees the real bar to a march on Rome as the massive amount of provisions the Punic army would need *en route* (elaborate calculations, Shean, 167–75). But if so, this limitation should have immobilized it more or less as soon as it left north Italy in spring 217. On the possibilities for besieging Rome: Seibert, *Hann.* 200. For swift movement even over unsuitable terrain, it is worth noting how in 1807 a *retreating* Spanish army covered over 300 miles/500 kilometres of trackless mountains during early winter (1 to 23 November) to reach the city of León, thus averaging 14 miles/22.4 kilometres a day—though it lost half its strength *en route* (Chandler (1965/1993) 636–7). Like an ancient army, this one had to move at foot's pace, while it also had to transport guns and ammunition.

13 Livy 22.51.4.

X HANNIBAL'S ITALIAN LEAGUE

1 Defections: Pol. 3.118.1–4; Livy 22.61.10–12 (both lists cover several years' worth, cf. Walbank, 1.448); Lazenby (1978) 89–90; Huss (1985) 335–6; Seibert, *Hann.* 203–4, 212–15. Mago sent south, Livy 23.1.4, 11.7. On the Samnite defections, E. T. Salmon, *Samnium and the Samnites* (Cambridge 1967) 298–9; on the Campanian, Frederiksen (1984) 238–41. On Hannibal's hopes in 217 for Capua's defection cf. chapter IX note 6. Links with Romans: Livy 23.2.6, 4.7 (Pacuvius Calavius' with Ap. Claudius Pulcher and M. Livius Salinator), 25.18.4–5 (Badii family's guest-friendship with Quinctii Crispini). Vibius Virrius, Livy 23.6.1–2; on the defection of Capua cf. Ungern-Sternberg (1975) chapter II.

2 Hannibal's treaty with Capua, Livy 23.7.1–2 ('more like pro-Carthaginian nonbelligerency than a genuine fighting alliance', Salmon (see note 1), 298); arrest of Decius Magius, 23.10.3–13 (Magius escaped to Alexandria). Atella, Calatia (and the obscure Sabatini): 26.33.12, 34.6, 34.11; Salmon, 298 note 4; Frederiksen (1984) 36, 242–3. Capua seen as 'an indispensable source of provisions and industrial wealth' for Hannibal: Frederiksen, 241. For what it is worth, note that artisans ('fabri') serving the Punic garrison at Locri were paid: Livy 29.6.4.

3 Defection of Locri, Livy 23.30.8, 24.1.2–13 (with pact, 24.1.13; cf. Schmitt, *SVA* 3.245; Kukofka (1990) 16 note 29). Treaty with Tarentum: Pol. 8.25.1–2; Livy 25.8.8; Schmitt, *SVA* no. 531. Samnites' complaints, Livy 23.42 (especially 42.11). Bruttians and Lucanians defeated, 24.14–16. Bruttians at Tarentum in 209, 27.15.9; Appian, *Hann*. 49.212.

4 Livy 24.2.8 ('[ut] senatus Romanis faveret, plebs ad Poenos rem traheret'); cf. 23.14.7, and Plutarch, *Marcellus* 10.1 (pro-Hannibal commons at Nola). Locri: Livy 23.30.8 (quoted), 24.1.5–8 (fuller details), 29.6.5. Arpi, 24.47.6–10; Etruria, e.g. 27.24.2–5 (Arretium), 29.36.10–12, 30.26.12 (investigation 'de coniurationibus principum'). See Harris (1971) 142–3; Ungern-Sternberg (1975) 63–76 (defecting to Hannibal 'fast durchweg von Angehörigen der führenden Schicht ins Werk gesetzt wurde', 69); Lazenby (1978) 88; Kukofka (1990) 154–7. Hannibal as democrat: Groag (1929) 112 note 1; Picard (1967) 135–6 (cf. (1968)); Brisson (1973) 154–5, 206 ('il favorisait de toutes ses forces tout ce qu'il y avait de démocratique dans l'Italie romaine'), 212–13, 233, 235; Huss (1985) 347; contrast Nicolet (1978) 2.612, 617–18 (Barcid democratic inclinations at home, but in Italy Hannibal did not push democracy).

5 Hannibal and Tarentum in 214, Livy 24.13.1–5; its defection, Pol. 8.24–31; Livy 25.7.10–10.10. Date: Walbank 2.5; Lazenby (1978) 110. Metapontum and Thurii, 25.15.5–17; Heraclea, Appian, *Hann*. 35.149.

6 The 'clouds gathering in the west', Pol. 5.104.10 (Agelaus of Naupactus), cf. Gruen (1984) 1.322–5; Seibert, *FzH* 15 note 57. Treaty between Philip V and Hannibal: Pol. 7.9; Livy 23.33.9–34.2 (a libellous version); Schmitt, *SVA* 3.247–50 no. 528. Gelo of Syracuse's attitude: Livy 23.30.10–12; Marino (1988) 31–4. Syracusan demands about Sicily: Pol. 7.4.1–7, 5.4–7; Livy 24.6.7–8. Hieronymus' dealings with Hannibal and Carthage: Pol. 7.2, 7.4; Livy 24.6.1–9; Schmitt, 3.251–2 no. 529. Hannibal's agent Hannibal: Pol. 7.2.3, terming him 'trierarch'; Livy 24.6.2 ('a young nobleman', perhaps misreading Polybius). Lenschau, *RE* 7.2,351, suggests he may have been the Hannibal nicknamed Monomachus of Pol. 9.24.5 (on whom see above, chapters VII note 2, VIII note 18) which is possible enough (despite Walbank, 2.32; Brizzi (1984) 15 note 20). Monomachus was a friend of the general, and a trusted lieutenant if he could perpetrate atrocities yet stay unpunished: and the position of trierarch was held by trusted friends or kinsmen (like Hasdrubal under Hamilcar in Spain; cf. Walbank, 1.109, 153).

7 Hannibal to his Roman PoWs, Livy 22.58.2–3 ('non internecivum sibi esse cum Romanis bellum; de dignitate atque imperio certare'), cf. Hoyos (1983) 176, 180 note 9. Carthalo 'nobilis Carthaginiensis', 22.58.7–9, probably the same as the skilful cavalry general in 217 (22.15.8). De Sanctis supposes Carthalo's mission a fiction (3.2.216 note 33—describing it wrongly as 'd'offrir pace'); so too Seibert, *Hann*. 203, on the grounds that Hannibal was waiting on the Romans to make the overtures (but that was precisely Carthalo's brief) and that sending Carthalo was incompatible with his personal sense of honour (a subjective verdict). Incidentally, the Carthaginians and other Hellenistic states continued to obey the dictum that crushing defeats required peace. After three in North Africa in 203–202 the Carthaginians capitulated; after one major battle, Cynoscephalae in 197, so did Philip V of Macedon; likewise his son Perseus in 168 after losing his army at Pydna. Antiochus III of Syria came to terms after a defeat in Greece in 191 and a major battle in Asia in 189.

8 Hannibal's promises, Pol. 7.9.12 and 15. Discussions of the treaty are many: e.g. G. Egelhaaf, 'Analekten zur Geschichte des zweiten punischen Krieges', *HZ* 53/NF 17 (1885) 456–61; and (1922) 13–16; Groag (1929) 80–90, 132–5;

E. Bickerman, *AJP* 73 (1952) 1–23; A. J. Chroust, *Classica et Medievalia* 15 (1954) 60–107; Picard (1967) 26–35; Walbank, 2.42–56; Eucken (1968) 62–71; M. Barré, *The God-List in the Treaty between Hannibal and Philip V of Macedonia* (Baltimore and London 1983); Huss (1985) 341–3; R. M. Errington, *CAH²* 8.96–8; Seibert, *Hann.* 240–6; Lancel, *Hann.* 192–4. Seibert, *FzH* 271–2 gives a lengthy bibliography going back to 1885. Treaty bound Carthaginian state: Hoyos (1994) 254–5 and note 13. For Illyrian events in 216, e.g. Lazenby (1978) 158–9.

9 'For honour and power' ('de dignitate atque imperio', note 7 above): cf. Appendix §10. That Hannibal did not envisage the destruction of the Roman state or city, but instead the reduction of Roman power, was early stressed by G. Egelhaaf (*HZ* (1885) 456–65, and (1922) 13–16, 39–40), Kromayer ((1909/1974) 247–50) and de Sanctis (3.2.11–12); doubted by Groag ((1929) 80–95); reaffirmed with modifications by Hoffmann ((1957/1974) 40–3, 56–9), Nicolet ((1978) 619–20), Huss ((1985) 343), Seibert (*Hann.* 63–5), Lazenby ((1996) 42–6), and Barceló ((1998) 65–6).

10 Virrius' assurances, Livy 23.6.1–3; Hannibal's, 23.10.2. Bruttians attack Petelia and Croton, 23.20.4–10, 30.1–7; 24.2.2–3.15; Locri, 24.2.1. On other resurfacing antagonisms cf. J.-M. David, *The Roman Conquest of Italy* (tr. A. Nevill, Oxford 1996 (from French edn 1994)) 58–9; cf. Seibert, *Hann.* 224, 253, 484, 543.

11 Annexation: Seibert makes a similar deduction (*FzH* 159–61; *Hann.* 64–5). Citizenship promised to soldiers: Ennius, *Annales* 234–5, ed. Skutsch; Livy 21.45.6; cf. chapter VI note 7. Italy claimed as gain of war: Pol. 3.111.9; Livy 23.33.11 (treaty), 23.5.13 (Varro), cf. 24.6.8; Zon. 9.4.2. Promises before Ticinus: Livy 21.45.5–8, a programme too carefully itemized to look like mere Roman invention; it could go back to Silenus or Sosylus even if Livy, or a predecessor like Coelius, chose to put it in at a dramatic rather than historically suitable moment (but the rite Livy imagines accompanying Hannibal's promises is a borrowed Roman one: cf. 1.24.7–9 and R. M. Ogilvie, *A Commentary on Livy Books 1–5* (Oxford 1965) 70–1, 112). Barceló's view that Hannibal meant to enforce simply 'das Prinzip des Gleichgewichts der Mächte' ((1998) 65–6) is over-simple.

12 Reinforcements via southern Gaul: thus Seibert (1989); *FzH* 183, 193–4; *Hann.* 110, 222. Picard sees southern Gaul as virtually annexed by Hannibal in 218 ((1967) 163–7), but rather than reinforcements by that route he infers later Bruttian and Lucanian recruits (198). So had others, e.g. de Sanctis, 3.2.213–14; Gsell, *HAAN* 2.339; Groag (1929) 100 note 3 (on p. 102). Bomilcar's corps: Livy 23.13.7, 41.10, 43.6; the figure for the funds sent over is missing (13.7) but was probably '500' (cf. Conway and Walters' comment (Oxford text) on the passage). Another 1,000 talents were voted later (23.32.5) though not sent. Reinforcements diverted to Spain, 32.5–6; forces to Sardinia, 32.12; Mago sent to Spain for fresh troops, 13.8. The elephants mentioned once with Hannibal in Campania in 215 (Livy 23.18.6) are probably later annalists' anticipation of the corps that later arrived with Bomilcar (de Sanctis, 3.2.227 note 52; Peddie (1997) 110, 215, 222, supposes the Carthaginians might have sent some in 216). Despite writing on 'gli eserciti annibalici', Barreca (1983–4) has nothing on the army after Cannae, nor has Peddie's discussion, 101–4; contrast Wise (1982) 12, 22–3.

13 Northern and southern Punic armies: Seibert, *Hann.* 211–15. Not heard of after 211: Kukofka (1990) 83. Garrisons: at Capua, Livy 23.7.5, 25.15.3, and 26.5.6, 6.3, 12.10–11, 14.7; Appian, *Hann.* 36.153–4; Livy 24.47.2 (Arpi), 26.38.11 and Val. Max. 3.8 ext. 1 (Salapia); 27.1.1–2 (Marmoreae and Meles in Samnium), 25.11.8; 27.15.9–12, 15.18, 16.5 (Tarentum), 29.6.5–7.10 (Locri). Still other Punic garrisons are mentioned at Tisia in Bruttium (Appian, *Hann.* 44.188–90), among the Hirpini and Lucanians (Livy 27.15.2) and at Metapontum (27.16.12, 42.16).

Passing comment in Livy: 27.43.11. Lazenby (1996) 45, like Livy 26.38.1–2, is over-pessimistic about Hannibal's capacity to garrison places, though it is obviously true the general could never hope—or need—to garrison everything. Punic army at the Calor, 24.14.1, 15.2 (most of the cavalry were Numidians and Mauretanians). Bruttian levies in 207, 27.42.16; cf. 27.12.5 for Bruttian deserters in 209. Polybius (11.19.4) includes Italians in his generalized list of the nationalities represented in Hannibal's army from 218 to 203.

14 Italian troops in Hannibal's army: cf. Appian, *Hann.* 59.247 (stressing their high quality). Recalcitrant Italian troops massacred in 203: Livy 30.30.6; Diod. 27.9; Appian 59.247–9; below, chapter XIV §III. Veterans at Zama: Pol. 15.11.2 (Hannibal's speech, 11.6–12), 12.7; Livy 30.33.5, 35.9; cf. Appian, *Lib.* 40.170 (terming them entirely Italian). For Kahrstedt (1913) 561, they were some 15,000 survivors from 218 and Bomilcar's reinforcement, plus 'ein paar Tausend' Italians; for de Sanctis, 3.2.531, a mixture of invasion-veterans and Italian recruits; Picard (1967) 198, 204; Wise (1982) 22–3. Hallward (1930) 104, estimates 8,000 survivors of the original army and 7,000 Italians; Connolly (1981) 203–4, 4,000-odd of the original African troops; similarly G. T. Griffiths, *The Mercenaries of the Hellenistic World* (London 1935) 229–33. For Brisson (1973) 293, Hannibal took to Africa only 'les vétérans des premières années de campagne'.

15 Bomilcar's reinforcements: note 12. Punic army sent to Sicily, Livy 24.35.1–3; cf. Thiel (1946) 79–80. On the war in Spain see for instance Lazenby (1978) chapter V. Hannibal's control of Punic war-effort, Pol. 9.22.1–6. Mottones: Walbank, 2.150 with references; Lazenby (1978) 119, 172, 292 note 44; Seibert, *Hann.* 317 note 95.

16 Hasdrubal the Bald: Livy 23.32.11, 34.16–17, 40.6–41.1. Himilco in Sicily: 24.35.3–36.10, 39.10; 25.26.3–14. Hanno: 26.40.3–11. Hasdrubal son of Gisco: chapter XI §III.

17 Mago's report to the senate at Carthage: Livy 23.11.7–13.8 ('a small extra effort', 13.6), cf. Seibert, *Hann.* 215–16. Hannibal and supporters at Carthage: chapter VII §I. On dealings with Syracuse see note 6 above; Hoffmann (1961/1974) 351 also stresses Hannibal's initiative. Letter of Hannibal to Carthage: Livy 24.35.4–5. Epicydes and Hanno: 25.40.5–13 and 41.3–7; 26.40.11. Mottones: Pol. 9.22.4; Livy 25.40; 26.40.3–8; 27.5.6–7; *SEG* 585 no. 32; de Sanctis, 3.2.299 note 170; Walbank, 2.150. Hanno as anti-Barcid: Hoffmann, 356; Huss (1985) 369 note 266.

18 Hasdrubal ordered to march to Italy: Livy 23.27.9–10, 28.1–8, 29.16–17; Oros. 4.16.13. Romans worried: Pol. 3.97.4. Date of battle of the Ebro: de Sanctis, 3.2.235 note 71. Seibert, *Hann.* 220–2, views the marching orders as a Roman fiction to glorify the Scipios' victory.

19 Fresh army from Spain envisaged: previous note. On the encirclement strategy cf. Hallward (1930) 60–1. Sardinian rebellion, Livy 23.32.10–17, 40.1–41.7; Dyson (1985) 251–4.

20 Pro-Carthaginian versus pro-Roman factions: Ungern-Sternberg (1975) 65–70; Kukofka (1990) 154–6. Arpi: Livy 24.45.1, 47.4–8. Salapia: Livy 26.38.1–11; Val. Max. 3.8 ext. 1; Appian, *Hann.* 45.191–47.205. Importance of Castra Claudiana (Monte Cancello above Maddaloni): de Sanctis, 3.2.243, cf. his Map IV; Connolly (1981) 190.

21 For operations in Italy in the first five years after Cannae see (e.g.) de Sanctis, 3.2 chapter VII; Hallward (1930) 72–82; Lazenby (1978) chapter IV; Connolly (1981) 188–95; Briscoe (1989) 52–6; Seibert, *Hann.* 198–220, 230–46, 254–62, 287–96, 301–14.

XI INDECISIVE WAR

1 On the brothers Scipio in Spain see Hoyos (2001b); cf. note 7 below. Philip V's defeat, Livy 24.40; de Sanctis, 3.2.398; Lazenby (1978) 160; Seibert, *Hann.* 267–8. The war in Sicily: Hallward (1930) 63–9; Lazenby, 102–8, 115–19; Eckstein (1987) chapters V–VI; Seibert, *Hann.* 262–5, 278–83, 296–9, 314–18, 335–7.

2 Desertions from Hannibal's army: Livy 23.46.6–7, 24.47.8, 27.12.5–6.

3 Significance of Tarentum *et al.* defecting: Kukofka (1990) 68–9. On supply-areas note Bruttium as a (diminishing) source of food for Hannibal, Livy 28.12.7. First battle of Herdonea: sceptics include de Sanctis, 3.2.445 and note 28; Hallward (1930) 81; Huss (1985) 366 note 246; Briscoe (1989) 54; Kukofka, 87–91. By contrast it is accepted by F. G. Moore, *Livy Books XXVI–XXVII* (Loeb edn (1943)) 206 note 1; Broughton, *MRR* 1.271 note 2; Lazenby (1978) 114; Caven (1980) 169, 189; Seibert, *FzH* 237, *Hann.* 295. Roman irregulars beaten in 213: Livy 24.20.1–2, 25.1.3–4 (more detailed report), 25.3.9. A force under M. Centenius Paenula crushed in 212, 25.19.9–17; see also Appendix §11. Tarentines defeat Roman naval squadron, 26.39.1–19.

4 Roman armies and commanders: see the tables in de Sanctis, 3.2.614–17, 619, cf. 306–16; Hallward (1930) 104–5 insert. Twenty-five legions in 212: Brunt (1971) 418; naval strength, 421–2.

5 On campaigning in Italy and Sicily from 212 to 208 see for instance Lazenby (1978) 110–24, 158–81; Marino (1988) 70–83; Seibert, *Hann.* 290–9, 302–18, 330–7, 344–50, 363–7. Hannibal's famous march on Rome in 211 is widely discussed, notably by Lazenby, 121–3; Scullard (1974) 163–4; Walbank, 2.118–33; G. Leidl, 'Appians "Annibaike"', in *Aufstieg und Niedergang der Römischen Welt*, 34.1, ed. H. Temporini *et al.* (Berlin and New York 1993) 456–7; Seibert, *FzH* 238–41, *Hann.* 304–11.

6 'Hannibal ad portas' (proverbial): Cicero, *De Finibus* 4.22, *Philippics* 1.11. Roman recapture of Tarentum: Broughton, *MRR* 1.285; Lazenby (1978) 175–6. Death of Fulvius Centumalus: Broughton, 1.280; Lazenby, 170–1.

7 The sources for the Spanish campaigns are printed and discussed by Schulten (1935) 23–166. See also Lazenby (1978) chapter V; *Historia de España*, chapter I; Richardson (1986) chapter III; and Seibert, *Hann.*, has a Spanish section for each year in his annalistic account of the war. Hasdrubal appointed by Hannibal, chapter VIII §II; and see Pol. 11.2.1–4, 9–11 (praise, cf. Diod. 26.24); 9.11.1–4; 10.7.3, 37.2 (quarrels with Mago and Hasdrubal son of Gisco), cf. Livy 26.41.20; Walbank, 2.136. Gauls at battle of the Metaurus: Pol. 11.3.1; Livy 27.48.17–18. Hanno commandant beyond the Ebro, chapter VIII note 15; Scipio's strength in 218 (about 25,000): Lazenby, 125; Richardson, 35–6.

8 Battle of the Ebro: Pol. 3.95–6; Livy 22.19.1–20.3. Seibert, *Hann.* 178–9, plays down the extent of the Roman success; but that makes Hasdrubal's further inactivity still more peculiar. Reinforcements to Hasdrubal: note 9. Land battle near the Ebro, 23.29 (usually called the 'battle of Hibera' but in fact near a different, unnamed town, cf. 23.28.11–12); cf. de Sanctis, 3.2.235 note 71; Hoyos (2001b) 74. Seibert, *Hann.* 220–3, thinks the defeat less serious than Roman tradition and many moderns suppose, and does not believe Livy (23.27.9–12) that Hasdrubal had been ordered to Italy.

9 Hostile Celtiberi (217), Livy 22.21.7–8; Tartessian revolt (216), 23.26.4–27.8, 24.41.1; rebels in 214 (or 212, cf. notes 12 and 13 below), 24.41.1–2. Reinforcements to Hasdrubal in 216–215: Livy 23.26.2, 28.2, 32.5–6, 32.11. Celtiberians hired by Scipios: Pol. 10.6.2, 7.1; Livy 24.49.7–8, 25.32.11. Hasdrubal versus Carpetani (209), Pol. 10.7.5; Carpetani and others released from Hannibal's army

(218), chapter VIII note 15. Spaniards disliked serving abroad, Livy 23.29.8. Indibilis' and Mandonius' defection: Pol. 9.11.3–4, 10.35.6–8; Livy 27.17.3.

10 Barcid Hasdrubal recalled against Syphax, Appian, *Iber.* 15.59–60; believed by Lenschau, *RE* 2471; de Sanctis, 3.2.237, 431 note 2; Hallward (1930) 70; *Historia de España*, 21; Lazenby (1978) 129; Huss (1985) 357; Briscoe (1989) 57; Seibert, *Hann.* 283 note 77, 284 note 84. But Appian also claims Scipionic victories in Hasdrubal's absence and has him, Mago and Hasdrubal son of Gisco all sent from Africa to Spain together afterwards, around 212: in reality Mago was in Spain from 215, Livy has no such Roman victories, and his account of the war with Syphax (24.48.13–49.6) does not mention Hasdrubal the Barcid.

11 Roman coastal raiding, Livy 22.20.3–10, cf. Thiel (1946) 51–2. Supposed advance to the *saltus Castulonensis* (the Sierra Morena), 22.20.11–12; but cf. Pol. 3.97.5; Hoyos (2001b) 71–2.

12 Battle of Hibera: note 8. Recovery of hostages from Saguntum: Pol. 3.97.2–99.9; Livy 22.22.3–21; Zon. 9.1.2–3; believed by Walbank, 1.432, Lazenby (1978) 128, and Eckstein (1987) 200; rejected by de Sanctis, 3.2.233 note 65; Seibert, *Hann.* 180–1. Campaign of '214'—really 212—with Castrum Altum, Mons Victoriae and Castulo: Livy 24.41–2, cf. chapter IV note 20. Sceptics include de Sanctis, 3.2.237 note 76; Lazenby, 129; Seibert, *Hann.* 266–7; and Richardson (1986) 40 thinks some details misplaced from 211. But a misdating of the campaign from 212 (note restoration of Saguntines, 24.42.9–11) is likelier: cf. Appian, *Iber.* 16.60–1, with the Scipios wintering at Castulo and 'Orson'—probably his ultimate source meant not Urso near modern Seville but, like Castulo, a town of the Orissi/Oretani (chapter V note 17; see Hoyos (2001b) 79). Scipios' catastrophe was in 211: de Sanctis, 3.2.431–2; Seibert, *FzH* 255–6.

13 Saguntines restored, Livy 24.42.9–10 (but the punishment of their noxious neighbours (*ibid.* 11) may be a mistaken anticipation, cf. 28.39.11–12); correct date 212 and not Livy's 214, cf. Schulten (1935) 85; Lazenby (1978) 129; Hoyos (2001b) 77–9. Seibert, *FzH* 256–8, disbelieves the episode. Destruction of the Scipio brothers (211), retreat of surviving troops to safety: Pol. 10.6.2, 7.1; Livy 25.32–9; Appian, *Iber.* 16.61–3; other sources listed by Broughton, *MRR* 1.274–5. See Hoyos (2001b) 83–90.

XII THE DEFEAT OF HASDRUBAL

1 Punic raid on Sardinia in 210, Livy 27.6.13–14. Roman military effort in 211: cf. Brunt (1971) 418–22. Bomilcar's fleets in 212: Livy 25.25.11–13, 27.2–12. Roman raids on North Africa: Livy 22.31.1–5 (in 217), 23.21.2 (216), 23.41.8–9 (215), 25.31.12–15 (211), 27.5.1 and 5.8–13 (210). There were to be more raids, in 208, 207 and 205: Lazenby (1978) 196–7; cf. Rankov (1996) 55–6.

2 Eminence of Hasdrubal son of Gisco: Livy 28.12.13, 29.28.7; Silius 17.175 ('qui rerum agitarit habenas'); cf. Appian, *Lib.* 10.37; Lenschau, *RE* 7.2,474–5; de Sanctis, 3.2.519–20 ('dei Barcidi era stato socio, se pur rivale', and equally bellicose). Groag (1929) 104 note 1, sums him up as a 'professional battle-loser' ('berufsmässige Schlachtenverlierer')—harsh but not all that unfair. Perhaps brother of the Hamilcar son of Gisco who surrendered Malta to the Romans in 218 (Livy 21.51.2). Supposedly anti-Barcid: Kahrstedt (1913) 559; Groag (1929) 105 note 1; Hoffmann (1962) 92–3, 101–3, 141–2; Picard (1967) 202; Picard and Picard, *LDC* 260, 264 (contrast 273); Caven (1980) 183. Livy does once report him disagreeing, about Spanish loyalties, with Hasdrubal and Mago (27.20.4–5), but the brothers in 211–208 were themselves at odds (chapter XI note 7).

Hanno son of Hamilcar, in 204: Livy 29.34.1–15 (cf. 35.2); Appian, *Lib.*

14.57–60, and Zon. 9.12.3–5, give a rather different account (and Zonaras terms his father Hasdrubal son of Gisco!); cf. Lenschau, *RE* 7.2,359. T. A. Dorey and C. W. F. Lydall, *Livy XXIX* (Havant 1968) 109, think his father was Hamilcar son of Gisco (Livy 21.51.2) but that is a guess. Sophoniba: Livy 30.12.11–22, 15.6–8; Diod. 27.7; Appian, *Lib.* 10.37–8, 27.111–28.120 (romanticized account). Barcids' political position: Picard too thinks that Hannibal lost popularity in the later war-years ((1967) 202); cf. Hoffmann (1962) 91–2, 141–2. Hasdrubal and the Barcid faction rallied the Carthaginians in 203: Livy 30.7.7. His operations in later 203: Appian, *Lib.* 24.97–8, 29.122–30.127, 36.151; sound scepticism in Gsell, *HAAN* 2.269. Hannibal still the ultimate supreme commander: chapter XIV §I.

3 *Ordo iudicum*, Livy 33.46.1; above, chapter VI §III. Huss (1985) 369 note 266, wonders if the year 212 saw 'die beginnende Formierung einer antibarqidischen Opposition' (cf. Hoffmann (1962) 91–2); but Hanno the Great and his friends had been there all along (Livy 30.42.12–21, 44.5).

4 Fall of Tarentum: Livy 27.15.9–16.11; cf. chapter XI §II. Scipio's first actions in Spain: sources in Broughton, *MRR* 1.280, 287; Liddell Hart (1926) chapters II–III; Scullard (1970) chapter II; Lazenby (1978) 132–40; Seibert, *Hann.* 350–7. Livy's notion (26.20.5) that the Punic generals from the start were strangely afraid of him is patriotic imagination.

5 Punic generals mutually antagonistic: chapter XI note 7. Campaign of Baecula: Pol. 10.34–40; Livy 27.17–20; Liddell Hart (1926) chapter IV; Walbank, 2.245–55; Scullard (1970) chapter III; Seibert, *Hann.* 371–3. Why Scipio did not pursue Hasdrubal: Pol. 10.39.9; Livy 27.20.2.

6 Hasdrubal's Italian design (208): Pol. 10.37.3–5. First mooted in 215: chapter XI note 8.

7 Roman force mauled, Livy 27.26.4–6; cf. chapter XI note 3. Marcellus and his colleague Crispinus: Broughton, *MRR* 1.289–90; Lazenby (1978) 178–80; cf. Baker's remarks (1929) 229–30. Failure to take Salapia, Livy 27.28.4–12; relief of Locri, *ibid.* 13–17. Commandant at Locri was 'The Samnite': de Sanctis, 3.2.462 note 55; Huss (1985) 387 note 102. Comment after loss of Tarentum: Plutarch, *Fabius* 23.

8 Elections and military dispositions for 207: Livy 27.33.9–35.14, 36.10–14; cf. Lippold (1963) 193–6; Lazenby (1978) 180–2; Briscoe (1989) 72; Seibert, *Hann.* 379–81. Though Livius at first refused Fabius' urging, he and Nero did finally agree to be reconciled (27.35.6–9), which scarcely justifies the widespread view of them being anti-Fabius.

9 On Hasdrubal's route: Lehmann (1905) 193–203; de Sanctis, 3.2.547–8; Lazenby (1978) 182. Siege of Placentia, Livy 27.39.10–14.

10 Seibert, *Hann.* 385, infers that as soon as he reached Italy Hasdrubal had got a message through to Hannibal, but this does not really follow from Livy 27.39.10–14.

11 Livy 27.40.1–42.17; Hasdrubal's unlucky messengers, 43.1–5. Deserters: Hasdrubal had gathered over 3,000 Roman captives before his defeat (49.7; cf. Zon. 9.9.11; Oros. 4.18.14) and it is unlikely that no deserters at all had joined him.

12 Hannibal's movements as reported by Livy (27.40.10–42.17) are discussed by de Sanctis, 3.2.553–4; Lazenby (1978) 184–6; Hoyos (1983) 178–9; Huss (1985) 392–3; Kukofka (1989) 121–4; Seibert, *Hann.* 382–3. On some debated aspects of the campaigning in 207 see Appendix §12. The alleged Punic losses in the Apulian battles total a most improbable 17,000 (Livy 27.40.11, 42.7, 42.15).

13 Canusium as Hannibal's intended junction-point: Seibert, *Hann.* 382–4; see Appendix §12. Hasdrubal's despatch perhaps meant to mislead the Romans: Lazenby (1978) 183–4. Garrisons in the south: Locri was not captured until 205

(Livy 29.6–9), Clampetia and other strongpoints in Bruttium not till 204 (29.38.1). Latin colonies refuse troops (209), 27.9.1–6; not dealt with until 204, 29.15.2–15; those in the Umbria–Etruria region were Nepet, Sutrium and Narnia.

14 Etruscans restive (209–207): Livy 27.21.6–7, 24.1–9, 38.7; 28.10.4–5. Discontent still in 204, 29.36.10–12; Harris (1971) 136–43. Etruscan epitaph for a 106-year-old, Larth Felsnas, who in youth served 'with Hannibal's people (*hanipaluscle*)': A. J. Pfiffig, *Studi Etruschi* 35 (1967) 659–63.

15 Metaurus campaign and battle: Pol. 11.1–3 (battle only); Livy 27.43.1–49.9; later sources, adding little, listed in Broughton, *MRR* 1.294. Date: note 12 above. Surviving Punic forces, Livy 27.48.16, 49.8–9 ('uno agmine'); cf. Appian, *Hann.* 53.224. On Hasdrubal's original strength and losses: de Sanctis, 3.2.556–8, and Walbank, 2.273–4 (30,000–35,000); Lazenby (1978) 190 (20,000–30,000); Seibert, *Hann.* 388 note 58 (20,000–25,000). Pol. 11.3.2–3 records 10,000 killed, Livy 27.49.6 has 5,400 prisoners—not necessarily an underestimate. Hasdrubal's head: Livy 27.51.11–13; Silius 15.813–21; Frontinus 2.9.2; Zon. 9.9.12. See also Appendix §12.

16 Hasdrubal's death admired: Pol. 11.2.1–10; Livy 27.49.3–4; Silius 15.740–805. That Hasdrubal's virtual suicide was ill-timed was also held by Thomas Arnold, *The Second Punic War* (1842; ed. W. T. Arnold (London 1886) 289–90). Resistance in Cisalpine Gaul after 201: W. V. Harris in *CAH²* 8.107–13. The Punic officer Hamilcar: Livy 31.10.2, etc.; Lenschau, *RE* 7.2,308–9; Briscoe (1973) 82–4, 115, 293.

17 Honour to fallen consuls: Livy 22.7.5 and 52.6, 27.28.1; Cicero, *De Senectute* 75 (Marcellus); other sources in Broughton, *MRR* 1.247, 290. Three proconsuls: the brothers Scipio and, at Herdonea in 210, Cn. Fulvius Centumalus.

18 'The fortune of Carthage': Livy 27.51.12; cf. Horace, *Odes* 4.5.69–72. On Nero's speed of march, and efforts to defend Hannibal's inactivity, see Appendix §12.

XIII AFRICA INVADED

1 Roman raids on Africa: chapter XII note 1. New army and general to Spain, and Silanus' victory: Livy 28.1.1–2.12. Punic strength at Ilipa: Pol. 11.20.2, plausibly defended by Lazenby (1978) 145; Livy 28.12.13–14 gives 50,000 foot and 4,500 horse while mentioning the larger figure. Mago's resistance after Ilipa: Livy 28.36.1–37.2. His reputed town-foundation (modern Mahón) on the isle of Menorca: chapter XVI note 15.

2 Scipio and Hasdrubal visit Syphax: Livy 28.17.4–18.12 (wrongly claiming Scipio made a treaty with the king); Appian, *Iber.* 29.115–30.119, with the usual improbable embroideries; Seibert, *Hann.* 404–5. Huss (1985) 398 doubts the story, unnecessarily (cf. Seibert, 405 note 24). Barcid niece's royal Numidian marriages, Livy 29.29.12–13; dissensions in royal family and Syphax's takeover, 29.29.4–33.10; cf. Thompson (1981); Eckstein (1987) 234–40. Masinissa's contacts with the Romans: 28.16.11–12 (in Spain), 29.3.14 ('aperta defectione' known at Rome by 205), cf. 29.4.7–9 (interview with Laelius during African raid); Walsh (1965) 150.

3 Mago's expeditionary force, Livy 28.46.7; reinforced, 29.4.6 (note 'magna pecunia ad conducenda auxilia'), 5.2. On his uselessness in Liguria cf. Hoyos (1983) 175. Roman fleet in Sicily reduced: Livy 28.10.16 (cf. 27.22.9); Thiel (1946) 139–40.

4 Punic fleets: e.g. 83 ships fought Laevinus' 100 in 208 (27.29.7–8; he captured 18); 30 and then 25 joined Mago in 205 (28.46.7, 29.4.6). Laevinus' alleged victory in 207 over a 70-strong fleet, capturing 17 (28.4.5–7), is probably a doublet

of the previous year's (de Sanctis, 3.2.461 note 52), though both are accepted by Thiel (1946) 130–2; Lazenby (1978) 197; and Siebert, *Hann.* 377 note 82, 398. Punic fleet burned in 202, Livy 30.43.11–12 (some of his sources reported 500 craft of all sizes); Thiel, 182.

5   Pol. 9.22.1–6; cf. Hoyos (1994) 254–5. Hanno son of Bomilcar: Appian, *Lib.* 24.98, 29.122–30.126 (an involved and implausible story of treachery to Hasdrubal son of Gisco), 31.133. Hannibal's nephew: de Sanctis, 3.2.678, in Index; Picard and Picard, *LDC* 264; Caven (1980) 243. Hannibal saves Hasdrubal: note 8 below. Bomilcar last heard of in 211: Pol. 9.9.11, cf. Livy 26.20.7. Walbank, 2.230, supposes he commanded the fleet sent to Greece in 209, but this is an assumption. Punic effort in 205 to supply Hannibal: note 11 below.

6   The campaign of 206: Pol. 11.20–33; Livy 28.12.10–16.5; Appian, *Iber.* 25.96–38.155; Walbank, 2.296–312; Lazenby (1978) 145–56; Corzo Sánchez (1975) 234–40; Millán León (1986); Seibert, *Hann.* 404–9.

7   Carthaginians less interested in Hannibal, more so in Spain: Livy 28.12.9. Moderns who see Hannibal as let down by his home government include Mommsen, *HR* 2.144, 146, 201; Egelhaaf (1922) 16–17, 40; Groag (1929) 104–7; Thiel (1946) 161; Hoffmann (1962) 92–3, 98, 113, 141–2; Caven (1980) 156, 183, 257–8; Lancel (1992) 418; Seibert, *Hann.* 340 note 81, 369–70, 412; Santosuosso (1997) 181–2. 'Hannibal's complaint' in 203: Livy 30.20.1–4; Silius 17.187–235; Appian, *Lib.* 33.138.

8   Laelius' raid in 205 and Punic reactions: Livy 29.3.9–5.1. Mood at Carthage in 203–202: Pol. 14.9.6–10.1, 15.1.1–3.2. Carthaginians' reaction after destruction of the camps: 14.6.6–13; Livy 30.7.6–8. But Appian's picture of a bellicose, fickle and foolish citizenry, hostile even to Hannibal for not being warlike enough (*Lib.* 31.131, 34.143–35.150, 38.157–9, etc.), is an obvious distortion, whether going back to an author like Silenus or more likely a Roman annalist. Hannibal saves Hasdrubal, Appian, *Lib.* 36.151. He later silences an opponent of peace: Pol. 15.19.1–3; Livy 30.37.7–9 names the man Gisco. Hasdrubal 'the Kid', Livy 30.42.12–21, 44.5; Appian, *Lib.* 34.145, also 49.213–53.228 (an improbable oration to Scipio).

9   Appian, *Hann.* 40.173.

10 On the tribunal of One Hundred and Four earlier: chapter VI §III. Supremacy of Carthage's 'ordo iudicum' by 196: Livy 33.46.1.

11 The debate on invading Africa: Livy 28.40.1–45.9 ('let there be peace in Italy', 41.9). Legions in 205: Lazenby (1978) 195. Hannibal's Cape Lacinium inscription: Pol. 3.33.18, 56.4; Livy 28.46.16; cf. Seibert's comment (*Hann.* 416), 'er sah wohl den Krieg als beendet an'. Groag (1929) 107–8 implausibly imagines it was accompanied by unrecorded peace-overtures to the Romans. Loss of Locri: 29.6–7; de Sanctis, 3.2.499–500. Hannibal's camp: Pliny, *NH* 3.95, mentions a Castra Hannibalis on the coast near Scylletium at the narrowest part of Italy (cf. Seibert, 417 note 24). But he spent only part of his time there, if Pol. 15.1.11 is correct in giving him two years at Cape Lacinium; and this was at least 85 miles (140 kilometres) from Locri. Epidemic and food shortage: Livy 28.46.15, 29.10.1. Bruttium too small to supply Punic army: 28.11.7–8 (from 206). Punic supply fleet in 205: Livy 28.46.14 citing Coelius; Appian, *Hann.* 54.226 has 100 ships. The later annalist Valerius Antias (Livy, *ibid.*) had the Punic fleet transporting Etruscan and other booty and captives from Mago's expedition—but Mago was still stagnant in 205 and never in fact invaded Etruria.

12 Scipio's invasion and early operations: de Sanctis, 3.2.502–11, 562–7; Scullard (1970) chapter VI. Hannibal's doings in Italy in 204–203: Livy 29.36.4–9, 30.19.10–12; Seibert, *Hann.* 428–9, 435, 449. Seibert rhetorically questions the

Romans' alleged successes in 204 over Hannibal (e.g. 'warum griffen sie das Lager Hannibals nicht an und trieben ihn endlich außer Landes, wenn sie so deutlich gesiegt hatten?', 428) but does not ask why Hannibal was still hanging on in Italy. Cf. Groag (1929) 107, wondering why Hannibal did not even earlier leave a lieutenant in charge and return to Carthage (to confront his supposedly hostile government); while Huss (1985) 400 note 244 sees the leaders at Carthage still nursing illusory hopes. Livy depicts the general as bitter about departing in 203 (30.19.12–20.9; cf. Silius 17.184–200), but this is imagination. Roman naval forces increased in 203: Thiel (1946) 162–3.

13 Hasdrubal's pre-eminence at Carthage by 204: chapter XII §I. Negotiations in winter 204–203: Pol. 14.1.9; Livy 30.3.5–7; Appian, *Lib.* 17.69–70; Dio frg. 57.72 = Zon. 9.12.7. Appian and Dio have Spain among the lands explicitly mentioned: probably an inference that goes back to their ultimate sources, for Spain could not be ignored (even if Syphax and Hasdrubal might have preferred this). Hannibal and Scipio before Zama: below, chapter XIV note 19. Huss (1989) struggles to find a theme of 'Pan-African' solidarity in the alliance of the Carthaginians and Syphax.

14 Scipio and countrymen aimed to limit the Carthaginians in Africa and had geopolitical goals too ('il dominio del mondo', no less): de Sanctis, 3.2.510–11. Secure peace required Hannibal's own defeat: Scullard (1970) 125; cf. Scullard (1980) 234 (Rome needed compensation for sufferings). Scipio himself later claimed—or so it was said—that he *would* have destroyed Carthage had he had the time; but this smacks of postwar pride and pique (Livy 30.44.3—contrast 30.36.11; cf. Scullard (1970) 155–6). Eckstein (1987) 248–9, cf. 262–3, sees it as his original aim, in part thanks to Livy and in part because reportedly the Carthaginians in 203 were fearing it. Casualties at Zama: Seibert, *Hann.* 470 note 42. Consuls' attempts to take command in Africa: Livy 30.24.1–3 (in 203), 27.1–5 (202), 40.7–16 (201); cf. Harris (1979) 139. Attack on the camps: Lazenby (1978) 207–8 with references.

15 Thirty days for Hasdrubal and Syphax to rendezvous with new armies at Great Plains: Pol. 14.7.9. This looks almost too short an interval: possibly Polybius wrote the Greek numeral Ν ('50') and it was later miscopied as Λ ('30') thanks to the initial letter of the next word, ΠΕΡΙ. The disaster at the camps was at the start of spring (14.2.1; late February in North Africa?) and Syphax was later defeated and captured by Masinissa on '22 June' by the Roman calendar (Ovid, *Fasti* 6.769–70; Walbank, 2.440). Though scholars disagree over how accurate the calendar then was (Derow (1976); Seibert, *FzH* 306), all this fits suitably. Fifty days would put the rendezvous at the Great Plains in late April, the battle two to three weeks later (cf. Pol. 14.8.1–4) in May, and Syphax's capture some while after that (for Derow, 266–8, cf. 272–3, it was 23 May). Though Syphax's son Vermina and some lesser chieftains held out against Masinissa and for the Carthaginians (Pol. 15.3.5–7; Livy 30.36.8; Appian, *Lib.* 33.139, 141) they proved of little moment.

16 Attack on Roman fleet: Pol. 14.10.6–12; Livy 30.10; Appian, *Lib.* 24.100–25.103, 30.127–8, calling the admiral Hamilcar but telling of two attacks. It would be a rather typical coda if the Hasdrubal afterwards appointed admiral was still the son of Gisco (Livy 30.24.11, 25.5; cf. Kahrstedt (1913) 558; Lazenby (1978) 330, in Index), though Appian has the latter become a guerrilla leader and finally commit suicide (*Lib.* 24.97–8, 29.122–30.127, 36.151, 38.169; similarly Zon. 9.12.10–11, 14.10)—none of this mentioned by Polybius or Livy, and very pro-Hasdrubal in flavour. The suicide may be factual since Hasdrubal now vanishes from the record. Hanno son of Bomilcar: note 5 above. Hannibal's nephew: de Sanctis, 3.2.678, in Index; Picard and Picard, *LDC* 264; Caven (1980) 243.

XIV DEFEAT

1 Carthage's countryside rebellious: Pol. 14.9.5. Carthaginians decide to seek terms, recall Barcids and prepare for siege: Pol. 14.9.7–10.1; Livy 30.9.7; Silius 17.149–83; Appian, *Hann.* 58.243, *Lib.* 31.129; other sources cited by Seibert, *Hann.* 449 note 66. Carthage divided between Barcid supporters and pro-peace anti-Barcids: de Sanctis, 3.2.519–20, 522, 532; Hoffmann (1962) 103; Warmington (1964) 230–2; Picard (1967) 203; Picard and Picard, *LDC* 264; Scullard (1970) 134; Caven (1980) 246. Hanno the Great's group excluded: chapter XIII note 8. Inner 'sacred council' of senate: chapter II §IV.

2 Laelius: note 6 below. Livy's claim (30.16.14–15) that the Carthaginians negotiated only to buy time may draw on Polybius, whose account of the talks does not survive. For Seibert, 'hatten beiden Seiten . . . kein ehrliches Spiel gespielt . . . Beide Verhandlungspartner wollten Zeit gewinnen', and Scipio wished 'den Krieg mit einem Sieg über Hannibal zu beenden' (*Hann.* 459–60, cf. 446; cf. too Groag (1929) 108). But it suited Scipio far better to finish the war quickly, provided he could impose the terms he wanted. Senate ordered consuls of 203 to keep Hannibal and Mago in Italy: Livy 30.21.1; cf. Hoyos (1983) 179. The consul Caepio in 203 eager to supplant Scipio: chapter XIII note 14 above. One of those in 202 was similarly keen: Broughton, *MRR* 1.319 for references.

3 Prostrate envoys: Pol. 15.1.6–7; Livy 30.16.4 supposes it a normal Punic custom; so too Picard (1967) 203 'cérémonial égyptien'; Seibert, *Hann.* 445 note 48. The envoys tried it again after Zama, if we can believe Appian (*Lib.* 49.214) supported by hints in Polybius (15.17.1–2) and Livy (30.36.10). Envoys blamed Hannibal: cf. chapter VI §III.

4 Scipio's terms: Schmitt, *SVA* 291–3; Mantel (1991) 105–6; Scardigli (1991) 297–313; Seibert, *Hann.* 445–8. Appian claims that Scipio set the future boundary of Punic Africa at the 'Phoenician Trenches' (*Lib.* 32.135), but on these see chapter XV §I.

5 Pol. 15.1.2, 8.8, and *P. Rylands* no. 491 (Roberts (1938) 114–17 with Plate 5), lines 2–4, on the armistice-oaths (cf. Scardigli (1991) 315); Livy 30.17 (Laelius' arrival at Rome), 21.1–2 (news of Barcids' departure), 22–3 (Punic envoys face Roman senators); Appian, *Lib.* 31.131–2.136; Dio, frg. 57.74 = Zon. 9.13.8. On *P. Rylands* 491 see M. Treu, *Aegyptus* 33 (1953) 30–56, with earlier bibliography; Lippold (1963) 64–6; Walbank, 2.441–2; Lehmann (1974) 182–6; Eckstein (1987) 251–4; Mantel (1991) 111–17, 124–8; Seibert, *FzH* 307–8; Hoyos (2001a). Senate wished to keep Hannibal and Mago in Italy: note 2 above.

   Seibert, *Hann.* 448, accepts Dio's report of the Senate's refusal to negotiate while Punic armies were still in Italy, seeing it conform to 'allgemeinem römischen Usus' (*ibid.* note 60); next (453–8) he accepts most of Livy's account, adds to it Appian's senatorial commission sent to Africa, and then infers from Pol. 15.1.3 and 4.8 that the Roman citizen-Assembly prodded the Senate to agree to terms after all—but harsher ones, thereby provoking the Carthaginians to fight on ('Was sie erregte, war die Tatsache, daß die Römer die Begingungen wesentlich verschärft hatten', 457). This reconstruction is unconvincing, and in any case the Senate's supposedly harsher additions (*Hann.* 455) to Scipio's terms (446–7) include a limit on the size of the Punic navy which Livy in fact ascribes to Scipio (30.16.11) while the other additions are minor—a ban on hiring Ligurian and Gallic mercenaries, and a precise figure for the indemnity the Carthaginians already knew they would have to pay.

6 'Scipionem in eo positam habuisse spem pacis si Hannibal et Mago ex Italia non revocarentur' (said Laelius and his colleague Fulvius, Livy 30.23.6). Tränkle (1977) 237–8 sees Livy as using not Polybius, but a later author 'der die ganze

Geschichte stärker in einem römisch nationalen und antikarthagischen Sinne ausgeformt hatte', but it is likelier, as usual, that Livy draws on both Polybius and other sources together to produce a composite—and not always well-judged—narrative. Seibert judges the Senate's initial rejection of the terms as genuine, holding that Roman annalists would not invent it as this would make it impossible for them to describe the ensuing Carthaginian attack on the food convoy as a breach of the terms (*Hann.* 454 note 94). But annalists got round this difficulty—in Livy, Scipio accuses the enemy of violating the armistice and the law of nations (30.25.2, 25.9–10, 37.6), not the 'rejected' terms; contrast Pol. 15.1.2 and 9.

7 Mantel (1991) 126–7, 133, infers Valerius Antias as Livy's source. Coelius' use of Silenus: Cicero, *De Divinatione* 1.49, cf. chapter VIII note 18; C. B. R. Pelling, *OCD*³ 355. Dramatic invention by Coelius: notably a fearsome storm that nearly wrecks Scipio's crossing to Africa in 204, whereas all other sources give him a calm sea (Livy 29.27.14–15 = Coelius, frg. 40P; cf. P. G. Walsh, *Livy: His Historical Aims and Methods* (Cambridge 1963) 132; Badian (1966) 16). Silius borrows the storm for Hannibal's crossing in 203 (17.236–91). On Valerius Antias and other annalists see, e.g., Badian (1966).

8 Hannibal now in Africa: Pol. 15.1.10–11, cf. 15.3.5. Leaves Italy: Livy 30.20.5; Appian, *Hann.* 58.243; *Lib.* 31.129; Thiel (1946) 170–1; Seibert, *Hann.* 450–1. Thiel thinks that the interval between summons and departure points to Hannibal having to build the ships. Capture of Syphax: chapter XIII note 15. Summons to Hannibal: note 1 above. Chronology: de Sanctis, 3.2.571–2. Scipio's forces and fleet in 204: Lazenby (1978) 203; Seibert, *Hann.* 432.

9 Massacre: Diod. 27.9; Livy 30.20.6 (but contrast 42.3.6); Appian, *Hann.* 59.249; cf. chapter VIII §IV. Silius, interestingly, has no massacre (17.158–202). Kukofka (1990) 149 is disposed to believe one did occur; Connolly (1981) blames it on the Romans after Hannibal's exit. Horses: Diodorus (3,000) and Appian (4,000), *ibid.*; cf. Seibert, *Hann.* 432 Both Diodorus (27.10) and Appian (*Lib.* 33.140) then tell an implausible tale of Hannibal in Africa massacring 4,000 Numidian cavalry deserters from Masinissa to acquire their horses. Polybius on mutiny-free expedition, 11.19.3–5, 23.13.1–2; echoed by Diod. 29.19, Livy 28.12.3–4.

10 Mago's death: Livy 30.19.5. Nepos reports him still alive in 195 (*Hann.* 7.3–4, 8.2; accepted by Seibert, *Hann.* 448 note 63, 513–14) but Polybius' and Livy's details of the Zama campaign—and Livy's account of Hannibal's sufetate in 196—know nothing of him, while Dio, frg. 56.77 (= Zon. 9.13.10), has the Carthaginians before Zama send him back to Italy! Cf. de Sanctis, 3.2.526 note 151, 604; below, chapter XV note 16.

11 Carthaginian urgings to Hannibal: Pol. 15.5.1–2. Hannibal's niece: chapter XIII §I. The ousted Mazaetullus fled to Punic territory with his puppet king, before returning to Numidia under assurances from Masinissa and against Punic wishes (Livy 29.30.10–13). Tychaeus: Pol. 15.3.5–7, cf. Appian, *Lib.* 33.139; Walbank, 2.444. 'Mesotylus': Appian, *Lib.* 33.141, accepted by Lazenby (1978) 217–18. Appian imagines Syphax's son Vermina bringing aid too—but in reality he arrived only after Zama (Livy 30.36.7–8; Seibert, *Hann.* 472).

12 Fresh supplies to Scipio: Scardigli (1991) 336 note 174 sees the Carthaginians as obliged to keep Scipio supplied, but this is not what Livy (30.16.12) reports. Provision-fleets sent in early spring 202: Thiel (1946) 174; Walbank, 2.441. In January, i.e. winter: Kahrstedt (1913) 557–8, 560 note 1, implausibly. Roman transports seized, Livy 30.24.5–12. It is not likely that the transports reaching Aegimurus could be seen from Carthage 30 miles (50 kilometres) away (despite Livy, Thiel (1946) 174, *et alii*), though this would be true of those driven ashore at

Aquae Calidae on the Cape Bon coast near modern Korbous. Tribulations of Scipio's envoys: Pol. 15.1.3–2.15; Livy 30.25.1–10; Appian, *Lib.* 34.144–5. These episodes a Roman fabrication to justify Scipio's renewal of hostilities: Hoffmann (1941) 279–82; M. Treu, *Aegyptus* 33 (1953) 48–53; Lippold (1963) 64–5; Huss (1985) 414 note 90; Seibert, *Hann.* 458–9. Yet the Carthaginians had recalled Hannibal so as to renew hostilities (thus too Seibert, 457–8) and he was now in Africa, so Roman tradition had no need to invent a pretext for Scipio to do so (cf. note 6). Besides, Scipio's preliminary peace-terms after Zama included compensation for Punic 'misdeeds' during the armistice (Pol. 15.18.3; Livy 30.37.6 more specifically writes of compensation for the seizures; cf. Eckstein (1987) 259). See also Appendix §13.

13 Attitudes at Carthage: Pol. 15.2.2–3; Diod. 27.11.1; Appian, *Iber.* 34.143–5, 35.149–50; cf. Livy 30.24.10–11. Fabius Pictor's anti-Barcid claims: chapter VI §III. That the return of the forces from Italy cast a supposed 'peace party' out of power at Carthage and restored the 'war party' (e.g. de Sanctis, 3.2.532–3) is not persuasive; nor that the Carthaginians were thereby reinvigorated to fight (Huss (1985) 414, 'ein bedeutsamer Meinungsumschwung'). Oaths at armistice: note 5 above. 'Sent out men bearing war instead of peace': *P. Rylands* 491, lines 39–42, ἀπέστειλαν φέροντας ἀντὶ τῆς εἰρήνης τὸν πόλεμον; Hoyos (2001a) 75.

14 Diehards prompted Hasdrubal to attack: Pol. 15.2.4–8. Unclear if they or he alone responsible: Livy 30.25.5. Mantel (1991) 111–16 argues that the Carthaginians' seizure of the supplies and attack on the ambassadorial ship did not amount to a rupture of the peace-terms, but this is a very legalist argument. Seibert, *Hann.* 458–9, holds that the Carthaginians wanted to hear their envoys' report and this did not justify Scipio's ensuing actions in the countryside. Scipio's anger: Pol. 15.4.2, and stressed by Eckstein (1987) 254 as 'probably . . . the proconsul's basic motivation' even though 'he had little to gain politically . . . while militarily he was risking much'—but this is not persuasive.

15 Desire to bring Hannibal to battle: Lazenby (1978) 217. Date of Zama: de Sanctis, 3.2.582–5, 671; Walbank, 2.446; Seibert, *FzH* 316–17.

16 Punic fleet's station: Pol. 15.2.7; cf. Lazenby (1978) 217. Larger Roman war-fleets in Africa for 202: Livy 30.24.6–7, 27.5, 36.2, 41.6–7; Thiel (1946) 176–7 thinks Roman politics the main cause, but Lazenby stresses the military situation. Appian supplies an implausible detailed account of campaigning before Zama (33.141–40.167), which includes Hannibal operating in Numidia (so too Zon. 9.13.10), a siege of Carthage simultaneous with a cavalry battle at Zama, a truce between the generals, etc. Eutropius 3.22 encapsulates the same fictitious tradition (cf. note 10). Masinissa's arrival: Pol. 15.5.11 is preferable to Livy 30.29.4; cf. Lazenby, 219.

17 Cf. Huss (1985) 415 (Hannibal delayed battle to build and train his forces).

18 Site of Zama: Seibert, *FzH* 311–14, discussing the possibilities, with bibliography. Spies and interview: Pol. 15.5.4–9.1; Livy 30.29.2–31.10. Doubted for instance by Groag (1929) 99 note 2; Hampl (1983–4) 17–22; Seibert, *FzH* 315, and *Hann.* 465–6 ('Legenden'); de Sanctis, 3.2.578, rejects only the spies. Xerxes had done the same with Greek spies (Herodotus 7.147–8) but this is scarcely ground for disbelieving Polybius. Masinissa's arrival (note 16) and Scipio's stratagem: thus Lazenby (1978) 219.

19 Hannibal intended cavalry-sacrifice at Zama: Scullard (1970) 150; Connolly (1981) 204; Seibert, *Hann.* 467, 469 note 35; Lancel, *Hann.* 280; Santosuosso (1997) 195; but Walbank, 2.468–9, and Lazenby (1978) 223, have doubts, and Goldsworthy (2000) 304–5 disbelieves. Meeting with Scipio: Hampl (1983–4) 21–2 note 17 sceptically points to other anciently noted confrontations, like

Lycurgus' with Thales and Polycrates' with King Amasis of Egypt. But these are not meetings between two opposing leaders—and Alexander the Great, for instance, does not interview his foe Darius in any tradition, while his famous meeting with King Porus happened *after* Porus' defeat (Plutarch, *Alexander* 60; N. G. L. Hammond, *A History of Greece to 323 BC* (Cambridge 1959) 631).

20 Scipio's demand, Pol. 15.8.14 (Loeb tr.); cf. Walbank, 2.453.

21 Zama is much discussed: e.g. de Sanctis, 3.2.536–9, 572–98; Liddell Hart (1926) chapter XI; Walbank, 2.445–64; Scullard (1970) chapter VI; Lazenby (1978) 220–6; Seibert, *FzH* 308–17 (with extensive bibliography), *Hann.* 466–71; Lancel, *Hann.* 276–83; R. J. A. Wilson, *OCD*³ 1,633, and J. Lazenby, *OCD*³ 1,633–4; Santosuosso (1997) 194–7; Goldsworthy (2000) 300–7. Single combat between Hannibal and Scipio: Appian, *Lib.* 45.188–9. Hannibal gathered 6,500 foot and horse after Zama, just possibly a genuine detail (Appian, 55.241, shakily supported by Nepos, *Hann.* 6.4), but urged peace (Appian, *ibid.*). Silenced a diehard senator: Pol. 15.19.2; Livy 30.37.7–8 (more dramatically placing it in the citizen-assembly). Suicide of Hasdrubal son of Gisco: chapter XIII note 16.

22 Not so in Huss' view: 'Die barqidische "Partei" verlor keineswegs ihren Einfluss—im Gegenteil!' ((1985) 426). But his only argument for this is that Hannibal later won the sufeteship; on this see chapter XV.

XV POSTWAR ECLIPSE

1 Punic envoys: note 8 below. Peace terms of 201: Schmitt, *SVA* 3.296–308; Scardigli (1991) chapter VIII; see also de Sanctis, 3.2.599–605; Walbank, 2.465–71; Lazenby (1978) 227–30; Eckstein (1987) 255–67; Seibert, *Hann.* 473–5; Lancel, *Hann.* 284–6. Polybius supplies most of the terms (15.18) but Appian (*Lib.* 54.234–8)—despite some improbable extra items, like a clause demanding Mago's recall from Italy (plainly a carryover from his version of the terms in 203)—can be believed on the ban against mercenary-levying (also in Dio, frg. 57.82). Masinissa clause not intended to undermine Carthage: Eckstein, 259–60, plausibly. Scipio's concern: in 201 one consul, Cn. Cornelius Lentulus—the third consul in as many years—strove to take over the command in Africa (Broughton, *MRR* 1.319; cf. chapter XIV note 2).

2 Appian on Zama-aftermath: *Lib.* 55.239–56.244; cf. Gsell, *HAAN* 2.271–3. Fleet burned: Livy 30.43.11.

3 Scipio's demarcation of Punic boundaries, Livy 34.62.8–11. 'Phoenician Trenches': Appian, *Lib.* 54.236 (cf. 32.135); Eumachus, *FGrH* 178 F2, from a *periegesis*; Gsell, *HAAN* 2.101–3, 3.290; Scardigli (1991) 340 note 324; Lancel (1992) 283–4; cf. map in *CAH*¹ 8 (1930) facing p. 99, or Picard and Picard, *LDC* 179. Walsh (1965) 156 disbelieves them. *Fossa regia*: Pliny, *NH* 5.25; *ILS* 5,955 (of Vespasian's time). Younger Scipio's delimitation: Pliny, *ibid.*; Gsell, 3.326–7, 404; Lancel (1992) 283–4, *Hann.* 286.

4 Down-payment and indemnity after First Punic War: chapter I §v. Hannibal's reproof to the Carthaginians (abbreviated tr.), Livy 30.44.4–11; 'first' indemnity-payment, 32.2.1. One might try attaching the anecdote instead to the payment of compensation for Scipio's seized supply-ships—the Romans calculated this at 25,000 pounds of silver, more than 300 talents—which had to be paid at once (Livy 30.37.6, 38.1–2; de Sanctis, 3.2.600); but this would be a guess and would not cancel the other objections.

5 Nepos, *Hann.* 6.4–7.4; believed by Lenschau, *RE* 7.2,348; Groag (1929) 114 (Hannibal continues as *strategos* of Libya for some years—even though Nepos 7.1 explicitly dates his recall to 200); Hallward (1930) 468; Picard (1967) 213–14;

Kotula (1983–4) 89; Seibert, *Hann.* 497–8; Goldsworthy (2000) 326. In contrast Lancel, *Hann.* 289, is sceptical. More boldly but unpersuasively, Cresci Marrone (1978) interprets Nepos 7.4 as meaning that Hannibal became sufete in 199 and held a lesser office in 197. Olive-trees planted over 'Africae pleraque': Aurelius Victor, *Caesares* 37.2–3. Roman embassy in 200 and Hamilcar the renegade: Livy 31.11.4–12, 19.1–6; on his later fate, Lenschau, *RE* 7.2,308–9; Briscoe (1973) 82–3, 115. Seibert (*Hann.* 497) prefers Nepos (7.2) for a Punic embassy to Rome instead. Punic hostages freed without ransom: Livy 30.43.5–8.

6 Victor a North African: *Caesares* 20.6, cf. 40.19. Garrison in Utica: to be inferred from Scipio's lengthy and unsuccessful siege (Lazenby (1978) 206–9). Note Appian giving Hannibal 6,500 troops in the aftermath of Zama (chapter XIV note 21); he also has a plausible garrison at Hadrumetum (47.206) and earlier (30.128) tells of Scipio making an attempt on Hippou Acra after his victories in 203, again unsuccessfully which would imply another strong garrison—as is likely, even though trusting Appian's unsupported word on these African operations is unsafe (Gsell, *HAAN* 3.235–6; chapter XIV notes 11 and 16). Libyans inclined to rebellion by 203: chapter XIV note 1.

7 Nepos, *Hann.* 7.4, 'praetor factus est, postquam rex fuerat, anno secundo et vicesimo'. Properly 'in the twenty-second year' means after twenty-one years and this would point to the year 200 (cf. Picard (1963) 276), but Nepos has just (7.2) had Hannibal continue in army command until 199. Nepos' notion that he moved straight from army command to 'praetura' (cf. note 5) is as fuzzy—and unreliable—as his contradictions in applying these Latin terms to Punic offices: having Hannibal become 'praetor' with the explanation that, like the consuls at Rome, so too at Carthage two 'reges' (tautologically, 'quotannis annui bini reges') were elected yearly; then terming Hannibal's year of office 'praeturam' (7.6). Picard's efforts to excuse these oddities do not convince (274–8)—for instance declaring the statement about 'reges' a gloss by Nepos' late Roman editor Aemilius Probus.

8 Dio, frg. 57.86 = Zon. 9.14.13; rejected by (e.g.) Gsell, *HAAN* 2.273; Groag (1929) 111. Envoys at Tunes, Livy 30.6.9; those to Rome, 30.42.11 ('longe primi civitatis'); Hasdrubal's speech to Senate, 42.14–19; he blames 'paucorum cupiditatem', 42.13; that this blaming occurs separately—*not* in the speech—perhaps supports its genuineness. Appian's speech for The Kid at Tunes, *Lib.* 50.215–52.228; silence too on Hannibal in Livy's and Appian's versions of Scipio's reply (30.37.1–6; *Lib.* 53.230–54.238).

9 Hanno the Great: an envoy to Scipio at Tunes according to Appian (49.213), but if still alive in 202—doubted by Lenschau, *RE* 7.2,357; de Sanctis, 3.2.541 note 174—he would be near 80 and cannot have survived much longer (despite Appian, *Lib.* 68.304: cf. chapter XVI note 19).

10 Competences of the One Hundred and Four: chapter I §III. 'Everyone's possessions', etc., Livy 33.46.2; on his source for Hannibal's sufeteship see chapter XVI note 1. *Ordo iudicum* = the One Hundred and Four: Groag (1929) 116–18, 127; Hallward (1930) 468–9; M. P. Charlesworth, *CAH¹* 8.486; Hoffmann (1962) 112, 115; Warmington (1964) 148, 240; de Sanctis, 3.1.54; Picard (1967) 216–18; Görlitz (1970) 153, 155; Briscoe (1973) 336; Bacigalupo Pareo (1977) 71–7; Huss (1985) 427, 464; Scullard (1989a) 491; Lancel (1992) 422; Seibert, *Hann.* 501–2. Contrast Sznycer (1978) 580, 584 (implicitly rejects); Gsell, *HAAN* 2.207–8 (doubtful). Hasdrubal's possible measures on the Hundred and Four: chapter VI §III. 'Barcina factio' still in 193: Livy 34.61.11 (Hannibal's expectations, 60.5). Proliferation of abuses by 195: 33.46.8–47.2.

11 Critics harassed: Livy 33.46.2, 'nec accusator apud infensos iudices deerat'. Aristotle on plurality of offices: *Pol.* 2.11.8, 1273b; above, chapter II §IV.

12 Flawed indemnity payment (Livy 32.2.1–2) due to Punic state's impoverishment: Gsell, *HAAN* 2.323; Seibert, *Hann.* 497–8. Due to corrupt dealings: Hallward (1930) 467; Warmington (1964) 240. Silver coinage debased during war: Howgego (1995) 114. It is possible that the Carthaginians had to produce special pure issues for the indemnity (cf. Gellius 7.5.1) and that of 199 was found defective—which would point to chicanery all the more.

13 Gifts of grain: Livy 31.19.2; 36.4.5 (in 191); 43.6.11–14 (170). On cereal output cf. Tlatli (1978) 124–5 (estimating 1.5 million quintals in Punic times, i.e. about 20 million *modii*); R. M. Haywood, *An Economic Survey of Ancient Rome*, 4 (Baltimore 1938) 43–4 (estimating 160 million *modii* for Tunisia and Algeria by AD 14). Economic recovery: Lancel (1992) 423–5, *Hann.* 292–7. The notion that Spain was now lost as a market (Kotula (1983–4) 89) confuses economics with politics.

14 Loss of state revenues: Livy 33.46.8–9. Hannibal's reforms: Livy 33.47.1–2. Raids on North Africa during war: chapter XII §I. Scipio's armistice-promise to stop ravaging 'eo die', Livy 30.37.2. It is unfoundedly optimistic to claim that the Romans left the countryside 'ungeschmälert' (Lenschau, *RE* 10 (1919) 2233), or with Lancel (1992) 292 to limit the destruction, for reasons unclear, to the territory around Utica and the Bagradas valley. Aristotle and Polybius on money at Carthage: *Pol.* 2.11.8–12, 1273a (cf. 6.5.9, 1320b, on usefulness of bribery); Pol. 6.56.1–4; Gsell, *HAAN* 2.235–6; Walbank, 1.741.

15 Hannibal's fondness for money: chapter VII note 1. Postwar supporters: Görlitz (1970) 151 assumes that most of his war-comrades had passed away.

16 General tax levy proposed for 196: Livy 33.46.9. Hamilcar the renegade: note 5 above.

17 Hannibal's popularity in office: Livy 33.46.7, cf. 48.9–11. 'Democratic' or 'popular' terminology: available to Appian for a report of politics at Carthage in the 150s (*Lib.* 68.304–5) but not used by Livy for the 190s though he stresses Hannibal's popularity (cf. chapter XVI). Mago *frater* joining Hannibal in exile: Nepos, *Hann.* 8.2; chapter XIV note 10. Mago the Samnite and Mago the relative: chapters IV note 5, VII note 2; on the former cf. H. Volkmann, *Kl P* 3.889. Interestingly among the leaders of the 'democratic' party 40-odd years later was one Hamilcar 'the Samnite' (Appian, 68.305)—a descendant with inherited political ties as well as nickname? (cf. Walbank, 1.110, 2.153–4). Kotula (1983–4) 92–7 denies any democratic tendency in Hannibal's sufeteship; similarly Seibert, *Hann.* 501–2.

18 Accusations by enemies: Livy reports them only in 195 and as following his actions as sufete (33.45.6–8, cf. 47.3); cf. Justin 31.1.7–9. Mommsen, *HR* 2.202, Picard and Picard, *LDC* 274, 277, and Seibert, *Hann.* 499, think them plausible. Hannibal's journeys to Syria and then Ephesus: Livy 33.49.5–7. Antiochus' dealings with the Romans and uninterest in fighting them: Hoffmann (1957/1974) 64; R. M. Errington, *CAH²* 8.270–82; Ma (1999) 94–102. Hannibal advises him on war: Livy 34.60, 35.19.

19 Carthage's foremost citizen: Livy 33.48.10 'principem civitatis'. Links with Tyre, 33.48.3, 34.61.2–3; levees, 33.48.9; dinner-parties and the like, cf. 34.61.5.

XVI HANNIBAL SUFETE

1 Polybius as Livy's likely source for events at Carthage: Briscoe (1973) 335–6. Silenus and Sosylus 'cum eo in castris fuerunt simulque vixerunt, quamdiu fortuna passa est' (Nepos, *Hann.* 13.3; Brizzi's fancies of a Sosylus increasingly disillusioned by his hero's unsentimental behaviour are unconvincing (1984) 7–29,

117–18). Nepos mentions them only as sources for the Second Punic War, but one or both might have taken the story down to 195 or even to his death, even if separated from him, despite Zecchini's suggestion that Sosylus published his work around 197 ((1997) 1,065–6). Failing them, other possibilities would be Chaereas, Eumachus and Xenophon (on these, Hoyos (1998) 233–4, 281; (2001a) 77). Terentius Culleo: Livy 33.47.7; devotion to Scipio, 30.43.11, 45.5 (cf. Plutarch, *Moralia* 196D); still active in 171, Livy 42.35.7; cf. Scullard, *RP* 114, 141, 284. Polybius in Italy: Walbank (1972) 6–13, 166–70.

2　Date of sufeteship: M. Claudius Marcellus, one of the ensuing Roman envoys (Livy 33.47.7), was almost certainly the consul of 196 (Broughton, *MRR* 3.341, 342 n.3) and so could not become an envoy until 195 at earliest. Nepos dates the exile to 'anno post praeturam, M. Claudio L. Furio consulibus' (*Hann.* 7.6), i.e. 196, yet terms 193 the 'anno tertio' after it (8.1), not 'quarto' as in normal inclusive reckoning; on his chronology for these years cf. chapter XV note 7. Appian's date of 196: *Syr.* 4.14–1, believed by de Sanctis 4.1.112 note 3. See also Gsell, *HAAN* 2. 275 note 1; Groag (1929) 114 note 4; Scullard, *RP* 284 (sound arguments for 196); Briscoe (1973) 335; Seibert, *Hann.* 499 note 17; Ma (1999) 93.

3　That the clash was over the state finances is generally assumed: e.g. Groag (1929) 119; Hallward (1930) 468; Hoffmann (1962) 115; Picard (1967) 217; Seibert, *Hann.* 500–1; Lancel, *Hann.* 291. Finance reform a separate item: Livy introduces it with 'adiecit et aliud', 33.46.8. On the 'quaestor' in 196 see Appendix §14.

4　Hannibal overstepped powers: Groag (1929) 119 note 1; Picard (1967) 216–18; Picard and Picard, *LDC* 275; Lancel (1992) 421–2; cf. Gsell, *HAAN* 2.276. Against this view: Seibert, *Hann.* 501 note 23. Speed of events: Livy 33.46.5–7 (note 'legem *extemplo* promulgavit pertulitque'); thus Groag's more complicated interpretation does not persuade. On the Roman *contio*, cf. A. H. J. Greenidge, *Roman Public Life* (London 1901) 158–60; A. W. Lintott, *OCD*[3] 385. Livy's source if Greek would not have used the Roman term, but quite possibly reported the legislative meeting as coming afterwards.

5　Tribunal's functions had changed: chapter VI §III, with note 8. Sufetes by 193 were hearing cases: chapter VI note 8.

6　The Hundred and Four to be popularly elected: Livy uses the verb 'legerentur' ('were to be chosen') which does not expressly confirm this, and Seibert accepts no changes save to the judges' term of office (*Hann.* 501–2, 'Hannibal hatte . . . keine Kompetenzen entzogen, ebensowenig den Personenkreis, der für die Einhundertvier gewählt werden konnte, erweitert'). But politically that would have been suicide. The 'electing' verb *creare* was used only for magistrates while *legere* was the proper Latin verb for appointing judges (e.g. *Lex Acilia* of 123 (*Corpus Inscriptionum Latinarum* 1[2].583) lines 12, 14, etc.; Cicero, *Pro Milone* 21), though at Rome the appointing was done by the relevant magistrate. Hannibal's reform of only limited impact: Kotula (1983–4) 91–7; Seibert, *ibid.* On the other hand Groag (1929) 121 has no warrant for supposing that the reform was applied also to the inner 'sacred' council of Carthage (on which see chapter II §IV).

7　Groag (1929) 121, 126, too optimistically supposes that *all* of the 104, not to mention both new sufetes and most of the senate, were Barcid supporters in 195 thanks to the reform; similarly Hoffmann (1962) 115.

8　Livy 33.46.8–47.1; Nepos, *Hann.* 7.5 'novis vectigalibus', garnering enough money not only to pay the indemnity but also 'ut . . . superesset quae in aerario reponeretur'. Groag (1929) 121–2 has the new taxes affect only 'die besitzende Klasse' at Carthage. Seibert, *Hann.* 502, 543, considers Hannibal's finance measures just as limited as the judicial—yet also (541) judges him to have tackled abuses in both areas 'gründlich und mit dauerhaftem Erfolg'.

9 On Carthaginian state revenues see chapter II §III. 'Outstanding funds', etc.: Livy 33.47.1–2 'omnibus residuis pecuniis exactis, tributo privatis remisso'; E. Sage's Loeb translation of *residuis pecuniis* as 'the revenues not otherwise used' scarcely suits the context. All embezzled funds to be repaid: thus Gsell, *HAAN* 2.275–6; Picard (1967) 218 'une véritable révolution sociale', and (1968) 276; Lancel, *Hann.* 291–2.

10 'Vectigalia publica partim neglegentia dilabebantur, partim praedae ac divisui et principum quibusdam et magistratibus erant', Livy 33.46.8.

11 'Kept his promise' ('praestitit promissum'), 33.47.2. Carthaginian offers in 191, Livy 36.4.7–9 (the manuscript numerals for the wheat and barley are corrupt). Nepos: note 8 above. Shipbuilding skills: Scullard (1989a) 496–7; Lancel (1992) 137–51. On the ports see chapter II §II and note 5.

12 Byrsa development: Lancel *et al.* (1980); Picard and Picard (1983) 56–8; Rakob (1992) 33–5; and especially Lancel (1992) 172–92, 423, and *Hann.* 296–7 (backing 'l'hypothèse qu'Hannibal, au cours de son suffétat, en ait été le concepteur et qu'il ait posé la première pierre'). Mago's town in Minorca: Mela 2.124, 'castellum'; Pliny, *NH* 3.77, a *civitas*; *ILS* 6958, 'r(es) p(ublica) Mag(onensium)'; Huss (1985) 400 note 242. Early second-century shoreline mansions: Picard and Picard (1983) 56; Lancel (1992) 171–2 and Fig. 76.

13 Groag (1929) 125–6 implausibly supposes a senate in 195 entirely pro-Barcid, cf. note 7 above; contrast Seibert, *Hann.* 505. Servilius: the consul of 203 (P. Willems, *Le Sénat de la République romaine* (Louvain 1878–85, repr. Darmstadt 1968) 1.311, 2.498; Broughton, *MRR* 1.341, 342 note 3), not politically friendly with Scipio (F. Càssola, *I gruppi politici Romani nel III secolo a.C.* (Trieste 1962, repr. Rome 1968) 415–16; Scullard, *RP* 78–83, 277–8). Justin 31.2.1 imagines he was the sole envoy. Punic senate's reply, Livy 33.49.4; Hannibal proscribed, Nepos, *Hann.* 7.7.

14 Aristo episode, Livy 34.61.1–62.1; Appian, *Syr.* 8.30–3; Justin 31.4.1–3; debate, Livy 34.61.12–13; varying attitudes ('principibus . . . senatui, senatu . . . populo suspecto') and Masinissa's moves, 62.1–4.

15 Allegations began after the finance-reforms, Livy 33.45.8 ('recenti facto'); cf. Justin 31.1.7. Scipio 'long' impeded intervention, 33.47.4–5; cf. Val. Max. 4.1.6. Cato's attitude: not recorded but neither are most of his doings as consul (A. Astin, *Cato the Censor* (Oxford 1978) 24). Hannibal fled Carthage in mid-summer (Livy 33.48.5) while Cato left Rome for Spain only then or later—just when is debated (Briscoe (1981) 65–6 puts it later than does Astin, 308–10; cf. Richardson (1986) 80, and Harris, *CAH²* 8.123). Ill-will towards Scipio: Astin, 12–16, 60–2, 70–3; Scullard, *RP* 114 and (1970) 188–9; and Ridley (1987) 159 all go rather too far in seeing the despatch of the embassy as really an attack on Scipio directed by Cato. Hannibal's flight: Livy 33.47.10–48.8; Nepos, *Hann.* 7.6–7; Justin 31.2.2–5 (where 'rus urbanum' probably imagines Hannibal's property as being in the Megara district).

16 Envoys might have demanded handover: so too Mommsen, *HR* 2.202; cf. Groag (1929) 125, who sees Hannibal as patriotically choosing self-exile to save Carthage from domestic strife and Roman attack; echoed by Warmington (1964) 241; Görlitz (1970) 156. Demands for Hannibal's handover: chapter VIII §IV (in 218); Pol. 21.17.7, 43.11 (in 188); Nepos, *Hann.* 12.2; Livy 39.51.1–3; Appian, *Syr.* 11.43; Plutarch, *Flamininus* 20; Pausanias 8.11.11; Justin 32.4.8 (in 183); Walbank, 3.158–9; Seibert, *Hann.* 521, 523 note 9, 527. Accusations by the envoys, Livy 33.49.1–2. Ships sent in pursuit, Nepos 7.7.

17 33.49.3 (E. Sage's Loeb tr.).

18 Penalties: Nepos 7.7. Groag (1929) 126–7 argues that they were not voted until

after the Aristo episode in 193, believing as he does that the senate in 195 was Barcid to a man and that in any case Carthage's leading men would not so abase themselves at a nod from Rome; contrast Seibert, *Hann.* 505 note 44.

19 Factions: Appian, *Lib.* 68.304–5 (οἱ δὲ ἐδημοκράτιζον). Perhaps the Hanno the Great Appian mentions was yet another one (Picard and Picard, *LDC* 286; Huss (1985) 432) but we would need a more reliable source than Appian for us to see that as plausible. People's vote to banish pro-Masinissa leaders, *Lib.* 70.316; cf. statements put forward by citizens ἐς τὸ μέσον, 'in public', pretty clearly indicating at an assembly (94.443, 111.527). Senate directing foreign affairs: *Lib.* 91.429–31 (Punic envoys in 149 report consuls' ultimatum to senate first), 93.439 (senate decrees war; not the tribunal of Hundred and Four, as Goldsworthy (2000) 339 assumes). Hannibal's measures soon repealed: Gsell, *HAAN* 2. 279, and Groag (1929) 127 (tribunal reform); Picard (1967) 221–2 (ditto); Kotula (1983–4) 94 (all).

20 Cf. Caven's comment on the tragedy of 146: 'the Romans could well have afforded to leave her [Carthage] in peace on her peninsula, stripped of her territorial possessions' ((1980) 293, cf. 271–2)—though going on to offer generalized censorious claims about the Carthaginians' moral and cultural unattractiveness (293–4).

21 Masinissa's claim in 174: Livy 41.22.1–3.

XVII THE END OF THE BARCIDS

1 Hobnobbing with Roman envoys: Pol. 3.11.2–3; Livy 35.14.1–4, based on Polybius. A legend makes Scipio Africanus one of the envoys (Briscoe (1981) 165–6; Seibert, *Hann.* 511–12), and his supposed conversation with his old foe (Livy 35.14.5–12; Appian, *Syr.* 9.34–10.42; other sources, Seibert, 511 note 28) may be another, unless Scipio made a separate, but poorly attested, visit to Ephesus that year (cf. Scullard (1970) 198, 285–6 note 163, citing earlier discussions based on *Inscriptiones Graecae* 11.4.712, an inscription at Delphi honouring Scipio, and Zon. 9.18.12–13). Oath story: chapter IV §II.

2 Comment to Antiochus on army, Gellius 5.5 ('satis, plane satis credo esse Romanis, etiamsi avarissimi sunt'); the pun might come from Greek (e.g. ἱκανοὶ εἰσιν Ῥωμαίοις) and so need not automatically be due to a Latin writer, even if Gellius' own source was probably in Latin (*libri veterum memoriarum*, 5.5.1). Phormio story ('multos se deliros senes saepe vidisse, sed qui magis quam Phormio deliraret vidisse neminem'), Cicero, *De Oratore* 2.75–6.

3 Hannibal's proposal in 194–193: Livy 34.60.2–6 ('somewhere in Italy' 60.6, but cf. 36.7.16); Nepos, *Hann.* 8.1; Appian, *Syr.* 7.26–9; Justin 31.3.5–10; cf. Seibert, *Hann.* 508–9. Aristo episode: chapter XVI §IV.

4 Nepos, *Hann.* 8.1–2, a tale believed by Lenschau, *RE* 7.2,348–9, and Seibert, *Hann.* 513–14; disbelief, Kahrstedt (1913) 590; but Hoffmann (1962) 121 is unsure while Picard (1967) 227–8 redates it to 190. More likely a confused blend of the abortive project reported by Livy (35.18.8, 42.2–43.1) and Hannibal's putative Cyrene stopover in 195 *en route* to Tyre (note how the episode ends with a bald 'Hannibal ad Antiochum pervenit'—rather than, say, *rediit*). Livy makes plain that the project envisaged only smaller, undecked ships (35.42.3; on *naves apertae* cf. 32.21.27, 37.22.4, and Cicero, *II Verrines* 5.104; Thiel (1946) 269; McDonald and Walbank (1969)), so Nepos' 'five' may rightly report its intended strength even if he has garbled the rest. See also Appendix §15.

5 Livy 36.7.1–8.1, very probably from Polybius and, as Seibert emphasizes (*Hann.* 508 note 13), not a copy of Hannibal's previous advice; Appian, *Syr.* 13.53–14.58

and Justin 31.5.3–9 supply variously recast versions (cf. Briscoe (1981) 229). Seibert, 515, supposes that Hannibal at Demetrias proposed descending on Etruria, Liguria or Cisalpina, but see note 3. Lancel (1992) 319–20 sees the advice as fiction.

6 Antiochus' expeditionary fleet to Greece, Livy 35.43.3; Seleucid naval strength in 192–189, Thiel (1946) 273–76. Hannibal's invasion schemes: Groag (1929) 135–41 judges them highly practicable; not so Hoffmann (1957/1974) 66–71; Hoyos (1983) 179; Seibert, *Hann.* 508, 516.

7 Battle of Side: Livy 37.23–4; Thiel (1946) 338–45; Seibert, *Hann.* 519–21. Hannibal's last years: Seibert, *Hann.* 522–9, with full references. His travels are not in Livy, Appian or Dio, which indicates that the details in Nepos, *Hann.*, Justin *et al.* come from non-annalistic sources: a continuator of Silenus or Sosylus, or from Coelius? At Gortyn: Nepos, *Hann.* 9.1; Justin 32.4.3–5. Seibert, 522, perhaps rightly thinks the story of the treasure-deception a slander for a genuine offering to Artemis. Artaxata: Plutarch, *Lucullus* 31; Strabo 11.14.6, C528. Poison-snakes battle: Nepos, 10.3–11.7; Justin 32.4.6–7; Frontinus 4.7.10–11; but Seibert, 526, feels 'erhebliche Zweifeln'. Prusa: Pliny, *NH* 5.148. On the various versions of Hannibal's suicide, Seibert, *Hann.* 527–8. Date: Polybius gave it as Olympiad 149, 2, i.e. mid-183 to mid-182 (Nepos, 13.1; Livy 39.52.1; Walbank, 3.235–9; Walsh [1994] 172); Livy opts for 183, the consulate of M. Claudius Marcellus and Q. Fabius Labeo. Since the Roman envoys left Rome in the second half of 183 (Walbank, 3.221–2, 237; despite Seibert, 529), the suicide can be placed in winter 183/182. Hannibal's tomb: Pliny, *NH* 5.148; [Victor], *De Vir. Ill.* 42.6, claiming the simple epitaph 'Here lies Hannibal' still existed in the author's day; Tzetzes, *Chiliades* 1 (cf. chapter V note 15), lines 804–5 on Severus' construction; A. R. Birley, *The African Emperor: Septimius Severus* (London 1988) 148; Seibert, 529.

8 Barcids, and Hannibal especially, as Hellenized and pro-diversity: Kromayer (1909/1974) 269–74; Groag (1929) 141–3 (Hannibal the 'Vorkämpfer der Völkerfreiheit', in effect resisting 'nicht allein den Untergang der hellenischen Freiheit, sondern auch die Vernichtung oder Zersetzung unermeßlicher Menschheitswerte und Kulturgüter'); Picard (1967) 10, 103–14, 231–8 (Barcids were 'les créateurs et les propagateurs d'une forme originelle de la civilisation hellénistique', 231), and (1983–4) 75–81; Brizzi (1983), (1984) 101–18, and cf. 'Hannibal—Punier und Hellenist', *Das Altertum* 37 (1991) 201–10; Barceló (1998) 46–7, envisaging the hero as spokesman (*Sprachrohr*) and defender, à la Picard, of 'phönikisch-hellenische' civilization against Rome (cf. *ibid.*, 14–15). A more nuanced view of the Barcids, as a virtually independent *Potenz* like the Hellenistic despots, allying with other Mediterranean states to defeat the Roman menace, in Hoffmann (1962) 129–35. Cf. the surveys of Christ (1974) 9–13, and Seibert, *FzH* 64–82. Carthaginian borrowings from Greece, chapter II §II; Greeks in Punic service, chapter V §VI. Hannibal's Greek compositions: Nepos, *Hann.* 13.2. Reforms drew on Sosylus' reports of Cleomenes III's policies during the 220s at Sparta: Groag 119 note 4, followed by Picard and Picard, *LDC* 277 and Kotula (1983–4) 100.

9 Against Appian's claim that Hasdrubal went over to Africa in about 214–213, see chapter XI note 10.

10 Scipio's supposed meeting with Hannibal at Ephesus: note 1 above. Cato on Hamilcar, Plutarch, *Cato Maior* 8.14; on the attack against Saguntum, *Origines* frg. 84 Peter; cf. Hoyos (1998) 175, 221.

11 Polybius' views of the Barcids: 1.64.6 (very pro-Hamilcar), 2.13.1 (on his successor Hasdrubal), 2.36.1–2 (Hasdrubal and Hannibal), 3.71.6 (Mago), 11.2 (Hamilcar's son Hasdrubal); on Hannibal's virtues and vices, 9.22, 9.24–6, 11.19,

23.13. Hannibal in the right in 218: 3.30.3–4, cf. 3.15.10–11; Hoyos (1998) 164–5, 278. Acted too soon: 11.19.6–7. Polybius' expected readership: Walbank (1972) 3–5, 27–8. Livy on Hannibal: 21.4.2–10 (portrait), 22.58.1–4, 28.12.1–9 (based on Polybius), 39.51.9–12 (last words). Dio's character-portrayal, frg. 54; Brizzi (1984) 105 is more impressed by it ('il migliore e più attendibile rittrato del Barcide trasmessoci dall'antichità').

12 Against the frequent view of Hanno the Great's group as North African expansionists, Hoyos (1994) 264–6, 278. That the Carthaginians should have limited themselves to North Africa and thus avoided further clashes with the Romans is argued by de Sanctis, 3.1.390–3.

XVIII SOURCES

1 Aristotle, *Politics* 2.11.1–9, 1272b–1273b; 4.7.11, 1293b; cf. chapter II §IV.

2 Philinus is studied, with all the rigours of firm *Quellenkritik*, by V. La Bua, *Filino–Polibio Diodoro–Sileno* (Palermo 1966) who sees him as a better historian than Polybius and, just as unconvincingly, thinks he narrated the Mercenaries' War too; cf. E. Badian's review, *Rivista di Filologia e Istruzione Classica* 96 (1968) 203–11. On Fabius Pictor's contemporary narrative: M. Gelzer, *Kleine Schriften* (Wiesbaden 1964) 3.51–92; B. W. Frier, *Libri Annales Pontificum Maximorum: The Origins of the Annalistic Tradition* (Rome 1979) 225–84, arguing for the early close; against this, Hoyos (2001a) 77–9. Philinus on the background and outbreak of the First Punic War: B. D. Hoyos, *Classical Quarterly* 35 (1985) 92–109, and (1998) 7–11, 82–104. Fabius on Hasdrubal and Hannibal: chapter VI §III. Both writers' honest intent: Pol. 1.14.2. On *P. Rylands* 3.491: chapter XIV note 5.

3 Hannibal's inscription: chapter XIII note 11; 'aram . . . cum ingenti rerum a se gestarum titulo' (Livy 28.46.16). Polybius and its statistics: chapter VIII §IV. Treaty with Philip V: Pol. 7.9; chapter X §III. On a fictitious letter supposedly from Hannibal to the Athenians (*P. Hamburg.* 129): Seibert, *FzH* 5–6; Brizzi (1984) 85–102.

4 Silenus and Sosylus: chapter V note 16, chapter XVI note 1. Sosylus' fragment: *FGrH* 176 F1; cf. Walbank, 1.430–1; Seibert, *FzH* 12; Zecchini (1997), who is enthusiastic but unconvincing. Hannibal's dream: chapter VIII §V. Polybius on Sosylus, 3.20.5; on Hannibal's supposed divine guides, 3.47.6–9. Silenus on booty from New Carthage: Livy 26.49.3, contrasting his figures for captured siege-engines with the wildly inflated ones of Livy's near-contemporary Valerius Antias.

5 Chaereas, Eumachus, Xenophon: *FGrH* nos. 177–9; cf. K. Meister, *Historische Kritik bei Polybios* (Wiesbaden 1975) 167–72; Seibert, *FzH* 13; Hoyos (2001a) 77. Cincius Alimentus: Livy 21.38.3–5; Appendix §8. Cato: Badian (1966) 6–11; B. D. Hoyos, *Ancient History Bulletin* 1 (1987) 112–21, and 4 (1990) 31–6; Maharbal's remark: chapter IX §IV, with note 3.

6 Coelius: Badian (1966) 15–17; W. Hermann, *Die Historien des Coelius Antipater: Fragmente und Kommentar* (Meisenham/Glan 1979). Scipio's storm, chapter XIV note 7.

7 Claudius and Valerius: Badian (1966) 18–22 ; Luce (1977) 139–84 (mostly on Livy's use of them and others in Books 31–45). A Clodius Licinus, cited once (Livy 29.22.10), may have been the consul of AD 4 who was a historian (Suetonius, *De Grammaticis* 20, and perhaps also Plutarch, *Numa* 1); thus Kukofka (1990) 142 note 61. But Livy wrote Books 21–30 probably around 20 BC (cf. Luce, 5 note 5), which would put this Clodius' historical opus many decades before his consulate—not an unthinkable span, but difficult. More likely Livy's Clodius was

the historian whom Cicero names as one of Coelius' inferior successors (*De Legibus* 1.2.6; so too Badian, 17, 20).

8 On Polybius see F. W. Walbank's study (1972) and of course his *Commentary*; also A. E. Astin, in *CAH²* 8.3–8. On *symploke:* Vollmer (1990).

9 Polybius at Carthage, 38.19, 21–2. 'How, and through what type of political system', 1.1.5. Later decision to extend the *History:* 3.4–5.

10 Zama: Pol. 15.9–19; Livy 30.33–7; Walbank, 2.453–71; H. E. Butler and H. H. Scullard, *Livy, Book XXX* (6th edn, London, 1954) 122–9. Lengthy listing of Second Punic War Livian variants from Polybius in Kukofka (1990) 165–7, who in impeccable *quellenkritisch* style ascribes all variants not to Livy but to a writer between Polybius and Livy, like Coelius Antipater. On Livy's use of Polybius: P. G. Walsh, *Livy: His Historical Aims and Methods* (Cambridge 1963), esp. 142–63; Luce (1977); Tränkle (1977).

11 Mercenaries' War an awful warning: Pol. 1.65.2–7, 67.4–6, 81.5–11. Relevant to Hannibal's war: 67.8–9 (not that Polybius clearly explains how). Gisco in 203: Pol. 15.19.2; Livy 30.37.7–8. Sufete (βασιλεύς) in 218: Pol. 3.33.3; on Picard's unconvincing notion that this was Bomilcar, brother-in-law of Hannibal, cf. chapter IV note 5. Democratic leanings at Carthage by 218: Pol. 6.51.6; cf. chapter VI §III.

12 Sardinia: chapter IV §I; Hoyos (1998) 132–43. Carthaginians in the right in 218: Pol. 3.30.3–4; see chapter VII §IV. A Roman city-sack: 10.15.4–16.9 (New Carthage in 209); not totally representative of all sackings, cf. A. Ziolkowski, '*Urbs direpta*, or how the Romans sacked cities', in J. Rich and G. Shipley (eds.), *War and Society in the Roman World* (London 1993) 69–91. On Polybius' life and activities, Walbank (1972) is an outstanding guide; for Polybius' improvements to fire-signalling see Pol. 10.43–7; interview with Masinissa, 9.25.4–6; with eyewitnesses of Hannibal's passage of the Alps, 3.48.12.

13 On Diodorus generally: K. S. Sacks, *Diodorus Siculus and the First Century* (Princeton 1990). La Bua (1966) and Loreto (1995) analyse his sources for Books 22–5 with rigid *Quellenkritik;* cf. note 1 above and, on Loreto, Hoyos (1999). Diodorus on 264: Hoyos (1998) 82–6, cf. 85 note 6.

14 On Livy generally see Walsh (note 10 above); Luce (1977); J. D. Chaplin, *Livy's Exemplary History* (Oxford 2000). V. M. Warrior sees greater coherence and accuracy, at least in a later book, than usually credited to him: *The Initiation of the Second Macedonian War: An Explication of Livy Book 31* (Stuttgart 1996), especially 23–35, 52–73, 91–3.

15 On *Hannibalica:* Leidl (1993) 428–62, arguing (446–59) that Appian uses a pre-Livian source who, he thinks, is Coelius. Appian on the 'Ebro': *Iber.* 6.24; chapter VI §VI. Events in Africa from 204: e.g. the gory capture of 'Locha' (*Lib.* 15.62–3; Livy (29.35.4) has a town Salaeca taken without incident); Syphax's machinations before Scipio's attack on the enemy camps (*Lib.* 17.68–18.74) and his rôle, after capture, in the story of Sophoniba (27.113–16); and most notably Hannibal's supposed activities, including a truce with Scipio, before Zama (36.151–39.161). Appian incidentally sites this battle near a town 'Cilla' and knows nothing of names like Naraggara or Zama (40.165): cf. Walbank, 2.449; Seibert, *FzH* 310–11. Cannae: Appian, *Hann.* 19.83–26.114. On the Iber-accord and Appian's version of it, which incidentally dates it to Hamilcar's time (*Hann.* 2.6): Hoyos (1998) 158, 160, 167–71, 292–3. Appian and the elder Scipios in Spain: Hoyos (2001b) 70–1, 78–89, 84–5, 88. Younger Scipio's operations in 208–206: *Iber.* 24.93–36.146. Scipio versus Hannibal at Zama, *Lib.* 45.188–9. Unsatisfied with this touch of epic, Appian follows up with a Masinissa–Hannibal clash during the pursuit (46.195–7).

16 Italian traders and other items in 241–237: chapters III §III, IV §I. Hannibal's oath: chapter IV note 7; army-strength, chapter VIII note 15. Trasimene: Appian, *Hann.* 10.39–43. Italian troops massacred: chapter XIV §IV.

17 *Iber.* 9.33–5, *Hann.* 3.9–10 (Hannibal causes war); *Hann.* 5.17, 14.60 (kills prisoners), 31.132 (burns alive traitor's family at Arpi), 43.183 (Lucanian mistress). On Hannibal's plus side: *Hann.* 10.43 (mild to Italian prisoners), 26.111 (brilliance of Cannae), 35.152 (honours to Gracchus), 50.216–17 (to Marcellus); *Lib.* 37.155–38.158 (his foiled peace-effort), 55.241 (peace counsel after Zama). Leidl fails to persuade that this portrayal is largely hostile (1993) 441–2.

18 Coelius the basic source: Schwarte (1983) 26–7, 31–6; Leidl (1993) 456–9.

19 Nepos on Hannibal's later life: *Hann.* 7–13; years of exile, 8–12. On 216 to 203: *Hann.* 5; much of it in fact concerns 217 (5.1–3). A verdict of 'solid and reliable' on Nepos' Hannibalic chronology is too kind (J. Geiger, *Cornelius Nepos and Ancient Political Biography* (Stuttgart 1985) 110–11). Hannibal's postwar position, *Hann.* 7.1–4; see chapter XV §II.

20 Dio's Roman envoys in 219, Zon. 8.21; Hannibal after Trasimene, 8.25; treaty with Philip V, 9.4; Metaurus campaign, 9.9. Romans initially reject peace terms in 203: Dio, frg. 57.74 = Zon. 9.13; cf. chapter XIV §III.

21 Scipio's true parentage: Silius 13.615–20. On Silius cf. C. Reitz in *Der Neue Pauly* 11 (2001) 557–9; D. W. T. C Vessey in *The Cambridge History of Classical Literature* (Cambridge 1982) 2.590–6. Silius used against Polybius and Livy: Schwarte (1983), especially 1–36. Against this: B. D. Hoyos, 'Polybius mendax?', *Liverpool Classical Monthly* 10 (1985) 135–9, 153–6; cf. Hoyos (1998) 226–32.

22 Eutropius 2.18–3.23 (Punic Wars period); also 4.5 (Hannibal's suicide). Justin on the Barcids: notably 44.5.4–7 (in Spain), 29.1.7 (Hannibal's *odium Romanorum*), 31.1.7–2.8 (his exile), 31.3.5–6.3 (dealings with Antiochus; the lengthiest episode), 32.2–12 (last years and laudatory obituary).

23 On Valerius Maximus, Frontinus, Florus, Polyaenus and Orosius see, conveniently, *OCD*³. Oros. 4.7–19 reports the Punic wars to 201. *De Viris Illustribus:* the manuscripts claim Pliny the Younger as author while in early modern times the fourth-century epitomizing historian Aurelius Victor was suggested; the real author remains unknown (F. Pichlmayr in his Teubner edition of Victor and *De Vir. Ill.* (1911; revised by R. Gruendel, 1970) x–xi).

BIBLIOGRAPHY

Abbreviations

AS	Kromayer and Veith, *Antike Schlachtfelder*
AHB	*Ancient History Bulletin*
AJP	*American Journal of Philology*
Appian, *Hann.*	Appian, *Hannibalica*
Appian, *Iber.*	Appian, *Iberica*
Appian, *Lib.*	Appian, *Libyca*
Appian, *Sic.*	Sic
Appian, *Syr.*	Appian, *Syriaca*
Broughton, *MRR*	Broughton, *The Magistrates of the Roman Republic*
CAH[1], *CAH*[2]	*Cambridge Ancient History*, 1st and 2nd edns
Cassiod.	Cassiodorus
CP	*Classical Philology*
Degrassi, *ILLRP*	Degrassi, *Inscriptiones Latinae Liberae Rei Publicae*
Diod.	Diodorus
Eutrop.	Eutropius
frg.	fragment
FGrH	Jacoby, *Die Fragmente der griechischer Historiker*
Gsell, *HAAN*	Gsell, *Histoire ancienne de l'Afrique du Nord*
HZ	*Historische Zeitschrift*
ILS	*Inscriptiones Latinae Selectae*, ed. H. Dessau (Berlin 1892–1916)
Itin. Ant.	*Itinerarium Antonini*
Itin. Rav.	*Itinerarium Ravennatis*
Kl P	*Der Kleine Pauly*
Livy, *Epit.*	Livy, *Epitome*
LSJ	Liddell, Scott and Jones, *Greek Lexicon*, 6th edn (Oxford 1968)
NF	Neue Folge [New Series]
OCD[3]	*Oxford Classical Dictionary*, 3rd edn
Oros.	Orosius

Picard and Picard, *LDC*	Picard and Picard, *The Life and Death of Carthage*
Pliny, *NH*	Pliny, *Naturalis Historia*
Pol.	Polybius
RE & Supplbd.	*Paulys Realencyclopädie der Altertumswissenschaft*, and supplements
RÉL	*Revue des Études Latines*
RhM	*Rheinisches Museum für Philologie*
RSA	*Rivista di Storia Antica*
Schmitt, *SVA*	Schmitt, *Die Staatsverträge des Altertums*, vol. 3
Schulten, *FHA*	Schulten, *Fontes Hispaniae Antiquae*
SEG	*Sylloge Epigraphica Graeca*
Seibert, *FzH*	Seibert, *Forschungen zu Hannibal*
Seibert, *Hann.*	Seibert, *Hannibal*
St. Byz.	Stephanus of Byzantium
Val. Max.	Valerius Maximus
Zon.	Zonaras

Works cited

Ancient

Appian, *Hannibalica, Iberica, Libyca*, Sic, *Syriaca*

Aristotle, *Politics*

Aurelius Victor, *Caesares*

Cassiodorus, *Chronica*

Cato, *Origines*: in H. Peter (ed.), *Historicorum Romanorum Reliquiae* (2 vols: Leipzig 1906–14)

Cicero (various works)

Dio (L. Cassius Dio), *Historia Romana*

Diodorus, *Bibliotheca Historica*

Ennius, *Annales*, ed. O. Skutsch (Oxford 1985)

Eutropius, *Compendium Historiae Romanae*

Florus, *Epitome*

Frontinus, *Strategemata*

Gellius, *Noctes Atticae*

Itinerarium Antonini

Itinerarium Ravennatis

Justin, *Trogi Pompei Historiarum Philippicarum Epitome*

Livy, *Ab Urbe Condita* [cited as Livy]

Livy, *Epitome* [cited as Livy, *Epit.*]

Mela, *De Chorographia*

Nepos, *Hamilcar*

Nepos, *Hannibal*

Orosius, *Historia adversus Paganos*

Pausanias, *Periegesis tes Hellados* [*A Tour of Greece*]
Pliny the Elder, *Naturalis Historia*
Plutarch (various works)
Polyaenus, *Strategemata*
Polybius, *Historiae*
Pseudo-Scylax, *Periplus*
Ptolemy, *Geographia*
Silius Italicus, *Punica*
Stephanus of Byzantium
Strabo, *Geographia*
Valerius Maximus, *Facta et Dicta Memorabilia*
[Victor], *de Viris Illustribus*
Zonaras, *Historiae*

Modern

Works cited only once in the text are not as a rule included.

Acquaro, E. (1974), 'Il tipo del toro nelle monete puniche di Sardegna e la politica barcide in occidente', *Rivista di Studi Fenici* 2, 105–7
—— (1983–4), 'Su i "rittrati barcidi" delle monete puniche', in *Studi Annibalici: RSA* 13–14, 83–6
Alföldy, G. (1987), *Römisches Städtewesen auf der neukastilischen Hochebene: Ein Testfall für die Romanisierung* (Heidelberg: Abhandlungen der Heidelberger Akademie der Wissenschaften, Philosophisch-historische Klasse, Jg. 1987, Abh. 3)
Ameling, W. (1993), *Karthago: Studien zu Militär, Staat und Gesellschaft* (Munich)
Bacigalupo Pareo, Enrica (1977), 'I supremi magistrati di Cartagine', in *Contributi di Storia Antica in Onore di Albino Garzetti* (Genoa) 61–87
Badian, E. (1966), in T. A. Dorey (ed.), *Latin Historians* (London) 1–38
Baker, G. P. (1929), *Hannibal* (New York)
Barceló, P. (1988), *Karthago und die Iberische Halbinsel vor den Barkiden: Studien zur Karthagischen Präsenz im Mittelmeerraum von der Gründung von Ebusus (VII. Jhr. v. Chr.) bis zum Übergang Hamilkars nach Hispanien (237 v. Chr.)* (Bonn)
—— (1989), 'Beobachtungen zur Entstehung der barkidischen Herrschaft in Hispanien', in Devijver and Lipinski, 167–84
—— (1996), 'Rom und Hispanien vor Ausbruch des 2. punischen Krieges', *Hermes* 124, 45–57
—— (1998), *Hannibal* (Munich)
Barré, M. L. (1983), T*he God-List in the Treaty between Hannibal and Philip V of Macedonia: A Study in Light of the Ancient Near Eastern Treaty Tradition* (Baltimore and London)
Barreca, F. (1983–4), 'Gli eserciti annibalici', in *Studi Annibalici*, 43–68
Beltrán, A. (1964), 'Algunos datos para el estudio del lugar del muerto de Amílcar Barca', *Caesaraugusta* 23–4, 87–94
Bender, P. (1997), 'Rom, Karthago und die Kelten', *Klio* 79, 87–106
Bengtson, H. (1952) 'Zur karthagischen "Strategie"', *Aegyptus* 32, 158–62 [= *Kl. Schr. zur Alten Geschichte* (Munich 1974) 110–14]

Blázquez Martínez, J. M., and García-Gelabert Pérez, M. P. (1991), 'Los Bárquidas en las península ibérica', in *Atti del II Congresso Internazionali di Studi Fenici e Punici, Roma 9–14 Novembre 1987*, 2 vols (Rome), 1.27–50

Bosch Gimpera, P., and Aguado Bleye, P. (1955), 'La conquista de España por Roma', in R. Menéndez Pidal (ed.), *Historia de España* vol. 2: *España Romana*, 1st edn (Madrid) 1–282 [cited as Bosch Gimpera (1955)]

Briscoe, J. (1973), *A Commentary on Livy Books XXXI–XXXIII* (Oxford)

—— (1981), *A Commentary on Livy Books XXXIV–XXXVII* (Oxford)

—— (1989), 'The Second Punic War', chap. III in *CAH²* 8.44–80

Brisson, J.-P. (1973), *Carthage ou Rome?* (Paris)

Brizzi, G. (1983), 'Ancora su Annibale e l'ellenismo: la fondazione di Artaxata e l'iscrizione di Era Lacinia', in *1° Congresso Internazionale di Studi Fenici (Roma 1979)*, 3 vols (Rome), 2.243–51

—— (1984), *Studi di Storia Annibalica* (Florence: Epigrafia e Antichità 6)

Broughton, T. R. S., *The Magistrates of the Roman Republic*: vols 1–2 (with M. L. Patterson: Philadephia 1951–2); vol. 3, *Supplement* (Atlanta 1986) [cited as Broughton, *MRR*]

Brunt, P. A. (1971), *Italian Manpower 225 BC–AD 14* (Oxford)

Cambridge Ancient History, ed. S. A. Cook *et al.*, 1st edn: vol. 7, *The Hellenistic Monarchies and the Rise of Rome*; vol. 8, *Rome and the Mediterranean, 218–133 BC* (Cambridge 1928–30) [cited as *CAH¹*]

Cambridge Ancient History, ed. F. W. Walbank *et al.*, 2nd edn: vol. 7 part 2, *The Rise of Rome to 220 BC*; vol. 8, *Rome and the Mediterranean to 133 BC* (Cambridge 1989) [cited as *CAH²*]

Carey, W. L. (1996), 'Nullus videtur dolo facere: the Roman seizure of Sardinia in 237 BC', *CP* 91, 203–22

Caven, B. (1980), *The Punic Wars* (London)

Chandler, D. (1965/1993), *The Campaigns of Napoleon* (London; reprinted 1993)

Christ, K. (ed.) (1974), *Hannibal* (Darmstadt)

Chroust, A.-H. (1954), 'International treaties in antiquity', *Classica et Medievalia* 15, 60–107

Connolly, P. (1981), *Greece and Rome at War* (London)

Cornell, T. (1996), 'Hannibal's legacy: the effects of the Hannibalic War on Italy', in Cornell, Rankov and Sabin, 97–117

Cornell, T., Rankov, B., and Sabin, P. (eds) (1996), *The Second Punic War: A Reappraisal* (London)

Corzo Sánchez, F. (1975), 'La segunda guerra púnica en la Bética', *Habis* 6, 213–45

Cresci Marrone, G. (1978), 'Nota a Nep. Hann., 74', *Aevum: Rassegni di Scienze Storiche, Linguistiche, Filologiche* (Milan) 52, 85–7

Degrassi, A., *Inscriptiones Latinae Liberae Rei Publicae*, 2 vols: vol. 1, 2nd edn (Florence 1965); vol. 2 (Florence 1963) [cited as Degrassi, *ILLRP*]

Delbrück, H. (1920/1975), *History of the Art of War in the Framework of Political History*, 3rd edn: vol. 1, *Antiquity*, tr. W. R. Renfroe, Jr. (Westport, CN and London)

Derow, P. S. (1976), 'The Roman calendar, 218–191 BC', *Phoenix* 30, 265–81

de Sanctis, G. (1967–8), *Storia dei Romani*, 2nd edn, vol. 3 parts 1 and 2 (Florence) [cited as de Sanctis, 3.1, 3.2]

—— (1969), *Storia dei Romani*, 2nd edn, vol. 4 part 1 (Florence) [cited as de Sanctis 4.1]

Develin, R. (1985), *The Practice of Politics at Rome 366–167 BC* (Brussels: Collection Latomus 188)

Devijver, H., and Lipinski, E. (eds) (1989), *Studia Phoenicia*, vol. 10: *Punic Wars* (Leuven)

Domínguez-Monedero, A. J. (1986), 'La campaña de Anibal contra los Vacceos: sus objetivos y su relación con el inicio de la segunda guerra púnica', *Latomus* 45, 241–58

Dyson, S. L. (1985), *The Creation of the Roman Frontier* (Princeton)

Eckstein, A. M. (1983), 'Two notes on the chronology of the outbreak of the Hannibalic War,' *RhM* 126, 255–72

—— (1987), *Senate and General: Individual Decision-Making and Roman Foreign Relations, 264–194 BC* (Berkeley, Los Angeles and London)

—— (1989), 'Hannibal at New Carthage: Polybius 3.15 and the power of irrationality', *CP* 84, 1–15

Egelhaaf, G. (1922), *Hannibal: ein Charakterbild* (Stuttgart)

Ennabli, A. (ed.) (1992), *Pour Sauver Carthage: exploration et conservation de la cité punique, romaine et byzantine* (Paris and Tunis)

Erdkamp, P. (1998), *Hunger and the Sword: Warfare and Food Supply in Roman Republican Wars (264–30 BC)* (Amsterdam)

Erskine, A. (1993), 'Hannibal and the freedom of the Italians', *Hermes* 121, 58–62

Errington, R. M. (1970), 'Rome and Spain before the Second Punic War', *Latomus* 29, 25–57

—— (1971), *Dawn of Empire: Rome's Rise to World Power* (London)

Eucken, H.-C. (1968), *Probleme der Vorgeschichte des zweiten punischen Krieges* (Inaugural Dissertation, Freiburg im Breisgau)

Fantar, M'hamed Hassine (1995), *Carthage: la cité punique* (Tunis: Coll. Patrimoine de la Méditerranée)

Fentress, E. W. B. (1979), *Numidia and the Roman Army* (Oxford: BAR International Series 53)

Fernández Castro, María Cruz (1995), *Iberia in Prehistory* (London)

Fitton Brown, A. D. (1959), 'After Cannae', *Historia* 8, 365–71

Frank, T. (1933), *An Economic Survey of Ancient Rome*, vol. 1: *Rome and Italy of the Republic* (Baltimore) [complete series in 5 vols., 1933–40]

Frederiksen, M. (1984), *Campania*, ed. N. Purcell (Rome)

Goldsworthy, A. (2000), *The Punic Wars* (London)

González Wagner, C. (1989), 'The Carthaginians in ancient Spain: from administrative trade to territorial annexation', in Devijver and Lipinski, 145–56

Görlitz, W. (1970), *Hannibal: eine politische Biographie* (Stuttgart, Berlin, Cologne and Mainz)

Groag, E. (1929), *Hannibal als Politiker* (Vienna [anastatic reprint Rome 1967])

Gruen, E. S. (1984), *The Hellenistic World and the Coming of Rome*, 2 vols (Berkeley, Los Angeles and London)

Gsell, S., *Histoire ancienne de l'Afrique du Nord*, 2nd edn: vol. 2, *L'État carthaginois*; vol. 3, *Histoire militaire de Carthage* (Paris 1921–4) [cited as Gsell, *HAAN*]

Guadán, A. M. de (1969), *La Numismática Ibérica e Ibero-Romana* (Madrid)

Hahn, I. (1974), 'Die Hellenisierung Karthagos und die punisch griechischen Beziehungen im 4. Jahrhundert v.u.Z.', in Elizabeth Welskopf (ed.), *Hellenische Poleis* (4 vols), 2.841–54

Hallward, B. L. (1930), 'Hannibal's invasion of Italy' (chap. II), 'The Roman defensive' (chap. III), 'Scipio and victory' (chap. IV), 'The fall of Carthage' (chap. XV, sections I–IV), in *CAH*[1] 8.25–115, 466–84

Hampl, F. (1983–4), 'Einige Probleme der Forschung zum Hannibalischen Krieg in alter und neuerer Sicht', in *Studi Annibalici*, 9–29

Hans, L.-M. (1983), *Karthago und Sizilien: Die Entstehung und Gestaltung der Epikratie . . . (VI.–III. Jahrhundert v. Chr.)* (Hildesheim: Historische Texte und Studien 7)

—— (1991), 'L'immagine di Amilcare Barca presso i Romani', in *Atti del II Congresso Internazionali di Studi Fenici e Punici, Roma 9–14 Novembre 1987*, 2 vols (Rome), 1.113–17

Harris, W. V. (1971), *Rome in Etruria and Umbria* (Oxford)

—— (1979), *War and Imperialism in Republican Rome, 327–70 BC* (Oxford)

Harrison, R. J. (1988), *Spain at the Dawn of History* (London)

Historia de España (1982): Á. Montenegro Duque and J. M. Blázquez Martínez (eds.), *Historia de España*, 2nd edn, vol. 2 part 1: *España Romana (218 a. de JC–414 de JC): La Conquista y la Explotación Económica* (Madrid)

Hoffmann, W. (1941), 'Ein Papyrusfund zum Frieden von 203', *Hermes* 76, 270–82

—— (1957/1974), 'Hannibal und Rom', in Christ, 40–74 [= *Antike und Abendland* 6 (1957) 7–26]

—— (1961/1974), 'Hannibal und Sizilien,' in Christ, 335–57 [= *Hermes* 89 (1961) 478–94]

—— (1962), *Hannibal* (Göttingen)

Howgego, C. (1995), *Ancient History from Coins* (London)

Hoyos, B. D. (1983), 'Hannibal: what kind of genius?', *Greece and Rome* 30, 171–80

—— (1994), 'Barcid "proconsuls" and Punic politics, 237–218 BC', *RhM* 137, 246–72

—— (1998), *Unplanned Wars: The Origins of the First and Second Punic Wars* (Berlin and New York: Untersuchungen zur antiken Literatur und Geschichte 50)

—— (1999), 'A modern view of Carthage's "Truceless War" (241–237 BC)', review-discussion of Loreto (1995), in *Electronic Antiquity* 5.1: see <http://scholar. lib.vt.edu/ejournals/ElAnt/V5N1/loreto.html>

—— (2000a), 'Towards a chronology of the "Truceless War", 241–237 BC', *RhM* 143, 369–80

—— (2000b), 'Maharbal's *bon mot*: authenticity and survival,' *CQ* 50, 610–14

—— (2001a), 'Polybius and the papyrus: the persuasiveness of *P. Rylands* 3.491', *Zeitschrift für Papyrologie und Epigraphik* 134, 71–9

—— (2001b), 'Generals and annalists: geographic and chronological obscurities in the Scipios' campaigns in Spain, 218–211 BC', *Klio* 83, 68–92

—— (2001c), 'Identifying Hamilcar Barca's heights of Heircte', *Historia* 50, 490–5

—— (2002), 'Hannibal's Olcades', *Habis* 33, 131–40

Huss, W. (1979), 'Die Stellung des rb im karthagischen Senat', *Zeitschrift der Deutschen Morgenländischen Gesellschaft* 129, 217–32

—— (1983), 'Der karthagische Sufetat', *in Althistorische Studien H. Bengtson zum 70. Geburtstag Dargebracht*, ed. H. Heinen (Wiesbaden: Historia-Einzelschrift 43), 24–43

—— (1985), *Geschichte der Karthager* (Munich: Handbuch der Altertumswissenschaft, Abteilung 3, Teil 8)

—— (1989), 'Der panafrikanische Gedanke im zweiten römischen Krieg', in Devijver and Lipinski, 185–91

—— (1991), 'Probleme der karthagischen Verfassung', in *Atti del II Congresso Internazionale di Studi Fenici e Punici, Roma, 9–14 Novembre 1987*, ed. E. Acquaro *et al.*, 3 vols (Rome), 1.117–30

Jacob, P. (1985), 'Notes sur la toponymie grecque de la côte méditerranéenne de l'Espagne antique', *Ktema* 10, 247–71

Jacobs, M. (1990), *A Guide to Andalusia* (London)

Jacoby, F., *Die Fragmente der Griechischen Historiker*: several vols, texts and commentary (Berlin, 1923–58)

Jenkins, G. K., and Lewis, R. B. (1963), *Carthaginian Gold and Electrum Coins* (London)

Kahrstedt, U. (1913), *Geschichte der Karthager*, vol. 3 (Berlin) [see also Meltzer]

Der Kleine Pauly: Lexicon der Antike, ed. K. Ziegler and W. Sontheimer, 5 vols (Munich 1975)

Knapp, R. C. (1980), 'Cato in Spain, 195/194 BC: chronology and geography', in *Studies in Latin Literature and Roman History*, vol. 2, ed. C. Deroux (Brussels), 21–56

Kotula, T. (1983–4), 'Hannibal-Sufet und seine vermeintlich demokratische Reform in Karthago', in *Studi Annibalici*, 87–101 [revised version of article in Polish in *Eos* 57 (1967/8)]

Kromayer, J. (1909/1974), 'Hannibal als Staatsmann', in Christ, 241–74 [= *HZ* 103 (1909) 237–73]

Kromayer, J., and Veith, G. (1912), *Antike Schlachtfelder*, vol. 3: *Italien und Afrika* (Berlin) [cited as Kromayer and Veith, *AS*]

Kukofka, D.-A. (1990), *Süditalien im zweiten punischen Krieg* (Frankfurt am Main, Bern, New York and Paris)

La Bua, V. (1966), *Filino–Polibio Diodoro–Sileno* (Palermo)

Lancel, S. (1992), *Carthage* (Paris) (= *Carthage: A History*, Eng. tr. A. Nevill (London 1995))

—— (1995), *Hannibal* [cited as Lancel, *Hann.*]

Lancel, S., Robine, S., and Thuillier, J.-P. (1980), 'Town-planning and domestic architecture of the early second century BC on the Byrsa, Carthage', in Pedley, 13–27

Lautensach, H. (1964), *Die Iberische Halbinsel* (Munich)

Lazenby, J. (1978), *Hannibal's War: A Military History* (Warminster)

—— (1996), *The First Punic War* (London)

Lehmann, G. A. (1974), 'Polybios und die ältere und zeitgenössische griechische Geschichtsschreibung: einige Bemerkungen', in *Entretiens sur l'antiquité classique (Fondation Hardt)*, vol. 20: *Polybe* (Vandœuvres-Geneva) 145–200

Lehmann, K. (1905), *Die Angriffe der Drei Barkiden nach Italien* (Leipzig)

Leidl, C. G. (1993), 'Appians "Annibaike"', *ANRW* 34.1, 428–62

Liddell Hart, B. H. (1926), *A Greater than Napoleon: Scipio Africanus* (Edinburgh and London) [facsimile repr. New York 1994]

Lippold, A. (1963), *Consules: Untersuchungen zur Geschichte des römischen Konsulates von 264 bis 201 v. Chr.* (Bonn: Antiquitas, Reihe 1: Abhandlungen zur alten Geschichte 8)

Loreto, L. (1995), *La Grande Insurrezione Libica contro Cartagine del 241–237 a.C.* (Rome: Mélanges de l'École française de Rome 211)

Luce, T. J. (1977), *Livy: The Composition of His History* (Princeton)

Ma, J. (1999), *Antiochus III and the Cities of Western Asia Minor* (Oxford)

McDonald, A. H., and Walbank, F. W. (1969), 'The treaty of Apamea (188 BC): the naval clauses', *JRS* 59, 30–9

McKnight, S. (1998), 'Cannae, 2 August 216 BC: the double envelopment', in J. Pimlott (ed.), *The Hutchinson Atlas of Battle Plans: Before and After* (Oxford), 3–14

Manni, E. (1981), *Geografia fisica e politica della Sicilia antica* (Rome: Testimonia Siciliae Antiquae I.1)

—— (1990), 'Su alcune recenti proposte d'identificazione di centri antichi della Sicilia', *Sikelika kai Italika* [Rome], 1.355–67

Mantel, N. (1991), *Poeni Foedifragi: Untersuchungen zur Darstellung römisch-karthagischer Verträge zwischen 241 und 201 v. Chr. durch die römische Historiographie* (Munich: Münchener Arbeiten zur alten Geschichte 4)

Marino, R. (1988), *La Sicilia dal 241 al 210 a.C.* ([Rome]: Testimonia Siciliae Antiquae I.12)

Mattingly, D. J. (1994), *Tripolitania* (Ann Arbor, MI)

Meltzer, O. (1879, 1896), *Geschichte der Karthager*, 2 vols (Berlin)

Millán León, J. (1986), 'La batalla de Ilipa', *Habis* 17, 283–303

Miller, K. (1916/1964), *Itineraria Romana: Römische Reiswege an der Hand der Tabula Peutingeriana* (Stuttgart 1916, reprinted Rome 1964)

Mommsen, T., *The History of Rome*, tr. W. P. Dickson (London 1880–1) [cited as Mommsen, *HR*]

Montenegro Duque, Á. (1982): see *Historia de España*

Morgan, M. G. (1977), 'Calendars and chronology in the First Punic War', *Chiron* 7, 89–117

Müller, C. (1883), *Claudii Ptolemaei Geographia: Libri I–V* (Paris)

—— (1855/1965), *Geographi Graeci Minores*, 3 vols (orig. edn Paris 1855; reprinted Hildesheim 1965)

Nicolet, C. (1977–8) (ed.) *Rome et la conquête du monde méditerranéen*, 2 vols (Paris: L'Histoire et ses Problèmes 8)

Niemeyer, H.-G., Rindelaub, A. and Schmidt, K. (1996), *Karthago: die alte Handelsmetropole: eine archäologische Grabung* (Hamburg)

Oxford Classical Dictionary, 3rd edn, ed. S. Hornblower and A. Spawforth (Oxford 1996) [cited as *OCD³*]

Peddie, J. (1997), *Hannibal's War* (Phoenix Mill, Glos.)

Pedley, J. G. (ed.) (1980), *New Light on Ancient Carthage* (Ann Arbor, MI)

Picard, G. C. (1961), *Daily Life at Carthage in the Time of Hannibal* [tr. A. E. Foster] (London) [orig. French edn 1958]

—— (1963), 'Les sufètes de Carthage dans Tite-Live et Cornelius Nepos', *RÉL* 41, 269–81

—— (1964), *Carthage*, English tr. by M. and L. Kochan (London) [orig. French edn 1956]

—— (1966), 'L'administration territoriale de Carthage', in *Mélanges offerts à André Piganiol* (Paris), 3.1257–65

—— (1967), *Hannibal* (Paris)

—— (1968), 'La révolution démocratique de Carthage', *Conférences de la Société des Études Latines de Bruxelles 1965–66* (Brussels 1968) 113–30

—— (1983–4), 'Hannibal hégémon hellénistique', in *Studi Annibalici*, 75–81

Picard, G. C. and Picard, C. (1968), *The Life and Death of Carthage* (London) [cited as Picard and Picard, *LDC*]

—— (1983), *Karthago: Leben und Kultur* [revised German edn of Picard (1961): tr. I. Miller] (Stuttgart)

Proctor, Sir D. (1971), *Hannibal's March in History* (Oxford)

Rakob, F. (1992), 'L'habitat ancien et le système urbanistique', in Ennabli, 28–37

Rankov, B. (1996), 'The Second Punic War at sea', in Cornell, Rankov and Sabin, 49–57

Rawlings, L. (1996), 'Celts, Spaniards and Samnites: warriors in a soldiers' war', in Cornell, Rankov and Sabin, 81–95

Rich, J. W. (1976), *Declaring War in the Roman Republic in the Age of Transmarine Expansion* (Brussels: Collection Latomus 149)

—— (1996), 'The origins of the Second Punic War', in Cornell, Rankov and Sabin, 1–37

Richardson, J. S. (1986), *Hispaniae: Spain and the Development of Roman Imperialism, 218–82 BC* (Cambridge)

—— (1996), *The Romans in Spain* (Cambridge, MA)

Ridley, R. T. (1987), *History of Rome: A Documented Analysis* (Rome: Problemi e Ricerche di Storia Antica 8)

Roberts, C. H. (1938), *Catalogue of the Greek and Latin Papyri in the John Rylands Library, Manchester*, vol. 3: *Theological and Literary Texts (nos 457–551)* (Manchester)

Robinson, E. S. (1956/1978), 'Punic coins of Spain and their bearing on the Roman Republican series', in R. A. G. Carson and C. H. V. Sutherland (eds), *Essays on Roman Coinage Presented to H. Mattingly* (Oxford 1956; separately reprinted, Chicago 1978) [cited from the 1978 offprint]

Rouillard, P. (1982), 'Les colonies grecques du sud-est de la péninsule ibérique: état de la question', *La Parola del Passato* 37, 417–31

Ruiz Rodríguez, A. (1997), 'The Iron Age Iberian peoples of the upper Guadalquivir valley', in M. Díaz-Andrieu and S. Keay (eds.), *The Archaeology of Iberia: The Dynamics of Change* (London and New York), 175–91

Sabin, P. (1996), 'The mechanics of battle in the Second Punic War', in Cornell, Rankin and Sabin, 59–77

Salmon, E. T. (1982), *The Making of Roman Italy* (London)

Samuels, M. (1990), 'The reality of Cannae', *Militärische Mitteilungen* (Freiburg-im-Bremen) 47, 7–29

Sanctis, de: see de Sanctis

Santosuosso, A. (1997), *Soldiers, Citizens and the Symbols of War: From Classical Greece to Republican Rome, 500–167 BC* (Boulder, CO)

Scardigli, B. (1991), *I Trattati Romano-Cartaginesi: Introduzione, edizione critica, traduzione, commento e indici* (Pisa)

Schmitt, H. H., *Die Staatsverträge des Altertums*, vol. 3 (1969) [cited as Schmitt, *SVA*]

Schulten, A. (1935), *Fontes Hispaniae Antiquae*, vol. 3: *Las Guerras de 237–154 ADJC* (Barcelona) [cited as Schulten, *FHA*]

—— (1952), *Fontes Hispaniae Antiquae*, vol. 6: *Estrabón, Geografía de Iberia* (Barcelona)

Schwarte, K.-H. (1983), *Der Ausbruch des zweiten punischen Krieges: Rechtsfrage und Überlieferung* (Wiesbaden: Historia-Einzelschriften 43)

Scullard, H. H. (1970), *Scipio Africanus: Soldier and Politician* (London)

—— (1973) *Roman Politics, 220–150 BC*, 2nd edn (Oxford) [cited as Scullard, *RP*]

—— (1974), *The Elephant in the Greek and Roman World* (London)

—— (1980), *A History of Rome 753–146 BC*, 4th edn (London)

—— 'Carthage and Rome,' chapter 11 in *CAH²* 7.2.486–569

—— (1989b), 'The Carthaginians in Spain,' chapter 2 in *CAH²* 8.17–43

Seibert, J. (1989), 'Zur logistik des Hannibal-Feldzuges: Nachschub über die Alpen?', in Devijver and Lipinski, 213–21

—— (1993) *Forschungen zu Hannibal* (Darmstadt) [cited as Seibert, *FzH*]

—— (1993) *Hannibal* (Darmstadt) [cited as Seibert, *Hann.*]

Shean, J. (1996), 'Hannibal's mules: the logistical limitations of Hannibal's army and the battle of Cannae, 216 BC', *Historia* 45, 159–87

Starr, C. G. (1980), T*he Beginnings of Imperial Rome: Rome in the Mid-Republic* (Ann Arbor, MI)

Studia Phoenicia: see Devijver and Lipinski

Studi Annibalici, in *RSA* 13–14 (1983–4)

Sumner, G. V. (1966), 'The chronology of the outbreak of the Second Punic War', *Proceedings of the African Classical Associations* 9, 5–30

—— (1967), 'Roman policy in Spain before the Hannibalic War', *Harvard Studies in Classical Philology* 72, 205–46

—— (1972), 'Rome, Spain and the outbreak of the Second Punic War: some clarifications', *Latomus* 31, 469–80

Susemihl, F., and Hicks, R. D. (1894), *The Politics of Aristotle: Books I–V* (London)

Sznycer, M. (1978), 'Carthage et la civilisation punique', in Nicolet, 2.545–93

Tarn, W. W. (1930), *Hellenistic Military and Naval Developments* (Cambridge; reprinted Chicago 1984)

Thiel, J. H. (1946), *Studies on the History of Roman Sea-Power in Republican Times* (Amsterdam)

—— (1954), *A History of Roman Sea-Power before the Second Punic War* (Amsterdam)

Thompson, L. A. (1981), 'Carthage and the Massylian *coup d'état* of 206 BC', *Historia* 30, 120–6

Tlatli, S.-E. (1978), *La Carthage punique: étude urbaine* (Paris and Tunis)

Tränkle, H. (1977), *Livius und Polybios* (Basel and Stuttgart)

Tusa, V. (1974), 'La civiltà punica', in *Popoli e Civiltà dell'Italia Antica* (Rome) 2.9–142

Ungern-Sternberg, J. von (1975), *Capua im zweiten punischen Krieg: Untersuchungen zur römischen Annalistik* (Munich: Vestigia: Beiträge zur Alten Geschichte 23)

Veith, see Kromayer

Verbrugghe, G. P. (1976), *Sicilia* (*Itinera Romana: Beiträge zur Strassengeschichte des römischen Reiches*, ed. G. Walser, 2: Berne)

Villaronga, L. (1973), *Las Monedas Hispano-Cartaginesas* (Barcelona)

Vollmer, D. (1990), *Symploke: Das Übergreifen der römischen Expansion auf den griechischen Osten* (Stuttgart: Hermes-Einzelschriften 54)

Wagner: see González Wagner

Walbank, F., *A Historical Commentary on Polybius*, vols 1 (1957), 2 (1967), 3 (1979) (Oxford) [cited as Walbank, 1, 2 and 3]

—— (1972), *Polybius* (Berkeley, Los Angeles and London: Sather Classical Lectures 42)

Walsh, P. G. (1965), 'Masinissa', *JRS* 55, 149–60

—— (1994), *Livy: Book XXXIX* (Warminster)

Warmington, B. H. (1964), *Carthage* (Harmondsworth)

Warmington, E. H. (1935, 1936), *Remains of Old Latin*, vol. 1, *Ennius and Caecilius*; vol. 2, *Livius Andronicus, Naevius, Pacuvius and Accius* (Cambridge, MA, and London: Loeb Classical Library)

Whittaker, C. R. (1978), 'Carthaginian imperialism in the fifth and fourth centuries', in P. D. A. Garnsey and C. R. Whittaker (eds), *Imperialism in the Ancient World* (Cambridge), 59–90

Wise, T. (1982), *Armies of the Carthaginian Wars 265–146 BC*, plates by R. Hook (Osprey Men-at-Arms Series 121: Botley)

Zecchini, G. (1997), 'Ancora sul Papiro Würzburg e su Sosilo', *Akten des 21. Internationalen Papyrologenkongresses: Berlin 13–19.8.1995* (Stuttgart: Archiv für Papyrusforschung, Beiheft 3: 2 vols), 1,061–7

INDEX

Very frequent names (*e.g.* Carthage, Hannibal, Livy, Polybius, Rome, Sicily) are not included